Annual Editions:
Psychology, 45/e

Edited by R. Eric Landrum
Boise State University

http://create.mcgraw-hill.com

ISBN-10: 1259153312   ISBN-13: 9781259153310

Contents

Preface

Why does a person need to purchase a book that contains a collection of articles about psychology (the science of human behavior)? Why not just google the term and read what is available for free? I believe that is a fair question. Go ahead and google "psychology" sometime—when I did this in September 2013, there were 197 million results—that's right, 197,000,000 web pages related to psychology. So I suppose with enough time you could identify (and read) some great articles about psychology, but I hope you have plenty of time for reading. Please also remember that not everything on the Internet is free—you'd have to pay per article to access some of the works provided in this book. Of course, to be fair, this book isn't free either—but with the culling of key articles done for you and all the permissions fees paid on your behalf, we believe we've created a usable and readable resource that can help you better understand psychology, whether you're enrolled in an introductory psychology course or just looking to read more about a fascinating topic—our own human behavior—and what can be more fascinating than that?

Like any academic or professional discipline, psychology is filled with jargon and nuance—characteristics that are challenging for those new to any topic to absorb. For this reason, McGraw-Hill publishes *Annual Editions*—an anthology of current, clearly written, and highly understandable articles about psychology. The editorial staff at McGraw-Hill has designed *Annual Editions: Psychology* to meet the needs of lay people and students who are curious about psychological science and its applications. *Annual Editions: Psychology* provides a large selection of readable, informative articles primarily from popular magazines and newspapers. Many of these articles are written by journalists, but some are authored by psychologists. The articles for this volume are representative of current research and thinking in psychology. In fact, you'll see that the organization of the units and articles presented may follow quite nicely with the same order of topics and chapters you'll be studying in an introductory psychology class.

This is a series that has been successful for quite some time. How do some articles get added to *Annual Editions: Psychology* whereas others are dropped? Were the articles that were dropped from the previous edition not very good? No, that's not the case at all! As new research emerges, a book like *Annual Editions: Psychology* allows both faculty member and student to stay abreast of current changes. So for some articles, it was time to update the work to more recent sources. McGraw-Hill also values instructor feedback highly, so sometimes an article on an important topic just didn't work out well when students are trying to read and comprehend the content. Results from instructor surveys were also instrumental in helping determine what should absolutely stay, and what areas might be updated.

What would be the best way to get the most out of this book? Read it. Seriously—the book won't do you any good without reading it. As you read about the biological bases of behavior in your introductory psychology course, also read *Annual Editions: Psychology.* Concepts you may find difficult to understand from your textbook or from your instructor may become clearer to you once you read about the same topics when discussed by a knowledgeable journalist, or the actual researcher. Read and engage with the articles provided in *Annual Editions: Psychology* and you'll be on your way to a better understanding of the science of human behavior—psychology.

EDITOR

R. Eric Landrum is a professor of psychology at Boise State University, receiving his PhD in cognitive psychology from Southern Illinois University-Carbondale. His research interests center on the educational conditions that best facilitate student advancement. Eric is a member of the American Psychological Association, a fellow in APA's Division Two (Society for the Teaching of Psychology or STP). He served as STP secretary (2009–2011) and will serve as the 2014 STP President.

Academic Advisory Board

Members of the Academic Advisory Board are instrumental in the final selection of articles for each edition of ANNUAL EDITIONS. Their review of articles for content, level, and appropriateness provides critical direction to the editors and staff. We think that you will find their careful consideration well reflected in this volume.

John Billingsley, Jr.,
American Intercontinental University

Bernardo J. Carducci,
Indiana University Southeast

Sharon Chacon-Mineau,
Northeast Wisconsin Technical College

Thomas C. Davis,
Nichols College

Carlos A. Escoto,
Eastern Connecticut State University

Christian Fossa-Andersen,
DeVry University – South Florida

Nicholas Greco IV,
Adler School of Professional Psychology

Deborah Harris-Sims,
University of Phoenix

Correlation Guide

The *Annual Editions* series provides students with convenient, inexpensive access to current, carefully selected articles from the public press. **Annual Editions: Psychology, 45/e** is an easy-to-use reader that presents articles on important topics such as development, motivation, psychological disorders, and many more. For more information on other McGraw-Hill Create™ titles and collections, visit www.mcgrawhillcreate.com.

This convenient guide matches the articles in **Annual Editions: Psychology, 45/e** with **The Science of Psychology: An Appreciative View, 3/e** by King.

The Science of Psychology: An Appreciative View, 3/e By King	Annual Editions: Psychology, 45/e
Chapter 1: What is Psychology?	Psychology Is a Hub Science
Chapter 2: Psychology's Scientific Method	Dangerous Distraction The 10 Commandments of Helping Students Distinguish Science from Pseudoscience in Psychology
Chapter 3: Biological Foundations of Behavior	The Left Brain Knows What the Right Hand Is Doing Political Attitudes Vary with Physiological Traits Reflections on Mirror Neurons A Scientific Pioneer and a Reluctant Role Model
Chapter 4: Sensation and Perception	The Color of Sin: White and Black Are Perceptual Symbols of Moral Purity and Pollution Increasing Speed of Processing with Action Video Games Mini-Multitaskers Uncanny Sight in the Blind
Chapter 5: States of Consciousness	Corporeal Awareness and Proprioceptive Sense of the Phantom Dangerous Distraction
Chapter 6: Learning	The Epidemic of Media Multitasking While Learning Finding Little Albert: A Journey to John B. Watson's Infant Laboratory The Perils and Promises of Praise Pigeons, Like Humans, Can Behave Irrationally Will Behave for Money
Chapter 7: Memory	A Scientific Pioneer and a Reluctant Role Model
Chapter 8: Thinking, Intelligence, and Language	Does Thinking Really Hard Burn More Calories? Evolutionary Psychology and Intelligence Research Harnessing the Wisdom of the Ages How Good Are the Asians? Refuting Four Myths about Asian-American Academic Achievement The Secret Life of Pronouns by James Pennebaker: What Do "I" and "We" Reveal about Us?
Chapter 9: Human Development	The Benefits of Positive Parenting Blessed Are Those Who Mourn—and Those Who Comfort Them For Kids, Self-Control Factors into Future Success The Mind at Midlife The Recession's Toll on Children That Elusive Birth Order Effect and What It Means to You
Chapter 10: Motivation and Emotion	Need Motivation? Declare a Deadline A Single Brain Structure May Give Winners That Extra Physical Edge What Does Guilt Do?
Chapter 11: Gender, Sex, and Sexuality	Women at the Top: Powerful Leaders Define Success as Work + Family in a Culture of Gender
Chapter 12: Personality	Enough about You Physical Order Produces Healthy Choices, Generosity, and Conventionality, Whereas Disorder Produces Creativity Resisting Temptation
Chapter 13: Social Psychology	Gross National Happiness in Bhutan: The Big Idea from a Tiny State That Could Change the World The Psychology and Power of False Confessions Replicating Milgram We're Wired to Connect
Chapter 14: Industrial and Organization Psychology	Psychological Science and Safety: Large-Scale Success at Preventing Occupational Injuries and Fatalities Self-Efficacy in the Workplace: Implications for Motivation and Performance 13 Practical Tips for Training in Other Countries Women at the Top: Powerful Leaders Define Success as Work + Family in a Culture of Gender
Chapter 15: Psychological Disorders	Bringing Life into Focus Hypochondria: The Impossible Illness Phobias: The Rationale behind Irrational Fears Post-Prozac Nation: The Science and History of Treating Depression The Roots of Mental Illness

(continued)

(concluded)

Chapter 16: Therapies	Addiction Interaction, Relapse and Recovery
	More Support Needed for Trauma Interventions
	Post-Prozac Nation: The Science and History of Treating Depression
	PTSD Treatments Grow in Evidence, Effectiveness
	When Do Meds Make the Difference?
	Yes, Recovery Is Possible
Chapter 17: Health Psychology	Improving Health, Worldwide
	The Kids Aren't All Right

This convenient guide matches the articles in **Annual Editions: Psychology, 45/e** with **Psychology and Your Life, 2/e** by Feldman.

Psychology and Your Life, 2/e By Feldman	Annual Editions: Psychology, 45/e
Chapter 1: Introduction to Psychology	Psychology Is a Hub Science
	The 10 Commandments of Helping Students Distinguish Science from Pseudoscience in Psychology
Chapter 2: Neuroscience and Behavior	The Left Brain Knows What the Right Hand Is Doing
	Political Attitudes Vary with Physiological Traits
	Reflections on Mirror Neurons
	A Scientific Pioneer and a Reluctant Role Model
Chapter 3: Sensation and Perception	The Color of Sin: White and Black Are Perceptual Symbols of Moral Purity and Pollution
	Increasing Speed of Processing with Action Video Games
	Mini-Multitaskers
	Uncanny Sight in the Blind
	You Do Not Talk about Fight Club If You Do Not Notice Fight Club: Inattentional Blindness for a Simulated Real-World Assault
Chapter 4: States of Consciousness	Corporeal Awareness and Proprioceptive Sense of the Phantom
	Dangerous Distraction
Chapter 5: Learning	The Epidemic of Media Multitasking While Learning
	Finding Little Albert: A Journey to John B. Watson's Infant Laboratory
	The Perils and Promises of Praise
	Pigeons, Like Humans, Can Behave Irrationally
	Will Behave for Money
Chapter 6: Thinking: Memory, Cognition, and Language	Does Thinking Really Hard Burn More Calories?
	Evolutionary Psychology and Intelligence Research
	Harnessing the Wisdom of the Ages
	The Secret Life of Pronouns by James Pennebaker: What Do "I" and "We" Reveal about Us?
Chapter 7: Motivation and Emotion	Need Motivation? Declare a Deadline
	Self-Efficacy in the Workplace: Implications for Motivation and Performance
	A Single Brain Structure May Give Winners That Extra Physical Edge
	What Does Guilt Do?
Chapter 8: Development	The Benefits of Positive Parenting
	Blessed Are Those Who Mourn—and Those Who Comfort Them
	For Kids, Self-Control Factors into Future Success
	The Mind at Midlife
	The Recession's Toll on Children
	That Elusive Birth Order Effect and What it Means to You
Chapter 9: Personality and Individual Differences	Enough about You
	How Good Are the Asians? Refuting Four Myths about Asian-American Academic Achievement
	Physical Order Produces Healthy Choices, Generosity, and Conventionality, Whereas Disorder Produces Creativity
	That Elusive Birth Order Effect and What It Means to You
Chapter 10: Psychological Disorders	Bringing Life into Focus
	Hypochondria: The Impossible Illness
	Phobias: The Rationale Behind Irrational Fears
	Post-Prozac Nation: The Science and History of Treating Depression
	The Roots of Mental Illness
Chapter 11: Treatment of Psychological Disorders	Addiction Interaction, Relapse and Recovery
	The Kids Aren't All Right
	More Support Needed for Trauma Interventions
	Post-Prozac Nation: The Science and History of Treating Depression
	PTSD Treatments Grow in Evidence, Effectiveness
	When Do Meds Make the Difference?
	Yes, Recovery Is Possible
Chapter 12: Social Psychology	Gross National Happiness in Bhutan: The Big Idea from a Tiny State that Could Change the World
	Psychological Science and Safety: Large-Scale Success at Preventing Occupational Injuries and Fatalities
	The Psychology and Power of False Confessions
	Replicating MilgramWe're Wired to Connect

This convenient guide matches the articles in **Annual Editions: Psychology, 45/e** with **Psychology: An Introduction, 11/e** by Lahey.

Psychology: An Introduction, 11/e By Lahey	Annual Editions: Psychology, 45/e
Chapter 1: Introduction to Psychology	Psychology Is a Hub Science The 10 Commandments of Helping Students Distinguish Science from Pseudoscience in Psychology
Chapter 2: Research Methods in Psychology	Dangerous Distraction
Chapter 3: Biological Foundations in Behavior	The Left Brain Knows What the Right Hand Is Doing Political Attitudes Vary with Physiological Traits Reflections on Mirror Neurons
Chapter 4: Interplay of Nature and Nurture	Comprehensive Soldier Fitness and the Future of Psychology That Elusive Birth Order Effect and What it Means to You
Chapter 5: Sensation and Perception	The Color of Sin: White and Black Are Perceptual Symbols of Moral Purity and Pollution Increasing Speed of Processing with Action Video Games Mini-Multitaskers Uncanny Sight in the Blind You Do Not Talk about Fight Club If You Do Not Notice Fight Club: Inattentional Blindness for a Simulated Real-World Assault
Chapter 6: States of Consciousness	Corporeal Awareness and Proprioceptive Sense of the Phantom Dangerous Distraction
Chapter 7: Basic Principles of Learning	The Epidemic of Media Multitasking While Learning Finding Little Albert: A Journey to John B. Watson's Infant Laboratory The Perils and Promises of Praise Pigeons, Like Humans, Can Behave Irrationally Will Behave For Money
Chapter 8: Memory	A Scientific Pioneer and a Reluctant Role Model
Chapter 9: Cognition, Language, and Intelligence	Does Thinking Really Hard Burn More Calories? Evolutionary Psychology and Intelligence Research Harnessing the Wisdom of the Ages How Good Are the Asians? Refuting Four Myths about Asian-American Academic Achievement The Secret Life of Pronouns by James Pennebaker: What Do "I" and "We" Reveal about Us?
Chapter 10: Developmental Psychology	The Benefits of Positive Parenting Blessed Are Those Who Mourn—and Those Who Comfort Them For Kids, Self-Control Factors into Future Success The Mind at Midlife The Recession's Toll on Children That Elusive Birth Order Effect and What It Means to You
Chapter 11: Motivation and Emotion	Need Motivation? Declare a Deadline A Single Brain Structure May Give Winners That Extra Physical Edge What Does Guilt Do?
Chapter 12: Personality	Enough about You Physical Order Produces Healthy Choices, Generosity, and Conventionality, Whereas Disorder Produces Creativity That Elusive Birth Order Effect and What It Means to You
Chapter 13: Stress and Health	Improving Health, Worldwide The Kids Aren't All Right
Chapter 14: Abnormal Behavior	Bringing Life into Focus Hypochondria: The Impossible Illness Phobias: The Rationale Behind Irrational Fears Post-Prozac Nation: The Science and History of Treating Depression The Roots of Mental Illness
Chapter 15: Therapies	Addiction Interaction, Relapse and Recovery More Support Needed for Trauma Intervention Post-Prozac Nation: The Science and History of Treating Depression PTSD Treatments Grow in Evidence, Effectiveness When Do Meds Make the Difference? Yes, Recovery Is Possible
Chapter 16: Social Psychology	Replicating Milgram The Psychology and Power of False Confessions We're Wired to Connect Gross National Happiness in Bhutan: The Big Idea from a Tiny State that Could Change the World
Chapter 17: Psychology Applied to the Environment and to Professions	Psychological Science and Safety: Large-Scale Success at Preventing Occupational Injuries and Fatalities Women at the Top: Powerful Leaders Define Success as Work + Family in a Culture of Gender Self-Efficacy in the Workplace: Implications for Motivation and Performance 13 Practical Tips for Training in Other Countries

Topic Guide

This topic guide suggests how the selections in this book relate to the subjects covered in your course.

All the articles that relate to each topic are listed below the bold-faced term.

Unit 1

UNIT

Prepared by: Eric Landrum, *Boise State University*

The Science of Psychology

Contemporary psychology is defined as the science of human behavior. Compared to other sciences (like chemistry or physics), psychology is a younger discipline. Some aspects of modern psychology are particularly biological, such as neuroscience, perception, psychophysics, and behavioral genetics. In fact, many of our recent advances in understanding, thinking, and behavior emerge from neuroscience—with examples of both men and women succeeding in this important field.

Modern psychology encompasses the full spectrum of human behavior, thought, and emotion. There is no aspect of human life that does not fall under psychology's purview. In fact, if you can think of a behavior, then there is surely a branch of psychology that focuses on the study of that behavior. From home life to the workplace to the athletic field to the church, synagogue, and mosque, psychologists seek to understand the causes of our behaviors and our thoughts. Some psychologists work to understand these behaviors simply for the sake of advancing new knowledge. Other psychologists take this new knowledge and apply it to improving the quality of everyday life. Still other psychologists focus exclusively on the most challenging problems facing the world today—war, hunger, poverty, sexual and other forms of abuse, drug and alcohol addiction, environmental change and global warming, and so on.

Psychologists work in varied settings. Many psychologists are academics, teaching and conducting psychological research on college and university campuses. Others work in applied settings such as hospitals, mental health clinics, industry, local, state, and federal government, and schools. Other psychologists work primarily in private practice in which they see clients for personal therapy and counseling sessions. Despite this diversity of settings, psychologists share a keen interest in understanding and explaining human thought and behavior. Psychologists receive rigorous training in their respective subfields of psychology. Undergraduates who are interested in becoming professional psychologists apply for and attend graduate school to receive specialized training. Some of these students earn their master's degree in psychology, whereas others go on to complete their doctorate (PhD or PsyD). For some subfields of psychology, such as clinical psychology, individuals must obtain a license to practice psychology. In this case, in addition to completing the graduate degree, the individual must also complete an internship in which he or she receives advanced and closely supervised training in the specialty.

Psychology is an incredibly diverse discipline that offers valuable insights into work, play, suffering, and love. It addresses many fascinating issues, dilemmas, and questions. Not only are individual psychologists successful in advancing careers, but psychologists on the whole continue to be successful in advancing our knowledge about human behavior. This unit offers you a glimpse at some of the pressing challenges that face psychologists in their work today and offers considerable insight into what you can expect from your study of psychology.

Article

Prepared by: Eric Landrum, *Boise State University*

The 10 Commandments of Helping Students Distinguish Science from Pseudoscience in Psychology

SCOTT O. LILIENFELD

"Professor Schlockenmeister, I know that we have to learn about visual perception in your course, but aren't we going to learn anything about extra-sensory perception? My high school psychology teacher told us that there was really good scientific evidence for it."

"Dr. Glopelstein, you've taught us a lot about intelligence in your course. But when are you going to discuss the research showing that playing Mozart to infants increases their I.Q. scores?"

"Mr. Fleikenzugle, you keep talking about schools of psychotherapy, like psychoanalysis, behavior therapy, and client-centered therapy. But how come you've never said a word about sensory-motor integration therapy? My mother, who's an occupational therapist, tells me that it's a miracle cure for attention-deficit disorder."

Learning Outcomes

After reading this article, you will be able to:

- Distinguish between science and pseudoscience.

- Understand the common criticisms of the scientific basis of psychology.

The Pseudoscience of Popular Psychology

If you're like most introductory psychology instructors, these sorts of questions probably sound awfully familiar. There's a good reason: much of the popular psychology "knowledge" that our students bring to their classes consists of scant more than pseudoscience. Moreover, our students are often fascinated by dubious claims on the fringes of scientific knowledge: extra-sensory perception, psychokinesis, channeling, out-of-body

experiences, subliminal persuasion, astrology, biorhythms, "truth serum," the lunar lunacy effect, hypnotic age regression, multiple personality disorder, alien abduction reports, hand-writing analysis, rebirthing therapy, and untested herbal remedies for depression, to name but a few. Of course, because some of these claims may eventually be shown to contain a core of truth, we should not dismiss them out of hand. Nevertheless, what is troubling about these claims is the glaring discrepancy between many individuals' beliefs in them and the meager scientific evidence on their behalf.

Yet many introductory psychology instructors accord minimal attention to potentially pseudoscientific topics in their courses, perhaps because they believe that these topics are of, at best, marginal relevance to psychological science. Moreover, many introductory psychology textbooks barely mention these topics. After all, there is already more than enough to cover in psychology courses, so why tack on material of doubtful scientific status? Furthermore, some instructors may fear that by devoting attention to questionable claims they will end up sending students the unintended message that these claims are scientifically credible.

Benefits of Teaching Students to Distinguish Science from Pseudoscience

So why should we teach psychology students to distinguish science from pseudoscience? As personality theorist George Kelly (1955) noted, an effective understanding of a construct requires an appreciation of both of its poles. For example, we cannot grasp fully the concept of "cold" unless we have experienced heat. Similarly, students may not grasp fully the concept of scientific thinking without an understanding of pseudoscientific beliefs, namely those that at first blush appear scientific but are not.

Moreover, by addressing these topics, instructors can capitalize on a valuable opportunity to impart critical thinking skills, such as distinguishing correlation from causation and recognizing the need for control groups, by challenging students' misconceptions regarding popular psychology. Although many students find these skills to be "dry" or even deadly dull when presented in the abstract, they often enjoy acquiring these skills in the context of lively and controversial topics (e.g., extrasensory perception) that stimulate their interest. Students often learn about such topics from various popular psychology sources that they seek out in everyday life, such as magazine articles, Internet sites, and television programs.

Indeed, for many beginning students, "psychology" is virtually synonymous with popular psychology. Yet because so much of popular psychology consists of myths and urban legends, such as most people use only 10 percent of their brains, expressing anger is usually better than holding it in, opposites attract in interpersonal relationships, high self-esteem is necessary for psychological health, people with schizophrenia have more than one personality, among a plethora of others, many students probably emerge from psychology courses with the same misconceptions with which they entered. As a consequence, they often depart college incapable of distinguishing the wheat from the chaff in popular psychology.

Teaching students to distinguish science from pseudoscience can prove immensely rewarding. Foremost among these rewards is producing discerning consumers of the popular psychology literature. Indeed, research evidence supports the efficacy of teaching psychology courses on pseudoscience and the paranormal. For example, Morier and Keeports (1994) reported that undergraduates enrolled in a "Science and Pseudoscience" seminar demonstrated a statistically significant reduction in paranormal beliefs relative to a quasi-control group of students enrolled in a psychology and law class over the same time period (see also Dougherty, 2004). They replicated this effect over a 2-year period with two sections of the course. Wesp and Montgomery (1998) found that a course on the objective examination of paranormal claims resulted in a statistically significant improvement in the evaluation of reasoning flaws in scientific articles. Specifically, students in this course were better able to identify logical errors in articles and provide rival explanations for research findings.

The 10 Commandments

Nevertheless, teaching students to distinguish science from pseudoscience brings more than its share of challenges and potential pitfalls. In my introductory psychology course (in which I emphasize strongly the distinction between science and pseudoscience in psychology) and in my advanced undergraduate seminar, "Science and Pseudoscience in Psychology," I have learned a number of valuable lessons (by first making just about every mistake about which I'll warn you).

In the following section, I summarize these teaching tips, which I refer to as the "10 Commandments" of teaching psychology students to distinguish science from pseudoscience. To avoid being accused of failing to separate Church from State, I have worded all of these injunctions in the positive

rather than the negative to distinguish them from the (only slightly better known) biblical 10 Commandments. I urge readers of this column to inscribe these commandments on impressive stone tablets to be mounted outside of all psychology departments.

First Commandment

Thou shalt delineate the features that distinguish science from pseudoscience. It's important to communicate to students that the differences between science and pseudoscience, although not absolute or clear-cut, are neither arbitrary nor subjective. Instead, philosophers of science (e.g., Bunge, 1984) have identified a constellation of features or "warning signs" that characterize most pseudoscientific disciplines. Among these warning signs are:

- A tendency to invoke ad hoc hypotheses, which can be thought of as "escape hatches" or loopholes, as a means of immunizing claims from falsification.
- An absence of self-correction and an accompanying intellectual stagnation.
- An emphasis on confirmation rather than refutation.
- A tendency to place the burden of proof on skeptics, not proponents, of claims.
- Excessive reliance on anecdotal and testimonial evidence to substantiate claims.
- Evasion of the scrutiny afforded by peer review.
- Absence of "connectivity" (Stanovich, 1997), that is, a failure to build on existing scientific knowledge.
- Use of impressive-sounding jargon whose primary purpose is to lend claims a facade of scientific respectability.
- An absence of boundary conditions (Hines, 2003), that is, a failure to specify the settings under which claims do not hold.

Teachers should explain to students that none of these warning signs is by itself sufficient to indicate that a discipline is pseudoscientific. Nevertheless, the more of these warning signs a discipline exhibits, the more suspect it should become.

Second Commandment

Thou shalt distinguish skepticism from cynicism. One danger of teaching students to distinguish science from pseudoscience is that we can inadvertently produce students reflexively dismissive of any claim that appears implausible. Skepticism, which is the proper mental set of the scientist, implies two seemingly contradictory attitudes (Sagan, 1995): an openness to claims combined with a willingness to subject these claims to incisive scrutiny. As space engineer James Oberg (see Sagan, 1995) reminded us, we must keep our minds open but not so open that our brains fall out. In contrast, cynicism implies close-mindedness. I recall being chastised by a prominent skeptic for encouraging researchers to keep an open mind regarding the efficacy of a novel psychotherapy whose rationale struck him as farfetched. However, if we foreclose the possibility that our preexisting beliefs are erroneous, we are behaving unscientifically. Skepticism entails a willingness to entertain novel claims; cynicism does not.

Third Commandment

Thou shalt distinguish methodological skepticism from philosophical skepticism. When encouraging students to think critically, we must distinguish between two forms of skepticism: (1) an approach that subjects all knowledge claims to scrutiny with the goal of sorting out true from false claims, namely methodological (scientific) skepticism, and (2) an approach that denies the possibility of knowledge, namely philosophical skepticism. When explaining to students that scientific knowledge is inherently tentative and open to revision, some students may mistakenly conclude that genuine knowledge is impossible. This view, which is popular in certain postmodernist circles, neglects to distinguish knowledge claims that are more certain from those that are less certain. Although absolute certainty is probably unattainable in science, some scientific claims, such as Darwin's theory of natural selection, have been extremely well corroborated, whereas others, such as the theory underpinning astrological horoscopes, have been convincingly refuted. Still others, such as cognitive dissonance theory, are scientifically controversial. Hence, there is a continuum of confidence in scientific claims; some have acquired virtual factual status whereas others have been resoundingly falsified. The fact that methodological skepticism does not yield completely certain answers to scientific questions and that such answers could in principle be overturned by new evidence does not imply that knowledge is impossible, only that this knowledge is provisional. Nor does it imply that the answers generated by controlled scientific investigation are no better than other answers, such as those generated by intuition (see Myers, 2002).

Fourth Commandment

Thou shalt distinguish pseudoscientific claims from claims that are merely false. All scientists, even the best ones, make mistakes. Sir Isaac Newton, for example, flirted with bizarre alchemical hypotheses throughout much of his otherwise distinguished scientific career (Gleick, 2003). Students need to understand that the key difference between science and pseudoscience lies not in their content (i.e., whether claims are factually correct or incorrect) but in their approach to evidence. Science, at least when it operates properly, seeks out contradictory information and—assuming that this evidence is replicable and of high quality—eventually incorporates such information into its corpus of knowledge. In contrast, pseudoscience tends to avoid contradictory information (or manages to find a way to reinterpret this information as consistent with its claims) and thereby fails to foster the self-correction that is essential to scientific progress. For example, astrology has changed remarkably little over the past 2,500 years despite overwhelmingly negative evidence (Hines, 2003).

Fifth Commandment

Thou shalt distinguish science from scientists. Although the scientific method is a prescription for avoiding confirmatory bias (Lilienfeld, 2002), this point does not imply that scientists are free of biases. Nor does it imply that all or even most scientists are open to evidence that challenges their cherished beliefs. Scientists can be just as pigheaded and dogmatic in their beliefs as anyone else. Instead, this point implies that good scientists strive to become aware of their biases and to counteract them as much as possible by implementing safeguards against error (e.g., double-blind control groups) imposed by the scientific method. Students need to understand that the scientific method is a toolbox of skills that scientists have developed to prevent themselves from confirming their own biases.

Sixth Commandment

Thou shalt explain the cognitive underpinnings of pseudoscientific beliefs. Instructors should emphasize that we are all prone to cognitive illusions (Piatelli-Palmarini, 1994), and that such illusions can be subjectively compelling and difficult to resist. For example, class demonstrations illustrating that many or most of us can fall prey to false memories (e.g., Roediger & McDermott, 1995) can help students to see that the psychological processes that lead to erroneous beliefs are pervasive. Moreover, it is important to point out to students that the heuristics (mental shortcuts) that can produce false beliefs, such as representativeness, availability, and anchoring (Tversky & Kahneman, 1974), are basically adaptive and help us to make sense of a complex and confusing world. Hence, most pseudoscientific beliefs are cut from the same cloth as accurate beliefs. By underscoring these points, instructors can minimize the odds that students who embrace pseudoscientific beliefs will feel foolish when confronted with evidence that contradicts their beliefs.

Seventh Commandment

Thou shalt remember that pseudoscientific beliefs serve important motivational functions. Many paranormal claims, such as those concerning extrasensory perception, out-of-body experiences, and astrology, appeal to believers' deep-seated needs for hope and wonder, as well as their needs for a sense of control over the often uncontrollable realities of life and death. Most believers in the paranormal are searching for answers to profound existential questions, such as "Is there a soul?" and "Is there life after death?" As psychologist Barry Beyerstein (1999) noted (in a play on P.T. Barnum's famous quip), "there's a seeker born every minute" (p. 60). Therefore, in presenting students with scientific evidence that challenges their paranormal beliefs, we should not be surprised when many of them become defensive. In turn, defensiveness can engender an unwillingness to consider contrary evidence.

One of the two best means of lessening this defensiveness (the second is the Eighth Commandment) is to gently challenge students' beliefs with sympathy and compassion, and with the understanding that students who are emotionally committed to paranormal beliefs will find these beliefs difficult to question, let alone relinquish. Ridiculing these beliefs can produce reactance (Brehm, 1966) and reinforce students' stereotypes of science teachers as close-minded and dismissive. In some cases, teachers who have an exceptionally good rapport with their class can make headway by challenging students' beliefs with good-natured humor (e.g., "I'd like to ask all of you who believe in psychokinesis to please raise my hand"). However, teachers must ensure that such humor is not perceived as demeaning or condescending.

Eighth Commandment

Thou shalt expose students to examples of good science as well as to examples of pseudoscience. In our classes, it is critical not merely to debunk inaccurate claims but to expose students to accurate claims. We must be careful not merely to take away students' questionable knowledge, but to give them legitimate knowledge in return. In doing so, we can make it easier for students to swallow the bitter pill of surrendering their cherished beliefs in the paranormal. Students need to understand that many genuine scientific findings are at least as fascinating as are many scientifically dubious paranormal claims. In my own teaching, I have found it useful to intersperse pseudoscientific information with information that is equally remarkable but true, such as lucid dreaming, eidetic imagery, subliminal perception (as opposed to subliminal persuasion, which is far more scientifically dubious), extraordinary feats of human memory (Neisser & Hyman, 2000), and appropriate clinical uses of hypnosis (as opposed to the scientifically unsupported use of hypnosis for memory recovery; see Lynn, Lock, Myers, & Payne, 1997). In addition, we should bear in mind the late paleontologist Stephen Jay Gould's (1996) point that exposing a falsehood necessarily affirms a truth. As a consequence, it is essential not only to point out false information to students, but also to direct them to true information. For example, when explaining why claims regarding biorhythms are baseless (see Hines, 2003), it is helpful to introduce students to claims regarding circadian rhythms, which, although often confused with biorhythms, are supported by rigorous scientific research.

Ninth Commandment

Thou shalt be consistent in one's intellectual standards. One error that I have sometimes observed among skeptics, including psychology instructors who teach critical thinking courses, is to adopt two sets of intellectual standards: one for claims that they find plausible and a second for claims that they do not. The late psychologist Paul Meehl (1973) pointed out that this inconsistency amounts to "shifting the standards of evidential rigor depending on whose ox is being gored" (p. 264). For example, I know one educator who is a vocal proponent of the movement to develop lists of empirically supported therapies, that is, psychological treatments that have been shown to be efficacious in controlled studies. In this domain, he is careful to draw on the research literature to buttress his assertions

regarding which psychotherapies are efficacious and which are not. Yet he is dismissive of the research evidence for the efficacy of electroconvulsive therapy (ECT) for depression, even though this evidence derives from controlled studies that are every bit as rigorous as those conducted for the psychotherapies that he espouses. When I pointed out this inconsistency to him, he denied emphatically that he was adhering to a double standard. It eventually became apparent to me that he was casting aside the evidence for ECT's efficacy merely because this treatment struck him as grossly implausible. Why on earth, he probably wondered, should inducing an epileptoid seizure by administering electricity to the brain alleviate depression? But because surface plausibility is a highly fallible barometer of the validity of truth claims, we must remain open to evidence that challenges our intuitive preconceptions and encourage our students to do so as well.

Tenth Commandment

Thou shalt distinguish pseudoscientific claims from purely metaphysical religious claims. My final commandment is likely to be the most controversial, especially for skeptics who maintain that both pseudoscientific and religious beliefs are irrational. To appreciate the difference between these two sets of beliefs, we must distinguish pseudoscience from metaphysics. Unlike pseudoscientific claims, metaphysical claims (Popper, 1959) cannot be tested empirically and therefore lie outside the boundaries of science. In the domain of religion, these include claims regarding the existence of God, the soul, and the afterlife, none of which can be refuted by any conceivable body of scientific evidence. Nevertheless, certain religious or quasi-religious beliefs, such as those involving "intelligent design" theory, which is the newest incarnation of creationism (see Miller, 2000), the Shroud of Turin, and weeping statues of Mother Mary, are indeed testable and hence suitable for critical analysis alongside of other questionable naturalistic beliefs. By conflating pseudoscientific beliefs with religious beliefs that are strictly metaphysical, instructors risk (a) needlessly alienating a sizeable proportion of their students, many of whom may be profoundly religious; and (b) (paradoxically) undermining students' critical thinking skills, which require a clear understanding of the difference between testable and untestable claims.

Conclusion

Adherence to the Ten Commandments can allow psychology educators to assist students with the crucial goal of distinguishing science from pseudoscience. If approached with care, sensitivity, and a clear understanding of the differences between skepticism and cynicism, methodological and philosophical skepticism, the scientific method and the scientists who use it, and pseudoscience and metaphysics, incorporating pseudoscience and fringe science into psychology courses can be richly rewarding for teachers and students alike. In a world in which the media, self-help industry, and Internet are disseminating psychological pseudoscience at an ever-increasing pace, the critical thinking skills needed to distinguish science from pseudoscience should be considered mandatory for all psychology students.

References

Beyerstein, B. L. (1999). Pseudoscience and the brain: Tuners and tonics for aspiring superhumans. In S. D. Sala (Ed.), *Mind myths: Exploring popular assumptions about the mind and brain* (pp. 59–82). Chichester, England: John Wiley.

Brehm, J. (1966). *A theory of psychological reactance.* New York: Academic Press.

Bunge, M. (1984, Fall). What is pseudoscience? *Skeptical Inquirer, 9,* 36–46.

Dougherty, M. J. (2004). Educating believers: Research demonstrates that courses in skepticism can effectively decrease belief in the paranormal. *Skeptic, 10*(4), 31–35.

Gilovich, T. (1991). *How we know what isn't so: The fallibility of human reason in everyday life.* New York: Free Press.

Gleick, J. (2003). *Isaac Newton.* New York: Pantheon Books.

Gould, S. J. (1996, May). Keynote address, *"Science in the age of (mis)information."* Talk presented at the Convention of the Committee for the Scientific Investigation of Claims of the Paranormal, Buffalo, New York.

Hines, T. (2003). Pseudoscience and the paranormal: A critical examination of the evidence. Buffalo, NY: Prometheus.

Kelly, G. A. (1955). *The psychology of personal constructs, Vols. 1 and 2.* New York: Norton.

Lilienfeld, S. O. (2002). When worlds collide: Social science, politics, and the Rind et al. child sexual abuse meta-analysis. *American Psychologist, 57,* 176–188.

Lilienfeld, S. O., Lohr, M., & Morier, D. (2001). The teaching of courses in the science and pseudoscience of psychology. *Teaching of Psychology, 28,* 182–191.

Lilienfeld, S. O., Lynn, S. J., & Lohr, J. M. (2003). *Science and pseudoscience in clinical psychology.* New York: Guilford.

Lynn, S. J., Lock, T. G., Myers, B., & Payne, D. G. (1997). Recalling the unrecallable: Should hypnosis be used to recover memories in psychotherapy? *Current Directions in Psychological Science, 6,* 79–83.

Meehl, P. E. (1973). *Psychodiagnosis: Selected papers.* Minneapolis, MN: University of Minnesota Press.

Miller, K. (2000). *Finding Darwin's God: A scientist's search for common ground between God and evolution.* New York: Cliff Street Books.

Morier, D., & Keeports, D. (1994). Normal science and the paranormal: The effect of a scientific method course on students' beliefs in the paranormal. *Research in Higher Education, 35,* 443–453.

Myers, D. G. (2002). *Intuition: Its powers and perils.* New Haven: Yale University Press.

Neisser, U., & Hyman, I. E. (2000). *Memory observed: Remembering in natural contexts.* New York: Worth Publishers.

Piatelli-Palmarini, M. (1994). *Inevitable illusions: How mistakes of reason rule our minds.* New York: John Wiley & Sons.

Popper, K. R. (1959). *The logic of scientific discovery.* New York: Basic Books.

Roediger, H. L., & McDermott, K. B. (1995). Creating false memories: Remembering words not presented in lists. *Journal of Experimental Psychology: Learning, Memory, and Cognition, 21,* 803–814.

Ruscio, J. (2002). *Clear thinking with psychology: Separating sense from nonsense.* Pacific Grove, CA: Wadsworth.

Sagan, C. (1995). *The demon-haunted world: Science as a candle in the dark.* New York: Random House.

Shermer, M. (2002). *Why people believe weird things: Pseudoscience, superstition, and other confusions of our time.* New York: Owl Books.

Stanovich, K. (1997). *How to think straight about psychology* (4th ed.). New York: HarperCollins.

Tversky, A., & Kahneman, D. (1974). Judgment under uncertainty: Heuristics and biases. *Science, 185,* 1124–1131.

Wesp, R., & Montgomery, K. (1998). Developing critical thinking through the study of paranormal phenomena. *Teaching of Psychology, 25,* 275–278.

Critical Thinking

1. In what key ways does pseudoscience differ from real science?
2. How accurate is the popular media in its portrayal of psychology?
3. What suggestions do you have for critically reading the popular literature in psychology?

Create Central

www.mhhe.com/createcentral

Internet References

Distinguishing science from pseudoscience
https://webspace.utexas.edu/cokerwr/www/index.html/distinguish.htm

Science and pseudo-science
http://plato.stanford.edu/entries/pseudo-science

Article Prepared by: Eric Landrum, *Boise State University*

Comprehensive Soldier Fitness and the Future of Psychology

MARTIN E. P. SELIGMAN AND RAYMOND D. FOWLER

Whom shall I send? And who will go for us?
And I said, "Here am I. Send me!"
—Isaiah 6:8

Learning Outcomes

After reading this article, you will be able to:

- Explain the historical role of psychology within the U.S. Army.
- Evaluate how psychologists are using positive psychology to improve the mental health of U.S. soldiers.

The history of American psychology has been shaped by national need. This has been true of both the science of psychology and the practice of psychology. In this article, we look at past turning points and then describe why we believe that the Comprehensive Soldier Fitness (CSF) program is another such turning point.

In the past century, psychologists were among the first professionals to offer assistance to the nation. The work of psychologists in World Wars I and II helped to improve the effectiveness of the military, and it made enduring changes in psychology's identity and in the public recognition and acceptance of psychology.

Psychology in the United States was first recognized as an independent discipline in 1892 with the establishment of the American Psychological Association (APA). It began as a research–academic discipline with little interest in applications, and for the most part it remained so in its early years, with some notable exceptions. For example, two of the founders of American psychology were William James, who treated mentally ill patients with psychotherapy and medication, and Lightner Witmer, who established the first psychological clinic at the University of Pennsylvania in 1896 and is viewed as the founder of clinical psychology. But the first big leap into the application of psychology took place in the context of World War I.

In 1917, as war raged through Europe and American involvement seemed imminent, Robert Yerkes, a 40-year-old Yale professor of biopsychology and president of APA, proposed that APA help to create within the U.S. Army a psychology unit to select recruits and determine their duties. In a letter to the APA Council of Representatives, Yerkes (1918) wrote, "Our knowledge and our methods are of importance to the military service of our country, and it is our duty to cooperate to the fullest extent and immediately toward the increased efficiency of our Army and Navy" (p. 191).

A detailed plan was approved by the National Research Council and submitted to the Surgeon General of the Army. A unit was quickly established under the overall direction of Yerkes, who was commissioned a major. One group developed two new intelligence tests, the Army Alpha and the Army Beta, and administered them to more than 2 million soldiers. A second group interviewed and classified 3,500,000 soldiers and developed proficiency tests for military specialties.

The response of APA members to Yerkes's call for service was immediate. Although APA then had fewer than 300 members, Yerkes was able to compile a list of 150 psychologists who were willing to serve as civilian or uniformed psychological examiners, 24 of whom were available for service within a week. By the end of the war, several hundred psychologists were overseeing the work of several thousand men in personnel units throughout the military.

The effects of the program extended far beyond the military. Psychology, as a scientific and applied discipline, gained the recognition and support of the public, and psychological and educational testing centers were established in colleges and universities and in business and industry.

After the armistice, some of the participants in the Army program remained in military service to work in the 43 Army rehabilitation hospitals that had been established. Others left the service to develop tests for business and industry, but most returned to academic positions. Among those who served in the program were people who became the nation's leading psychologists, including J. R. Angell, E. K. Strong, E. G. Boring, Lewis Terman, E. L. Thorndike, L. L. Thurstone, and John B. Watson.

The attention given to psychology, and the increased number of academic programs, brought about a rapid increase in the number of psychologists. In the years following World War I, APA's membership grew tenfold, from approximately 300 members to 3,000. Doctoral production rose rapidly through the 1920s, and by the end of the decade, at least 35 universities had established doctoral programs, most of which included programs in applied psychology.

In 1939, as war again ravaged Europe, 50 psychologists met together to celebrate the 20th anniversary of their demobilization as members of the Army's Committee on Classification of Personnel. The meeting was attended by a representative from the Army Adjutant General's office, who drew attention to the worsening situation in Europe. Yerkes, representing APA, and Walter Bingham, representing APA's practitioner counterpart, began working to establish psychologists' roles in the coming war. Bingham was commissioned as a colonel, appointed chief psychologist for the Army, and given responsibility for personnel classification.

Yerkes, still vigorous as he approached retirement age but too old for military service, spent his time contacting high-level officials in the government and military to promote a broader role for psychology to include treatment, enhancement of morale, and training of military psychologists. By early 1941, he had drafted a comprehensive plan for the military that also aimed to transform the role of professional psychology. Yerkes wrote,

> Psychology must stand as a basic science for such universally desirable expert services as the guidance and safeguarding of an individual's growth and development, education and occupational choice, social adjustments, achievement and maintenance of balance, poise and effectiveness, contentment, happiness, and usefulness. (Yerkes, 1941, quoted in Capshew, 1999, p. 50)

Just six months after Pearl Harbor, there were over 100 psychologists working in Washington, DC. At the request of the Selective Service, a list of 2,300 psychologists qualified to help local draft boards determine the mental capacity of registrants was compiled, and efforts were made to ensure that some 1,500 psychologists eligible for the draft were placed in positions where their background and training could be utilized. Soon, hundreds of psychologists were spread throughout the military and in government agencies.

Personnel psychology in the military thrived in the war years, as it had in World War I. As psychologists developed many new tests of achievement, knowledge, and aptitude, the Army established the largest and most diversified testing program in history. Millions of tests were administered; for example, The Army General Classification Test (AGCT) was administered to 9 million men, one seventh of the U.S. male population.

At the start of World War II, clinical psychology, as opposed to personnel psychology, had little recognition in the military, and not much more in the wider world. Later in the war, psychologists began to serve in mental illness settings in the military, primarily because of the actions of psychiatrist William C. Menninger, newly appointed chief of neuropsychiatry. An acute shortage of psychiatrists led to the appointment of a chief clinical psychologist, the commissioning of 250 men who had experience in clinical psychology, and the establishment of permanent divisions of clinical psychology in the military services. By the end of the war, clinical psychology had become a full-fledged mental health profession, and the election in 1946 of Carl Rogers as the first clinical psychologist to be APA president confirmed its new status.

Building a productive relationship between psychology and the military was not without problems, but as the war drew to a close, both seemed pleased with the partnership. Surveys indicated that psychologists were more satisfied with their utilization in the military than were physicists, chemists, and geologists. And the military demonstrated its appreciation of the work of psychologists by continuing to recruit them: Demand for psychologists exceeded supply throughout the war (Napoli, 1981, p. 105). The Navy representative on the National Defense Research Committee said, "I believe that the application of psychology in selecting and training men, and in guiding the design of weapons so they would fit men, did more to help win this war than any other single intellectual activity" (Smith, 1948, quoted in Napoli, 1981, p 105). Psychology's contribution received praise from senior military officers and from the Army's chief psychiatrist, William C. Menninger, who foresaw a continuing role for psychologists in clinical work (Napoli, 1981, p. 106).

In 1946, the Veterans Administration, faced with an estimated 40,000 war casualties, launched a major program to fund training for new clinical psychologists. Subsequently, the National Institute of Mental Health and the U.S. Public Health Service provided millions of dollars in training and research grants to psychology graduate programs. The military services, especially the Navy, continued to fund psychological research. In the first 30 years after World War II, the federal government spent over $1.2 billion on psychological research, and over half of the members of APA received some government support (Napoli, 1981, p. 137).

Federal support through the military helped to build psychology into a major scientific discipline and profession and APA into the largest doctoral-level scientific society in the world. There are now approximately 3,000 psychologists in the Department of Veterans Affairs (VA) and over 1,500 serving in the military. And psychologists, with their research and applied work, continue to provide services to a wide spectrum of American society.

The Current National Need

The first author (Martin E. P. Seligman) was initially visited by Colonel Jill Chambers in August 2008 to discuss the problems of returning warriors, and this led to a meeting with U.S. Army Chief of Staff General George W. Casey Jr. and his advisers in the Pentagon in early December 2008. They outlined two sets of national needs and asked what psychology's response could be.

One national need was the unprecedented rates of posttraumatic stress disorder (PTSD), depression, suicide, and divorce among military personnel. Two facts stood out about this need: (a) The Army and the VA system were expending huge resources to treat these clinical issues, but their question was not how to provide more treatment but rather how to prevent these problems. (b) Related to this question was the identification of who was most at risk for PTSD: The Millennium Cohort Study found that the bottom 15% in mental and physical fitness accounted for 58% of the cases of PTSD (LeardMann, Smith, Smith, Wells, & Ryan, 2009). The other national need was for a resilient fighting force in our small, all-volunteer Army that would be capable of meeting the challenge of the persistent warfare and repeated redeployments that loom in the Army's future.

Seligman responded by suggesting that the human response to high adversity, such as combat, is normally distributed: On the left of the distribution are the minority who collapse—exhibiting what is called variously PTSD, depression, or anxiety. In the middle are the great majority who are resilient; they return to their normal level of functioning after a brief period of disruption. On the right-hand side of the distribution are those who grow: people who after adversity attain a higher level of functioning than they began with or, in other words, exhibit posttraumatic growth. The aim of any prevention program, Seligman suggested, should be to move the entire distribution toward growth. This aim would lower PTSD, increase resilience, and increase the number of people who grow.

Other important ideas, as well as a concrete plan, emerged from this meeting. The former Surgeon General of the United States, Richard Carmona, advised that civilian medicine was perversely incentivized: Of the $2 trillion the United States spends annually on health care, 75% goes into chronic disease and end-of-life care. In contrast, Army medicine is rationally incentivized—its mission is to produce health, not cure disease, and by producing health preventively, it will reduce later disease. This could be a model for civilian medicine.

The Surgeon General of the Army, Lieutenant General Eric Schoomaker, suggested constructively to General Casey that the program should not be part of his Medical Corps. Moving it from medicine to education and training would help remove any stigma and be much more in line with a universal training purpose. Seligman said that his model for preventive training was positive education: The Penn Resilience Program teaches teachers the skills of resilience and positive psychology, and the teachers then embed these skills into the teaching of their students. This reliably produces less depression and anxiety among the students (Seligman, Ernst, Gillham, Reivich, & Linkins, 2009). General Casey said that this model fits the Army's training process well: The teachers of the Army are the drill sergeants, and they would become the teachers of resilience and positive psychology. He further hoped that a successful demonstration of the effects of resilience training in soldiers and their families would provide a model for the civilian education of young people.

General Casey then set the new plan for Comprehensive Soldier Fitness into motion: It was assigned to education and training, under Brigadier General Rhonda Cornum, not to medicine. The four components detailed in this special issue of

the *American Psychologist* were fleshed out over the next three months: creating the Global Assessment Tool (GAT); creating self-improvement courses for the emotional, social, family, and spiritual fitness dimensions measured on the GAT; beginning to provide resilience training and positive psychology training throughout the Army; and beginning to identify and train master resilience trainers from Army personnel and civilian psychologists. These four components have involved dozens of psychologists over the past two years. We have worked in test creation and validation, in course creation, in writing and refining resilience and positive psychology training materials, and in serving as data analysts, as research designers, and as the trainers and facilitators of live courses with Army personnel. Of critical interest is the Soldier Fitness Tracker (Fravell, Nasser, & Cornum, 2011, this issue). This powerful platform creates an unprecedented, hypermassive database in which psychological variables, medical variables, and performance variables are merged. All of these activities continue as we write, in active collaboration with our peers from the Army.

Future Opportunities

We can only speculate about what the future may hold. The validation of the GAT, the effects of the fitness courses, the effects of resilience and positive psychology training, and the efficacy of the master resilience trainers will all be carefully measured by the Army over the months and years to come. We underscore the importance of delineating the four dimensions of psychological "fitness": emotional, social, family, and spiritual (Cornum, Matthews, & Seligman, 2011, this issue). These are the capacities that underpin human flourishing not only in the Army but in schools, corporations, and communities, and the building of these fitnesses may help define the role of the practicing psychologist of the future. The Army will rigorously ask whether building these fitnesses decreases rates of PTSD, depression, and anxiety; improves performance and morale; improves mental and physical well-being; and helps soldiers and their families in the successful transition back to civilian employment.

If the results are positive, we hope to see expanded collaboration between the military and psychology in creating an Army that is just as psychologically fit as it is physically fit. Among the future possibilities are the following:

- Training of all ranks of soldiers and of civilian employees of the Army in resilience and positive psychology
- Parallel training offered for all family members of soldiers
- Mobile training units for resilience training in far-flung outposts
- Comprehensive Military Fitness: the training of *all* the armed services and their employees in the techniques of resilience and positive psychology
- Expanded online and in-person courses for the military in emotional, social, family, and spiritual fitness

- One million soldiers taking the GAT is an unprecedented database for the prospective longitudinal study of the effects of psychological variables on physical health, mental health, and performance. The Soldier Fitness Tracker is the backbone of this longitudinal study, and we predict that this database will become a national treasure for psychological and medical research.

The use of resilience training and positive psychology in the Army is consciously intended as a model for civilian use. The bulk of health care costs in civilian medicine go not to building health but rather to treating illness. The Army's emphasis on building psychological fitness preventively is intended to be a model for the future of medicine generally. Imagine that building emotional, social, family, and spiritual fitness among young soldiers noticeably reduces morbidity, mortality, and mental illness, offers a betters prognosis when illness strikes, and cuts down on treatment costs. We should know whether this is the case in the next decade. If the CSF program turns out to work, it should—in any rational system—revolutionize the balance between treatment and prevention and radically reform how civilian health care is provided.

The implications for public education and for the corporation may be just as sweeping. Positive education claims that teaching young people the skills of emotional fitness along with teaching the traditional goals of education will enable youth to perform better at school and to perform better later in the workplace. And, more important, perhaps these young people will enjoy lives that have more positive emotion, engagement, and meaning and better relationships. All of these claims will be directly tested prospectively in the CSF program: The resilience training and the fitness courses offered are almost exact parallels of the courses we use in positive education (Seligman et al., 2009). If it turns out that soldiers given this training perform better in their jobs, are more engaged, have more meaning in their lives, enjoy better relationships, and have more fruitful employment when they return to civilian society, this will ground a new model for our public schools. Again we will know whether this is so within the next decade.

Objections

We are not unmindful of those segments of American society, including some psychologists, who look askance on working with the military in any way.

The task of the military is to provide the capability of defending the nation from threat. Revulsion toward war is understandable, but it is not the military that sets the nation's policies on war and peace. The military carries out the policies that emerge from our democratic form of government. Withholding professional and scientific support for the people who provide the nation's defense is, we believe, simply wrong. Psychologists are as diverse in their views as any other group of citizens, but the American Psychological Association has, for six decades, been solid in its support on behalf of the men and women who serve in our armed forces.

Here, in unvarnished form, are three of the objections that might be raised to working with the military, and our responses:

- Psychology should devote its scarce resources to helping those who are suffering, not those who are well.

Positive psychology seeks to broaden the scope of psychological science and practice. It seeks to build more positive emotion, engagement, and meaning and better relationships among all people, and it has developed new interventions to do just that. It is a supplement, not a replacement, for the science and practice of relieving suffering. We believe that soldiers with PTSD, depression, anxiety, and other disorders should continue to receive the best of treatments. We are also mindful, however, that the known treatments are of limited effectiveness (Seligman, 1993, 2006). The CSF program will not subtract from the treatment resources; rather it is a preventive program that will likely reduce the need for them by effectively preventing suffering.

- Psychology should do no harm: Aiding the military will make people who kill for a living feel better about killing and help them do a better job of it.

If we had discovered a way of preventing malaria—mosquito netting, draining swamps, quinine—and our soldiers were fighting in a malaria-infested theater, would these voices also counsel withholding our discoveries? We would not withhold our help: The balance of good done by building the physical and mental fitness of our soldiers far outweighs any harm that might be done. The alleged harm—making healthier killers or helping them to feel better—turns also on the final objection.

- Psychology should not aid the foreign policy of the United States.

Three ideologies have arisen in the past century that have sought to overthrow democracy by force: fascism, communism, and jihadist Islam. It should be noted that without a strong military and the will to use force responsibly in self-defense, our victories would not have happened, and defense against current and future threats would be impossible. Psychology materially aided in the defeat of the first two threats, and in doing so it carved out its identity. We are proud to aid our military in defending and protecting our nation right now, and we will be proud to help our soldiers and their families into the peace that will follow.

References

Capshew, J. H. (1999). *Psychologists on the march: Science, practice, and professional identity in America, 1929–1969.* Cambridge, England: Cambridge University Press. doi:10.1017/CBO9780511572944

Cornum, R., Matthews, M., & Seligman, M. (2011). Comprehensive Soldier Fitness: Building resilience in a challenging institutional context. *American Psychologist, 66,* 4–9. doi:10.1037/a0021420

Fravell, M., Nasser, K., & Cornum, R. (2011). The Soldier Fitness Tracker: Global delivery of Comprehensive Soldier Fitness. *American Psychologist, 66,* 73–76. doi:10.1037/a0021632

LeardMann, C. A., Smith, T. C., Smith, B., Wells, T. S., & Ryan, M. A. K. (2009). Baseline self reported functional health and vulnerability to post-traumatic stress disorder after combat deployment: Prospective US military cohort study. *British Medical Journal, 338,* 1–9. doi:10.1136/bmj.b1273

Napoli, D. S. (1981). *Architects of adjustment: The history of the psychological profession in the United States.* Port Washington, NY: Kennikat Press.

Seligman, M. E. P. (1993). *What you can change and what you can't.* New York, NY: Knopf.

Seligman, M. E. P. (2006). Afterword: Breaking the 65 percent barrier. In M. Csikszentmihalyi & I. Selega (Eds.), *A life worth living: Contributions to positive psychology* (pp. 230–236). New York, NY: Oxford University Press.

Seligman, M. E. P., Ernst, R. M., Gillham, J., Reivich, K., & Linkins, M. (2009). Positive education: Positive psychology and classroom interventions. *Oxford Review of Education, 35,* 293–311. doi:10.1080/03054980902934563

Smith, L. P. (1948). Foreword. In C. Bray (Ed.), *Psychology and military proficiency: A history of the Applied Psychology Panel of the National Defense Research Committee.* Princeton, NJ: Princeton University Press.

Yerkes, R. M. (1918). Psychology in relation to the war. *Psychological Review, 25,* 85–115. doi:10.1037/h0069904

Yerkes, R. M. (1941). Psychology and defense. *Proceedings of the American Philosophical Society, 84,* 527–542.

Critical Thinking

1. Historically, what role has psychology played in the armed services? How is this role changing today?

2. What is positive psychology and what role might it play in helping combat veterans readjust to life after war?

3. What are some of the objections that some psychologists may have in working with the military, and how do psychologists address these objections?

Create Central

www.mhhe.com/createcentral

Internet References

Ready Army: Comprehensive soldier fitness
www.acsim.army.mil/readyarmy/ra_csf.htm

Building the warrior within
www.stripes.com/building-the-warrior-within-comprehensive-soldier-fitness-program-aims-to-boost-soldiers-psychological-resiliency-1.119529

Seligman, Martin E. P.; Fowler, Raymond D. From *American Psychologist*, January 2011, pp. 82–86. Copyright © 2011 by American Psychological Association. Reprinted by permission via Rightslink.

Article   Prepared by: Eric Landrum, *Boise State University*

Improving Health, Worldwide

Psychology is ramping up efforts to improve global health and well-being.

KIRSTEN WEIR

Learning Outcomes

After reading this article, you will be able to:

• Describe the nature of the looming healthcare crisis regarding healthcare needs.

• Provide an example of how economics can specifically effect the delivery of effective healthcare.

A serious shortage of health-care providers threatens well-being around the world. With the planet's population soaring, the global health crisis stands to get even worse. According to the World Health Organization, 57 countries have fewer than 23 health workers for every 10,000 citizens, and 13 low- and middle-income countries have fewer than one hospital per million people.

Those proportions are expected to deteriorate by 2045, when the world's population is predicted to swell to 9 billion, from 7 billion today.

Clearly, there's work to be done to meet the world's burgeoning health-care needs, especially within the developing world. But more medicine and more doctors aren't the only answers. Most global health concerns—including HIV, obesity, malnutrition and sanitation—have a behavioral component, says Robert Balster, PhD, a psychologist at Virginia Commonwealth University and currently a Jefferson science fellow at the United States Agency for International Development (USAID). As a result, he says, "focusing on behavior change would have huge benefits."

"Regardless of the kind of health-care intervention, psychology needs to be at the table," adds Chris Stout, PsyD, who directs the Center for Global Initiatives and is a clinical professor at the College of Medicine, University of Illinois, Chicago. "Psychologists are probably better trained than any other health-care professional to have cultural awareness and sensitivity, and that queues us up to be really helpful when we deal with global health issues."

Psychologists are gradually becoming more tuned into global health, says Merry Bullock, PhD, senior director of APA's Office of International Affairs. The International Congress of Psychology, (/news/events/2012/international-congress-psychology.aspx), scheduled to be held in Cape Town, South Africa, in July, features health as a central topic and will include a symposium on models of health care around the world, organized by APA's Senior Science Advisor Ellen Garrison, PhD, Bullock says. And APA President Suzanne Bennett Johnson, PhD, serves on a committee for the International Council of Science, which recently issued a global call for research on a systems approach to global health issues. Those collaborations, Bullock says, "make opportunities available for broader international exchange."

Psychological Perspective

Among the greatest threats to human life is infectious disease. In 2010, malaria alone killed 655,000 people—a tragedy made even more heartbreaking by the fact that the disease is both preventable and curable.

In the poverty-stricken regions where malaria is endemic, however, prevention and treatment are hard to come by. Most malaria-carrying mosquitoes bite at night, and insecticide-treated bed nets are one of the most effective and affordable defenses against the deadly disease. "[Bed nets] are a very cheap intervention and they're quite available," says Balster. "The trick is to get people to use them, and use them properly."

To do that, health workers have implemented a variety of behavior-change initiatives in countries throughout Africa, Balster says. USAID-supported behavior-change workers took steps to make it easy for people to obtain bed nets, encouraged local leaders to endorse their use and recruited community health workers to go door-to-door distributing nets and explaining how to use them. They distributed pamphlets, broadcast radio campaigns, held town hall meetings, and led community workshops. The efforts paid off. In nine countries where baseline data are available, bed net ownership more than doubled from 2004 to 2010, Balster says, with corresponding improvement in malaria rates. In Ethiopia, for instance, villages that received malaria prevention and treatment programs saw malaria cases fall by 73 percent between 2005 and 2010.

Educating communities about the importance of bed nets is one thing. Health workers face bigger hurdles when trying to convince people to change their sexual behavior. HIV/AIDS (/topics/hiv-aids/index.aspx) infects some 34 million people worldwide. Much of the effort to control AIDS focuses on bio-medical advances such as vaccines and anti-retroviral medications. Those are clearly important, says Balster. "[But] an equally important and effective use of resources is in prevention."

Among the psychologists applying their talents to AIDS prevention is Kathleen Sikkema, PhD, a professor of psychology and neuroscience at the Duke Global Health Institute. Sikkema, who studies HIV prevention and mental health in South Africa and other developing nations, argues that mental health treatment should be a key element in any HIV prevention program (*AIDS and Behavior,* 2010). After all, she says, researchers have compiled strong evidence of the link between HIV transmission risk and mental health. A person with a poor mental health status is more likely to engage in risky sexual behaviors and less likely to adhere to drug treatment protocols that could minimize the spread of the disease.

To address these issues, Sikkema and her colleagues are developing and testing a number of HIV interventions in South Africa and elsewhere. One project promotes adaptive coping among HIV-positive men and women with a history of childhood sexual abuse. Another teaches coping skills to young children of HIV-positive mothers, while a third aims to reduce risky behavior among women who drink alcohol in informal drinking establishments where gender-based violence is prevalent. With these projects, she and her colleagues hope to identify effective techniques to ultimately reduce the spread of HIV.

Of course, infectious diseases such as malaria and HIV make up just one subset of the global health agenda. Worldwide, rates of chronic, non-communicable diseases such as heart disease, lung disease, diabetes and cancer have been rising sharply alongside skyrocketing obesity (*The Lancet,* 2011). Many people think of obesity and related diseases as plights of prosperity, but in fact, nearly 80 percent of deaths from chronic, non-communicable diseases occurred in low- and middle-income countries in 2008, according to the WHO.

With primary risk factors such as poor diet, tobacco use and inactivity, those diseases have a clear behavioral component. And that's where psychologists like Gary Bennett, PhD, also at the Duke Global Health Institute, can help. Bennett has developed obesity interventions in the United States, and is now working to adapt some of those successful interventions for China. It's a good place to start. "There are more than 1.5 billion overweight people in the world, and at least a quarter of them are in China," he says.

He's testing an innovative project that provides tailored diet and exercise goals to participants via text message. In China, as in many other countries around the world, nutrition labeling on food is inconsistent. And as the country becomes more prosperous, eating out is becoming much more popular. As a result, he says, "counting calories is a real challenge." The text message program provides accessible, understandable goals that ultimately help people reduce their caloric intake and increase their activity levels—even if they aren't charting every calorie they swallow.

Bennett is still testing the intervention, but he's hopeful that it can be adapted to communities and cultures around the world.

Access to technology is growing at a rapid pace. "Cell phone towers are now found in most remote parts of the world," he says. Unfortunately, the same cannot be said for psychologists. "Obesity and other health behaviors present major opportunities for psychology," he says. "I think, frankly, we need many more psychologists focusing on these issues."

Another important area where psychologists are making a difference is at the intersection of early nutrition and behavior, says Maureen Black, PhD, a psychologist at the University of Maryland School of Medicine. Scientists have learned a lot about the relationship between psychology and nutrition over the last decade, Black says. Maternal depression, for instance, puts children at risk of nutritional deficiencies, poor growth and cognitive delays (*Bulletin of the World Health Organization,* 2011). On the flip side, maternal education and protective factors such as breastfeeding and early cognitive and socio-emotional opportunities can reduce a child's future health risks, as Susan Walker, PhD, at the University of the West Indies, with Black and other colleagues from the Global Child Development Group, reported last fall (*The Lancet,* 2011). Together with economists, psychologists have shown that ensuring early child development puts children on a positive trajectory to benefit from educational opportunities, become productive citizens and enhance the social capital of the society, Black says.

Such findings now form a basis for global policy recommendations, she says, and international agencies such as the WHO, the World Bank and UNICEF are incorporating a psychological angle into their strategies to promote early childhood development and nutrition.

Mental health experts can also help improve people's use of health-care services, says Balster. People in resource-poor regions may not take advantage of opportunities such as vaccination and prenatal care. As experts in behavior, psychologists can help identify and address the underlying reasons to help people make the most of health-care resources. "It's one thing to have medicines," Balster says, "but people have to take them properly."

Local Knowledge

When working in other countries, the best approaches aren't always the most intuitive. Sometimes it makes sense to adapt models from the United States to fit the needs of a developing country or community. In other instances it's better to create a program from scratch for a particular place and culture. "Understanding cultural context and adaptation to the local community are essential for interventions to be effective," Sikkema says.

As health workers implement behavior-change programs, they must also ensure their strategies are good for the long haul, Balster says. "Historically, there's been too much of Western nations coming in, dumping a lot of money on a problem and disappearing when the money runs out." Fortunately, that appears to be changing, he says.

Stout, who works with communities around the world through the Center for Global Initiatives, has also witnessed a growing emphasis on involving locals to create sustainable programs. Drawing on local experience just makes sense, he says.

"Natural healers in South Africa provide services that you and I would see as pretty close to counseling," he points out. "In Cambodia and Vietnam, midwives become the de facto medical responders." When global health workers collaborate with these local sources of knowledge, they stand to reach more people and continue to benefit communities well into the future, he says.

Nevertheless, the psychology angle still sometimes gets short shrift among global health initiatives. That's gradually changing, Stout says, as researchers continue to demonstrate the value of psychology to global health. Black adds that, in her view, most global health agencies and organizations are happy to include the psychological perspective—especially when that perspective includes a preventive point of view. "I think psychologists would be much better positioned to have a global impact if they took their theories, which are strong and effective in promoting positive behavioral changes, and put them in a public health perspective," she adds. "Don't wait until the problem has occurred. Think about prevention, or better yet, health promotion."

Ultimately, Balster adds, psychologists are poised to make an important contribution to global health. "There are associations of psychology in most every country of the world," he notes. "Psychology has the wherewithal to be an organized global presence."

Critical Thinking

1. How is the growing population on the planet impacting the provision of health care services? Is supply keeping up with demand?

2. Provide an example of a behavior change intervention that can have an impact on the spread of infectious disease. What psychological principles are in play here with regard to behavior change?

3. What, if anything, is the link between HIV transmission risk and mental health?

Create Central

www.mhhe.com/createcentral

Internet References

How science is crucial to improving health worldwide
 www.huffingtonpost.com/susan-blumenthal/public-health-how
 -science_b_784726.html

Maternal and child health
 www.globalhealth.gov/global-health-topics/maternal-and-child-health

KIRSTEN WEIR is a writer in Minneapolis.

Article

Prepared by: Eric Landrum, *Boise State University*

Psychology Is a Hub Science

JOHN T. CACIOPPO

Learning Outcomes

After reading this article, you will be able to:

- Explain what a hub science is and the role it plays in relation to other scientific endeavors.

- Understand the notion of 'proximity' regarding other sciences in relation to psychology.

In an issue of the magazine *Scientific American,* the editors observed that "whenever we run articles on social topics, some readers protest that we should stick to 'real' science" (The Peculiar Institution, 2002, p. 8). You and I are confident about the scientific stature of psychology, but who in APS hasn't felt the icy skepticism of a fellow traveler on a flight after you respond to the question, "What is your occupation?" You may therefore be pleasantly surprised by a scientometric study entitled "Mapping the Backbone of Science" (Boyack, Klavans, & Borner, 2005).[1] The article is must reading for deans who oversee scientific psychology departments. I will explain why shortly. But first, some background.

In the Middle Ages, theology and philosophy were a dynamic duo of hub disciplines around which the other sciences were organized. These two areas influenced thinking across the various fields of scholarship (Leydesdorff, 2006).

The past three centuries have seen unparalleled advances in science. During this time, there have been scientific theories of invisible forces operating with measurable effects, such as in the case of magnetism, gravity, and dark matter. Natural philosophy became identified with physics, which, with mathematics, took on the role of the hub discipline of science.

Scientific research during the past century has continued to accelerate in terms of quantity and impact. People may reminisce about the good old days, but thanks to science and technology the amount of total income spent on the necessities of food, clothing, and shelter dropped from 80 percent in 1901 to 50 percent in 2002/2003 (United States Department of Labor, 2006). The explosion in the number of scientists, scientific specializations, journals, and research articles over the past century has been just as extraordinary. Given these dramatic changes, are the sciences still organized around a central discipline or two? Has the rapid period of expansion produced several hub disciplines? Or have all the scientific disciplines matured independently and sufficiently such that there is no central, inherent overall structure in the sciences?

Boyack and colleagues sought to answer these and similar questions. Scientometric and bibliometric analyses have been in place to identify clusters of authors, papers, or references, but only recently have computing capabilities, computational algorithms, and visualization techniques emerged that permit the analysis of large-scale document datasets. Boyack and colleagues quantified the patterns of scientific influence within and across the sciences based on citation data from more than one million journal articles appearing in 7,121 natural and social sciences journals published in 2000. For a source of high-quality citation data, they turned to the Science Citation Index (SCI) and the Social Science Citation Index (SSCI). The use of the SCI and SSCI also made it possible to use individual journal articles, rather than entire journals, as the unit of analysis. Among the limitations of using the SCI and SSCI are that conference and workshop proceedings are not indexed and that non-English-language journals are less likely to be included.

Eight different approaches to quantifying citation patterns were used to ensure structural accuracy, where accuracy means that journals within the same subdiscipline were grouped together, and groups of journals that cite each other were close to each other. Additionally, new visualization techniques were used to generate a two-dimensional spatial map of the sciences based on each metric. Finally, the validity of these maps was compared using two different accuracy measures. The best measures converged on the landscape of scientific influence. The resulting mapping of science provides a visual depiction of where each scientific discipline is, what is around it, what its relationships are to its neighboring disciplines, and how strong its impact is on the neighboring disciplines.

Not surprisingly, given scientific specialization over the past century, contemporary sciences no longer originate from a single source. Instead, seven hub sciences can be identified: mathematics, physics, chemistry, earth sciences, medicine, psychology, and the social sciences. Yes, psychology emerged as one of the hub disciplines of science!

The location of many of the disciplines has face validity as well. Electrical and nuclear engineering fall between mathematics and physics, chemical engineering and analytic chemistry fall between physics and chemistry, and statistics falls between mathematics and the social sciences. More interestingly here, public health, neuroscience, neurology, radiology, cardiology, and genetics are among the sciences that fall between psychology and medicine, whereas education and gerontology fall between psychology and the social sciences.

The more insular the field, the closer a field will lie to the outside of the map. Those with many interdisciplinary linkages are more likely to lie toward the middle of the map. It is interesting, therefore, to note that psychiatry, law, political science, and economics all lie along the outside, whereas psychology is closer to the middle, reflecting its interdisciplinary nature. Another map depicting the linkages among scientific fields confirmed that psychology is a hub discipline—that is, a discipline in which scientific research is cited by scientists in many other fields. For instance, medicine draws from psychology most heavily through neurology and psychiatry, whereas the social sciences draw directly from most of the specialties within psychology.

During a period in which our national leaders appear more likely to identify psychology with the work of Dr. Phil and Dr. Laura than with the thousands of scientists worldwide who make up the membership of the Association for Psychological Science, it is imperative that institutions of higher education make clear the centrality and influence of psychological science as well as the importance of maintaining and promoting its growth. Indeed, Boyack et al. (2005) noted: "Our interest in mapping science stems from a desire to understand the inputs, associations, flows, and outputs of the Science and Technology enterprise in a detailed manner that will help us guide that enterprise (or at least that portion of it operating in our institutions) in more fruitful directions" (p. 352). Most universities are organized along more traditional disciplinary boundaries, but decisions about both faculties and facilities could benefit from knowledge about the scientific disciplines that are especially central and influential. The results of Boyack et al. (2005) indicate that scientific contributions in psychology advance not only the discipline but many other scientific fields as well.

I began this column with the observation by the editors of *Scientific American* that whenever they run articles on "social" science topics they receive protests from some readers who advise them to stick to real science. The editors of *Scientific American* went on to say that they seldom hear these complaints from working physical or biological scientists: "They are the first to point out that the natural universe, for all its complexity, is easier to understand than the human being. If social science seems mushy, it is largely because the subject matter is so difficult, not because humans are somehow unworthy of scientific inquiry" (The Peculiar Institution, 2002, p. 8). The importance and centrality of psychological science may not be fully understood by politicians, but the evidence is clear: The mapping of

science shows psychology to be a hub discipline with a great deal to offer (and learn from) other scientific disciplines.

Note

1. The study was kindly sent to the author by Eliot Smith.

References

Boyack, K.W., Klavans, R., & Börner, K. (2005). Mapping the backbone of science. *Scientometrics, 64,* 351–374.

Editors. (2002). The peculiar institution. *Scientific American, 286,* 8.

Leydesdorff, L. (2006). Can scientific journals be classified in terms of aggregated journal-journal citation relations using the *Journal Citation Reports? Journal of the American Society for Information Science and Technology, 57,* 601–613.

United States Department of Labor (2006). *100 years of United States consumer spending.* Washington, D.C. (Also available at http://www.bls.gov/opub/uscs/)

Critical Thinking

1. The notion of hub sciences has been around for years—what were considered to be the first of the hub sciences?

2. Based on recent scientometric and bibliomentric analyses, psychology emerged as one of seven hub sciences. What does that mean, exactly?

3. What is the tension between the sciences and the social sciences, and why does it matter?

Create Central

www.mhhe.com/createcentral

Internet References

Is psychology the other-than-science science?
www.apa.org/ed/precollege/ptn/2012/08/other-science.aspx

Hey what's your minor?
www.psychologytoday.com/blog/career-minded/200806/hey-whats-your-minor

JOHN T. CACIOPPO is the Tiffany and Margaret Blake Distinguished Service Professor at The University of Chicago and the Director of the Center for Cognitive and Social Neuroscience. His current research falls under the rubric of social neuroscience, with an emphasis on the effects of social isolation and the mechanisms underlying effective versus ineffective social connection.

Article   Prepared by: Eric Landrum, *Boise State University*

A Scientific Pioneer and a Reluctant Role Model

Erin Millar

Learning Outcomes

After reading this article, you will be able to:

- Understand the challenges for women entering neuroscience fields.

- Comprehend some of the challenges in working in the neuroscience field.

In the early 1950s, Wilder Penfield, one of the world's leading neurosurgeons at the time, performed what should have been a straightforward elective surgery. The patient, an engineer who headed his department, had come to the Montreal Neurological Institute and Hospital, affiliated with McGill University, with epileptic seizures. The results of the surgery were catastrophic. "He couldn't remember anything that happened. He couldn't go out for dinner and follow a conversation," recalls the neuropsychologist Brenda Milner. "He had to be demoted to draftsman. But there was no loss of intelligence, no loss in reasoning."

Dr. Milner was then a 30-something PhD candidate, one of the few women employed by The Neuro (as those who work there call it). "Dr. Penfield was shocked. He didn't know what happened." She and the master surgeon wrote up the case, not knowing what would come of it. Soon after, she received an invitation from a neurosurgeon at Harvard. He had a similar case he hadn't thought significant; did she have any interest?

"I couldn't imagine why he would invite a young woman to study this case," remembers Dr. Milner, who at 94 continues her research full-time. The patient, identified for decades only as H.M., became the most important case study in the history of neuroscience, leading to many discoveries about how the brain creates memories. Although doctors had assumed H.M. was unable to form any new memories, Dr. Milner's groundbreaking research showed that he could develop new motor skills and spatial memories, proving for the first time that there are different types of memory. The Nobel Laureate Eric Kandel credited Dr. Milner with creating a whole new field called cognitive neuroscience.

On November 21, Dr. Milner became the ninth woman to be named to the Canadian Science and Engineering Hall of Fame, joining 53 other history-making researchers such as Alexander Graham Bell and J. Armand Bombardier. But she doesn't like to to be recognized as being one of the few women who have reached the highest ranks of science in Canada.

After her Hall of Fame acceptance speech, a group of young female scientists swarmed her eagerly to snap photos with her, showing how Dr. Milner, albeit somewhat unwillingly, has become an icon of what female scientists can accomplish in a male-dominated field.

"I have not set myself up to be a role model for women, but it does seem to be more of an issue than it used to be," Dr. Milner explains, recalling how she increasingly gets mobbed by women after public lectures in the past five years. "There is rarely a man in the group."

Although the landscape, particularly at medical schools, has changed significantly since Dr. Milner began her career, women continue to be underrepresented in many scientific fields. They make up only 39 per cent of students in physical sciences and 17 per cent in engineering and computer science. According to a recent study from the Council of Canadian Academies, only a third of faculty members in Canada are women, and that number shrinks to 15 per cent in the physical sciences, engineering and computer science.

Yet the toughest competition that Dr. Milner says she ever faced was against other women. When she was in high school she announced her intention to pursue mathematics against her headmistress's wishes she go into languages. The best science students in her native Britain went to Cambridge, yet the school's rigid college system only allowed for 400 female students to enroll. "It was tremendously difficult to get in," she says. "My competition was all women." Her all-girls school didn't have the calibre of teacher in math and physics to get her up to a competitive level, so they sent her elsewhere to a male lecturer.

For the rest of her career, however, Dr. Milner was determined to compete with the best scientists, male or female. "She never wanted to win prizes that were only for women, she wanted to win prizes open to both genders so she could beat the men," says Denise Klein, who has worked at The Neuro since starting a post-doc with Dr. Milner in 1992.

Early in her studies at Cambridge, Dr. Milner realized she would never be a great mathematician and switched to psychology, earning her degree in 1939. She met her husband Peter Milner while working for the military during the Second World War. They hastily married when he was asked to launch Canada's atomic energy program, and moved to Montreal.

After a teaching stint at the Université de Montréal, she realized that "in North America you were nobody if you didn't have a PhD." Dr. Milner wanted more than a teaching career. "I knew I had it in me to do something big," she says.

When she arrived at The Neuro in June, 1950, to begin her PhD, she was one of few women. "The institute was authoritarian," Dr. Milner recalls. "People who were junior would not speak out of turn. But it was not sexist." Dr. Klein goes a step further in describing it as a "chauvinistic environment."

Dr. Milner's response to the male-dominated atmosphere was to challenge stereotypes about psychology being a less rigorous approach to brain science than the work of the primarily male neurosurgeons. "She took what she did seriously enough that other people took her seriously and did not dismiss her work as soft science," says Dr. Klein. "She showed people that her field could be as scientific, as useful and as data-driven as other fields that are taken more seriously." During this period before brain imaging, when surgery was required to see what was happening in the brain, Dr. Milner's behaviour-based diagnostic work was eventually seen as crucial.

Dr. Milner insists she never encountered any barriers because of her gender. Her resistance to being recognized as an outstanding woman seems to stem from her desire to be a great scientist in general. "Brenda was good at showing people she was necessary," says Dr. Klein. "She showed people that the pieces of information she was providing from thinking about the brain and behaviour were important. She told me to make myself useful and I would have a job."

Far from being dismissed as a woman, Dr. Milner intimidated people. "Remember that she was a very strong woman," explains Gabriel Leonard, a clinical scientist at The Neuro. "There were very few people that had the courage and the necessary tenacity to fight her. She was a formidable person to debate, with a large vocabulary and a great knowledge of literature."

Three years ago, Dr. Milner received the prestigious international Balzan Prize, netting $1-million for her research. Now, she is in the midst of launching into a new research area looking at how the hemispheres of the brain interact. This year she is taking on two new post-docs and her colleagues reckon that she may be the oldest scientist in the world to do so.

Critical Thinking

1. Thinking about your own career trajectory, are there goals that you have that may be impacted by your gender? Explore and explain.

2. What role do you think one's involvement in a famous study may help or hinder advancement in one's particular chosen field?

Create Central

www.mhhe.com/createcentral

Internet References

The Finkbeiner test
www.doublexscience.org/the-finkbeiner-test

Psychology's feminist voices
www.feministvoices.com/Brenda-Milner

Unit 2

UNIT

Prepared by: Eric Landrum, *Boise State University*

Biological Bases of Behavior

As a child, Angel vowed that she did not want to turn out like either of her parents. Angel's mother was passive and silent about her father's drinking. When her father was drunk, her mom always called his boss to report that he was "sick" and then acted as if there was nothing wrong at home. Angel's childhood was a nightmare. Her father's behavior was erratic and unpredictable. If he drank a little, he seemed to be happy. If he drank a lot (which was usually the case), he often became belligerent.

Despite vowing not to become like her father, as an adult Angel found herself as an in-patient in the alcohol rehabilitation unit of a large hospital. Angel's employer could no longer tolerate her on-the-job mistakes or her unexplained absences from work. Angel's supervisor referred her to the clinic for help. As Angel pondered her fate, she wondered whether her genes preordained her to follow in her father's drunken footsteps or whether the stress of her childhood had brought her to this point in her life. After all, being the adult child of an alcoholic is difficult.

Psychologists are concerned with discovering the causes (when possible) of human behavior. Once the cause is known, treatments for problematic behaviors can be developed. In fact, certain behaviors might even be prevented when the cause is

identified early enough. But for Angel, prevention was too late. One of the paths to understanding human behavior is the task of understanding its biological underpinnings. Genes and chromosomes, the body's chemistry (as found in hormones, neurotransmitters, and enzymes), and the central and peripheral nervous systems are all implicated in human behavior.

Physiological psychologists, biopsychologists, and neuroscientists examine the role of biology in behavior. These experts often utilize one of a handful of techniques to understand the biology–behavior connection. Animal studies involving manipulation, stimulation, or destruction of certain parts of the brain offer one method of study, but these studies remain controversial with animal rights activists. There is an alternative technique that involves the study of individuals born with unusual or malfunctioning brains or those whose brains are damaged by accidents or disease—some case studies of these individuals are famous in psychology for the insights yielded. By studying an individual's behavior in comparison to both natural and adoptive parents, or by studying identical twins reared together or apart, we also can begin to understand the role of genetics and environment on human behavior.

Article

Prepared by: Eric Landrum, *Boise State University*

The Left Brain Knows What the Right Hand Is Doing

New research explores how brain lateralization influences our lives.

Michael Price

Learning Outcomes

After reading this article, you will be able to:

- Understand and explain brain lateralization.

- Describe how brain lateralization influence common human traits.

Browse through a list of history's most famous left-handers and you are likely to see Albert Einstein's name. You may even see people tying Einstein's genius to his left-handedness. The problem is, Einstein's left-handedness is a myth. Myriad photos show him writing on a chalkboard with his right hand, for example.

But handedness has its roots in the brain—right-handed people have left-hemisphere-dominant brains and vice versa—and the lefties who claim Einstein weren't all that far off. While he was certainly right-handed, autopsies suggest his brain didn't reflect the typical left-side dominance in language and speech areas. His brain's hemispheres were more symmetrical—a trait typical of left-handers and the ambidextrous.

By comparison, 95 percent of righties have brains that strictly divvy up tasks: The left hemisphere almost exclusively handles language and speech, the right handles emotion and image processing—but only about 20 percent of lefties have brains that divide up these duties so rigidly.

Brain hemisphere specialist Michael Corballis, PhD, a psychologist at the University of Auckland in New Zealand, points out that having the hemispheres manage different tasks might increase the brain's efficiency.

"There's an advantage to cerebral dominance because it localizes function to one hemisphere," he says. "Otherwise, information has to cross back and forth across the corpus callosum, and that can sometimes cause problems."

A strongly symmetrical brain, like Einstein's, leaves people open to mental dysfunction, but it also paves the way for creative thinking. Researchers are exploring these unusually balanced brains and finding out why that's the case.

Righties Rule

About 90 percent of people are right-handed, says Corballis. The remaining 10 percent are either left-handed or some degree of ambidextrous, though people with "true" ambidexterity—i.e., no dominant hand at all—only make up about 1 percent of the population.

That means the vast majority of people on this planet have strongly lateralized brains. That's probably no accident, Corballis says. Early in human history, and possibly even in our pre-human ancestors, evolution delegated different cognitive responsibilities to the brain's two hemispheres, he posits. It would be inefficient for both sides to, for example, process a person's speech when one hemisphere can do that just fine on its own. That frees up the other hemisphere to do something else, such as sort out the speech's emotional content.

Researchers used to think that minor brain damage early in development caused left-handedness, he notes.

"But if that's true, that's probably the minority of cases," Corballis says. There are just too many lefties for brain damage to be the major culprit, "so we look to genetics."

In 2007, geneticists identified a gene on chromosome 2, LRRTM1, that seems to be present in most lefties (*Molecular Psychiatry,* Vol. 12, No. 12). The gene has also been linked to schizophrenia, which fits with earlier research showing that people with schizophrenia are significantly more likely to be left-handed or ambidextrous.

Less-lateralized brains may also be linked to lower IQ scores, suggests a study by Corballis, published in *Neuropsychologia* (Vol. 46, No. 1). The study found that left-handers and right-handers had similar IQ scores, but people who identify as ambidextrous had slightly lower scores, especially in arithmetic, memory and reasoning.

Lateral of the Sexes

One curious fact about handedness is that men appear to be ever so slightly more prone to left-handedness than women. Over the past few decades, a number of studies have turned up this peculiarity, but there was nothing concrete, nothing consistent. But a recently published meta-analysis in September's *Psychological Bulletin* (Vol. 134, No. 5) seems to prove the point.

In their analysis of 144 handedness and brain laterality studies—accounting for a total of nearly 1.8 million individuals—University of Oxford psychologists Marietta Papadatou-Pastou, PhD, and Maryanne Martin, PhD, found that males are about 2 percent more likely to be left-handed than females. In other words, they note in the paper, if exactly 10 percent of a population's women were left-handed, then around 12 percent of men would be, too.

Interestingly, they found that in places such as Japan and Mexico, with high levels of "cultural masculinity," which is associated with highly differentiated social roles for men and women, there was an even stronger correlation between males and left-handedness. This suggests a cultural dimension of handedness, the authors point out.

So what else might account for the sex difference? One answer might be basic morphology. Some studies, the researchers note, have found that left-handed and ambidextrous people have larger corpus callosums—brain regions that connect the two hemispheres—than right-handed people, which might be linked to differences in brain development between men and women.

Another possibility Papadatou-Pastou and Martin suggest is testosterone. One theory holds that testosterone accelerates right hemisphere growth in the brain, which could lead to more cases of right hemisphere dominance and, consequently, more left-handedness, although this idea is debated.

There may also be a genetic component. No one has discovered a smoking gene or genes for left-handedness, but if it turns out to be linked to the X chromosome and recessive, like red-green colorblindness, it would make sense for more males to be left-handed.

It's even possible that all of these factors play some role in males' penchant for left-handedness, say Papadatou-Pastou and Martin.

—M. Price

These results dovetail with Corballis's previous findings that ambidextrous people also rate higher on a "magical ideation" scale, which measures people's propensity to, for example, think that people on television are talking directly to them or that they can sense when people are talking about them (*Laterality*, Vol. 7, No. 11).

The link among these three findings—the slight propensity for schizophrenia, lower IQ scores and magical ideation—may suggest that the brain is more likely to encounter faulty neuronal connections when the information it's processing has to shuttle back and forth between hemispheres, says Corballis.

Ambidexterous Payback

"That poses an evolutionary question," Corballis says. "If this [right-handed] gene is so advantageous, why are there still left-handers?"

Research suggests that there might be a big advantage to a less constrained brain: It might lead to less constrained thinking.

For years, anecdotal evidence has suggested that lefties might think more creatively than right-handers, and recent research supports this link. A 2007 paper in *Journal of Mental and Nervous Disease* (Vol. 195, No. 10) found that musicians, painters and writers were significantly more likely to be left-handed than control participants.

Corballis has a theory as to why: Just as information is prone to errors as it traverses between brain hemispheres, it's also more likely to encounter novel solutions. Righties might dismiss an idea as too radical, but nonrighties might be willing to entertain the thought nonetheless, and develop a solution that a right-hander's brain would skip right over.

"It's good to have a few people in any society who think outside the square," Corballis says.

Left-handers are taking that creativity straight to the bank, too, says Christopher Ruebeck, PhD, an economist at Lafayette College in Easton, PA. In a study published in *Laterality*, he found that lefties earn slightly more money than their right-handed peers who work at the same jobs. These results were most pronounced in left-handed college-educated men, Ruebeck says, who, on average, earn 15 percent more than righties. In fields where creative thinking is valuable, lefties might get the edge and earn more accordingly.

"Left-handed men seem to get a higher return on their education," he says.

The study found this effect in men but not in women, Ruebeck adds, though he's unsure why that might be. And because his study is one of only a few that have looked into this area so far, he cautions against overgeneralizing these results; at the moment, it remains an interesting correlation.

Also, equating left-handedness with creativity glosses over the fact that 20 percent of left-handed people do have strongly lateralized brains and are probably no more creative than right-handers. The idea of lefties as creative types "probably refers to the subgroup of [left-handers] who lack clear dominance in the hemispheres," Corballis says.

So what's the final verdict? Well, in a way, the human condition itself might be summed up as the balance between the brain's asymmetries and symmetries—rationality versus creativity, novel ideas versus traditional solutions.

"The asymmetrical brain might even represent science and the symmetrical brain, religion," Corballis speculates. "An exaggeration, no doubt, but it's fun to think along these lines."

Critical Thinking

1. What is brain lateralization?
2. How important is brain lateralization in influencing common human traits?

3. What, if any, are the differences between men and women with regard to handedness? Does it matter?

Create Central

www.mhhe.com/createcentral

Internet References

Right brain-left brain: A primer
www.dana.org/media/detail.aspx?id=40274

Right, left, right, wrong: An investigation of handedness
www.rightleftrightwrong.com/sources.html

Article Prepared by: Eric Landrum, *Boise State University*

Reflections on Mirror Neurons

TEMMA EHRENFELD

Learning Outcome

After reading this article, you will be able to:

- Describe mirror neurons and explain their role in influencing observational behavior and communication.

In 1992, a team at the University of Parma, Italy discovered what have been termed "mirror neurons" in macaque monkeys: cells that fire both when the monkey took an action (like holding a banana) and saw it performed (when a man held a banana). Giacomo Rizzolati, the celebrated discoverer, will deliver the Keynote Address at the APS Convention in Washington DC, USA, on May 26, 2011, and report on his latest findings. To tide us over until then, here's a report on the state of mirror neuron science.

Like monkeys, humans have mirror neurons that fire when we both perceive and take an action. Locating the tiny cells means attaching electrodes deep inside the brain. As this has hardly been practical in humans, studies have had to rely on imaging, which shows which areas of the brain "light up" in different circumstances. By last year, a meta-analysis of 139 imaging studies confirmed mirroring activity in parts of the human brain where, in monkeys, mirror neurons are known to reside. Because the lit-up areas contain millions of neurons, for humans most researchers speak of a "mirror system," rather than mirror cells. Last year, single mirror neurons were recorded in humans for the first time, using in-depth electrodes, in 21 epileptic patients.

The cells showed up unexpectedly in an area known for memory, the medial temporal lobe, as well as in areas where they were expected. The discovery suggests that memory is embedded in our mirror system, says Marco Iacoboni (University of California, Los Angeles), a leading authority in the field and a co-author of the epilepsy study. Perhaps, he says, we form memory "traces" whenever we see or observe an action. "It's a lovely idea," says Rizzolati, though he adds that it's too early to say.

The mirroring system includes a mechanism that helps the brain record the difference between seeing and acting. In the epilepsy study, some neurons fired more during action and others fired more during observation. These same cells, Iacoboni proposes, help us distinguish between the self and others.

That's an important issue, to say the least. We often confuse our own actions with those of other people. In a study published recently in *Psychological Science,* Gerald Echterhoff, University of Muenster, Germany, and his co-authors reported that people who had watched a video of someone else doing a simple action—shaking a bottle or shuffling a deck of cards—often mistakenly recalled two weeks later that they had done so themselves. The mistake occurred even when participants were warned that they could mix up other people's actions with their own. Echterhoff and a co-author, Isabel Lindner, of the University of Cologne, Germany, plan to conduct imaging studies to test if the phenomenon is related to mirroring.

Mirror neurons are present in infant monkeys. Three years ago, the first abstract appeared reporting that surface electrodes had recorded mirroring in monkeys one- to seven-days old as they watched humans stick out their tongues and smack their lips. Says Pier Francesco Ferrari, of the University of Parma, and co-author of an upcoming study, "This is the first evidence that infants have a mirror mechanism at birth that responds to facial gestures. Without any experience of stimulation, they are able to focus their attention on the most relevant stimuli and respond." Sometimes the days-old monkeys even stuck out their tongues when they saw the human tongue, Ferrari says.

In monkeys, mirror neurons are present in the insula, an emotion center. Despite all the claims linking mirror neurons to empathy, Rizzolatti says he is only now reporting the discovery of a few mirror neurons in the insula in monkeys, "a reservoir for disgust and pain. Many other factors control how we react," he says, "but mirror neurons are how we recognize an emotion in others neurally."

Mimicry, linked to mirror neurons, makes monkeys bond. The idea that mimicry helps humans bond is well-accepted, but the first controlled experiment, with a monkey, came last year, Ferrari says. In that study, reported in *Science,* his team presented monkeys with a token and rewarded them with treats if they returned it. The monkeys had a choice of returning the token to either of two investigators, only one of whom was imitating the monkey. The monkeys consistently chose to return the token to the person who imitated them and spent more time near that investigator.

Mimicry in humans reflects social cues. The idea that we're primed in one part of our brain to like those who mimic us doesn't rule out other discriminations. Unconscious mimicry is deeply social and, as such, reflects prejudice, says Rick van Baaren of Radboud University in the Netherlands. In a 2009 overview of the science of mimicry published in the *Philosophical Transactions of The Royal Society,* he points out that people are more likely to mimic a member of the same ethnic group, less likely to mimic a stigmatized person who is obese or has a scar, and less likely to mimic members of a group we view with prejudice. In fact, humans tend to react badly when mimicked by someone from an "out group."

The mirror systems of two people can move in tandem. Many researchers had proposed that the brains of two people "resonate" with each other as they interact, with one person's mirror system reflecting changes in the other. Last spring, *the Proceedings of the National Academy of Sciences* reported on the brain activity of people playing the game of charades. The observer and gesturer performing the charade did move neurologically in tandem, says co-author Christian Keysers, of the University Medical Center in Groningen, The Netherlands. Keysers says the discovery backs up the idea that mirroring plays a key role in the evolution of language. We're exquisitely responsive to gestures, he says; "Nobody had ever shown that during gestural communication the observer's mirror system tracks the moment to moment state of the gesturer's motor system."

Mirror neurons respond to sound. In monkeys, mirror neurons fire at sounds associated with an action, such as breaking a peanut or tearing paper. Mirroring has been discovered in birds hearing bird song, and in humans. Recent work, led by Emiliano Ricciardi at the University of Pisa, Italy, found that blind people, using their hearing, interpret the actions of others by recruiting the same human mirror system brain areas as sighted people.

Mirror neurons code intentions. Whether mirror neurons register the goal of an action or other higher-level systems must chip in to judge other people's intentions has been the subject of much debate. The evidence is accumulating that mirror neurons "implement a fairly sophisticated and rather abstract coding of the actions of others," says Iacoboni. One clue is that while a third of all mirror neurons fire for exactly the same action, either executed or observed, the larger number—about two thirds—fire for actions that achieve the same goal or those that are logically related—for example, first grasping and then bringing an object to the mouth. And these neurons make fine distinctions: When a monkey observed an experimenter grasping an object and pantomiming the same action, the neurons fired when the experimenter grasped the object but not during the pantomime. "In academia, there is a lot of politics and we are continuously trying to figure out the 'real intentions' of other people," Iacoboni says. "The mirror system deals with relatively simple intentions: smiling at each other, or making eye contact with the other driver at an intersection."

Mirroring increases with experience. In the first studies, monkeys mirrored when they saw a person grasping food but not if the person used a tool. That made sense because monkeys don't use tools. In later research, monkeys did mirror humans using a tool; Iacoboni suggests that their brains had "learned," adjusting to seeing researchers with tools. In humans, more mirroring activity occurs when dancers see other dancers perform routines they know well. Mirroring in blind people is more active in response to more familiar action sounds.

Stimulating the mirror system helps stroke victims. If mirroring develops as we learn, perhaps triggering mirroring can teach. Two studies with stroke victims, for example, have found that stimulating the mirror system helped them recover particular motor actions, says Ferdinand Binkofski at the University of Luebeck, Germany. When stroke victims received "action observation therapy," in which they observed an action repeatedly, they regained more ability. Compared to a control group, the stroke victims also showed more mirroring in brain scans.

Children with autistic syndromes have mirroring defects. As early as 2001, researchers hypothesized that a deficit in the mirror neuron system could explain some of the problems of autistic patients. As of September, 2010 twenty published papers using brain imaging, magnetoencephalography, electroencephalography, and transcranial magnetic stimulation support this idea, and four failed to support it, according to Iacoboni.

The hope is that basic science in the mirror system could lead to a better understanding of emotional difficulties. As Ferrari points out, some infant monkeys separated from their mothers show "symptoms like those in autistic kids. You see them rocking and avoiding your gaze." Others develop normally. Ferrari and his colleagues plan to follow the infants they studied and measure whether strong mirror neuron activity in the first week of life indicates sociability later on. "We hope to create a picture of how brain activity interacts with the social environment to put some monkeys more at risk," he says. "The obvious direction is to translate this to humans."

Mirror neuron research continues to grow fast, across disciplines. Already the number of items produced by a PubMed search, for example, increased twenty-fold between 2000 and 2010, although that number only doubled for "Stroop and brain," another popular topic. The ongoing technical challenge remains: Mirror neurons are not the majority of cells in the brain areas where they are located, so it is still difficult to pinpoint their role when those areas show spiking activity. Iacoboni suggests that mathematical modeling will help make more of this data useful. Such modeling allowed Keysers, for example, to establish the existence of resonance in the charades study. So what can we expect next? Most likely, Iacoboni, says, more work with depth electrodes in neurological patients and studies like Ferrari's to test whether mirroring is a biomarker of sociality. A promising underexplored subject is the inhibitors that keep us from mimicking (but fail recovering addicts who relapse when they see others consume). Behind all this work will be a growing consensus that mirror neurons evolved in humans so we could learn from observation and communication.

References

Ertelt, D., Small, S., Solodkin, A., Dettmers, C., McNamara, A., Binkofski, F., & Buccino, G. (2007). Action observation has a positive impact on rehabilitation of motor deficits after stroke. *Neuroimage, 36*(Suppl 2), T164–T173.

Ferrari, P.F., Vanderwert, R., Herman, K., Paukner, A., Fox, N.A., & Suomi, S.J. (2008). Society for Neuroscience Abstract, *297,* 13.

Lindner, I., Echterhoff, G., Davidson, P.S., & Brand, M. (2010). Observation inflation: Your actions become mine. *Psychological Science, 21,* 1291–1299.

Mukamel, R., Ekstrom, A.D., Kaplan, J., Iacoboni, M., & Fried, I. (2010). Single-neuron responses in humans during execution and observation of actions. *Current Biology, 20,* 750–756.

Paukner, A., Suomi, S., Visalberghi, E., & Ferrari, P.F. (2009). Capuchin monkeys display affiliation toward humans who imitate them. *Science, 325,* 880.

Ricciardi, E., Bonino, D., Sani, L., Vecchi, T., Guazzelli, M., Haxby, J.V., Fadiga, L., Pietrini, P. (2009). Do we really need vision? How blind people "see" the actions of others. *Journal of Neuroscience, 29,* 9719-9724.

Schippers, M.B., Roebroeck, A., Renken, R., Nanetti, L., & Keysers, C. (2010). Mapping the information flow from one brain to another during gestural communication. *Proceedings of the National Academy of Sciences, USA, 107,* 9388–9393.

van Baaren, R., Janssen, L., Chartrand, T.L., & Dijksterhuis, A. (2009). Where is the love? The social aspects of mimicry. *Philosophical Transactions of the Royal Society of London, B: Biological Sciences, 364*(1528), 2381–2389.

Critical Thinking

1. What are mirror neurons and what role do they play in learning?

2. Generally speaking, what significance does understanding neural function hold for psychology?

3. How is the functioning of mirror neurons both similar and different when comparing their functions in monkeys and human infants?

Create Central

www.mhhe.com/createcentral

Internet References

The mind's mirror
www.apa.org/monitor/oct05/mirror.aspx

What's so special about mirror neurons?
http://blogs.scientificamerican.com/guest-blog/2012/11/06/whats-so-special-about-mirror-neurons

Article   Prepared by: Eric Landrum, *Boise State University*

Does Thinking Really Hard Burn More Calories?

Unlike physical exercise, mental workouts probably do not demand significantly more energy than usual. Believing we have drained our brains, however, may be enough to induce weariness

FERRIS JABR

Learning Outcomes

After reading this article, you will be able to:

- Identify the relationship between mental effort and the consumption of glucose during brain functioning.

- Apply the concept of resting metabolic rate to better understanding how cognitive activities are linked to burning calories and consuming energy.

Between October and June they shuffle out of auditoriums, gymnasiums and classrooms, their eyes adjusting to the sunlight as their fingers fumble to awaken cell phones that have been silent for four consecutive hours. Some raise a hand to their foreheads, as though trying to rub away a headache. Others linger in front of the parking lot, unsure of what to do next. They are absolutely exhausted, but not because of any strenuous physical activity. Rather, these high school students have just taken the SAT. "I was fast asleep as soon as I got home," Ikra Ahmad told The Local, a *New York Times* blog, when she was interviewed for a story on "SAT hangover."

Temporary mental exhaustion is a genuine and common phenomenon, which, it is important to note, differs from chronic mental fatigue associated with regular sleep deprivation and some medical disorders. Everyday mental weariness makes sense, intuitively. Surely complex thought and intense concentration require more energy than routine mental processes. Just as vigorous exercise tires our bodies, intellectual exertion should drain the brain. What the latest science reveals, however, is that the popular notion of mental exhaustion is too simplistic. The brain continuously slurps up huge amounts of energy for an organ of its size, regardless of whether we are tackling integral calculus or clicking through the week's top 10 LOLcats. Although firing neurons summon extra blood, oxygen and glucose, any local increases in energy consumption are tiny compared with the brain's gluttonous baseline intake. So, in most cases, short periods of additional mental effort require a little more brainpower than

usual, but not much more. Most laboratory experiments, however, have not subjected volunteers to several hours' worth of challenging mental acrobatics. And something must explain the *feeling* of mental exhaustion, even if its physiology differs from physical fatigue. Simply believing that our brains have expended a lot of effort might be enough to make us lethargic.

Brainpower

Although the average adult human brain weighs about 1.4 kilograms, only 2 percent of total body weight, it demands 20 percent of our resting metabolic rate (RMR)—the total amount of energy our bodies expend in one very lazy day of no activity. RMR varies from person to person depending on age, gender, size and health. If we assume an average resting metabolic rate of 1,300 calories, then the brain consumes 260 of those calories just to keep things in order. That's 10.8 calories every hour or 0.18 calories each minute. (For comparison's sake, see Harvard's table of calories burned during different activities.) With a little math, we can convert that number into a measure of power:

- Resting metabolic rate: 1300 kilocalories, or kcal, the kind used in nutrition
- 1,300 kcal over 24 hours = 54.16 kcal per hour = 15.04 gram calories per second
- 15.04 gram calories/sec = 62.93 joules/sec = about 63 watts
- 20 percent of 63 watts = 12.6 watts

So a typical adult human brain runs on around 12 watts—a fifth of the power required by a standard 60 watt lightbulb. Compared with most other organs, the brain is greedy; pitted against man-made electronics, it is astoundingly efficient. IBM's Watson, the supercomputer that defeated *Jeopardy!* champions, depends on ninety IBM Power 750 servers, each of which requires around one thousand watts.

Energy travels to the brain via blood vessels in the form of glucose, which is transported across the blood-brain barrier and used to produce adenosine triphosphate (ATP), the main currency of chemical energy within cells. Experiments with both animals and people have confirmed that when neurons in a particular brain region fire, local capillaries dilate to deliver more blood than usual, along with extra glucose and oxygen. This consistent response makes neuroimaging studies possible: functional magnetic resonance imaging (fMRI) depends on the unique magnetic properties of blood flowing to and from firing neurons. Research has also confirmed that once dilated blood vessels deliver extra glucose, brain cells lap it up.

Extending the logic of such findings, some scientists have proposed the following: if firing neurons require extra glucose, then especially challenging mental tasks should decrease glucose levels in the blood and, likewise, eating foods rich in sugars should improve performance on such tasks. Although quite a few studies have confirmed these predictions, the evidence as a whole is mixed and most of the changes in glucose levels range from the miniscule to the small. In a study at Northumbria University, for example, volunteers who completed a series of verbal and numerical tasks showed a larger drop in blood glucose than people who just pressed a key repeatedly. In the same study, a sugary drink improved performance on one of the tasks, but not the others. At Liverpool John Moores University volunteers performed two versions of the Stroop task, in which they had to identify the color of ink in which a word was printed, rather than reading the word itself: In one version, the words and colors matched—BLUE appeared in blue ink; in the tricky version, the word BLUE appeared in green or red ink. Volunteers who performed the more challenging task showed bigger dips in blood glucose, which the researchers interpreted as a direct cause of greater mental effort. Some studies have found that when people are not very good at a particular task, they exert more mental effort and use more glucose and that, likewise, the more skilled you are, the more efficient your brain is and the less glucose you need. Complicating matters, at least one study suggests the opposite—that more skillful brains recruit more energy.

Not So Simple Sugars

Unsatisfying and contradictory findings from glucose studies underscore that energy consumption in the brain is not a simple matter of greater mental effort sapping more of the body's available energy. Claude Messier of the University of Ottawa has reviewed many such studies. He remains unconvinced that any one cognitive task measurably changes glucose levels in the brain or blood. "In theory, yes, a more difficult mental task requires more energy because there is more neural activity," he says, "but when people do one mental task you won't see a large increase of glucose consumption as a significant percentage of the overall rate. The base level is quite a lot of energy—even in slow-wave sleep with very little activity there is still a high baseline consumption of glucose." Most organs do not require so much energy for basic housekeeping. But the brain must actively maintain appropriate concentrations of charged particles across the membranes of billions of neurons, even when those cells are not firing. Because of this expensive

and continuous maintenance, the brain usually has the energy it needs for a little extra work.

Authors of other review papers have reached similar conclusions. Robert Kurzban of the University of Pennsylvania points to studies showing that moderate exercise improves people's ability to focus. In one study, for example, children who walked for 20 minutes on a treadmill performed better on an academic achievement test than children who read quietly before the exam. If mental effort and ability were a simple matter of available glucose, then the children who exercised—and burnt up more energy—should have performed worse than their quiescent peers.

The influence of a mental task's difficulty on energy consumption "appears to be subtle and probably depends on individual variation in effort required, engagement and resources available, which might be related to variables such as age, personality and gluco-regulation," wrote Leigh Gibson of Roehampton University in a review on carbohydrates and mental function.

Both Gibson and Messier conclude that when someone has trouble regulating glucose properly—or has fasted for a long time—a sugary drink or food can improve their subsequent performance on certain kinds of memory tasks. But for most people, the body easily supplies what little extra glucose the brain needs for additional mental effort.

Body and Mind

If challenging cognitive tasks consume only a little more fuel than usual, what explains the feeling of mental exhaustion following the SAT or a similarly grueling mental marathon? One answer is that maintaining unbroken focus or navigating demanding intellectual territory for several hours really does burn enough energy to leave one feeling drained, but that researchers have not confirmed this because they have simply not been tough enough on their volunteers. In most experiments, participants perform a single task of moderate difficulty, rarely for more than an hour or two. "Maybe if we push them harder, and get people to do things they are not good at, we would see clearer results," Messier suggests.

Equally important to the duration of mental exertion is one's attitude toward it. Watching a thrilling biopic with a complex narrative excites many different brain regions for a good two hours, yet people typically do not shamble out of the theater complaining of mental fatigue. Some people regularly curl up with densely written novels that others might throw across the room in frustration. Completing a complex crossword or sudoku puzzle on a Sunday morning does not usually ruin one's ability to focus for the rest of the day—in fact, some claim it sharpens their mental state. In short, people routinely enjoy intellectually invigorating activities without suffering mental exhaustion.

Such fatigue seems much more likely to follow sustained mental effort that we do not seek for pleasure—such as the obligatory SAT—especially when we *expect* that the ordeal will drain our brains. If we think an exam or puzzle will be difficult, it often will be. Studies have shown that something similar happens when people exercise and play sports: a large component of physical exhaustion is in our heads. In related research, volunteers that cycled on an exercise bike following a 90-minute computerized test of sustained attention quit pedaling from exhaustion sooner than participants that watched emotionally neutral documentaries before exercising. Even if the attention test did not consume significantly more energy than watching movies, the volunteers reported feeling less energetic. That feeling was powerful enough to limit their physical performance.

In the specific case of the SAT, something beyond pure mental effort likely contributes to post-exam stupor: stress. After all, the brain does not function in a vacuum. Other organs burn up energy, too. Taking an exam that partially determines where one will spend the next four years is nerve-racking enough to send stress hormones swimming through the blood stream, induce sweating, quicken heart rates and encourage fidgeting and contorted body postures. The SAT and similar trials are not just mentally taxing—they are physically exhausting, too.

A small but revealing study suggests that even mildly stressful intellectual challenges change our emotional states and behaviors, even if they do not profoundly alter brain metabolism. Fourteen female Canadian college students either sat around, summarized a passage of text or completed a series of computerized attention and memory tests for 45 minutes before feasting on a buffet lunch. Students who exercised their brains helped themselves to around 200 more calories than students who relaxed. Their blood glucose levels also fluctuated more than those of students who just sat there, but not in any consistent way. Levels of the stress hormone cortisol, however, were significantly higher in students whose brains were busy, as were their heart rates, blood pressure and self-reported anxiety. In all likelihood, these students did not eat more because their haggard brains desperately needed more fuel; rather, they were stress eating.

Messier has related explanation for everyday mental weariness: "My general hypothesis is that the brain is a lazy bum," he says. "The brain has a hard time staying focused on just one thing for too long. It's possible that sustained concentration creates some changes in the brain that promote avoidance of that state. It could be like a timer that says, 'Okay you're done now.' Maybe the brain just doesn't like to work so hard for so long."

Critical Thinking

1. How does the rate of energy consumption of the brain relate, proportionally speaking, to the size of the brain compared to the size of the rest of the body?

2. What is the resting metabolic rate, and why does it matter?

3. What role does glucose play in supporting the energy consumption needs of the brain?

Create Central

www.mhhe.com/createcentral

Internet References

Do you burn more calories when you think hard?
    www.straightdope.com/columns/read/3083/do-you-burn-more
    -calories-when-you-think-hard
Does extra mental effort burn more calories?
    www.nytimes.com/2008/09/02/science/02qna.html?_r=0

Article   Prepared by: Eric Landrum, *Boise State University*

A Single Brain Structure May Give Winners That Extra Physical Edge

An extraordinary insula helps elite athletes better anticipate their body's upcoming feelings, improving their physical reactions

SANDRA UPSON

Learning Outcomes

After reading this article, you will be able to:

- Describe the role of the insular cortex and its relationship to athletic performance.
- Understand the process of interoception.

All elite athletes train hard, possess great skills and stay mentally sharp during competition. But what separates a gold medalist from an equally dedicated athlete who comes in 10th place? A small structure deep in the brain may give winners an extra edge.

Recent studies indicate that the brain's insular cortex may help a sprinter drive his body forward just a little more efficiently than his competitors. This region may prepare a boxer to better fend off a punch his opponent is beginning to throw as well as assist a diver as she calculates her spinning body's position so she hits the water with barely a splash. The insula, as it is commonly called, may help a marksman retain a sharp focus on the bull's-eye as his finger pulls back on the trigger and help a basketball player at the free-throw line block out the distracting screams and arm-waving of fans seated behind the backboard.

The insula does all this by anticipating an athlete's future feelings, according to a new theory. Researchers at the OptiBrain Center, a consortium based at the University of California, San Diego, and the Naval Health Research Center, suggest that an athlete possesses a hyper-attuned insula that can generate strikingly accurate predictions of how the body will feel in the next moment. That model of the body's future condition instructs other brain areas to initiate actions that are more tailored to coming demands than those of also-rans and couch potatoes.

This heightened awareness could allow Olympians to activate their muscles more resourcefully to swim faster, run farther and leap higher than mere mortals. In experiments published in 2012, brain scans of elite athletes appeared to differ most dramatically from ordinary subjects in the functioning of their insulas.

Emerging evidence now also suggests that this brain area can be trained using a meditation technique called mindfulness—good news for Olympians and weekend warriors alike.

Peak Performance

Stripped of the cheering fans, the play-by-play commentary and all the trappings of wealth and fame, professional sports reduced to a simple concept: The athletes who enthrall us are experts at meeting specific physical goals. They execute corporeal feats smoothly, without wasting a single drop of sweat.

Such performance is a full-brain phenomenon. The motor cortex and memory systems, for example, encode years of practice. Nerve fibers become ensconced in extra layers of a protective sheath that speeds up communication between neurons, producing lightning-fast reflexes. Understanding the brain at its athletic best is the goal of psychiatrist Martin Paulus and his colleagues at the OptiBrain Center. They propose that the insula may serve as the critical hub that merges high-level cognition with a measure of the body's state, to insure proper functioning of the muscles and bones that throw javelins and land twirling dismounts from the high bar. "The key idea we're after is how somebody responds when they get a cue that predicts something bad will happen," Paulus says. "The folks that are performing more optimally are the ones who are able to use that anticipatory cue to adjust themselves and return to equilibrium."

Slightly larger than a kumquat, the insula is part of the cerebral cortex, the thick folds of gray tissue that form the brain's outer layer. The densely rippled structure sits on the inside of the cortical mantle, resembling a tiny Japanese fan tucked neatly into the brain's interior. It is commonly thought of as the seat of interoception, or the sense of your body's internal state.

The insula generates this sense by maintaining a map of all your far-flung organs and tissues. Certain neurons in the insula respond to rumblings in the intestines, for example, whereas others fire to reflect a toothache. To manage the influx of messages bombarding it from throughout the body, the insula collaborates closely with the anterior cingulate cortex, an area crucial for decision-making, to evaluate and prioritize those stimuli. This raw representation of bodily signals has been hypothesized for more than a century to be the origin of emotions.

At first glance, pegging the insula as critical to anything can seem almost meaningless. It has been implicated in functions as diverse as decision-making, anticipation, timekeeping, singing, addiction, speech, even consciousness. The insula and the anterior cingulate cortex are the most commonly activated regions in brain-imaging experiments, according to a 2011 study, making it all the more difficult to discern their core functions.

Nevertheless, the case for the insula as the hub of athleticism has been building slowly for more than a decade. In the late 1990s neuroanatomist A. D. Craig at Barrow Neurological Institute was mapping the pathways that deliver pain and temperature sensations to the brain through the spinal cord. Upon discovering that these conduits led to the insula, he posited that one of the brain's core functions is to help the body maintain homeostasis, or equilibrium. For example, the body's internal temperature usually stays within a narrow range, and perturbations, registered by the insula, motivate us to restore it to that comfortable zone—perhaps by drinking cool water, seeking a shady patch or ceasing movement. Indeed, when scientists damaged the insula in rats, their ability to regulate their bodies was impaired.

When we exercise, we agitate our internal state. "Everything we do requires a calculation of how much energy it costs us, and this is what the insula seems to be performing," Craig says. By predicting how certain exertions will affect the body, the brain can initiate actions to temper those perturbations before they happen.

A compelling study from 2004 showed clear anatomical differences that matched variation in interoceptive ability. Hugo Critchley, now at the University of Sussex in England, asked participants to estimate the rate at which their hearts were beating without taking their own pulses. The people who guessed their heart rates most accurately had greater activity in the insula and more gray matter in this region. That last point is crucial, because it suggests that the physical size of the insula is directly related to differences in ability. This neural imprinting is similar to what is seen in professional violinists, whose motor cortex devotes greater real estate to the representations of fingers than is seen in an amateur's brain.

The OptiBrain researchers hypothesized that athletes need to be intensely aware of sensations such as heartbeat—and capable of recognizing the important ones and dismissing the red herrings. "The vast majority of NBA players are amazing athletes. But some of them stand out. It's not that Kobe Bryant or Derrick Rose has more energy, it's how they choose to expend that energy in critical moments that will decide their success," clinical psychologist Alan Simmons at the Veterans Affairs San Diego Healthcare System says.

Thinking Ahead

To test the idea that extremely fit individuals have superior interoception—and to investigate what this superiority looks like in action—Paulus and Simmons recently recruited a group of elite athletes to lie in a scanner and perform cognitive tests while an apparatus restricted their breathing. The feeling of shortness of breath is an unpleasant sensation that is known to rev up the insula.

Paulus and Simmons tested 10 of the world's most accomplished adventure racers—men and women who perform wilderness challenges that can include climbing, swimming, running and paddling. They asked the racers and 11 healthy control subjects to lie in a scanner and breathe through a tube while wearing a nose clip. While in the magnetic resonance imaging (MRI) machine, the subjects were instructed to view arrows pointing either left or right on a screen and press a button to note the direction. Sporadically, the researchers adjusted the airflow so that breathing became significantly more difficult. A change in the screen's color alerted the participants that breathing was about to become labored. The color change did not always accurately predict breathing restriction, however.

In all phases of the experiment, the insula was active, but to varying degrees. The healthy volunteers performed equally well on the arrow tests throughout the study—with no interference, when the screen's color changed and when struggling to inhale. But the adventure racers got more answers correct when either anticipating or undergoing the breathing load. Perturbing these individuals' interoceptive experience actually *improved* their performances. The racers also showed more brain activation when anticipating the breathing restriction but not while experiencing the restriction itself. It was as if the racers' brains made better use of cues to prepare themselves, thus gaining a cognitive edge. When the challenging moment arrived—when their breathing became labored—their insulas were comparatively placid.

Another study from Paulus's group, also published in 2012, adds nuance to this finding. The group sought to investigate elite athletes' cognitive flexibility. Considered a landmark of intelligence, this skill involves switching easily between opposing demands. Mental agility can plummet in a trying situation, however. Experiments on Navy SEALs and Army Rangers revealed that exposure to combatlike conditions impaired their reaction times, vigilance, learning, memory and reasoning. For Olympic-level athletes, too, grace under fire is a major objective.

To observe cognitive flexibility in action, Simmons asked 10 Navy SEALs and 11 healthy male civilians to perform a simple task in a brain scanner. Navy SEALs are extremely athletic individuals who are trained to cope with great demands on their physical, mental and emotional faculties. The exercise involved observing either a green or red shape followed by an emotionally laden photograph on a screen. Participants were to press one button when they saw a circle and another when they viewed a square. A green shape signaled that a positive image (such as a child playing) would follow; a red shape indicated that a negative picture (for example, a combat scene) would appear next. The subjects were then judged on their speed and accuracy in identifying the shapes.

Compared with healthy participants, the elite warriors sent more blood coursing through their insulas and a few other regions when the shapes' colors differed in consecutive trials. In short, they were more aware of the impending switch from positive to negative or vice versa and engaged brain systems involved in modulating emotional and interoceptive responses. They were quicker to prepare for a looming shift in their internal states, buying their brains time to tamp down their reactions.

Taken together, the studies indicate that men and women who have extreme physical abilities show greater insula activation when anticipating a change to their internal feelings, whether emotional or physical.

"To me that's really huge if you have a region of the brain that's anticipating a response and preparing the body for it," physiologist Jon Williamson at the University of Texas Southwestern Medical Center says. "If an athlete is approaching a hill and can anticipate the delivery of blood to muscles, he or she may perform better on that hill."

The studies so far have been small, however—it's not easy to corral top-tier athletes into brain-imaging labs—so larger experiments are still needed to firm up the observations. Even so, the results echo earlier findings on the insula's involvement in imagining the future, whether anticipating physical pain from, say, a boxer's punch or contemplating the purchase of an overpriced item.

To Simmons, the evidence suggests that the insula does not live in the present, but the future. "We're responding to information incorporated from physiology, cognition, our surroundings," Simmons says. "By the time we've integrated all that, it's part of the past." The ability to forecast can also backfire, producing disorders such as anorexia nervosa, which combines lapses in bodily awareness with a concern for how food consumption now will alter body image in the future. "It's the anticipation that's getting in your way," Simmons says. Indeed, brain scans of individuals with eating disorders and post-traumatic stress disorder show that insula activity diverges from that seen in healthy subjects, suggesting impairments in this area.

Train Your Interoception

For aspiring athletes or individuals who suffer insular dysfunction, there are reasons to hope interoception is trainable. A meditation technique called mindfulness encourages people to tune into their present thoughts, emotions and bodily sensations. Derived from Buddhist teachings, this training seeks to heighten awareness of feelings but also to temper our reactions to them. The OptiBrain researchers have collected preliminary data, not yet published, suggesting that healthy subjects and military personnel who received mindfulness training improved in cognitive performance during a stressful situation—as measured with a breathing-restriction task—and

reacted to challenges with less emotion, with the insular activation changes to match.

Small-scale studies on athletes, too, show benefit. This awareness of the feeling of the moment has been shown, for example, to improve the success of basketball players on the free-throw line. Sports psychologist Claudio Robazza at the University of Chieti in Italy has seen firsthand how mindfulness and similar techniques can single out successful athletes. He has worked for six years with Italy's Olympic shooting team, a mentally demanding sport that favors individuals who can still nail their targets when the pressure is highest. "Emotional states can reflect bodily changes, an increase in heart rate, muscular tension and breathing—all those things cause changes in the performance and the final outcome," Robazza says. "Certainly athletes need to be aware of their responses."

With tens of thousands of people gazing down from stadium seats, and millions more tuned in to television broadcasts, an Olympic athlete runs a high risk of choking. The stress of the moment can trigger many physical changes that interfere in the execution of even the most deeply ingrained maneuvers. A heightened awareness of the body's condition, facilitated by the insula, can alert a champion to tensed muscles or shallow breaths before these responses have a chance to undermine performance. The insula—where the body meets the brain—serves as the springboard from which athletic brilliance can soar.

Critical Thinking

1. What is the insular cortex, and how might it be related to athletic performance?

2. How does the protective sheath surrounding nerve fibers influence the speed of processing between neurons?

3. If damage were to occur to one's insular cortex, what would be the likely result to be observed?

Create Central

www.mhhe.com/createcentral

Internet References

Does the insula help elite athletes better anticipate their body's upcoming feelings, improving their physical reactions?
http://subrealism.blogspot.com/2012/07/does-insula-help-elite-athletes-better.html

Marines expanding use of meditation training
www.washingtontimes.com/news/2012/dec/5/marines-expanding-use-of-meditation-training/?page=all

Article   Prepared by: Eric Landrum, *Boise State University*

Mini-Multitaskers

For young people, a tendency to multitask may impoverish learning, productivity, and even friendships.

Rebecca A. Clay

Learning Outcomes

After reading this article, you will be able to:

- Articulate the idea of switching costs and how this concept applies to our understanding of multitasking.

- Describe how the formation of friendships is impacted by usage of social media.

Peek behind the bedroom doors of children and teens who are supposedly doing homework, and you may find they're doing that and much more—text messaging friends, surfing the Internet and listening to iPods.

In fact, according to a 2006 Kaiser Family Foundation study, almost two-thirds of 8- to 18-year-olds using a computer to do homework are also doing something else at the same time. And during a typical week, 81 percent of young people report "media multitasking" at least some of the time.

Multitasking may seem modern and efficient, but research suggests that it slows children's productivity, changes the way they learn and may even render social relationships more superficial.

Switching Costs

Like their adult counterparts, young people often believe multitasking boosts efficiency. But there is no such boost, says psychologist David E. Meyer, PhD, director of the Brain, Cognition and Action Lab at the University of Michigan in Ann Arbor. People who multitask actually take longer to get things done.

If a teen is trying to write an essay on Shakespeare while text messaging friends, says Meyer, that back-and-forth can cause "a kind of mental brown-out."

"You wind up needing to use the same sorts of mental and physical resources for performing each of the tasks," he explains. "You're having to switch back and forth between the two tasks as opposed to really doing them simultaneously."

Plus switching itself takes a toll: As you're switching, says Meyer, you're not concentrating on either task. And you need a mental warm-up to resume the suspended task.

In research published in 2001 in the *Journal of Experimental Psychology: Human Perception and Performance* (Vol. 27, No. 4), Meyer and colleagues found that people lost time switching from one task to another. The amount of time they lost increased significantly as the tasks became more complex or unfamiliar.

"As a result, the efficiency of getting the task done is much less than if you concentrated on one task from start to finish," says Meyer.

Less Flexible Learning

Despite teachers' best efforts, cell phones and other gadgets are infiltrating the classroom.

North Dakota school psychologist Tamara Waters-Wheeler, LSW, EdS, of the Morton Sioux Special Education Unit in Mandan estimates that the school confiscates an average of one or two cell phones every day.

Text messaging during class isn't just a high-tech version of passing notes. Because of its demands on attention, multitasking also may impair young people's ability to learn.

In particular, people with divided attention may not deeply integrate new information and may have trouble applying it later as a result, says Russell A. Poldrack, PhD, a neuroscience professor at the University of California, Los Angeles.

In a study published in 2006 in the *Proceedings of the National Academy of Sciences* (Vol. 103, No. 31), Poldrack and his colleagues asked participants to learn by trial and error to sort cards into different categories. Sometimes they could devote themselves exclusively to that task. At other times, they had to listen simultaneously to high- and low-pitched beeps and keep a mental tally of the high-pitched ones.

The participants learned the sorting task even when they were multitasking, but they didn't learn it in the same way. That's because they were using a different kind of memory to learn while multitasking, says Poldrack. They were relying on procedural memory rather than the more flexible declarative memory. As a result, they couldn't answer questions asking them to apply what they had learned while multitasking.

An fMRI study confirmed the behavioral findings. When participants focused on the task, they relied more on the hippocampus—the center of the declarative memory system. When they multitasked, they relied on the basal ganglia, one of the systems that builds less flexible memories.

Students with one eye on a teacher and one on a BlackBerry may be more likely to learn rote answers instead of developing a true understanding, says Poldrack.

And, he adds, the quest for new information made possible by cell phones and other gadgets can be addictive.

"The entire culture is starting to look like what you see in attention deficit disorder, where there's a difficulty in focusing and distractibility," he says.

A recent study published by Common Sense Media suggests that may be true. In a meta-analysis of research going back to 1980, researchers from the National Institutes of Health and Yale University found that 69 percent of the 13 studies that examined media exposure and ADHD found a statistically significant relationship.

Waters-Wheeler has noticed a similar trend in the classroom. "In the past, kids were more able to sit down and focus on things for much longer," she says. "Now they can only attend to things for a short period."

They're also easily distracted, she says. "It's not that they can't focus," she says. "It's that they focus on everything. They hear everything—even things they would normally be able to block out—because they are now so used to attending to many things at once."

Referrals for attention issues are up, she says. Many of these students don't have full-blown attention-deficit hyperactivity disorder, she says. Instead, she says, "it's just the way they've grown up—working short times on many different things at one time."

Superficial Friendships?

Much of children's and teens' texting and computer use centers on their friendships. A recent study by anthropologist Mizuko Ito, PhD, of the University of California, Irvine, found that digital media play an important role in the social development of the 800 young people she and her team interviewed. The MacArthur Foundation-funded study found that teens are using such media to hang out with friends and find communities that may not be represented in their own geographic area.

In doing so, the researchers say, they're learning important skills, such as managing large networks of friends and acquaintances.

But developmental psychologist Patricia Greenfield, PhD, isn't convinced that multitasking helps friendships any more than it helps learning.

"The same danger of superficiality applies," says Greenfield, who directs the Children's Digital Media Center LA and serves as a psychology professor at UCLA. "We evolved as human beings for face-to-face interaction. As more and more interaction becomes virtual, we could lose qualities like empathy that are probably stimulated by face-to-face interaction."

The effort to juggle multiple relationships is also problematic, Greenfield and co-authors say in a study published in the *Journal of Applied Developmental Psychology* (Vol. 9, No. 6). Noting that humans have traditionally had a few lifelong relationships, she says that young people using social networking sites like Facebook or MySpace often have more than 1,000 people in their networks.

"There's a danger that having a few long-term relationships is giving way to many superficial, fleeting relationships," she says.

Critical Thinking

1. For children, what is the behavioral relationship between multitasking and productivity?

2. What type of cost, if any, is there when a person switches between two or more different cognitive tasks?

3. Describe the current research findings regarding the formation of friendships and the roles social media play.

Create Central

www.mhhe.com/createcentral

Internet References

12 reasons to stop multitasking now!
www.health.com/health/gallery/0,,20707868,00.html

You'll never learn! Students can't resist multitasking, and it's impairing their memory
www.slate.com/articles/health_and_science/science/2013/05/
multitasking_while_studying_divided_attention_and_technological_
gadgets.html

REBECCA A. CLAY is a writer in Washington, D.C.

Unit 3

UNIT

Prepared by: Eric Landrum, *Boise State University*

Perceptual Processes

Marina and her roommate Claire have been friends since their first year of college. Because they share so much in common, they decided to become roommates in their sophomore year. They both want to travel abroad one day. They both enjoy the same restaurants and share the same preference for red wine. Both have significant others from the same hometown, both are education majors, and both want to work with young children someday. Today they are at the local art museum. As they walk around the galleries, Marina is astonished at Claire's taste in art. Whatever Claire likes, Marina finds hideous. The paintings and sculptures that Marina admires are the very ones to which her roommate turns up her nose. "How can our tastes in art be so different when we share so much in common?" Marina wonders. What Marina and Claire experience is a difference in perception—the interpretation of the sensory stimulation. Perception and sensation are closely connected topics in psychology, as well as the topic of this unit.

As you will learn in your study of psychology, the study of sensation and perception dates back to psychology's earliest beginnings, and even prior to psychology's formal start. Understanding how the physical energy of sound waves is translated to the language we hear and how waves of light are translated into the images we see are processes occurring in the nervous system and have long fascinated psychologists. Although the laboratory study of sensation and perception is well over 100 years old, psychologists are still seeking to further their understanding of these phenomena.

For many years, it was popular for psychologists to consider sensation and perception as two distinct processes. Sensation was defined in passive terms as the simple event of some stimulus energy (e.g., a sound wave) impinging on a specific sensory organ (e.g., the ear) that then reflexively transmitted the appropriate information to the central nervous system and brain. Perception, on the other hand, was defined as the interpretive process that the higher centers of the brain supposedly accomplish based on sensory information and available memories of similar events. Interesting abberations can occur, however, such as when individuals who suffer from the amputation of a limb still report pain from that missing limb (called phantom pain).

The dichotomy of sensation and perception is no longer widely accepted by today's psychologists. The revolution came in the mid-1960s, when a psychologist published a then-radical treatise in which he reasoned that perceptual processes included all sensory events that he believed were directed by an actively searching central nervous system. This viewpoint provided that certain perceptual patterns, such as recognition of a piece of art work, may be species specific. Thus, all humans, independent of learning history, should share some of the same perceptual repertoires. Optical illusions are intriguing because the sensations collected by the visual system, once the brain attempts to translate sensations into perceptions, cause humans to deduce that what was "seen" cannot be true. This is probably one of the reasons that magic tricks are so entertaining to so many people—and sometimes we are blind to events that occur right before our eyes. This unit on perceptual processes is designed to expand your understanding of these incredibly interesting processes.

As you will find, understanding perception is a complex process that made even more difficult by the fact that perception is fluid, continual, and often takes place below everyday levels of consciousness.

Article   Prepared by: Eric Landrum, *Boise State University*

Uncanny Sight in the Blind

Some people who are blind because of brain damage have "blindsight": an extraordinary ability to react to emotions on faces and even navigate around obstacles without knowing they can see anything.

BEATRICE DE GELDER

Learning Outcomes

After reading this article, you will be able to:

- Define blindsight and describe its basic features.
- Explain how researchers study blindsight.

The video my colleagues and I shot is amazing. A blind man is making his way down a long corridor strewn with boxes, chairs and other office paraphernalia. The man, known to the medical world as TN, has no idea the obstacles are there. And yet he avoids them all, here sidling carefully between a wastepaper basket and the wall, then going around a camera tripod, all without knowing he has made any special maneuvers. TN may be blind, but he has "blindsight"—the remarkable ability to respond to what his eyes can detect without knowing he can see anything at all. [To see the film of the experiment, go to www.ScientificAmerican.com/may2010/blindsight.]

TN's blindness is of an extremely rare type, caused by two strokes he suffered in 2003. The strokes injured an area at the back of his brain called the primary visual cortex, first on his left hemisphere and five weeks later on the right. His eyes remained perfectly healthy, but with his visual cortex no longer receiving the incoming signals he became completely blind.

What Is Blindsight?

Conscious vision in humans depends on a region of the brain called the primary visual cortex. Damage there causes blindness in corresponding areas of the visual field. "Blindsight" occurs when patients respond in some way to an item displayed in their blind area, where they cannot consciously see it. In a dramatic demonstration of the phenomenon, a patient called "TN" navigated an obstacle course despite his total blindness.

Visual Pathways

Signals from the retina go to the primary visual cortex via the lateral geniculate nucleus in the midbrain and ultimately to higher areas for conscious processing. Nerves also send visual information to areas such as the pulvinar nucleus and superior colliculus in the midbrain. Those areas do not seem to produce any conscious vision, but some must underlie blindsight.

Key Concepts

- Some people who are blind because of brain damage exhibit "blindsight"—responses to objects and images they cannot consciously see.
- Blindsight can detect many visual features, including colors, motion, simple shapes, and the emotion expressed by a person's face or posture.
- Researchers are mapping the ancient brain areas responsible for blindsight and exploring the limits of this remarkable ability.

This study of TN navigating along the hallway is probably the most dramatic demonstration of blindsight ever reported. Other patients who have lost vision because of damage to the primary visual cortex have exhibited less spectacular but equally mysterious cases of the phenomenon—responding to things they cannot consciously see, ranging from simple geometric shapes to the complex image of a person's face expressing an emotion. Scientists have also induced a similar effect in healthy people, by temporarily "switching off" their visual cortex or by outfoxing it in other ways.

Today research into blindsight seeks to understand the range of perceptual abilities that may be retained by the cortically blind and to determine which brain regions and neuronal pathways are responsible. The knowledge being gained says something about us all, because even if we never suffer a catastrophic injury resembling TN's, the same unconscious brain functions manifest in him as the astonishing ability to see without knowing are surely a constant, invisible part of our own daily existence.

A Controversial History

As long ago as 1917, doctors reported cases like blindsight—then called residual vision—in soldiers injured in World War I. Half a century would pass, however, before more organized and objective research into the capacity began. First, Lawrence Weiskrantz and his student Nicholas K. Humphrey, both then at the University of Cambridge, studied surgically altered monkeys in 1967. Then, in 1973, Ernst Pöppel, Richard Held and Douglas Frost of the Massachusetts Institute of Technology measured the eye movements of a patient and found he had a slight tendency to look toward stimuli that he could not see consciously.

These discoveries spurred further systematic investigations of animals lacking the primary visual cortex (also called V1, most of them conducted by Weiskrantz and his collaborators. A number of studies established that animals retain significant visual abilities after removal of their visual cortex (for example, detecting movement and discriminating shapes).

Weiskrantz and his co-workers also began studies in 1973 with a person known as DB who had recently lost part of his visual cortex in surgery to remove a tumor. The wider research community, however, initially greeted reports of human blindsight with great skepticism.

Disbelief about blindsight is not surprising, because the phenomenon seems counterintuitive, if not outright contradictory. After all, how could people see without knowing that they see? Just as it does not make sense to say that I do not know if I am in pain, it also does not make sense, on the face of it, to suggest that somebody can see something when he insists he is blind.

Yet we do not always know that we can see. Nor do we always know that we cannot. The relation between seeing and knowing is more complicated than we commonly assume. For instance, people with normal sight have a blind spot, although we are not usually aware of this hole in our sight or handicapped by it.

Another reason for disbelief was the paucity of human evidence: subjects with cortical blindness who can be studied are rare. The primary visual cortex is only a few centimeters across in adults, and brain damage is seldom restricted to just that area, knocking out the patient's vision yet leaving other faculties intact enough for meaningful research on what the brain continues to perceive. Even so, it is now clear that many more patients with damage to the visual cortex have blindsight than scientists realized in the past, and skepticism has abated.

It is now clear that many more patients with damage to the visual cortex have blindsight than scientists realized in the past.

Most of these patients still have some functioning in the primary visual cortex. Many have damage to only a small part of V1, leading to a small island of blindness in their visual field; others lose the entire left or right half of V1, leaving them blind across the corresponding half of their visual field. Blindsight in these cases involves detecting objects or images presented in the blind area, where the patient cannot see them consciously.

Traditional methods for studying vision in humans have relied on the viewers' verbal reports of what they perceive. Tested in that way, subjects will report not seeing anything in the blind part of their visual field. More indirect methods, however, can reveal that these unseen visual stimuli actually do influence how a patient responds.

In some experiments, patients show clear physiological changes, such as constriction of the pupil, as signs of unconscious seeing. And subjects can react differently to items shown in the intact visual field depending on what is presented at the same time in the blind field. When asked to guess which of several alternative items are displayed in the blind field, a patient may answer correctly almost every time.

Another important experimental tool is neuroimaging, which can provide direct evidence about the brain regions involved in blindsight and the pathways that the visual information travels. Brain imaging has been instrumental in dispelling lingering suspicions that some spared pieces of cortex might explain residual vision.

Collectively, these various kinds of experiments have revealed that people can unconsciously detect a wide range of visual attributes, including color, simple shapes such as X and 0, simple motion, and the orientation of lines or gratings. Large shapes, as well as very fine detail, seem hard to detect. For instance, patients detect features of a grating most effectively if its lines are comparable to Venetian blinds viewed from about 1.5 to 4.5 meters (five to 15 feet).

We were inspired to try the navigation experiment with TN by research Weiskrantz and Humphrey did in the 1970s: a monkey with no primary visual cortex freely moved around a room cluttered with objects without bumping into any of them. Nevertheless, we were amazed when TN made his way along the hallway with no collisions at all. Personalized psychophysical tests to assess his conscious vision had not found any visual functioning, including detection of big targets.

TN's ability to move down the corridor was reminiscent of sleepwalking, another phenomenon in which people exhibit a

What Can Be Detected?

Blindsight is strongest when visual details are about the size of a quarter viewed from five to 15 feet away. It can detect an assortment of basic visual properties, including:

- Simple shapes
- Arrays of lines
- Objects appearing or disappearing
- Movement
- Color
- Orientation of lines

Blindsight can also recognize emotions being expressed by a person, but not who the person is or what the person's gender is.

capacity to perform in some way without having any awareness of their actions. Indeed, when we questioned him afterward, he insisted he had simply walked along the hallway: he was not only unaware of seeing anything but also oblivious to how he had maneuvered around the unseen objects. He was at a loss to explain or even to describe his actions.

Blindsight for Emotions

Moving around is one of the most fundamental tasks an animal faces, so perhaps it should not be surprising that the brain has ways to support navigation even when the primary visual cortex and conscious vision are hobbled. As a social species, humans also depend for their survival on successful communication with others. They must recognize other people, along with their gestures and signs of what they are thinking. With such thoughts in mind, my collaborators and I began to wonder in the late 1990s if people with cortical damage could detect visual displays such as the emotion on a face or the meaning of a body posture in the usually inaccessible parts of their visual field.

In 1999 we started conducting tests using movies of faces. Vision researchers generally consider faces to be visually

---

Investigating Blindsight

Because total cortical blindness like patient TN's is rare, studies of blindsight often use patients blind on one side of their visual field. The patient stares at a fixed point while images are presented on each side. The subject may be asked to "guess" what is on the blind side or to press a button on seeing items on the sighted side. Equipment may monitor brain activity and measure involuntary responses such as tiny facial movements and pupil dilation.

Does Blindsight See Emotions?

Patients shown images on their blind side of people expressing emotions correctly guessed the emotion most of the time. Facial muscles used in smiling and frowning reacted in ways that matched the kind of emotion in the unseen image. Thus, the emotions were recognized without involving conscious sight. The effect worked with images of faceless bodies as well as faces, implying that patients were recognizing an emotion and not merely mimicking a facial expression unconsciously.

What Brain Areas Does Blindsight Use?

Researchers showed patients gray and purple squares, knowing the superior colliculus region in the midbrain receives no signals from the retina about purple objects. Gray squares but not purple ones triggered signs of blindsight such as greater pupil contractions. These results, along with neuroimaging of the patients in action, imply that the superior colliculus plays a critical role in blindsight.

Mapping Neural Pathways

Researchers are using advanced imaging techniques to attempt to trace the neural pathways that visual information travels in the brain to produce blindsight.

One such method is a kind of magnetic resonance imaging called diffusion tensor imaging, which relies on water diffusing more rapidly along neurons than across them.

Diffusion tensor imaging has mapped bundles of neurons that may be responsible for blindsight of emotions. The pathway connects the pulvinar nucleus and superior colliculus to the amygdala, which plays a key role in processing emotions.

---

complex—far more difficult to process than gratings and other elementary shapes—but a face is a very natural form for the human brain to handle. Our patient, GY, had lost all of his primary visual cortex on the left side in childhood, rendering him blind on the right side of his visual field. We found he could reliably guess the expression appearing on faces he did not consciously perceive, but he seemed truly blind to a variety of non-emotional facial attributes such as personal identity and gender.

To study blindsight of emotions further, in 2009 we exploited a phenomenon called emotional contagion, a tendency to match one's own facial expressions to those of others that we see. Researchers measure emotional contagion with a procedure called facial electromyography, by which electrodes on a subject's face record nerve signals going to muscles involved in smiling or frowning. We used this technique on GY and DB while showing them still images of faces and whole bodies expressing happiness or fear.

All the stimuli triggered emotional reactions as measured by electromyography, irrespective of whether the image was on the patient's sighted side or his blind side. In fact, surprisingly, the unseen images produced a faster response than those seen consciously. We also monitored pupil dilations, a measure of physiological arousal. The unseen fearful images produced the strongest effect—seemingly the more we are consciously aware of an emotional signal, the slower and weaker is our reaction.

One school of thought holds that emotional contagion arises because people unconsciously mimic the expressions they see, without necessarily recognizing the emotion itself. But because our patients reacted not only to faces but also to bodies (which had blurred faces), we concluded that they were perceiving and responding to the emotion.

Blindsight for All

Because the number of suitable patients for blindsight studies is extremely small, inducing the phenomenon temporarily in people with completely healthy brains is a valuable tool for conducting controlled experiments. One technique uses visual "masking," more popularly known as the use of subliminal images: a visual stimulus flashes before the experimental subject very briefly, followed immediately by a pattern in the same location. The pattern interferes with conscious processing of the fleeting subliminal image, leaving the subject with no conscious awareness of seeing it, but experiments can tease out objective evidence that it was seen. Other experiments temporarily disable the visual cortex by applying magnetic fields to the back of the head, a technique called transcranial magnetic stimulation.

Numerous studies have shown that healthy subjects can reliably "guess" the nature of a stimulus even when it is presented too briefly for them to perceive it consciously or when transcranial magnetic stimulation is disabling their visual cortex. Much research has also investigated how normally sighted observers react to emotional stimuli they cannot see consciously. Even before such blindsight experiments got under way, studies in animals and humans suggested that structures in the subcortex (areas of the brain that are deeper and more evolutionarily ancient than the cortex) can initiate appropriate responses before areas such as the visual cortex have analyzed the stimulus in detail. This nonconscious system seems to operate in parallel with the normal, predominantly cortical, processing routes. These subcortical areas that are activated by subliminal emotional stimuli are the leading suspects in processing emotions detected by blindsight in permanently blind patients.

Yet scientists continue to debate whether these temporary forms of blindness induced in normally sighted people are the true functional equivalent of blindsight in patients with permanent cortical damage. In particular, visual-masking techniques, such as the use of subliminal images, permit the visual cortex to process information as usual but interfere with further conscious processing. Consequently, "blindsight" of subliminal images could be a quite distinct phenomenon from blindsight in patients, involving its own characteristic assortment of brain regions. Transcranial magnetic stimulation presumably mimics cortical damage closely, but to know whether the resulting blindsight actually involves the same neuronal pathways requires experiments that combine the technique with neuroimaging.

Conversely, after an injury, a patient's brain (even an adult's) may start rewiring itself to compensate for the loss. Such neural plasticity could well create pathways for blindsight that are not present in the normally sighted people who are studied using transcranial magnetic stimulation and visual masking. Until these issues are better understood, studies of patients with injuries will remain crucial for fathoming how noncortical regions produce residual vision.

Neural Pathways

Research has not yet fully determined the neural structures responsible for blindsight in the cortically blind, but the most likely candidate to play a central role is a brain region called the superior colliculus (SC), which sits in a part of the subcortex called the midbrain. In nonmammals such as birds and fish, the SC is the main structure receiving input from the eyes. In mammals it is overshadowed by the visual cortex but remains involved in controlling eye movements, among other visual functions. Blindsight would exploit information that travels from the retina to the SC without first going through the primary visual cortex.

Last year my colleagues and I showed that this midbrain area is essential for translating a visual signal that cannot be consciously perceived into an action. Specifically, we had a patient press a button whenever we showed him a square on his sighted side. Sometimes we simultaneously presented a square on his blind side. Sometimes we used gray squares and sometimes purple ones. We chose a purple hue that only one type of light-detecting cone cell in the retina detects, knowing that the SC receives no inputs from that type; it is blind to this purple.

A gray square on our patient's blind side accelerated his response and made his pupils constrict more—a sign of processing the stimulus—whereas a purple square had neither effect. In other words, he exhibited blindsight of gray stimuli but not purple ones. Brain scans showed that his SC was most strongly activated only by the gray stimulus on his blind side. Some other areas in the midbrain have been suspected of being involved in blindsight instead of the SC, but in our experiment their activity seemed unrelated to the occurrence of blindsight.

These findings show that the SC acts in the human brain as an interface between sensory processing (sight) and motor processing (leading to the patient's action), thereby contributing to visually guided behavior in a way that is apparently separate from the pathways involving the cortex and entirely outside conscious visual experience. Blindsight of emotions displayed by people also involves the SC as well as other areas in the midbrain, such as the amygdala.

Blindsight has captured a lot of attention from philosophers, who are intrigued by the paradoxical idea of seeing without knowing that one sees. The idea, of course, is only a paradox if "seeing" is always taken to mean "consciously seeing." That mind-set was a stumbling block to acceptance of blindsight by scientists, delaying progress in understanding the role of unconscious seeing in human cognition.

It can also be a stumbling block for patients suffering from cortex-based loss of vision, preventing them from unlocking the potential of their residual visual skills in their everyday lives. For example, TN views himself as a blind person, and he will remain totally dependent on his white cane until he is convinced he can see without knowing it. Training may also help. After three months of daily stimulation, cortically blind patients were better at detecting targets in their blind field. Whether training in realistic conditions could lead to improved navigation skills is, like so many other features of blindsight, a question for future research.

Critical Thinking

1. What is blindsight?
2. How do researchers study this phenomenon?
3. What are the fundamental characteristics of blindsight?

Create Central

www.mhhe.com/createcentral

Internet References

Blinded by blindsight?

www.slate.com/articles/health_and_science/science/2013/05/
multitasking_while_studying_divided_attention_and_technological_
gadgets.html

Mystery of "blindsight" lets some people "see," study shows

http://news.nationalgeographic.com/news/2005/11/1101_051101_
blindsight.html

BEATRICE DE GELDER is professor of cognitive neuroscience and director of the Cognitive and Affective Neuroscience Laboratory at Tilburg University in the Netherlands. She is also on the faculty of the Athinoula A. Martinos Center for Biomedical Imaging in Charlestown, Mass. De Gelder investigates the neuroscience behind processing of faces and emotions and the ways cognition and emotion interact in both healthy and damaged brains.

More to Explore

Unseen Facial and Bodily Expressions Trigger Fast Emotional Reactions. Marco Tamietto et al. in *Proceedings of the National Academy of Sciences USA,* Vol. 106, No. 42, pages 17661–17666; October 20, 2009.

Collicular Vision Guides Nonconscious Behavior. Marco Tamietto et al. in *Journal of Cognitive Neuroscience,* Vol. 22, No. 5, pages 888–902; May 2010.

Affective Blindsight. Beatrice de Gelder and Marco Tamietto in *Scholarpedia,* Vol. 2, No. 10, page 3555; 2007. Available at www.scholarpedia.org/article/Affective_blindsight

Helen, a Blind Monkey Who Sees Everything. Video from 1971. Available at bit.ly/blindsightmonkey

---

Article   Prepared by: Eric Landrum, *Boise State University*

The Color of Sin

White and Black Are Perceptual Symbols of Moral Purity and Pollution

GARY D. SHERMAN AND GERALD L. CLORE

Learning Outcome

After reading this article, you will be able to:

* Describe the power of language to influence our perception of the world.

Abstract ideas can be clarified by comparisons with aspects of the physical world. "Love is like a rose," for example, invites people to appreciate the beauty and delicacy of love, and perhaps also the pain of its thorns. But beyond such rhetorical embellishment, some metaphors are so direct and compelling that their literal and metaphorical meanings may become conflated. For example, an admired person is often said to be "looked up to." This spatial metaphor may be so powerful that assertions about "high" or "low" status automatically evoke some of the processes involved in the perception of spatial location. Such a metaphor is "perceptually grounded," meaning that its comprehension involves an element of perceptual simulation appropriate to assertions about physical space (Barsalou, 1999; Lakoff & Johnson, 1980). For example, people have been found to attribute high status or power to individuals elevated in physical space and are able to identify powerful groups more quickly when those groups are positioned higher, rather than lower, than another group in space (Schubert, 2005). By being grounded in perceptual experience of the physical world, such analogical assertions achieve the authority of actual perceptions.

Moral cognition is embodied in this way. For example, physical purity is a metaphor for moral "purity" (Rozin, Millman, & Nemeroff, 1986). This explains why an evil person's clothing may be considered physically repulsive (Rozin, Markwith, & McCauley, 1994), and why reminders of one's moral transgressions can create desires for physical cleansing (Zhong & Liljenquist, 2006). An underappreciated, and understudied, aspect of this metaphor is that ideas of dirtiness and impurity are themselves grounded in the perceptual experience of the color black, which is seen not just as the opposite of white, but also as a potent impurity that can contaminate whiteness (Adams &

Osgood, 1973; Williams & Roberson, 1967). A white object, conversely, is universally understood to be something that can be stained easily and that must remain unblemished to stay pure. This is presumably at the heart of the culturally widespread practice of dressing brides in white, which by calling to mind the experience of physical purity, provides a compelling symbol for moral purity. One can see with one's own eyes that a drop of dark paint discolors white paint more readily than the reverse. By analogy, a single immoral act can counteract an otherwise exemplary reputation, whereas a single moral act cannot compensate for a life of questionable behavior.

Little is known about associations between immorality and blackness. Most of the relevant work has focused more generally on valence. That research has revealed that children tend to assume that black boxes contain negative objects and white boxes contain positive objects (Stabler & Johnson, 1972). Also, people are quicker to evaluate a negative word when it appears in black, rather than white (Meier, Robinson, & Clore, 2004), and perceive gray patches as darker after evaluating a negative word than after evaluating a positive word (Meier, Robinson, Crawford, & Ahlvers, 2007). More relevant to morality is a study in which sports players were perceived as more aggressive, and behaved more aggressively, when wearing black uniforms than when wearing nonblack uniforms (Frank & Gilovich, 1988).

Although associations between valence and blackness operate across many domains, the aforementioned research has focused on the domain-general aspects of these associations. Black has negative connotations for many reasons; it is the color of night, uncertainty, and danger. In the case of morality, however, its association with impurity is particularly noteworthy. Because of the shared connection of blackness and immorality with impurity, associations between darkness and valence in the moral domain have a metaphorical quality. Accordingly, the concept of immorality should activate "black," not because immoral things tend to *be* black, but because immorality *acts* like the color black (e.g., it contaminates).

In addition, past research has not examined how valence-blackness associations vary with contextual factors or individual differences. Making immorality salient is enough to evoke the moral-purity metaphor: In one study, people who recalled, or hand-copied, a first-person account of unethical behavior desired physical cleansing (Zhong & Liljenquist, 2006). It is during these times—when one is currently concerned with being morally "clean"—that immorality-blackness associations should be most evident. But such associations may also relate to more chronic concerns with purity and pollution. That is, they may be especially evident among people generally concerned with cleanliness. Support for these two predictions would provide multimethod, converging evidence that immorality-blackness associations exist and are a meaningful part of the moral-purity metaphor.

The Stroop (1935) color-word task served as our measure of word-color association (MacLeod, 1991). In this task, color names or color-related words appear in different colors. Color naming is slowed when the word and color are incongruent (e.g., "lemon" in blue ink; Klein, 1964) and speeded when they are congruent. Consequently, the more one associates immorality with black, the longer it should take to identify the color of immoral words (e.g., *sin*) when they appear in white, rather than black. After first documenting such a moral Stroop effect (Study 1), we tested whether experimentally priming immorality—a procedure known to encourage physical cleansing—would amplify the effect (Study 2) and whether the effect would be strongest for people who particularly like cleaning products (Study 3).

Study 1

Meier et al. (2004, Study 4) adapted the Stroop task to the study of valence-darkness associations and found that word color did not interact with valence (coded dichotomously) to predict naming times. We reanalyzed their data, taking into account the moral (rather than merely evaluative) connotation of the words.

Method
Participants

Participants were 22 undergraduates at North Dakota State University. Meier et al. (2004, Study 4) did not report the racial composition of their sample, but did note that their participant pool was 95% Caucasian.

Word Ratings

Two independent coders rated the words on the following dimensions: immoral versus moral, wrong versus right, unpleasant versus pleasant, and undesirable versus desirable. For each dimension, 1 represented one extreme (e.g., *very immoral*), 4 represented the neutral midpoint (e.g., *neither immoral nor moral*), and 7 represented the other extreme (e.g., *very moral*). There was substantial agreement between the raters (αs > .91), so their ratings were averaged. The first two dimensions formed a morality composite (α = .98), and the latter two a pleasantness composite (α = .99).

Stimuli and Procedure

Each of 100 words (50 positive, 50 negative; see Meier et al., 2004) appeared once in black or white font (randomly assigned) on a computer screen. Participants indicated the color of each word using the "1" ("black") and "9" ("white") keys.

Results and Discussion

Before analyzing the data, we adjusted reaction times (RTs) below 300 ms to 300 ms and RTs more than 3 standard deviations above the mean to that value (we followed the same procedure for cleaning the RT data in Studies 2 and 3). Additionally, RTs on the initial trials tended to be highly irregular; in Trials 1 and 2, a substantial percentage of participants took longer than 3 standard deviations above the mean to respond (86% for Trial 1, 27% for Trial 2). By Trial 3, participants' responses stabilized (0% > 3 SDs above the mean). We therefore excluded data from Trials 1 and 2 from analysis. (The same pattern characterized the other two studies, so we excluded Trials 1 and 2 in those studies as well.)[1]

Because the data were nested (trials within people), we used multilevel modeling (hierarchical linear modeling, HLM; Raudenbush, Bryk, Cheong, & Congdon, 2001). We predicted RT for correct trials (98%) from the word's color (-1 = white, 1 = black), its rated morality, and their interaction. There were no main effects of either color or morality (ts < 1.38, p_{rep}s < .76), but a significant Color × Morality interaction, β_3 = 8.10, $t(2106)$ = 2.99, p_{rep} = .97, indicated that the effect of morality on RT depended on word color. As predicted, for words in black, greater morality predicted slower RTs, β_1 = 6.26, $t(1054)$ = 1.83, p_{rep} = .86. For words in white, greater morality predicted faster RTs, β_1 = $-$12.72, $t(1052)$ = $-$3.01, p_{rep} = .97 (see Figure 1).[2] A separate analysis substituting pleasantness for morality found that pleasantness did not interact with color (t < 1), a finding consistent with the absence of an interaction between valence (coded dichotomously) and color in predicting RT in the original analysis reported by Meier et al. (2004, Study 4).

This is the first evidence that immorality-blackness associations operate quickly and automatically. These associations influenced performance on the Stroop task, a color-identification task that requires no moral evaluation and can be performed quickly (RTs around 500 ms). Just as the word *lemon* activates "yellow," so too do immoral words activate "black" and moral words activate "white."

Study 2

In Study 2, we sought to (a) replicate Study 1 ourselves with a new set of words and (b) test whether the moral Stroop effect is sensitive to conditions that make immorality salient. If immorality-blackness associations are part of the moral-purity metaphor, then they should be most evident when people are feeling morally dirty. That is, the same sort of manipulations that elicit the "Macbeth effect" (Zhong & Liljenquist, 2006) should also evoke immorality-blackness associations.

Method
Participants

Forty University of Virginia undergraduates (19 female, 21 male) participated for partial course credit. Two participants (1 female, 1 male) experienced a computer malfunction, leaving a final sample of 38. Of these, 27 were self-identified as Caucasian (71%), 6 as Asain (16%), 3 as African American (8%), and 2 as Hispanic (5%).

☐ White Font ■ Black Font

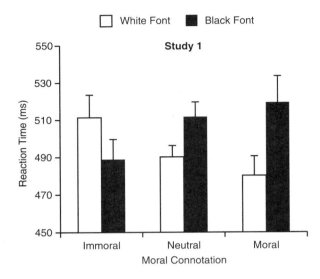

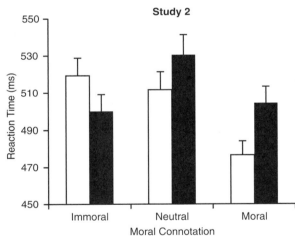

Figure 1 Reaction time during the Stroop color-word task as a function of font color and moral connotation in Study 1 (top) and the premanipulation phase of Study 2 (bottom). Although moral connotation was a continuous variable (7-point scale) in both studies, for illustrative purposes the words are binned into three categories: immoral (1–3), neutral (3.01–5), and moral (5.01–7). Error bars represent standard errors of the mean.

Word Ratings

At the end of the experiment, participants rated each word for morality and pleasantness (7-point scale, as in Study 1). We used each participant's ratings to predict his or her RTs.

Stimuli and Procedure

We generated a new list of 50 words that spanned the entire range of moral connotations (Table 1). Each word was presented once (order and color assigned randomly). Participants were instructed to indicate the color of each word as quickly and as accurately as possible. After incorrect responses, "incorrect"

Table 1 Words Used in Studies 2 and 3

Study 2
  abstain, abusive, brag, cheat, compete, confess, cruel, dieting, discipline, duty, erotic, evil, exciting, forgive, freedom, gambling, gossip, gratify, greed, hate, helping, honesty, humble, indulge, justice, kind, laugh, liar, lust, money, obey, pain, partying, pleasure, polite, pray, pride, profit, respect, revenge, sacrifice, seduce, selfish, sin, smile, steal, torture, vice, virtuous, work

Study 3
  Immoral: cheat, crime, devil, hell, neglect, sin, torment, vulgar
  Neutral: aspect, calm, concert, east, forecast, motion, recall, sum
  Moral: aid, angel, brave, charity, grace, honesty, saint, virtue

appeared on the screen in red font for 1.5 s. Five practice trials preceded the task.

To prime immorality, we asked participants to hand-copy a story, written in the first person. The story was about a junior partner at a law firm who was competing against a colleague for a promotion and found a document of great value to the colleague. The story ended with the character either giving the document to the colleague (ethical version) or shredding it (unethical version). The materials and cover story for this task (that it measured individual differences in handwriting) were identical to those used by Zhong and Liljenquist (2006, Study 2).

The four tasks in this study were completed in the following order: baseline Stroop task, writing task, postmanipulation Stroop task, and word-rating task.

Results and Discussion

To determine whether a moral Stroop effect was again present, we first analyzed baseline Stroop performance. In the model predicting RT for correct trials (98%), there were no main effects of either color or morality ($ts < 1.23$, $p_{rep}s < .72$), but the Color × Morality interaction was significant, $\beta_3 = 7.90$, $t(1792) = 2.30$, $p_{rep} = .93$. As in Study 1, the effect of morality depended on word color (see Figure 1). Separate models for the white and black fonts revealed that the effect was due primarily to white words, for which greater morality was associated with faster RTs, $\beta_1 = -10.72$, $t(923) = -2.33$, $p_{rep} = .92$. For words in black, the opposite pattern did not reach statistical significance, $\beta_1 = 4.73$, $t(869) = 0.92$, $p_{rep} = .60$.

We tested the effect of the writing task with a model predicting RT on the postmanipulation Stroop task from word color, word morality, and their interaction. Condition was a Level 2 (between-participants) predictor. To account for baseline Stroop performance, we computed a separate linear regression model for each participant, predicting RTs on the baseline Stroop task from word color, word morality, and their interaction. The standardized interaction coefficient—an estimate of that participant's Stroop effect—served as a Level 2 predictor, along with its interaction with condition (see Table 2).

The Color of Sin: White and Black Are Perceptual Symbols of Moral Purity and Pollution by Gary D. Sherman and Gerald L. Clore

55

Table 2 Hierarchical Linear Model Predicting Postmanipulation Stroop Performance (Reaction Time) in Study 2

Variable	Coefficient	t	df	p
Intercept, β_0				
Intercept, γ_{00}	470.94 (12.09)	38.95	34	< .001
Condition, γ_{01}	27.24 (12.31)	2.21	34	< .05
Baseline Stroop effect, γ_{02}	4.22 (11.23)	0.38	34	.71
Condition × Stroop Effect, γ_{03}	−18.60 (11.23)	−1.66	34	.11
Color, β_1				
Intercept, γ_{10}	−2.01 (2.58)	−0.78	1781	.44
Condition, γ_{11}	−5.64 (2.58)	−2.19	1781	< .05
Baseline Stroop effect, γ_{12}	−0.91 (2.17)	−0.42	1781	.68
Condition × Stroop Effect, γ_{13}	−0.47 (2.17)	−0.22	1781	.83
Morality, β_2				
Intercept, γ_{20}	−1.31 (3.33)	−0.39	1781	.69
Condition, γ_{21}	7.00 (3.28)	2.13	1781	< .05
Baseline Stroop effect, γ_{22}	1.42 (2.45)	0.58	1781	.56
Condition × Stroop Effect, γ_{23}	−1.43 (2.45)	−0.58	1781	.56
Color × Morality, β_2				
Intercept, γ_{30}	−2.82 (2.31)	−1.22	1781	.22
Condition, γ_{31}	0.09 (2.37)	0.04	1781	.97
Baseline Stroop effect, γ_{23}	−3.62 (2.09)	−1.73	1781	.08
Condition × Stroop Effect, γ_{33}	−7.94 (2.09)	−3.80	1781	< .001

Note. Standard errors are given in parentheses.

Compared with hand-copying an ethical story, hand-copying an unethical story slowed RTs overall, $\gamma_{01} = 27.24$, $t(34) = 2.21$, $p_{\text{rep}} = .90$, and speeded the color identification of (a) immoral, relative to moral, words (Condition × Morality), $\gamma_{21} = 7.00$, $t(1781) = 2.13$, $p_{\text{rep}} = .90$, and (b) black, relative to white, words (Condition × Color), $\gamma_{11} = -5.64$, $t(1781) = -2.19$, $p_{\text{rep}} = .91$. That is, the priming manipulation primed both immorality and blackness, providing converging evidence that people automatically associate immorality with blackness.

Additionally, condition interacted with baseline Stroop effect to predict the Color × Morality interaction, $\gamma_{33} = -7.94$, $t(1781) = -3.80$, $p_{\text{rep}} > .99$. That is, the effect of the writing task on the Stroop effect depended on baseline Stroop performance. Simple-slopes analysis (Aiken & West, 1991) testing the effect of condition at two levels of baseline Stroop effect (1 *SD* below and 1 *SD* above the mean) revealed that for participants who did not show the Stroop effect initially, the effect of condition was as predicted, $\gamma_{31} = 8.05$, $t(1781) = 2.80$, $p_{\text{rep}} = .96$: Participants who hand-copied the unethical story subsequently exhibited a significantly larger Color × Morality interaction (i.e., Stroop effect) than those who hand-copied the ethical story (see Figure 2). For participants who did show the Stroop effect initially, hand-copying the unethical story had the opposite effect: That is, it decreased the magnitude of the Stroop effect, $\gamma_{31} = -7.87$, $t(1781) = -2.30$, $p_{\text{rep}} = .92$.

This latter effect was unexpected and is particularly interesting. Stroop effects can be diminished by several factors (see MacLeod, 1991, for a review). Manipulations that decrease the attention-drawing power of the semantic content are especially effective. For example, exposing participants to a word before the trial in which it appears (Dyer, 1971) dampens its capacity to interfere with color naming. Our priming manipulation was designed to increase the salience of moral meaning in order to create Stroop interference, but among participants for whom moral meaning was already salient, hand-copying the unethical story may have made moral content sufficiently familiar to reduce its power to draw attention away from color naming. This could account for the observed decrease in the magnitude of the Stroop effect.

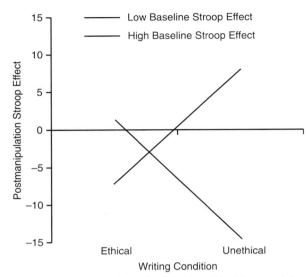

Figure 2 Regression slopes from the hierarchical linear modeling analysis in Study 2: postmanipulation Stroop effect (Color × Morality interaction) as a function of baseline Stroop effect (1 SD below and 1 SD above the mean) and writing condition.

Together, these findings attest to our measure's sensitivity. For people who showed no Stroop effect initially, simply exposing them to an instance of unethical behavior was sufficient to make immorality salient, which in turn allowed the morally relevant words in the Stroop task to activate their associated color. This finding suggests that whenever concerns about immorality (and perhaps also the sense of feeling morally dirty) are salient, so too are the purity-related colors of black and white. The unexpected finding for participants who had shown the Stroop effect initially suggests that moral content may lose its power with overexposure. If so, such "moral overexposure" might have troublesome behavioral consequences in that repeated thoughts or experiences of unethical behavior may cease to activate ideas of pollution and dirtiness.

Our immorality-salience manipulation is the same manipulation that in past research induced a desire for physical cleansing (Zhong & Liljenquist, 2006, Study 2). That this manipulation also primes "black" and alters the moral Stroop effect provides indirect evidence for the proposed link between immorality-blackness associations and notions of purity and contamination. In Study 3, we tested this link more directly.

Study 3

If associating sin with blackness reflects, in part, a concern with its polluting powers, then people who tend to make such associations should be those who are generally concerned with purity and pollution. Because purity concerns can manifest themselves as desires for physical cleansing (Zhong & Liljenquist, 2006), we assessed participants' liking of various products, including several cleaning products. We predicted that participants who considered cleaning products to be especially desirable would also show the moral Stroop effect.

Method
Participants

Fifty-three University of Virginia undergraduates (28 female, 25 male) participated for partial course credit. Two male participants did not complete the ratings task, leaving a final sample of 51. Of these, 30 were self-identified as Caucasian (59%), 11 as Asian (22%), 5 as African American (10%), 2 as Hispanic (4%), and 3 as "other" (6%).

Word Ratings, Stimuli, and Procedure

We created a new list of 24 words (8 immoral, 8 neutral, and 8 moral; see Table 1). To verify that the words had the intended moral connotation, at the end of the study we asked participants to rate the words themselves (as in Study 2). The ratings confirmed our categorization: All moral words had a mean rating greater than 6, all immoral words had a mean rating less than 2, and all neutral words were rated in between (minimum = 4.25, maximum = 5.66). Each word was selected from the MRC Psycholinguistic Database (Machine-Usable Dictionary, Version 2.00; see Wilson, 1988), which supplies values for various word attributes. The different categories did not differ in concreteness, familiarity, imageability, written frequency, number of letters, or number of syllables (Fs < 1).

The Stroop task was the same as in Study 2, except for the new words. Because we used fewer words than in Studies 1 and 2, we set the number of trials to 48. Each trial was randomly assigned 1 of the 24 words and one of the two colors. Also, participants were randomly assigned to one of two pairings of color and response key ("1" = black, "9" = white; "1" = white, "9" = black). Because the assigned pairings did not influence any result, we collapsed across them for all analyses.

After the Stroop task, participants rated the desirability of five cleaning products (Dove shower soap, Crest toothpaste, Lysol disinfectant, Windex cleaner, and Tide detergent) and five non-cleaning products (Post-it notes, Energizer batteries, Sony CD cases, Nantucket Nectars juices, and Snickers bars) on a 6-point scale (1 = *completely undesirable*, 6 = *completely desirable*). This measure was identical to the one used by Zhong and Liljenquist (2006, Study 2), who found that priming immorality increased the desirability of cleaning products.

At the end of the experiment, participants indicated their race, their political orientation (7-point scale: 1 = *very liberal*, 4 = *moderate*, 7 = *very conservative*), and the frequency with which they attended religious services (8-point scale: 0 = *never in my life*, 7 = *multiple-times per week*). The latter two measures were included to test whether any relation between the moral Stroop effect and liking of cleaning products could be explained by individual differences in religion or politics.

Results and Discussion

In an HLM model predicting RT for correct trials (99%), Level 1 predictors were word color, word morality, and their interaction. At Level 2 (between participants), we entered participants' average rating for the cleaning products and average rating for the non-cleaning products. At Level 1, there were no significant main effects of either color, $\gamma_{10} = 7.41$, $t(628) = 1.63$, $p =$

.10, or morality, $\gamma_{20} = -6.46$, $t(628) = -1.69$, $p = .09$, although both trends were notable. Unlike in Studies 1 and 2, the Color × Morality interaction was not significant, $\gamma_{30} = 5.90$, $t(628) = 1.46$, $p_{rep} = .77$, but it was in the predicted direction. Most important, this interaction was moderated by cleaning-product desirability, $\gamma_{31} = 22.36$, $t(628) = 4.04$, $p_{rep} > .99$, such that participants who rated cleaning products as more desirable had a larger Color × Morality interaction (i.e., moral Stroop effect). No such relationship was observed for non-cleaning products, $\gamma_{32} = -5.38$, $t(628) = -1.19$, $p = .24$. When political orientation and religious attendance were added as Level 2 predictors, they were also unrelated to the moral Stroop effect ($ts < 1$).

In supplementary analyses, each participant's interaction coefficient served as an estimate of his or her moral Stroop effect (as in Study 2). A series of multiple linear regression models predicted this estimate from product-desirability ratings. A model including the cleaning and noncleaning composite ratings replicated the HLM results: The cleaning composite was again a significant, positive predictor, $\beta = -.39$, $p_{rep} = .90$, whereas the noncleaning composite was unrelated to the moral Stroop effect, $\beta = -.07$, $p = .72$. To see which cleaning products were responsible for this relationship, we tested another model, with all 10 products as separate, simultaneous predictors. The only significant predictors were Crest toothpaste, $\beta = .46$, $p_{rep} = .94$, and Dove shower soap, $\beta = .35$, $p_{rep} = .90$. All other products were unrelated to the moral Stroop effect ($ts < 1$). Notably, the two items that were significant predictors are the only products that deal specifically with cleaning oneself. This result fits nicely with Zhong and Liljenquist's (2006) finding that people who had recalled a past unethical behavior preferred a hand-sanitizing antiseptic wipe to a pencil as a gift and that those who had actually cleansed their hands felt absolved of their moral guilt. Together, these findings suggest that the moral-purity metaphor may be particularly important for regulating one's own moral behavior. If the thought of acting immorally evokes images of dark, dirty impurities, it may facilitate avoidance of such behavior, thus protecting against moral contamination and ensuring that one's moral self stays clean and pure (i.e., "white").

General Discussion

There exists a moral-purity metaphor that likens moral goodness to physical cleanliness (Rozin et al., 1986; Zhong & Liljenquist, 2006). In three studies, we explored an unstudied, and underappreciated, aspect of this metaphor—its grounding in the colors black and white. We documented a moral Stroop effect indicating that people make immorality-blackness associations quickly and relatively automatically (Studies 1 and 2). Moreover, a manipulation known to induce a desire for physical cleansing primed both immorality and the color black (Study 2). The increased salience of immorality, in turn, altered the magnitude of the Stroop effect. Finally, individuals who showed the moral Stroop effect considered cleaning (especially self-cleaning) products to be highly desirable (Study 3), a finding indicating a direct link between immorality-blackness associations and purity concerns.

Although the metaphor of moral purity is well documented, this is the first demonstration that black and white, as representative of negative contagion (black contaminates white), are central parts of this metaphor. Sin is not just dirty, it is black. And moral virtue is not just clean, but also white. Our most unexpected finding—that the effect of priming immorality depended on an individual's baseline Stroop effect—contributes to understanding of embodied moral cognition by suggesting that seeing moral purity in black and white is not always a given. Just as easily as the metaphor can be evoked in people who do not generally show it, it can be diminished in those who do.

These findings may have implications for understanding racial prejudice. The history of race-related practices in the United States (e.g., the "one drop of blood" rule for racial categorization and segregation) has demonstrated that the tendency to see the black-white spectrum in terms of purity and contamination extends to skin color (for a discussion, see Rozin & Royzman, 2001). Given that both blackness and immorality are considered powerful contaminants to be avoided, and that the category labels "black" and "white" are often applied to race, dark skin might also be easily associated with immorality and impurity. This may explain, in part, why stereotypes of darker-skinned people often allude to immorality and poor hygiene, and why the typical criminal is seen as both dark skinned and physically dirty (MacLin & Herrera, 2006).

A morally virtuous person is said to be as "pure as the driven snow." In contrast to the pure whiteness of newly fallen snow, impurities are dirty, are dark, and visibly stain otherwise pristine surfaces. Equating immorality with these contaminants animates the abstract notions of sin and evil by grounding them in visceral, evocative qualities of one's experience of the physical world (Lakoff & Johnson, 1980). More than merely a rhetorical device for moral discourse, the moral-purity metaphor is a deep, embodied phenomenon covertly shaping moral cognition.

Notes

1. Because RT data are often positively skewed, we also analyzed the data using log-transformed RTs. The results were nearly identical to those reported here.

2. This interaction remained significant when we controlled for word extremity (provided by Meier et al., 2004) and written frequency (Kucera & Francis, 1967).

References

Adams, F.M., & Osgood, C.E. (1973). A cross-cultural study of the affective meanings of color. *Journal of Cross-Cultural Psychology, 4,* 135–156.

Aiken, L.S., & West, S.G. (1991). *Multiple regression: Testing and interpreting interactions.* Thousand Oaks, CA: Sage.

Barsalou, L.W. (1999). Perceptual symbol systems. *Behavioral and Brain Sciences, 22,* 577–609.

Dyer, F.N. (1971). The duration of word meaning responses: Stroop interference for different preexposures of the word. *Psychonomic Science, 25,* 229–231.

Frank, M.G., & Gilovich, T. (1988). The dark side of self- and social perception: Black uniforms and aggression in professional sports. *Journal of Personality and Social Psychology, 54,* 74–85.

Klein, G.S. (1964). Semantic power measured through the interference of words with color-naming. *American Journal of Psychology, 77,* 576–588.

Kucera, H., & Francis, W. (1967). *Computational analysis of presentday American English.* Providence, RI: Brown University Press.

Lakoff, G., & Johnson, M. (1980). *Metaphors we live by.* Chicago: University of Chicago Press.

MacLeod, C.M. (1991). Half a century of research on the Stroop effect: An integrative review. *Psychological Bulletin, 109,* 163–203.

MacLin, M.K., & Herrera, V. (2006). The criminal stereotype. *North American Journal of Psychology, 8,* 197–207.

Meier, B.P., Robinson, M.D., & Clore, G.L. (2004). Why good guys wear white: Automatic inferences about stimulus valence based on brightness. *Psychological Science, 15,* 82–87.

Meier, B.P., Robinson, M.D., Crawford, L.E., & Ahlvers, W.J. (2007). When 'light' and 'dark' thoughts become light and dark responses: Affect biases brightness judgments. *Emotion, 7,* 366–376.

Raudenbush, S., Bryk, A., Cheong, Y.F., & Congdon, R. (2001). *HLM5: Hierarchical linear and nonlinear modeling.* Chicago: Scientific Software International.

Rozin, P., Markwith, M., & McCauley, C. (1994). Sensitivity to indirect contacts with other persons: AIDS aversion as a composite of aversion to strangers, infection, moral taint, and misfortune. *Journal of Abnormal Psychology, 103,* 495–504.

Rozin, P., Millman, L., & Nemeroff, C. (1986). Operation of the laws of sympathetic magic in disgust and other domains. *Journal of Personality and Social Psychology, 50,* 703–712.

Rozin, P., & Royzman, E.B. (2001). Negativity bias, negativity dominance, and contagion. *Personality and Social Psychology Review, 5,* 296–320.

Schubert, T.W. (2005). Your highness: Vertical positions as perceptual symbols of power. *Journal of Personality and Social Psychology, 89,* 1–21.

Stabler, J.R., & Johnson, E.E. (1972). The meaning of black and white to children. *International Journal of Symbology, 3,* 11–21.

Stroop, J.R. (1935). Studies of interference in serial verbal reactions. *Journal of Experimental Psychology, 18,* 643–662.

Williams, J.E., & Roberson, J.K. (1967). A method for assessing racial attitudes in preschool children. *Educational and Psychological Measurement, 27,* 671–689.

Wilson, M. (1988). MRC Psycholinguistic Database: Machine-usable dictionary, version 2.00. *Behavior Research Methods, Instruments, & Computers, 20,* 6–10.

Zhong, C., & Liljenquist, K.A. (2006). Washing away your sins: Threatened morality and physical cleansing. *Science, 313,* 1451–1452.

Critical Thinking

1. In what interesting ways does language influence or shape our perception of life's experiences?

2. What are the stereotypes and associations typically made with the colors black and white?

3. One of the conclusions that the authors draw is that "sin is not dirty, it is black." What does that mean exactly?

Create Central

www.mhhe.com/createcentral

Internet References

The color of sin: Why the good guys wear white
 www.scientificamerican.com/article.cfm?id=the-color-of-sin

Mind games: Sometimes a white coat isn't just a white coat
 www.nytimes.com/2012/04/03/science/clothes-and-self-perception.html

Article

Prepared by: Eric Landrum, *Boise State University*

Increasing Speed of Processing with Action Video Games

MATTHEW W. G. DYE, C. SHAWN GREEN, AND DAPHNE BAVELIER

Learning Outcome

After reading this article, you will be able to:

- Explain why researchers believe that action-based video games may be useful in studying the tradeoff between reaction time and accuracy in responding.

Playing action video games—contemporary examples include *God of War, Halo, Unreal Tournament, Grand Theft Auto,* and *Call of Duty*—requires rapid processing of sensory information and prompt action, forcing players to make decisions and execute responses at a far greater pace than is typical in everyday life. During game play, delays in processing often have severe consequences, providing large incentive for players to increase speed. Accordingly, there is anecdotal evidence that avid game players react more readily to their environment. However, it remains unknown whether any reduction in reaction time (RT) really generalizes to tasks beyond video-game playing and, if it does, whether it makes gamers more impulsive and prone to making errors. In short, are expert video-game players (VGPs) just "trigger happy," or does video-game playing really improve RTs on a variety of tasks without a concomitant decrease in accuracy? The possibility of identifying a single training task that can lead to RT improvements across a variety of unrelated tasks is of great interest but remains controversial in the field of speeded-response-choice tasks (in which observers must choose among alternative responses or actions as rapidly as possible). On such tasks, decreases in RT are typically accompanied by decreases in accuracy. This is termed a speed–accuracy trade-off, with speeding up resulting in more mistakes. One exception is when individuals are trained on such speeded tasks. Performance on the trained task is then improved (faster RTs, but no speed–accuracy trade-off); however, little or at best limited transfer to new tasks is observed, limiting the benefits of training (Pashler & Baylis, 1991). Interestingly, flexible or integrated training regimens—requiring constant switching of processing priorities and continual adjustments to new task demands—have been argued to lead to greater transfer (Bherer et al., 2005). Action-video-game playing may be an extreme case of such flexible training.

Here we consider the possibility that action-video-game training leads to faster RTs on tasks unrelated to the training and, thus, for the first time may offer a regimen leading to generalized speeding across tasks in young adults.

Action Video Games and Speeded-Choice RT Tasks

The possibility that playing video games affects perceptual and cognitive skills has received much interest lately. Most past studies have compared VGPs to novice video-game players (NVGPs) using tasks that measure RTs in order to draw conclusions about performance. Although usually not the primary focus of these studies, they invariably show that the VGPs are faster overall than those who do not play such games (Bialystok, 2006; Castel, Pratt, & Drummond, 2005; Clark, Lanphear, & Riddick, 1987; Greenfield, deWinstanley, Kilpatrick, & Kaye, 1994). This is perhaps unsurprising given the fast pace of games considered in these studies. There are, however, two surprising characteristics of these RT decreases: (a) the consistency in speed-of-processing advantages for VGPs across a range of tasks, and (b) the fact that there is no speed–accuracy trade-off. These points are illustrated by the following meta-analysis, which examines the reported RTs of avid action gamers versus those of novices across a number of studies. . . .

It is important to note that a few studies (Clark et al., 1987; Green, 2008) have indicated that these faster RTs can be trained by action-video-game play, therefore establishing causality (as opposed to strictly correlative studies where population bias is a significant concern). RTs in NVGP individuals were assessed before and after action-video-game training, and these results were then compared to NVGP individuals trained on control non-action video games. The control video games were chosen to be as engrossing as the experimental game, minimizing differences in motivation across groups and thus controlling for both test–retest effects (i.e., improvement expected simply from taking the test a second time) and Hawthorne-like effects (wherein individuals who have an active interest taken in their behavior tend to, all other things being equal, outperform individuals in which no such interest is taken). Furthermore, by evaluating subject behavior a few days before and a few days

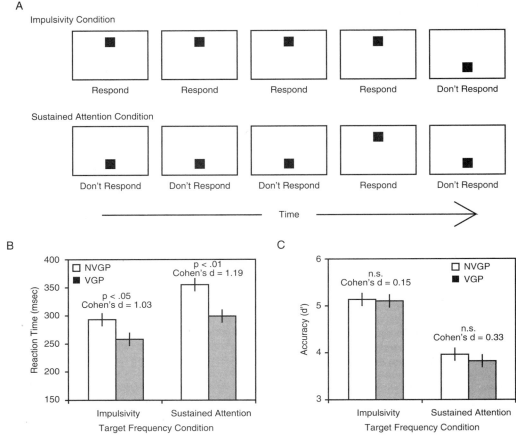

Figure 1 The Test of Variables of Attention (A), used to assess differences in impulsivity and sustained attention between non-video-game players (NVGPs) and expert video-game players (VGPs), and results for both reaction time (B) and accuracy (C) measures. VGPs were faster at responding than NVGPs on both the impulsivity and sustained attention measures, but the groups did not differ on the accuracy measure, suggesting that the faster responses of VGPs were not due to impulsive responses to the stimuli and that they did not have greater problems sustaining their attention (n.s. stands for nonsignificant; *p* values are given for statistical significance and Cohen's *d* for the strength of the effect).

after the end of training (rather than immediately prior to and after training), these training studies attempt to exclude possible short-term effects of gaming on behavior, such as changes in arousal state or frame of mind. . . .

Thus, unlike what has been reported in the majority of the literature on the training of speeded responses, the learning that occurs during action-video-game experience generalizes well beyond the act of playing games itself.

Action Video Games and Impulsivity

The increased speed of processing noted in VGPs is often viewed as a "trigger-happy" behavior, in which VGPs respond faster but make more anticipatory errors (responding incorrectly because they do not wait for enough information to become available). Available research suggests this is not the case. First, the metaanalysis above reveals that VGPs have equivalent accuracy to NVGPs in the face of an 11% decrease

in RTs. Second, a more direct evaluation of impulsivity using the Test of Variables of Attention (T.O.V.A.®) indicates equivalent performance in VGPs and NVGPs. Briefly, this test requires subjects to look at a computer monitor and make a timed response to shapes appearing at one location (targets), while ignoring the same shapes if they appear at another location (nontargets). In different parts of the experiment, the target can appear either often or very rarely (Figure 1A). The T.O.V.A. therefore offers a measure of both impulsivity (is the observer able to withhold a response to a nontarget when most of the stimuli are targets?) and a measure of sustained attention (is the observer able to stay on task and respond quickly to a target when most of the stimuli are nontargets?).

VGPs were selected based on self-reports of playing 5 hours per week (or more) of action video games in the previous year, and compared to NVGPs who reported little or no video gaming (and no action gaming for several years). VGPs responded more quickly than did NVGPs on both task components (Figure 1B), confirming increased processing speed in this group.

Crucially, accuracy did not differ for the two groups, this being the case for both the impulsivity and the sustained-attention measures (Figure 1C). VGPs were therefore faster but not more impulsive than NVGPs and were equally capable of sustaining their attention. Thus, in contrast to the "trigger-happy" hypothesis, VGPs did not compensate for their faster RTs by making more anticipatory errors than NVGPs.

Action Video Games and Accuracy Measures

Although earlier studies typically used speeded RT tasks, more recent studies of action-video-game players have focused on accuracy measures. This choice was motivated by the difficulty of making fair comparisons regarding cognitive processes across populations that have large differences in how quickly they make their responses. This problem is well acknowledged in the aging literature, and we refer the reader to Madden, Pierce, and Allen (1996) for a comprehensive discussion of the issue.

One area that has received considerable attention is the effect of action video games on visual cognition. Video-game players have been reported to show improved hand–eye coordination, increased visual processing in the periphery, enhanced mental-rotation skills, greater divided attention, and enhanced visuospatial memory. A series of published accuracy studies have established that playing action video games enhances performance on tasks thought to measure different aspects of visual attention, including the ability to (a) distribute attention across space, (b) efficiently perform dual tasks, (c) track several moving objects at once, and (d) process streams of briefly presented visual stimuli (Green & Bavelier, 2003, 2007). One such study focusing on visuospatial skills has suggested that action-game playing may provide a reliable training regimen to reduce gender differences in visuospatial cognition (Feng, Spence, & Pratt, 2007). In each of these instances, a causative role for action video games was demonstrated by conducting training studies with college students who did not play video games.

While these results in accuracy-based tasks have been previously interpreted as an increase in attentional resources in action-video-game players and/or an enhancement in the ability to allocate those resources across space and time, the Brinley plot in Figure 1 suggests an alternative hypothesis that parsimoniously explains the entire pattern of previous data, both RT-and accuracy-based. The consistent multiplicative VGP advantage in reaction time observed in the Brinley plot suggests a clear difference in the speed with which visual information is processed between the groups. In tasks in which RT is the primary dependent measure, this difference will be manifested as predictably faster RTs in VGPs than in NVGPs. However, such a difference in the speed of processing also predicts higher accuracy in VGPs in accuracy-based tasks in which the stimulus is typically quickly flashed or moving. This prediction was confirmed by Li, Polat, Makous, and Bavelier (2009), who show that VGPs acquire visual information more rapidly than NVGPs do. In fact, such a hypothesis predicts VGP advantages on virtually any task for which speeded visual processing is at the root of performance. To some

extent, this hypothesis can be thought of as the converse of the generalized-slowing hypothesis for cognitive aging—that is, the suggestion that the observed decrements on a wide range of tasks in the elderly can be explained by a single underlying mechanism, decreases in the speed of information processing.

Implications and Future Directions

A training regimen that efficiently increases processing speed is potentially greatly interesting, as faster RTs are reported to correlate with higher performance on tests of high-level cognition (Conway, Cowen, Bunting, Therriault, & Minkoff, 2002) and to be responsible for many of the observed changes in cognitive performance across the lifespan (Kail & Salthouse, 1994). For example, age-related declines in visual search, memory, and spatial-reasoning tasks appear to be largely due to task-independent slowing of processing speed in elderly subjects. Action-video-game training may therefore prove to be a helpful training regimen for providing a marked increase in speed of information processing to individuals with slower-than-normal speed of processing, such as the elderly or victims of brain trauma (Clark et al., 1987; Drew & Waters, 1986).

While the evidence reviewed here shows that these improvements generalize to a wide range of perceptual and attentional tasks, the extent of this generalization remains unknown. Because available work has focused on visual tasks, there is no information about generalization to other modalities, such as audition or touch. Similarly, because the focus has so far been on relatively fast tasks requiring decisions between just two alternatives (with RTs less than 2,000 milliseconds), it remains unknown whether more cognitively demanding tasks would benefit in any way.

While the mechanism of this generalization remains unknown, the need to maximize the number of actions per unit of time to achieve the greatest reward when playing action video games may well be a key factor. This will certainly be a promising avenue of research for future studies. A second important goal for future work is to gain a clearer understanding of the characteristics of the action-video-game play experience that favor performance enhancement. Much of what is currently known is descriptive (for instance, that fast-paced and visually complex games promote greater levels of learning than do slower games; see Cohen, Green, & Bavelier, 2007); there is a clear need to move toward more explanatory accounts. Hand-in-hand with such accounts, it will be important to isolate the characteristics of action video games that cause the observed changes and relate those characteristics to the mechanisms by which performance is altered. Finally, most of the games found to enhance performance are unsuitable for children in terms of their content and difficult for elderly gamers in terms of the dexterity of response and visual acuity required. Identifying which aspects of the games are relevant will allow the development of games that have a wide range of suitability and accessibility that can be used in clinical as well as educational applications. As with any research endeavor, a combination of basic theoretical research combined with evidence-led practical applications is the most likely to produce tangible results.

Recommended Reading

Green, C.S., & Bavelier, D. (2003). (See References). The first study reporting changes in several different aspects of visual attention as a result of action-video-game playing incorporating a training study designed to establish causality.

Green, C.S., & Bavelier, D. (2006). The cognitive neuroscience of video games. In P. Messaris & L. Humphreys (Eds.), *Digital Media: Transformations in Human Communication*. New York: Peter Lang. A review of existing studies on the effects of action video games on perception and cognition as well as brain organization.

Kail, R., & Salthouse, T.A. (1994). (See References). A discussion of the role of processing speed in cognition.

References

Bavelier, D., & Bailey, S. (2007). [N-back and pro-active interference memory tasks in action gamers]. Unpublished raw data.

Bherer, L., Kramer, A.F., Peterson, M.S., Colcombe, S., Erickson, K., & Becic, E. (2005). Training effects on dual-task performance: Are there age-related differences in plasticity of attentional control? *Psychology and Aging, 20,* 695–709.

Bialystok, E. (2006). Effect of bilingualism and computer video game experience on the Simon task. *Canadian Journal of Experimental Psychology, 60,* 68–79.

Cameron, E.L., Tai, J.C., Eckstein, M.P., & Carrasco, M. (2004). Signal detection theory applied to three visual search tasks—identification, yes/no detection and localization. *Spatial Vision, 17,* 295–325.

Castel, A.D., Pratt, J., & Drummond, E. (2005). The effects of action video game experience on the time course of inhibition of return and the efficiency of visual search. *Acta Psychologica, 119,* 217–230.

Clark, J.E., Lanphear, A.K., & Riddick, C.C. (1987). The effects of videogame playing on the response selection processing of elderly adults. *Journal of Gerontology, 42,* 82–85.

Cohen, J.E., Green, C.S., & Bavelier, D. (2007). Training visual attention with video games: Not all games are created equal. In H. O'Neil & R. Perez (Eds.), *Computer games and adult learning* (pp. 205–227). Oxford, England: Elsevier.

Conway, A.R.A., Cowan, N., Bunting, M.F., Therriault, D.J., & Minkoff, S.R.B. (2002). A latent variable analysis of working memory capacity, short-term memory capacity, processing speed, and general fluid intelligence. *Intelligence, 30,* 163–183.

Drew, D., & Waters, J. (1986). Video games: Utilization of a novel strategy to improve perceptual motor skills and cognitive functioning in the non-institutionalized elderly. *Cognitive Rehabilitation, 4,* 26–31.

Dye, M.W.G., Green, C.S., & Bavelier, D. (2009). The development of attention skills in action video game players. *Neuropsychologia, 47,* 1780–1789.

Feng, J., Spence, I., & Pratt, J. (2007). Playing action video games reduces or eliminates gender differences in spatial cognition. *Psychological Science, 18,* 850–855.

Green, C.S. (2008). *The effects of action video game experience on perceptual decision making.* Unpublished doctoral dissertation, University of Rochester, Rochester, NY.

Green, C.S., & Bavelier, D. (2003). Action video game modifies visual selective attention. *Nature, 423,* 534–537.

Green, C.S., & Bavelier, D. (2007). Action video game experience alters the spatial resolution of attention. *Psychological Science, 18,* 88–94.

Greenfield, P.M., deWinstanley, P., Kilpatrick, H., & Kaye, D. (1994). Action video games and informal education: Effects on strategies for dividing visual attention. *Journal of Applied Developmental Psychology, 15,* 105–123.

Kail, R., & Salthouse, T.A. (1994). Processing speed as a mental capacity. *Acta Psychologica, 86,* 199–225.

Li, R., Polat, U., Makous, W., & Bavelier, D. (2009). Enhancing the contrast sensitivity function through action video game training. *Nature Neuroscience, 12,* 549–551.

Madden, D.J., Pierce, T.W., & Allen, P.A. (1996). Adult age differences in the use of distractor homogeneity during visual search. *Psychology and Aging, 11,* 454–474.

Monsell, S., Sumner, P., & Waters, H. (2003). Task-set reconfiguration with predictable and unpredictable task switches. *Memory and Cognition, 31,* 327–342.

Palmer, J., Huk, A., & Shadlen, M. (2005). The effect of stimulus strength on the speed and accuracy of a perceptual decision. *Journal of Vision, 55,* 376–404.

Pashler, H., & Baylis, G. (1991). Procedural learning: I. Locus of practice effects in speeded choice tasks. *Journal of Experimental Psychology: Learning, Memory and Cognition, 17,* 20–32.

Critical Thinking

1. How can psychologists use video gaming to study human thought and action?

2. Why is the study of reaction time and response accuracy important topics in the study of psychology?

3. If you were able to train and to increase your own response times, what would be the expected impact on tests of cognition?

Create Central

www.mhhe.com/createcentral

Internet References

The positive effect of action video games: Speed of visual processing

www.psychologytoday.com/blog/ulterior-motives/201001/
the-positive-effect-action-video-games-speed-visual-processing

Train your brain with targeted video games, not with crossword puzzles

http://sharpbrains.com/blog/2013/05/06/train-your-brain-with-targeted
-videogames-not-with-crossword-puzzles/

Dye et al., Matthew W. G. From *Current Directions in Psychological Science*, vol. 18, no. 6, December 2009, pp. 321–326. Copyright © 2009 by the Association for Psychological Science. Reprinted by permission of Sage Publications via Rightslink.

Corporeal Awareness and Proprioceptive Sense of the Phantom by et. al. Melita Giummarra

63

Article

Prepared by: Eric Landrum, *Boise State University*

Corporeal Awareness and Proprioceptive Sense of the Phantom

MELITA J. GIUMMARRA ET AL.

Learning Outcomes

After reading this article, you will be able to:

- Understand some of the hypothesized theories as to why phantom limb pain occurs.

- Comprehend how survey methodology can be used to advance our knowledge of phantom limb pain.

Amputees invariably continue to perceive a ghost of their amputated limb as a phantom. The phantom limb is often plagued by unpleasant, annoying, or distressing phantom pain, but may also retain other features that suggest it is still highly represented in proprioceptive body maps. We report a large scale investigation of phantom limb experiences that systematically explored somatic and proprioceptive aspects of phantom phenomena. These include (a) the perception of bodily aspects of phantom limbs including the size (e.g., compared to the intact limb, thinner, or thicker/swollen), shape, posture, and telescoping (or shortening) of the phantom; (b) exteroceptive and proprioceptive sensations (e.g., touch, pressure, temperature, itching, vibration, pins, and needles, 'electric'/shooting; see also Hunter, Katz, & Davis, 2003); and (c) prosthesis embodiment. Embodiment involves the perception that one's sense of self is localized within one's bodily borders (Arzy, Thut, Mohr, Michel, & Blanke, 2006), but may extend to a habitually used tool or prosthesis that effectively extends the body's area of influence (Giummarra, Gibson, Georgiou-Karistianis, & Bradshaw, 2008). We do not presently report detailed data on phantom limb movement, even though they are principally relevant to phantom limb proprioception, as these observations have been reported elsewhere (Giummarra *et al.,*). The somatic and proprioceptive aspects of phantom phenomena offer a fascinating insight to corporeal bodily awareness.

Current accounts of somatic phantom limb awareness are typically based on anecdotal or incomplete descriptions (e.g., only exploring isolated features of the phantom, such as telescoping, position, shape, or size), based on small sample sizes or simply clinical observations of more extraordinary cases (e.g., limbs that can be moved through anatomically impossible ranges; Price, 1976). While various studies report the perception of somatic, non-painful phantom sensations (Aglioti, Smania, Atzei, & Berlucchi, 1997; Halligan, Marshal, Wade, Davey, & Morrison, 1993; Knecht *et al.*, 1995), few have systematically explored these aspects of phantom phenomena. Jensen, Krebs, Nielsen, and Rasmussen (1983) documented kinaesthetic sensations, present in 85% of amputees, over the first 6 months post-amputation. In particular, the phantom was perceived to be (a) normal length for 55% (43% at 6 months), longer for 7% (0 at 6 months), or shorter/telescoped for 7% (30% at 6 months); (b) normal volume for 48% (33% at 6 months), increased volume for 3% (4% at 6 months), or decreased volume for 9% (12% at 6 months). More recently, Fraser (2002) reported somatic qualities in the phantom limb in upper limb amputees. They found that a massive 64 of 66 upper limb amputees with phantom sensations experienced a phantom limb that resembled the limb prior to amputation in *shape and form;* however, for 28% the phantom was shortened/telescoped (but in some cases ultimately retained the pre-amputation shape and form), and for others the phantom was larger/magnified (8%). We intend to significantly extend these prior findings in both sample characteristics (with a much larger sample of both upper and lower limb amputees), and the types of sensations perceived to characterize the phantom.

The distal portion of the phantom is typically perceived either where it would be if the entire limb was present, or to be closer or attached to the stump (i.e., telescoped) in 28–67% of cases (Carlen, Wall, Nadvorna, & Steinbach, 1978; Fraser, 2002; Richardson, Glenn, Horgan, & Nurmikko, 2007), with approximately 30% reporting some telescoping within the first 6 months of amputation (Jensen *et al.*, 1983). Telescoping usually begins within weeks or months of amputation and the phantom limb may then disappear (Hunter *et al.*, 2003; Shukla, Sahu, Tripathi, & Gupta, 1982) or remain 'dangling' from the stump (Ramachandran & Hirstein, 1998). The telescoped phantom may resemble an ontogenetic form of the amputated limb, sometimes resembling the form of phocomelic limbs (e.g., from thalidomide) with portions of the limb shrunken, deformed, or absent. Phantom limbs apparently do not telescope in patients with pre-existing peripheral nerve injury, spinal cord transection, or brachial plexus avulsion, perhaps due to 'learned paralysis' and reinforcement of the 'extended' representation of the deafferented limb (Katz, 1992; Ramachandran & Hirstein, 1998). In amputees with telescoped phantoms, motor imagery of the phantom hand shows a medial shift in primary somatosensory cortex, activating cortical areas remote from the amputated limb (Flor, Nikolajsen, & Jensen, 2006), which suggests an association between changes in the perceived size or length of the phantom (i.e., telescoping) and perceptual remapping of primary somatosensory neurons subserving the amputated limb.

Phantom limbs are known to typically adopt a 'habitual' position and posture, resting at the side of the body, or in a posture that resembles that of the limb prior to amputation (Ramachandran & Hirstein, 1998). Often the phantom is stuck in a frozen or fixed position (Devor, 1997), particularly when moving other body parts (Fraser, 2002). The phantom may also assume an abnormal posture, such as the fingers twisted out of shape or grossly intertwined, or the thumb pushing through the palm (Bailey & Moersch, 1941; Henderson & Smyth, 1948). Kooijman, Dijkstra, Geertzen, Elzinga, and van der Schans (2000) report that abnormal shape and posture are perceived by 9 and 22% of upper limb amputees, respectively; however, the characteristics of abnormal phantom posture, and associations with aspects of amputation or other phantom limb phenomena, are not presently known. We would expect that pre-amputation history may affect the posture in the phantom; for example, functional impairment or immobilization prior to amputation may correspond to abnormal or fixed posture in the phantom.

Phantom limbs may be characterized by various exteroceptive or proprioceptive sensations, such as touch, pressure, temperature, itch, and vibration, tingling or buzzing (Hunter *et al.*, 2003; Jensen *et al.*, 1983; Weinstein, 1998). While these perceptions are frequently described they have rarely been examined with respect to aspects of amputation or other phantom limb phenomena. Jensen *et al.* (1983) indicated that 15% of their sample experienced exteroceptive sensations, including itching, tingling, cold, heat, and paraesthesia; however, they did not quantify the respective sensations. Richardson *et al.* (2007) found that 50% of amputees perceived pins and needles, 43% perceived itching, and 15% had 'super-added' sensations (primarily characterized by the perception of clothing on the phantom) in the phantom at 6 months. In a small study of 11 upper limb amputees, Hunter, Katz, and Davis (2008) reported a significant increase in the number of subjects experiencing additional exteroceptive sensations in the phantom over time (e.g., tickling, tingling, and 'pins and needles').

Evidently, while various studies have reported aspects of somatic and proprioceptive qualities that characterize phantom limbs, we aimed to systematically explored these phenomena in a large cohort of amputees.

Method
Participants
Two hundred and eighty-three amputees participated, aged 22–96 (mean = 59; SD = 15), and had been amputees for between 9 days and 70 years (median = 12.1 years, mean = 19 years; SD = 17.7 years).

Materials
Questionnaires assessed participants' neurological (e.g., stroke, peripheral neuropathy, or movement disorders), psychological, and surgical histories. The *Changes in Body Sensation Following Limb Loss* questionnaire (CIBS-questionnaire; see supplementary material for the full questionnaire) was developed for the present study, following appraisal of the literature on phantom limb phenomena, to explore aspects of phantom limb experience (e.g., perception of the size, shape, and posture of the phantom) that had not previously been quantified in a large sample of amputees. The CIBS-questionnaire is long, time consuming, and ultimately most useful when implemented in the manner for which it was designed: as an exploration of the perception of somatic and other qualities in the phantom limb following amputation, not as a clinical or diagnostic tool. While the questionnaire did not include 'control' questions, or measures of suggestibility, we did contact nearly all participants for a follow-up telephone interview to verify their answers.

The CIBS-questionnaire was implemented alongside existing pain [e.g., McGill Pain Questionnaire (Melzack, 1975) and the Brief Pain Inventory (Cleeland, 1989)], coping [e.g., Coping Strategies Questionnaire (Rosentstiel & Keefe, 1983)], mood [e.g., Hospital Anxiety and Depression Scale (Zigmond & Snaith, 1983)], and amputation scales [e.g., Trinity Amputation and Prosthetics Experiences Scales (Gallagher & MacLachlan, 2000)]. We report only a small portion of the results from the larger questionnaire study, findings from which are described elsewhere (Giummarra *et al.,*). The following questions from the CIBS-questionnaire were used in analyses for the present paper:

(a) *Information about limb loss* including: dates of amputation(s); side and level of each amputation; cause of limb loss, and duration and nature of functional impairment prior to amputation.

(b) *Information about prosthesis use,* including: prosthesis type, years/months of prosthesis use, frequency of use (all of the time, most of the time, some of the time, not often, never), and interaction between the phantom and prosthesis.

(c) *Information about phantom sensations and pain,* including: phantom limb perception; frequency of phantom limb perception now and in the past (always, a few times an hour, day, week, month, year, or very infrequently); duration of phantom limb perception now and in the past (seconds, minutes, hours, days, constantly); perception of the parts, size, shape, and posture of the phantom limb; static and dynamic changes in size or shape of the phantom limb (telescoping);

Corporeal Awareness and Proprioceptive Sense of the Phantom by et. al. Melita Giummarra

65

exteroceptive sensations in the phantom limb (including perception of itching, touching, pressure, vibration, electric sensations, or temperature in the phantom); referred sensations to the phantom limb; movement of the phantom (in particular, whether the phantom moves spontaneously, reflexively, or voluntarily); perception of pain in the phantom, stump, or residual limb now or in the past; Visual Analogue Scale (VAS) for current, and usual (during a typical episode of pain), intensity of phantom pain; VAS for current, and usual (during a typical episode of pain), intensity of stump pain. VASs comprised a line 10 cm long, with the left-most side labelled 'no pain' and the right-most side labelled 'worst possible pain'.

Procedure

Participants gave informed consent prior to inclusion in the study, which was approved by local university and hospital ethics boards, and met the ethical standards laid down in the 1964 Declaration of Helsinki. Participants were primarily recruited from the Caulfield General Medical Centre Amputee Unit, Australia. One thousand amputees were invited, 249 of whom responded, and 199 returned valid questionnaires (20% response rate). The true reason for the low response rate cannot be known; however, invitees who *no longer* perceived phantom sensations may not have volunteered as they assumed that they were not the target of the study (which was advertised as examining phantom limb perception). Furthermore, the letter of invitation requested volunteers with no personal history of mental illness or neurological condition, which would have further reduced the size of the eligible sample. Finally, the overall questionnaire was large and time consuming. The sample was heterogeneous—although likely comprising a larger proportion of upper limb and traumatic amputees than in the general amputee population—and is likely to be representative of the larger population of amputees perceiving phantom limb sensations.

The study was also reported in various Australian media (including mainstream television news programmes, and mainstream and regional newspapers) and resulted in another 108 amputees volunteering, of whom 84 returned valid questionnaires. Questionnaires were mailed to participants to be returned to the researchers in a reply paid envelope. The researchers then contacted each participant to clarify any ambiguities and verify their responses. Participants who did not return their questionnaires were sent a reminder letter, and a follow-up phone call requesting the return of the questionnaire.

Statistical Analyses

Univariate chi-square and Fisher exact tests (FET) were used to analyse the associations between dichotomous variables. Non-parametric (Mann–Whitney) analyses were performed to examine interval data that was not normally distributed (i.e., time since amputation and phantom limb posture). Factors potentially associated with somatic aspects of phantom limb phenomena (parts, size, telescoping, posture, and exteroceptive sensations) of the phantom limb perceived were examined. These included: cause of limb loss (trauma, vascular, diabetes),

functional impairment before amputation, time since amputation, level of limb loss (upper vs. lower limb; as well as level of loss in the respective limb), complications of amputation (e.g., gangrene or infection), and phantom pain. Ultimately, analyses were theory driven; for example, exploring the association between bent/fixed posture of the phantom and functional impairment or limb immobilization; and exploring the relationship between prosthesis embodiment and phantom limb sensations/pain, telescoping, and referred sensations.

Results

We separately report findings relating to parts of the phantom limb perceived, size of the phantom limb, telescoping, posture of the limb, exteroceptive and proprioceptive sensations, prosthesis use and embodiment.

Frequency of phantom sensations was not correlated with time since amputation; Spearman's $r = .11, p = .05$. This may be due to a recruitment bias in that amputees were more likely to participate if they were still experiencing phantom sensations or pain, particularly with the participants who volunteered following media exposure of the study who were more likely to experience phantom pain (82% media generated participants compared with 65% for invited participants); FET $\chi^2(1) = 8.14, p < .01$.

Parts of the Phantom Limb Perceived

The majority of amputees perceived the parts of their phantom limb to be similar to the limb before amputation. We have found, for the first time, that 11 (4.3%) primarily perceived proximal parts of the limb. Such amputees described that 'it is like an extension to the stump (but not foot), about 3 cm below the stump,' that they were 'just aware of the shin,' or that they just felt sensation 'below the stump.' Vascular amputees were more likely to perceive only the proximal portion of their phantom limb compared to other amputees (8.6% cf. 2.0%), and were less likely to report that their phantom resembled the shape (whole and/or deformed) of the limb as it was prior to amputation ($N = 21, 36.21\%$ cf. $N = 100, 50.50\%$); $\chi^2(3) = 8.53, p < .05$. Some amputees ($N = 17, 6.64\%$) perceived a 'whole' phantom limb, that was of an abnormal shape *unlike* the shape of the limb prior to amputation, and 19 (7.4%) did not perceive the parts/shape of their phantom limb.

Differences emerged in the parts of the phantom perceived according to the level of limb loss, $\chi^2(5) = 16.51, p < .01$. Upper limb amputees primarily perceived the phantom limb in its entirety as it was prior to amputation ($N = 27, 72.97\%$) with 18.91% ($N = 7$) perceiving only the distal portion of the limb, whereas lower limb amputees generally perceived their phantom to be either whole as it was prior to amputation ($N = 88, 41.71\%$) or to consist only of the distal portion of the limb ($N = 98, 46.45\%$).

Size of the Phantom Limb

The majority ($N = 213, 75.3\%$) of participant's phantom limbs were of a normal size, while some individuals could not perceive the size of their limb ($N = 34, 13.3\%$), and others reported that their limb was smaller/thinner ($N = 4$, 1.4%; e.g., foot feels smaller than the remaining foot; phantom limb feels thinner), or bigger ($N = 4$, 1.4%; e.g., phantom feels swollen; leg has become shorter [telescoped] and fatter) than it should be. The size of the phantom limb did not differ according to level of amputation or limb amputated. A higher proportion of participants with phantom pain ($N = 173$, 89.2%) perceived the size of their phantom limb compared with those without phantom pain ($N = 48$, 78.7%); FET $\chi^2(1) = 4.42$, $p < .05$.

Telescoping

Fifty-five (21.6%) participants reported that their phantom limb was telescoped, including 4 of 11 (36.4%) amputees with a brachial plexus avulsion. All participants with brachial plexus avulsion retained their limb for between 1 and 4 years following injury ($m = 2.28$ years, $SD = 1.11$). Upper limb amputees (35.1%) were more likely to experience a telescoped phantom than lower limb amputees (20.1%); FET $\chi^2(1) = 4.10$, $p < .05$. Furthermore, across upper and lower limb amputees, the higher the level of amputation (excluding finger/toe amputations) the more likely participants were to report telescoping; $\chi^2(4) = 13.42$, $p < .01$. Evidently, the finding that 35% of upper limb amputees experience a telescoped phantom limb, and 72% experience their limb as if it was whole could be seen to be contradictory. However, the seven amputees for whom this was the case described the distal portion of their phantom as being closer to the stump, or that the phantom was shortened, but still comprising the key joints and parts of the limb. An overlap between telescoping and perceiving the phantom as a 'whole' was also reported in 22 lower limb amputees. Similar observations (i.e., overlap between the phantom resembling the shape and form of the phantom, and being telescoped or shortened) have previously been reported by Fraser (2002).

Telescoping was less common among amputees with (a) vascular amputation ($N = 4$, 6.9%), which was nearly four times less likely to be associated with telescoping compared with other causes of limb loss ($N = 51$, 25.9%); FET $\chi^2(1) = 9.55$, $p < .01$; or (b) diabetic amputation ($N = 1$, 4%) compared with other causes of limb loss ($N = 54$, 23.5%); FET $\chi^2(1) = 5.06$, $p = .01$; and (c) functional impairment prior to limb loss ($N = 22$, 15%) compared with those without functional impairment ($N = 33$, 31%); FET $\chi^2(1) = 9.81$, $p < .01$. Telescoping was more common following (a) traumatic amputation [N(trauma) = 38, 29.7% compared with N(other) = 17, 13.4%; FET $\chi^2(1) = 10.01$, $p < .01$] and (b) cancer-related amputation [N(cancer) = 11, 44% compared with N(other) = 44, 19.1%; FET $\chi^2(1) = 8.24$, $p < .01$].

An aspect of telescoping not previously understood is that of *active* telescoping. Seven (2.5%) amputees reported that their phantom actively telescoped. For example, 'the phantom moves into the stump when in bed at night, not wearing the prosthesis', 'phantom withdraws towards the stump when taking the prosthesis off', or 'sometimes I wake up and it feels like whole leg is there, then I move it and it disappears back up towards the stump'.

Posture of the Limb

Most participants ($N = 203$, 79.3%) with phantom sensations perceived that their phantom occupied a normal or habitual position, and 30 (11.7%) reported that their limb occupied an abnormal position (see Figure 2 for participant illustrations of normal and abnormal postures). Abnormal and anatomically impossible postures consisted of the phantom (a) fingers or toes curled or clenched ($N = 5$); (b) in a fixed bent posture at the knee or elbow ($N = 10$); (c) limb twisted or pointing inwards/outwards ($N = 13$); (d) digits switched/crossed/confused or 'all over the place' ($N = 3$) and other ($N = 3$); data partially overlapping. Participants reporting anatomically impossible postures (c and d) were more likely to be traumatic amputees, FET $\chi^2(1) = 6.44$, $p = .01$.

Perception of normal posture was more common in those *with* functional impairment prior to limb loss, vascular and diabetic amputation, phantom pain, and lower limb amputation. Cancer-related amputation was less likely to result in perception of a normal posture. Among both upper and lower limb amputees, those with higher levels of amputation perceived more varied postures, such that those with higher levels of amputation were equally likely to perceive a normal posture, a telescoped (shortened) phantom in a normal posture (e.g., the phantom takes a habitual posture but is shorter, or that it switches between an extended and telescoped phantom in a normal/habitual posture), or an abnormal posture in the phantom, compared with those with lower levels of amputation who were more likely to perceive a normal posture; $\chi^2(3) = 68.87$, $p = .006$.

Ten amputees perceived their phantom to be in a fixed position where the limb was bent at the knee or elbow. This fixed position did not vary during prosthesis use when the phantom would typically dissociate from the prosthesis when walking, but merge when sitting. Amputees who perceived their phantom limb to be fixed in a bent position at the knee/elbow were more likely to have had their amputation for a longer time (median = 32.8 years; range: 22 months–61.7 years) than those who did not perceive their phantom limb in a fixed bent position (median = 10 years; range: 9 days–65 years); Mann–Whitney $U = 633.0$, $N_1 = 203$, $N_2 = 10$, $p < .05$, two-tailed. However, perception of a bent, fixed phantom knee/elbow did not differ according to functional impairment or immobilization prior to amputation, age at amputation, or present age. Furthermore, there was no apparent relationship with occupation (i.e., amputees with a fixed bent phantom knee/elbow did not perform sedentary jobs, but included an apprentice motor mechanic, architect, butcher, company director, computer programmer, disability support worker, electrical instrument maker, geologist, lecturer in mathematics, and television technician).

Nineteen (7.6%) amputees reported that the distal portion or the entire length of their phantom seemed to float at a distance from the stump, or that they could not perceive parts of the limb between the distal portion (e.g., the hand or foot) and the stump, but that the distal portion was at a distance from the stump. For example, one person explained that 'the phantom becomes dissociated from the limb when walking'. A further

17 reported that there was a space between their phantom and their stump, but that the phantom was not 'floating' *per se*.

Exteroceptive and Proprioceptive Sensations

At least half of all amputees with phantom sensations perceived one or more exteroceptive/proprioceptive 'super-added' (Richardson *et al.*, 2007) sensation. In particular, participants perceived itching ($N = 129$, 50%), pressure ($N = 92$, 36.7%), touch ($N = 41$, 16%), temperature [hot ($N = 43$, 16.6%), cold ($N = 40$, 15.6%), hot and cold ($N = 12$, 4.7%), and warm ($N = 14$, 17.6%)], electric sensations ($N = 120$, 43%; e.g., 'electrical nerve impulses', shooting/lightning bolt type pains, or electric shocks/jolts), vibration ($N = 32$, 11.5%), and pins and needles ($N = 49$, 17.6%). There were no differences in perception of any of these exteroceptive sensations according to cause of limb loss, functional impairment prior to amputation, infection or gangrene prior to amputation, or posture of the phantom limb. The only difference was found between upper and lower limb amputees, such that the former were more likely to report perceiving temperature in their phantom limb than the latter (52.78% cf. 41.04%); $\chi^2(5) = 12.582$, $p < .05$. While some medications used for relieving phantom pain can cause itching as a side effect, medication use was not significantly related to the perception of itching in the phantom.

Prosthesis Use and Embodiment

Nearly, all lower limb amputees used a prosthesis ($N = 202$, 88%) whereas only 59% ($N = 24$) upper limb amputees used a prosthesis; FET $\chi^2(1) = 22.45$, $p < .001$. Among lower limb amputees, those with higher levels of amputation used their prosthesis less often than those with below knee or lower amputations; $\chi^2(24) = 71.69$, $p < .001$. For example, no hindquarter amputees and 66.7% ($N = 40$) above knee amputees used their prosthesis all of the time compared with 78.1% ($N = 100$) of below knee amputees.

Of those who wore a prosthesis, 23 (11.6%) reported that their phantom limb 'becomes the prosthesis' or vice versa, and 34 (17.2%) reported that the phantom disappears, which may equally suggest that the prosthesis is embodied (i.e., the perception that one's sense of bodily self is localized within a 'tool' or prosthesis that extend the body's area of influence; Giummarra *et al.*, 2008) and the amputee therefore feels normal and whole. Experiences of embodiment included reporting that: 'the prosthesis fits like a glove/shoe'; 'it all feels like one . . . like it's in a shoe when I put the prosthesis on'; 'the artificial leg is my leg, if I have it off it is very strange'; and 'the phantom limb and prosthesis become one and the same'.

Among those who used a prosthesis 'most of the time' or 'all of the time' (i.e., excluding those who only wear their prosthesis 'some of the time' or 'never'), we combined participants who explicitly affirmed prosthesis embodiment and those who indicated that their phantom disappeared during prosthesis use as the 'prosthesis embodiment' group ($N = 57$), and compared these participants against others ($N = 170$) for differences in perception of phantom pain, frequency of phantom limb perception, and telescoping. Prosthesis embodiment was more frequent in amputees with an extended phantom ($N = 15/47$, 32%) compared to a telescoped phantom ($N = 18/118$, 15%); FET $\chi^2(1) = 5.83$, $p < .05$. Furthermore, prosthesis embodiment was more common in amputees who reported perceiving referred sensations from the amputated limb to the phantom ($N = 23/47$, 49%) than those without such referred sensations ($N = 40/120$, 33%); FET $\chi^2(1) = 3.50$, $p < .05$; although the accuracy of sensory maps in the amputated limb could not be verified using the present questionnaire-based method.

Prosthesis embodiment did not differ according to: perception of phantom pain or phantom pain intensity, level of amputation, limb amputated (upper vs. lower), whether the amputated limb was the dominant limb, frequency of phantom limb perception, or type of prosthesis used (functional vs. cosmetic; however, only 13 amputees used a cosmetic prosthesis most or all of the time).

Ten (3.5%) amputees indicated that the phantom did not embody their prosthesis, including all five with a phantom in a fixed bent posture who still used a prosthesis. Others described that their 'phantom sensations are completely independent of the prosthesis as it doesn't fit into the prosthesis', or that 'the phantom feels smothered because the prosthesis isn't long enough for the phantom limb'. Those who indicated that their phantom explicitly did not embody the prosthesis described a distinct perception of a mismatch between the phantom limb and the prosthesis. Those who reported 'no change', on the other hand, were more likely to explain that they had never noticed whether the phantom did or did not embody the prosthesis, or that they primarily perceived phantom pain rather than a phantom 'limb' *per se,* and could not relate to the concept of a phantom embodying the prosthesis.

Discussion

The present study examined the somatic and corporeal aspects of phantom phenomena. The properties that were found to define phantom limbs—including the size, shape, posture, and exteroceptive/proprioceptive qualities—parallel the sensations perceived in the intact body. Most amputees perceived a phantom that was of a normal size, and assumed a normal posture (whether extended or shortened/telescoped). Some perceived abnormal qualities in the phantom: the frequency (12%) of amputees with phantom limbs that occupied abnormal or anatomically impossible postures (e.g., the limb being twisted or pointing in the wrong direction, or digits on the phantom hand being switched, or crossed over) is quite high. Abnormal posture was more common following traumatic limb loss, and may be a consequence of the observation and perception of the affected limb occupying 'unnatural' positions during accidental injury (Anderson-Barnes, McAuliffe, Swanberg, & Tsao, 2009). Furthermore, upper limb amputees were more likely to perceive abnormal postures, which may relate to the higher degrees of freedom of movement of the joints of intact upper limbs compared to lower limbs. Upper limb amputees were also more likely to perceive temperature in their phantom, perhaps because temperature fluctuations are typically perceived more often in the upper limbs, which are often exposed and unprotected, compared with the lower limbs, which are typically enclosed in clothing and footwear.

The rare perception of the phantom being smaller/thinner or larger/swollen compared to the intact limb appears analogous to the perception of magnified or shrinking body parts in *Alice in Wonderland* illusions, which might result from reduced blood supply to the somatotopic representation of affected body parts (Kew, Wright, & Halligan, 1998). We have found for the first time that approximately 4% of amputees experienced the *proximal* portion of the phantom only. The finding that these patients were more likely to be vascular amputees may be because the distal portion of the limb contains finer vessels than proximal portions, and is more likely to have suffered prolonged sensory impairment leading to gradual reduction of somatosensory representation of the distal portion of the limb.

Telescoping was less frequent in the present sample than many previous studies (i.e., 21% compared with prior reports of 28–67%; Carlen *et al.,* 1978; Fraser, 2002; Richardson *et al.,* 2007), and was more common following proximal amputation. This is likely because the distal portion of the phantom can be apparently displaced (i.e., telescoped) a greater distance with more proximal amputation. Furthermore, cancer and traumatic amputees were more likely to experience telescoping, suggesting an association between telescoping and rapid limb loss compared with diabetic or vascular limb loss, which is characterized by more gradual sensory, neuropathic, and ischaemic changes prior to amputation. Contrary to prior reports (Katz, 1992; Ramachandran & Hirstein, 1998), over a third of patients with brachial plexus avulsion experienced a telescoped phantom, even though the physical limb was retained following injury for an average of 2 years and 4 months before amputation. Visual experience of a 'paralysed' limb does not, therefore, guarantee that the limb will be constrained by 'learned paralysis' and retain its extended form following amputation.

Consciously focusing on the phantom limb, as participants inevitably did in the present study, recruits the perceptual, conceptual, and emotional qualities (Gallagher & Cole, 1995) of the missing limb's body image (i.e., higher order, top-down bodily and perceptual representations; Gallagher, 2005; Kammers, van der Ham, & Dijkerman, 2006). Ordinarily, however, most amputees try not to allow their phantom limb to enter into conscious awareness because it is usually annoying or painful. Phantom limb awareness therefore likely results from much more complex mechanisms than mere conscious experience of the sensations of that limb. Most sensations typically occur spontaneously, and many properties that persist following amputation do so against one's wishes (e.g., itch, pressure, touch).

The present study was part of a larger study on phantom limb phenomena and phantom pain, and we have not presently examined phantom limb movement as these observations—and related literature—have been reported and discussed in depth elsewhere (Giummarra *et al.,*). However, we will briefly note these findings in order to satisfactorily account for the phantom limb's proprioceptive qualities—that is, the perception of feedback about limb position based on the combination of efferent information about limb movement and afferent information from somatosensory receptors (Tsakiris, Haggard, Franck, Mainy, & Sirigu, 2005). Key observations from our related substudy included the significant association between the *ability to move* the phantom and the perception of phantom pain, pain of a greater intensity, and an experience of phantom pain characterized by deep tissue-mediated qualities (e.g., cramping). Similarly, *spontaneous* phantom limb movements were associated with perception of heightened phantom and stump pain, and pain characterized by cramping, as well as electric-shooting pain, suggesting peripheral dysfunction. Furthermore, those who were able to wilfully move their phantom were more likely to perceive the size, shape, and posture of their phantom, suggesting that the body image of the limb was better preserved in those with voluntary phantom limb movement. Others have also described the perception of painful spontaneous phantom limb movements (Shukla *et al.,* 1982), and an association between voluntary phantom limb movement and phantom pain (Richardson *et al.,* 2007). Amputees suffering from phantom pain also exhibit decreased phantom limb motor control, taking longer to perform phantom limb movements (Gagne *et al.,* 2009). Increased phantom pain associated with phantom movement likely corresponds to an incongruence between sensory feedback and efference copy (Harris, 1999), consistent with forward prediction models (Blakemore, Wolpert, & Frith, 2002); that is, that we are unaware of the results of the comparison between predicted and intended outcome and sensory feedback from motor commands as long as the desired state is successfully achieved. In amputees, efferent and afferent information is in conflict. The associated phantom pain may be reduced with illusory phantom movement via mirrors, virtual reality, and prosthesis use, or mental imagery supplemented with observing others perform the imagined movement, thus involving mirror neuron systems (Giummarra *et al.,*).

Ultimately, rather than resulting from a mental image of the limb alone, perception of the corporeal phantom probably also stems from proprioceptive adjustments and minute, involuntary movements that occur during attempts to locate the limb in space. The phantom limb percept enters into awareness, or is even strengthened (Hunter *et al.,* 2003), during both non-conscious and intentional execution of motor schemata, including performance of automatic movements stored as limb-specific proprioceptive memories (Anderson-Barnes *et al.,* 2009). Various properties of the phantom may enter into conscious awareness as a result of non-conscious recruitment of body schemata (i.e., automatic, bottom-up sensory, and organizational processes that encode spatial and action capabilities of body parts; Gallagher, 2005; Giummarra *et al.,* 2008; Higuchi, Imanaka, & Patla, 2006) for the missing limb during proprioception, and maintenance of the (body) image of the limb (Gallagher, 1986; Gallagher & Cole, 1995; Paillard, 1991). This is somewhat analogous to the finding that the ability to see the visual illusion of apparent motion in *Enigma*, a display of closely spaced concentric rings and radiating black and white lines, relies upon the eyes making microsaccades (Troncoso, Macknik, Otero-Milian, & Martinez-Conde, 2008). The speed

Corporeal Awareness and Proprioceptive Sense of the Phantom by et. al. Melita Giummarra

69

of illusory motion is related to the rate of microsaccades, and if microsaccades cease or the eyes are immobilized (e.g., stabilized retinal image) then illusory motion ceases, or elements of the stimulus display disappear from vision, and one experiences a *ganzfeld* (Inhoff & Topolski, 1994). Likewise, when amputees are engaged in tasks that would not ordinarily require the use of the amputated limb or demand postural corrections (e.g., a lower limb amputee typing rapidly at the computer), or when occupied in a task that produces profound mental arousal (e.g., while working or engaged in socially stimulating activities), the proprioceptive sense of the phantom typically fades from awareness (Giummarra & Bradshaw, 2010).

The body image undoubtedly plays a large role in successful prosthesis use, as conscious awareness of the newly configured body is essential for this ambulatory transition. Not all amputees can use their prosthesis as a 'natural limb'—particularly those with proximal amputations for whom prosthesis use is more physically and mentally fatiguing (Smith, 2009)—and most continue to self-monitor, and consciously initiate movements using the body image and visual feedback. Prosthesis embodiment—which was reported by one third of prosthesis users—suggests successful merging of the phantom with the prosthesis in both body image and body schema. In some cases, the phantom did not 'fit' or embody the prosthesis (e.g., amputees with a permanently bent phantom). Prosthesis embodiment was more common in amputees with an extended phantom (i.e., not telescoped), which may suggest the importance of correspondence between the perceived proprioceptive and somatic qualities of the phantom and the physical and/or visual properties of the prosthesis. However, rubber limb embodiment seems not to depend upon correspondence between the visual properties of the rubber limb and visual and/or perceived somatic qualities in an amputee's limb/phantom (Giummarra, Georgiou-Karistianis, Gibson, Nicholls, & Bradshaw, 2010). The fundamental factor that appears to improve rubber limb embodiment in upper limb amputees is the presence of a 'sensory map' of sensations referred from the stump to the phantom (Ehrsson *et al.*, 2008). Likewise, we found that amputees reporting referred sensations from the stump and/or amputated limb were more likely to experience prosthesis embodiment; however, it was not possible to verify whether such referred sensations related to 'sensory maps' of the phantom on the stump or to more general referral or exacerbation of pain from the stump to the phantom.

Prosthesis use likely enables adaptive feed-forward mechanisms, reducing conflict between intended and actual movements of the amputated limb and its associated phantom, and provides for a 'surrogate' extension of kinaesthetic feedback. Functional prosthesis use, compared to cosmetic prosthesis use, among upper limb amputees has been found to correspond to maintenance of a more vivid phantom limb percept over time (Hunter *et al.*, 2008). Extensive prosthesis use, especially of a myoelectric prosthesis, is typically associated with decreased cortical reorganization, reduced phantom pain and likely preserved motor schemata for the phantom limb in upper limb amputees (Lotze *et al.*, 1999; Weiss, Miltner, Adler, Bruckner, & Taub, 1999); however, some studies have not replicated these findings (Hunter *et al.*, 2008; Kooijman *et al.*, 2000). We did not find any differences in prosthesis embodiment according to prosthesis type; however, only 13 amputees used a cosmetic prosthesis at least most or all of the time. Ultimately, the corporeal characteristics of non-painful phantom phenomena may affect the success of pain management strategies; e.g., the likely effectiveness of prosthesis training, mirror box therapy (Chan *et al.*, 2007; Ramachandran & Rogers-Ramachandran, 1996), or motor imagery (Moseley & Brugger, 2009) in alleviating phantom pain.

In summary, the phantom limb is, on the whole, characterized by properties that parallel the properties in the intact body—with respect to size, shape, and posture—with a small percentage experiencing anatomically impossible properties in the limb. While an amputee can deliberately focus on aspects of his or her phantom limb using the body image, this is unlikely to underlie ongoing and spontaneous phantom limb perception considering most phantom sensations are annoying. We therefore propose that phantom limb perception results in part from generation and maintenance of a conscious, long-term mental image of the missing limb (e.g., see O'Shaughnessy, 1995). Further studies should now compare and contrast the role of voluntary and involuntary proprioceptive adjustments (i.e., execution of *motor schemata* for the missing limb) in the maintenance of phantom limb phenomena.

References

Aglioti, S., Smania, N., Atzei, A., & Berlucchi, G. (1997). Spatio-temporal properties of the pattern of evoked phantom sensations in a left index amputee patient. *Behavioral Neuroscience, 111*(5), 867–872. doi:10.1037/0735-7044.111.5.867

Anderson-Barnes, V. C., McAuliffe, C., Swanberg, K. M., & Tsao, J. W. (2009). Phantom limb pain – a phenomenon of proprioceptive memory? *Medical Hypotheses, 73*, 555–558. doi:10.1016/j.mehy.2009.05.038

Arzy, S., Thut, G., Mohr, C., Michel, C. M., & Blanke, O. (2006). Neural basis of embodiment: Distinct contributions of temporoparietal junction and extrastriate body area. *Journal of Neuroscience, 26*(31), 8074–8081. doi:10.1523/JNEUROSCI.0745-06.2006

Bailey, A. A., & Moersch, F. P. (1941). Phantom limb. *Canadian Medical Association Journal, 45*(1), 37–42.

Blakemore, S.-J., Wolpert, D. M., & Frith, C. (2002). Abnormalities in the awareness of action. *Trends in Cognitive Sciences, 6*(6), 237–242. doi:10.1016/S1364-6613(02)01907-1

Carlen, P. L., Wall, P. D., Nadvorna, H., & Steinbach, T. (1978). Phantom limbs and related phenomena in recent traumatic amputations. *Neurology, 28*, 211–217.

Chan, B. L., Witt, R., Charrow, A. P., Magee, A., Howard, R., Pasquina, P. F., . . . Tsao, J. W. (2007). Mirror therapy for phantom limb pain. *New England Journal of Medicine, 357*, 2206–2207.

Cleeland, C. S. (1989). Measurement of pain by subjective report. In C. R. Chapman & J. D. Loeser (Eds.), *Advances in pain research and therapy: Issues in pain measurement* (Vol. 12, pp. 391–403). New York: Raven Press.

Devor, M. (1997). Phantom limb phenomena and their neural mechanism. In M. S. Myslobodsky (Ed.), *The mythomanias: The nature of deception and self-deception* (pp. 237–361). Hove, UK: Psychology Press.

Ehrsson, H. H., Rosen, B., Stockselius, A., Ragno, C., Kohler, P., & Lundborg, G. (2008). Upper limb amputees can be induced to experience a rubber hand as their own. *Brain, 131*, 3443–3452. doi:10.1093/brain/awn297

Flor, H., Nikolajsen, L., & Jensen, T. S. (2006). Phantom limb pain: A case of maladaptive CNS plasticity. *Nature Reviews Neuroscience, 7*(11), 873–881. doi:10.1038/nrn1991

Fraser, C. (2002). Fact and fiction: A clarification of phantom limb phenomena. *British Journal of Occupational Therapy, 65*(6), 256–260.

Gagne, M., Reilly, K. T., Hetu, S., & Mercier, C. (2009). Motor control over the phantom limb in above-elbow amputees and its relationship with phantom limb pain. *Neuroscience, 162*(1), 78–86.

Gallagher, P., & MacLachlan, M. (2000). Development and psychometric evaluation of the Trinity Amputation and Prosthesis Experience Scales (TAPES). *Rehabilitation Psychology, 45*, 130–154. doi:10.1037/0090-5550.45.2.130

Gallagher, S. (1986). Body image and body schema: A conceptual clarification. *Journal of Mind and Behavior, 7*, 541–554.

Gallagher, S. (2005). *How the body shapes the mind.* New York: Oxford University Press.

Gallagher, S., & Cole, J. (1995). Body image and body schema in a deafferented subject. *Journal of Mind and Behaviour, 16*, 369–390.

Giummarra, M. J., & Bradshaw, J. (2010). The phantom of the night: Restless legs syndrome in amputees. *Medical Hypotheses, 74*, 968–972. doi:10.1016/j.mehy.2009.12.009

Giummarra, M. J., Georgiou-Karistianis, N., Gibson, S. J., Nicholls, M. E. R., & Bradshaw, J. L. (2010). The phantom in the mirror: A modified rubber hand illusion in amputees and normals. *Perception, 39*(1), 103–118. doi:10.1068/p6519

Giummarra, M. J., Gibson, S. J., Georgiou-Karistianis, N., & Bradshaw, J. L. (2008). Mechanisms underlying embodiment, disembodiment and loss of embodiment. *Neuroscience and Biobehavioral Reviews, 32*, 143–160. doi:10.1016/j.neubiorev.2007.07.001

Giummarra, M. J., Gibson, S. J., Georgiou-Karistianis, N., Nicholls, M. E. R., Chou, M., & Bradshaw, J. L. Maladaptive plasticity in amputees: Imprinting of enduring, intense or 'core-trauma' experiences on phantom limb schemata.

Giummarra, M. J., Gibson, S. J., Georgiou-Karistianis, N., Nicholls, M. E. R., Chou, M., & Bradshaw, J. L. Maladaptive plasticity, phantom pain and movement.

Giummarra, M. J., Gibson, S. J., Georgiou-Karistianis, N., Nicholls, M. E. R., Chou, M., & Bradshaw, J. L. The menacing phantom: What pulls the trigger?

Halligan, P. W., Marshal, J. C., Wade, D. T., Davey, J., & Morrison, D. (1993). Thumb in cheek? Sensory reorganization and perceptual plasticity after limb amputation. *Neuroreport, 4*(3), 233–236. doi:10.1097/00001756-199303000-00001

Harris, A. J. (1999). Cortical origin of pathological pain. *Lancet, 354*, 1464–1466. doi:10.1016/S0140-6736(99)05003-5

Henderson, W. R., & Smyth, G. E. (1948). Phantom limbs. *Journal of Neurology, Neurosurgery and Psychiatry, 11*, 88–112. doi:10.1136/jnnp.11.2.88

Higuchi, T., Imanaka, K., & Patla, A. E. (2006). Action-oriented representation of peripersonal and extrapersonal space: Insights from manual and locomotor actions. *Japanese Psychological Research, 48*(3), 126–140. doi:10.1111/j.1468-5884.2006.00314.x

Hunter, J. P., Katz, J., & Davis, K. D. (2003). The effect of tactile and visual sensory inputs on phantom limb awareness. *Brain, 126*(3), 579–589. doi:10.1093/brain/awg054

Hunter, J. P., Katz, J., & Davis, K. D. (2008). Stability of phantom limb phenomena after upper limb amputation: A longitudinal study. *Neuroscience, 156*(4), 939–949. doi:10.1016/j.neuroscience.2008.07.053

Inhoff, A. W., & Topolski, R. (1994). Seeing morphemes: Loss of visibility during the retinal stabilization of compound and pseudocompound words. *Journal of Experimental Psychology: Human perception and Performance, 20*(4), 840–853. doi:10.1037/0096-1523.20.4.840

Jensen, T. S., Krebs, B., Nielsen, J., & Rasmussen, P. (1983). Phantom limb, phantom pain and stump pain in amputees during the first 6 months following limb amputation. *Pain, 17*, 243–256. doi:10.1016/0304-3959(83)90097-0

Kammers, M. P., van der Ham, I. J., & Dijkerman, H. C. (2006). Dissociating body representations in healthy individuals: Differential effects of a kinaesthetic illusion on perception and action. *Neuropsychologia, 44*(12), 2430-2436. doi:10.1016/j.neuropsychologia.2006.04.009

Katz, J. (1992). Psychophysiological contributions to phantom limbs. *Canadian Journal of Psychiatry, 37*, 282–298.

Kew, J., Wright, A., & Halligan, P. W. (1998). Somesthetic aura: The experience of 'Alice in Wonderland'. *Lancet, 351*, 1934. doi:10.1016/S0140-6736(05)78619-0

Knecht, S., Henningsen, H., Elbert, T., Flor, H., Höhling, C., Pantev, C., . . . Taub, E. (1995). Cortical reorganization in human amputees and mislocalization of painful stimuli to the phantom limb. *Neuroscience Letters, 201*, 262–264. doi:10.1016/0304-3940(95)12186-2

Kooijman, C. M., Dijkstra, P. U., Geertzen, J. H. B., Elzinga, A., & van der Schans, C. P. (2000). Phantom pain and phantom sensations in upper limb amputees: An epidemiological study. *Pain, 87*, 33–41. doi:10.1016/S0304-3959(00)00264-5

Lotze, M., Grodd, W., Birbaumer, N., Erb, M., Huse, E., & Flor, H. (1999). Does use of a myoelectric prosthesis prevent cortical reorganization and phantom limb pain? *Nature Neuroscience, 2*(6), 501–502. doi:10.1038/9145

Melzack, R. (1975). The McGill Pain Questionnaire: Major properties and scoring methods. *Pain, 1*(3), 277–299. doi:10.1016/0304-3959(75)90044-5

Moseley, G. L., & Brugger, P. (2009). Interdependence of movement and anatomy persists when amputees learn a physiologically impossible movement of their phantom arm. *Proceedings of the National Academy of Sciences of the United States of America, 106*(44), 18798–18802. doi:10.1073/pnas.0907151106

O'Shaughnessy, B. (1995). Proprioception and the body image. In J. L. Bermúdez, A. Marcel, & N. Eilan (Eds.), *The body and the self* (pp. 175–203). Cambridge, MA: MIT Press.

Paillard, J. (1991). Motor and representational framing of space. In J. Paillard (Ed.), *Brain and space* (pp. 163–182). New York: Oxford University Press.

Price, D. B. (1976). Phantom limb phenomena in patients with leprosy. *Journal of Nervous and Mental Disease, 163*, 108–116.

Ramachandran, V. S., & Hirstein, W. (1998). The perception of phantom limbs: The D.O. Hebb lecture. *Brain, 121*, 1603–1630. doi:10.1093/brain/121.9.1603

Ramachandran, V. S., & Rogers-Ramachandran, D. (1996). Synaesthesia in phantom limbs induced with mirrors.

Corporeal Awareness and Proprioceptive Sense of the Phantom by et. al. Melita Giummarra

71

Proceedings of the Royal Society of London B: Biological Science, 263, 377–386. doi:10.1098/rspb.1996.0058

Richardson, C., Glenn, S., Horgan, M., & Nurmikko, T. (2007). A prospective study of factors associated with the presence of phantom limb pain six months after major lower limb amputation in patients with peripheral vascular disease. *Journal of Pain, 8*(10), 793–801. doi:10.1016/j.jpain.2007.05.007

Rosentstiel, A. K., & Keefe, F. J. (1983). The use of coping strategies in chronic low back pain patients: Relationship to patient characteristics and current adjustment. *Pain, 17*(1), 33–44. doi:10.1016/0304-3959(83)90125-2

Shukla, G. D., Sahu, S. C., Tripathi, R. P., & Gupta, D. K. (1982). Phantom limb: A phenomenological study. *British Journal of Psychiatry, 141,* 54–58. doi:10.1192/bjp.141.1.54

Smith, J. (2009). We have the technology. *New Scientist,* 36–39. doi:10.1016/S0262-4079(09)60307-9

Troncoso, X. G., Macknik, S. L., Otero-Milian, J., & Martinez-Conde, S. (2008). Microsaccades drive illusory motion in the Enigma illusion. *Proceedings of the National Academy of Sciences of the United States of America, 105*(41), 16033–16038. doi:10.1073/pnas.0709389105

Tsakiris, M., Haggard, P., Franck, N., Mainy, N., & Sirigu, A. (2005). A specific role for efferent information in self-recognition. *Cognition, 96,* 215–231. doi:10.1016/j.cognition.2004.08.002

Weinstein, S. M. (1998). Phantom limb pain and related disorders. *Neurologic Clinics, 16*(4), 919–935. doi:10.1016/S0733-8619(05)70105-5

Weiss, T., Miltner, W. H. R., Adler, T., Bruckner, L., & Taub, E. (1999). Decrease in phantom limb pain associated with prosthesis-induced increased use of an amputation stump in humans. *Neuroscience Letters, 272*(2), 131–134. doi:10.1016/S0304-3940(99)00595-9

Zigmond, A. S., & Snaith, R. P. (1983). The Hospital Anxiety and Depression Scale. *Acta Psychiatrica Scandinavica, 67,* 361–370. doi:10.1111/j.1600-0447.1983.tb09716.x

Critical Thinking

1. Try to imagine that you no longer have the use of your right arm, and it has been amputated just above the elbow. Think about and brainstorm about all the different aspects of life that would be impacted by this event. See how many you can list. What do you think would be the most difficult behavioral change to adjust to, and why?

2. What is an "Alice in Wonderland" illusion, and how does it apply to the loss of a limb?

Create Central

www.mhhe.com/createcentral

Internet References

How to improve proprioception

www.bettermovement.org/2008/proprioception-the-3-d-map-of-the-body

Current treatments for phantom limb pain

www.practicalpainmanagement.com/pain/neuropathic/phantom-limb-syndrome/current-treatments-phantom-limb-pain

Article   Prepared by: Eric Landrum, *Boise State University*

You Do Not Talk about Fight Club if You Do Not Notice Fight Club: Inattentional Blindness for a Simulated Real-World Assault

Christopher F. Chabris et al.

Learning Outcomes

After reading this article, you will be able to:

- Understand the concept of inattentional blindness.
- Identify some of the key variables that influence the ooccurrence and intensity of inattentional blindness.

At 2:00 in the morning on 25 January 1995, Boston police officer Kenny Conley was chasing a shooting suspect who climbed over a chain-link fence. An undercover officer named Michael Cox had arrived on the scene moments earlier, but other officers had mistaken him for a suspect, assaulted him from behind, and brutally beat him. Conley chased the suspect over the fence and apprehended him some time later. In later testimony, Conley said that he ran right past the place where Cox was under attack, but he claimed not to have seen the incident. The investigators, prosecutors, and jurors in the case all assumed that because Conley could have seen the beating, Conley must have seen the beating, and therefore must have been lying to protect his comrades. Conley was convicted of perjury and obstruction of justice and was sentenced to thirty-four months in jail (Lehr 2009).

We have used the term 'illusion of attention' to denote the common but mistaken belief that people pay attention to, and notice, more of their visual world than they actually do (Chabris and Simons 2010; Levin and Angelone 2008). None of the principals in this case seem to have realized that Conley could have been telling the truth (Chabris and Simons 2010). He could have failed to notice the beating of Cox because of inattentional blindness (Mack and Rock 1998; Neisser 1979; Simons and Chabris 1999; Simons 2010): While his attention was focused on the suspect he was chasing, he may have been essentially blind to unexpected events that he otherwise would have seen easily.

This explanation is plausible, but generalization from studies using videos or computerized displays (eg, Most et al 2000) to real-world events is not necessarily valid. In laboratory studies participants are seated in front of a screen, under artificial light, indoors, tracking one or more objects within a confined display space at close range. Conley was running outdoors at night chasing a moving target at some distance.

Although some studies have examined inattentional blindness in relatively complex displays (eg, Haines 1991; Neisser 1979; Simons and Chabris 1999), and anecdotal evidence suggests that it plays a role in many real-world contexts (eg, the prevalence of 'looked but failed to see' driving accidents), to our knowledge, only one study has systematically documented a failure to notice an unexpected real-world event. Hyman and colleagues (2010) asked pedestrians whether they had noticed a clown that was riding a unicycle near where they were walking; many missed it, especially if they were talking on a mobile phone at the time. Here we ask whether inattentional blindness can occur under realistic conditions similar to those in the Conley-Cox scenario. In contrast to the clown study, our subjects knew they were participating in research, and they were assigned a task requiring focused attention.

In study 1 we asked 20 subjects (college students, tested individually, participating for money or course credit) to pursue a male confederate while he jogged a 400-meter route at night in an area lit with streetlamps. The confederate and subject ran at a speed of approximately 2.4 meters per second, for a total running time of about 2 minutes and 45 seconds. At the end of the run, the confederate's heart rate was approximately 148 beats per minute.

Subjects were told to maintain a distance of 30 feet (9.1 meters) while counting the number of times the runner touched his head. At approximately 125 meters into the route, in a driveway 8 meters off the path, three other male confederates staged a fight in which two of them pretended to beat up the third. These confederates shouted, grunted, and coughed during the fight, which was visible to subjects for at least 15 seconds before they passed by it. The runner touched his head three times with his left hand and six times with his right hand, following the same sequence on every trial. The touches always started 30 meters into the run and occurred at approximately 40-meter intervals.

At the end of the route, we first asked the subjects how many head-touches they had counted. Then we asked whether the subjects had seen anything unusual along the route, and then whether they had seen anyone fighting. Only 7 out of 20 subjects (35%) reported seeing the fight in response to at least one of these questions. All seven noticers were able to describe some details of the fight, such as the number of participants and the location. We asked about two additional events that we did not stage (someone dribbling a basketball and someone juggling), and no subjects falsely reported seeing either. These results demonstrate that under real-world visual conditions approximating those experienced by Kenny Conley, people can fail to notice a nearby fight.

In study 2 we asked whether the low rates of noticing resulted only from poor viewing conditions due to darkness. We repeated the procedure, on the same route, during the daytime. Now the fight first became visible to the subjects about 20 seconds into their run, and it remained visible for at least 30 seconds. Even so, only 9 out of 16 subjects (56%) noticed the fight, consistent with the inattentional blindness hypothesis.

One hallmark of inattentional blindness is that increasing the effort required by the primary task decreases noticing of unexpected events (eg, Jensen and Simons 2009; Simons and Chabris 1999). If the failure to notice the fight results from inattentional blindness, then manipulating the demands of the counting task should affect noticing rates. Study 3 used the same daytime protocol as study 2, but each of the 58 subjects was randomly assigned (by coin flip) to either keep separate counts of head touches by the runner's left and right hands (high load condition) or to follow the runner without counting (low load).

Under a high-attentional load 14 of 33 subjects noticed the fight (42%), but under a low load 18 of 25 noticed (72%). This difference was significant, $\chi^2(1) = 5.03$, $p = 0.02$, supporting the hypothesis that subjects who missed the unexpected event displayed inattentional blindness. Moreover, participants in the dual-counting condition who did notice the fight counted less accurately (off by $M = 1.1$ touches) than those who missed it (off by $M = 0.2$ touches), $t(31) = 2.65$, $p = 0.01$, $d = 0.86$, suggesting that engaging in the counting task had a direct impact on noticing. (In studies 1 and 2 there were no significant differences in accuracy between noticers and missers, $p > 0.30$ in both cases.) It is possible that the amount of physical exertion during the run, which varied among subjects, would also predict inattentional blindness in this task; future research should examine this.

In three studies with 94 total participants, a substantial number of subjects failed to notice a three-person fight as they ran past it. This real-world inattentional blindness happened both at night and during the day and was modulated by attentional load. Our results represent the first experimental induction of inattentional blindness outside the laboratory.

Kenny Conley eventually won an appeal, and the government decided not to retry him. The inattentional blindness explanation did not contribute to either of these decisions (Chabris and Simons 2010; Lehr 2009). Although no scientific study can prove or disprove a particular cause of a specific historical event, our results show that Conley's claim that he did not see the beating of Michael Cox, the claim that led to his indictment and conviction, might well have been truthful.

References

Chabris C, Simons D, 2010 *The Invisible Gorilla, and Other Ways Our Intuitions Deceive Us* (New York, NY: Crown)

Haines R F, 1991 "A breakdown in simultaneous information processing" in *Presbyopia Research* Eds G Obrecht, L W Stark (New York, NY: Plenum Press)

Hyman Jr I E, Boss S M, Wise B M, McKenzie K E, Caggiano J M, 2010 "Did you see the unicycling clown? Inattentional blindness while walking and talking on a cell phone" *Applied Cognitive Psychology* **24** 597–607 doi:10.1002/acp.1638

Jensen M, Simons D J, 2009 "The effects of individual differences and task difficulty on inattentional blindness" *Psychonomic Bulletin & Review* **16** 398–403 doi:10.3758/PBR.16.2.398

Lehr D, 2009 *The Fence: A Police Cover-up Along Boston's Racial Divide* (New York, NY: Harper-Collins)

Levin D T, Angelone B L, 2008 "The visual metacognition questionnaire: A measure of intuitions about vision" *The American Journal of Psychology* **121** 451–472 doi:10.2307/20445476

Mack A, Rock I, 1998 *Inattentional Blindness* (Cambridge, MA: MIT Press)

Most S B, Simons D J, Scholl B J, Jimenez R, Clifford E, Chabris C F, 2000 "How not to be seen: The contribution of similarity and selective ignoring to sustained inattentional blindness" *Psychological Science* **12** 9–17 doi:10.1111/1467-9280.00303

Neisser U, 1979 "The control of information pickup in selective looking" in *Perception and its Development: A Tribute to Eleanor J Gibson* Ed. A D Pick pp 201–219 (Hillsdale, NJ: Lawrence Erlbaum Associates)

Simons D J, 2010 "Monkeying around with the gorillas in our midst: Familiarity with an inattentional-blindness task does not improve the detection of unexpected events" *i-Perception* **1** 3–6 doi:10.1068/i0386

Simons D J, Chabris C F, 1999 "Gorillas in our midst: Sustained inattentional blindness for dynamic events" *Perception* **28** 1059–1074 doi:10.1068/p2952

Critical Thinking

1. If inattentional blindness commonly occurs, what does that say about the accuracy of eyewitness testimony? What is the consequence of not seeing what is before us?

2. Thinking about the concept of attentional load, how might that influence a student's ability to effectively study? How would a person know if he or she was in the midst of a high or low attentional load?

Create Central

www.mhhe.com/createcentral

Internet References

Dan Simons
www.dansimons.com/research.html
Inattentional blindness and conspicuity
www.visualexpert.com/Resources/inattentionalblindness.html

Acknowledgements—These studies were approved by the Union College Human Subjects Research Committee. Michael Corti, Joseph Dammann, Elon Gaffin-Cahn, Alexander Katz, Andrew McKeegan, Corey Milan, Timothy Riddell, and Jacob Schneider, all students at Union College who played the roles of the runner and the fighters, and otherwise assisted in the execution of these studies. Diana Goodman, Allie Litt, Lisa McManus, Robyn Schneiderman, and Rachel Scott provided suggestions for the design of these studies during a seminar course at Union College. Dick Lehr's brilliant journalism made us aware of the Boston case of Michael Cox and Kenny Conley and the possibility that inattentional blindness was involved in it. CFC designed and conducted the research, analyzed the data, and drafted the manuscript. AW helped to design and conduct the research. MF helped to conduct the research. DJS contributed to the research design and edited the manuscript.

Unit 4

UNIT

Learning

Prepared by: Eric Landrum, *Boise State University*

Do you remember your first week of college classes? There were so many new buildings and so many people's names to remember. You needed to remember accurately where all your classes were as well as your professors' names. Just remembering your class schedule was problematic enough. If you lived in a residence hall, you had to remember where your building was, recall the names of individuals living on your floor, and learn how to navigate from your room to other places on campus. Did you ever think you would survive college tests? The material, in terms of difficulty level and amount, was perhaps more than you thought you could manage, especially compared to high school. Or, it may be that it has been many years since you took tests in high school. What a stressful time you experienced when you first came to campus! Much of what created the stress was the strain on your learning and memory systems. Indeed, most students survive just fine—and with memories, learning strategies, and mental health intact.

Today, with their sophisticated experimental techniques, psychologists have identified several types of memory processes and have discovered what makes learning more efficient so that subsequent recall and recognition are more accurate. We also have discovered that humans aren't the only organisms capable of these processes. Nearly all types of animals can learn, even if the organism is as simple as an earthworm or amoeba.

You may be surprised to learn, though, that in addition to researching memory processes and the types of learning you most often experience in school, psychologists have spent a considerable amount of time and effort studying other types of learning, particularly classical conditioning, operant conditioning, and social learning. Classical conditioning is a form of learning that governs much of our involuntary responses to stimuli, such as environmental events and our emotions. Operant conditioning centers on how the consequences of our behavior shape and otherwise influence the frequency with which those behaviors subsequently occur and the circumstances under which they take place. Most of the time, these associations are beneficial to us, but sometimes individuals develop phobias, and operant conditioning can be used to help people "unlearn" the associations that result in irrational fears. Social learning happens when we learn from watching what other people do and how others' actions change the environment—that is, we sometimes learn vicariously from others.

Historically, psychologists used nonhuman laboratory animals as well as human participants to study learning processes. Such research has led to many widely accepted principles of learning that appear to be universal across many species. Although nonhuman laboratory research is still a popular area of psychological inquiry, many psychologists today test and extend the application of these principles to humans under a wide array of laboratory and non-laboratory settings. We explore these principles and their applications in the articles in this unit.

Article   Prepared by: Eric Landrum, *Boise State University*

Finding Little Albert
A Journey to John B. Watson's Infant Laboratory

In 1920, John Watson and Rosalie Rayner claimed to have conditioned a baby boy, Albert, to fear a laboratory rat. In subsequent tests, they reported that the child's fear generalized to other furry objects. After the last testing session, Albert disappeared, creating one of the greatest mysteries in the history of psychology. This article summarizes the authors' efforts to determine Albert's identity and fate. Examinations of Watson's personal correspondence, scientific production (books, journal articles, film), and public documents (national census data, state birth and death records) suggested that an employee at the Harriet Lane Home was Albert's mother. Contact with the woman's descendents led the authors to the individual they believe to be "Little Albert."

HALL P. BECK, SHARMAN LEVINSON, AND GARY IRONS

Learning Outcomes

After reading this article, you will be able to:

- Describe who "Little Albert" was and how identifying him solved an intriguing mystery in the annals of the history of psychology.

- Summarize the research involved in tracing the history and conditions surrounding Watson and Rayner's famous study with Little Albert.

In 1920, John Broadus Watson and Rosalie Alberta Rayner attempted to condition an 11-month-old boy, Albert B., to fear a laboratory rat. They subsequently reported generalization of the fear response to other furry objects (Watson & Rayner, 1920). Despite the investigation's lack of methodological rigor (Harris, 1979; Paul & Blumenthal, 1989; Samelson, 1980) and questionable ethics (Cornwell & Hobbs, 1976), the "Little Albert" study remains one of the most frequently cited articles in textbook psychology.

The interest created by Watson and Rayner's (1920) investigation is not due solely to the significance of the researchers' findings. Much of the attention the study has received has centered upon Albert. Without having been deconditioned, Albert moved from his home on the Johns Hopkins University campus, creating one of the greatest mysteries in the history of psychology. "Whatever happened to Little Albert?" is a question that has intrigued generations of students and professional psychologists (e.g., Blair-Broeker, Ernst, & Myers, 2003; Griggs, 2009; Harris, 1979; LeUnes, 1983; Murray, 1973; Resnick, 1974).

This article is a detective story, a narrative summarizing our efforts to resolve an almost 90-year-old cold case. It chronicles how seven years of searching, logic, and luck led my co-authors, my students, and me (Hall P. Beck) to the individual we believe to be Little Albert.

The investigation proceeded in two stages. First, we tried to learn as much as possible about Albert. Then we looked for an individual who matched these attributes. In this article, we introduce the lost boy's mother and surviving members of his family. We conclude by addressing the often-asked question: Whatever happened to Little Albert?

The Setting of the Watson and Rayner Study

The Albert study emerged during two of the most productive and turbulent years of John Watson's life. Between his return to Johns Hopkins University following World War I and his resignation from the faculty in October 1920 (Buckley, 1989), Watson conducted pioneering research on infant development, the psychology of emotion (Watson, 1919f), and sex education (Watson & Lashley, 1920). In addition, he planned tests of the effects of alcohol on manual and mental performance (Watson, 1920a), edited a major journal, promoted scientific psychology to the general public, and corresponded with such prominent scholars as Robert Yerkes, James McKeen Cattell, Edward B. Titchener, Edward Lee Thorndike, and Bertrand Russell.

Watson also became romantically involved with his graduate student, Rosalie Rayner. Their relationship resulted in a highly publicized divorce trial and Watson's dismissal. The Little Albert investigation was the last published research of Watson's academic career.

What Was Known about Albert

When we began our investigation, not a single fact had been verified about Albert after he left Johns Hopkins. Fortunately, more was known about Albert before he left the hospital. Watson's many descriptions of the study (e.g., Watson, 1924a, 1924b, 1925, 1928a, 1928b; Watson & Rayner, 1920; Watson & Watson, 1921) contain detailed reports of the conditioning procedures as well as personal information about Albert. Although there are troubling inconsistencies in Watson's various accounts (see Harris, 1979), his information offered the most reliable foundation from which we could begin to search for Albert.

According to Watson and Rayner (1920), Albert was assessed at 8 months 26 days, 11 months 3 days, 11 months 10 days, 11 months 15 days, 11 months 20 days, and 12 months 21 days of age. He "was reared almost from birth in a hospital environment" (p. 1). His mother was a wet nurse in the Harriet Lane Home for Invalid Children, a pediatric facility on the Johns Hopkins campus.

Albert was a healthy, unemotional child who rarely cried. The investigators chose him for conditioning because they reasoned that such a stolid child would experience "relatively little harm" (Watson & Rayner, 1920, p. 2). Convenience may also have influenced his selection. The Harriet Lane Home was adjacent to the Phipps Clinic, where Watson's Infant Laboratory was housed. A corridor connected the two buildings, which allowed the baby to be brought to the laboratory without exposing him to the winter air.

Although we cannot be sure why Albert's mother permitted him to be tested, financial incentives may have been offered. On January 12, 1920, Watson (1920b) wrote to Frank Goodnow, president of Johns Hopkins, that paying mothers $1.00 (2009 currency = $12.36, Bureau of Labor Statistics, 2009) per visit strained the departmental budget. One dollar may have been a significant sum to a young woman who supported herself and her child by selling breast milk.

A motion picture of the baby studies, made by Watson in 1919 and 1920 and distributed by the Stoelting Company in 1923 (Watson, 1923), provided a second valuable source of information. In 2004, Ben Harris kindly lent me a 16-mm version of Watson's movie that I converted to DVD format. The digitized images used in this investigation were made from Harris's copy.

The *Experimental Investigation of Babies* is the first (or one of the first) films made by a psychologist to disseminate research. In the initial scene, Watson and Rayner are shown preparing a baby for testing. Assessments were made of the baby's grasping, Babinski, nursing, and defensive reflexes as well as its infolded thumb, handedness, swimming movements, blinking, head steadiness, and reaching.

The film culminated in the sequences with Albert. A comparison of the movie and the Watson and Rayner (1920) article indicates that Albert was filmed at 8 months 26 days of age. During what today would be called baseline, he responded inquisitively but not fearfully to blocks, a marble, a crayon, a fire, a monkey, a dog, a rabbit, and a white laboratory rat. Overall, he fit Watson and Rayner's description of a robust and

somewhat phlegmatic baby. In the film, Albert appears to be Caucasian.

Watson made no effort to condition Albert until he was more than 11 months old. The film shows Albert's response after seven pairings of the rat and a loud noise. The previously innocuous rat now evoked what Watson interpreted as fear. Similar but less intense reactions were then observed to a rabbit, a dog, a fur coat, and a Santa Claus mask.

We do not know why Watson waited almost two months to begin the conditioning phase of the study. The university closed for Christmas vacation from December 24 through January 4 ("University Register 1919–20," 1919), but that accounts for only part of the interval. Perhaps other professional and personal affairs intervened.

Information from *The Experimental Investigation of Babies* and Watson's write-ups were the starting points for our inquiry. The facts they provided were critical, but they were known to many investigators. Why, then, had no one located Albert? The obvious answer was that crucial information was missing. Therefore, my students and I set out to learn more about Albert and Watson's baby studies.

When Did Watson and Rayner Test Albert?

Watson and Rayner (1920) reported Albert's age at each assessment, but they did not indicate the dates on which the study was performed. For their purposes, the testing dates were inconsequential. For our purposes, the testing dates were of great importance. If we could determine the assessment dates, then we could easily calculate Albert's birthday.

Most investigators (Beck, 1938; Buckley, 1989; Samelson, 1980) agree that the study was performed during the winter of 1919–1920. We hoped to narrow that time frame by concurrently examining Watson's descriptions of the study, his correspondence, and the film.

Mary Cover Jones (1974, 1975, 1976) recalled listening to Watson lecture on his work with Albert in the spring of 1919. However, the presence of Rosalie Rayner in many of the movie scenes, including those with Albert, is at odds with Jones's recollections. Rayner was taking classes at Poughkeepsie during the spring semester of 1919 ("Vassar College Transcript," 1919) and did not graduate until June 10, 1919 (D. M. Rogers, personal communication, September 30, 2008).

It is also unlikely that Albert was filmed in the summer or early fall. Watson left Baltimore to vacation in Ontario on June 6 and did not return until mid- or late September (Watson, 1919a). Classes started on September 30 ("University Register," 1919), at which time Rayner began working as Watson's graduate assistant. Watson may have been ready to film by early October, but an exchange of letters with President Goodnow reveals that he lacked the resources to do so.

During October and November, Watson made his case for the purchase of 1,000 ft (304.8 m) of film. The cost was $450.00 (2009 currency = $5,562.73), a considerable expenditure for the small, financially stressed university (Watson, 1919d). Although Goodnow (1919) doubted that the Budget

Committee would approve the appropriation, he agreed to present a letter from Watson (1919c) detailing the benefits of making the movie. Watson's letter and the president's probable endorsement proved effective. Funds to purchase the film were authorized on November 19.

In a letter dated December 5, Watson (1919b) thanked Goodnow for procuring money for the motion picture. He wrote that he was only "waiting for a warm spell to start in on the work." The Watson–Goodnow correspondence suggests that filming commenced around December 5, 1919.

Efforts to determine the exact date that shooting began were inconclusive. As his letter implies, Watson may have begun filming on or shortly after December 5. Other documents in the Alan Mason Chesney Medical Archives of the Johns Hopkins Medical Institutions, however, leave open the possibility that shooting started before the 5th. Watson frequently complained to Johns Hopkins officials of a lack of staff support. Among other duties, the departmental stenographer sometimes served as a research and editorial assistant (Watson, 1918).

If the stenographer was otherwise occupied, the December 5 letter may have been dictated or handwritten some days before. In 1920, Johns Hopkins was a small university, so Watson probably knew that funding had been approved on November 19, 1919. He may then have bought the film and started shooting before his "thank you" note to Goodnow was typed. Although a precise date cannot be established, a reasonable estimate is that the first filming session occurred within a two-week period between November 28 and December 12, 1919.

Subtracting 8 months 26 days (baseline) from these dates allows one to approximate Albert's birth date. Albert was born between March 2 and March 16, 1919. Given that he was last tested at 12 months 21 days of age, we estimate that the final assessment occurred between March 23 and April 6, 1920.

One important document is inconsistent with these calculations. The Watson and Rayner (1920) article was published in the February 1920 issue of the *Journal of Experimental Psychology (JEP)*. If *JEP* was printed on schedule, then the investigation must have begun much earlier than we anticipated. Conversely, if the publication was delayed, Watson could have completed data collection in late March or early April and still included the study in the February issue.

When Was the Watson and Rayner Study Published?

Watson was the founding editor of *JEP*, inaugurating the journal in 1915. By the time the United States entered World War I on April 6, 1917, two volumes had been printed and the journal was enjoying scholarly success. Publication was suspended as Watson and other psychologists joined the war effort. The Armistice was signed on November 11, 1918, and by early December, Watson was once more working at Johns Hopkins.

Before Watson could publish the third volume, he needed to solicit articles and reestablish subscriptions that had lapsed during the war. We wrote to the current editor of *JEP: General* hoping to discover when the first postwar issue was printed. Not unexpectedly, journal records do not go back to 1920

(F. Ferreira, personal communication, August 30, 2008). Searches of the Alan Mason Chesney Medical Archives and the Ferdinand Hamburger, Jr., Archives at Johns Hopkins as well as inquiries submitted to the Archives of the American Psychological Association and the Archives of the History of American Psychology at the University of Akron also failed to turn up any information on the publication date of the February issue.

An electronic mailing was sent to serialists throughout the United States asking if their libraries recorded when they received the first issue of Volume 3. A serialist at Johns Hopkins responded to a special request but was unable to find a receipt date. Fortunately, librarians at Kansas State University, Harvard University, and Cornell University located receipt stamps on their issues of the third volume (E. Cook, personal communication, July 14, 2008). The earliest of these was August 23, 1920, at Cornell. The stamp on that issue, however, is difficult to read; the year could be 1921. Two stamps were on the volume at Harvard, the first documenting receipt of Issues 1 through 5 and the second receipt of Issue 6. This might indicate that the first five issues were mailed as a package.

Our attempts to determine when the Watson and Rayner (1920) article was published included an examination of each page of the third volume for a telltale date. This effort furnished no pertinent information. We did uncover a letter to Adolf Meyer dated December 14, 1922, in which Watson (1922) commented that "the issues now come out on time." Presumably, Watson would not have made this statement unless previous issues of *JEP* were delayed.

Correspondence between Goodnow and Watson regarding the purchase of the film is also inconsistent with a February publication date. To illustrate, assume that the testing of Albert at 12 months 21 days occurred near the end of January 1920. That would place the filming of the baseline, when Albert was 8 months 26 days of age, in late September or early October of 1919.

Throughout October and November, Watson was seeking funds to buy film. Although investigators sometimes expend monies for which they are later reimbursed, Watson's letters to Goodnow imply that he had not yet purchased the film. In fact, Watson (1919c) claimed that "such a work has never hitherto been undertaken." Furthermore, he included four still photographs with his November 13, 1919, letter showing some of the tests he wanted to record.

It is hard to believe that Watson would have been so foolish as to try to mislead President Goodnow. If Watson were dishonest, his deception would have been revealed. The Phipps Clinic is a modest-sized building. Extensive filming could not have been conducted without the knowledge of Meyer, the clinic director, and other administrators.

Our estimation of the publication date also needed to account for the review process. Usually, several months or more pass between the submission and acceptance of a manuscript. As editor of *JEP*, however, Watson could have expedited publication by not sending the Albert article for review. Our searches found no document indicating that the Watson and Rayner (1920) study was ever reviewed.

The dates that universities received the journal, Watson's (1922) letter to Meyer, and his correspondence with Goodnow

(1919; Watson, 1919b) all suggest that the first issue of the third volume was substantially delayed. The initial issue was probably dated as February because *JEP* was a bimonthly publication and not because it was printed at that time. As Boring (1937) noted, it was not uncommon to print early psychological journals after the dates on the covers of the issue. Although we were unable to establish the month of publication, we found no evidence indicating that Watson did not complete data collection in late March or early April of 1920. He could then have included the Albert study in the February 1920 issue of *JEP.*

Traces of Albert

We had learned a great deal about Albert, but the most difficult part of our investigation, matching an individual to known Albert attributes, now awaited us. The early records from Johns Hopkins and the Harriet Lane Home (Park, 1957; Park, Littlefield, Seidel, & Wissow, 2006) mostly describe decisions and actions by administrators and physicians. They provide little information about the often nameless nurses, students, maids, cooks, and laundresses who labored in the university and its hospitals. We were especially interested in hearing the quiet voices of the wet nurses.

What evidence would Albert or those who knew him have left behind? Watson burned his papers late in life (Buckley, 1989), declaring, "When you're dead, you're all dead" (p. 182). No one knows whether those lost manuscripts included write-ups or notes on the baby studies.

If the child's actual name was Albert and if he had been treated at the hospital, then an examination of patient records might establish the boy's identity. Unfortunately, no patient records from the Harriet Lane Home remain from 1919–1920 (A. Harrison, personal communication, August 6, 2008). An attempt to examine the employee records for the names of wet nurses proved equally futile. All employee files from that time were either lost or destroyed (A. Harrison, personal communication, August 6, 2008).

There were no notes left by Watson and Rayner, no patient records, and no employee files. Although I could offer my students no direction at this point, Albert and his mother remained in the forefront of my thinking. I then remembered that 1920 was a census year. If a census taker came to Johns Hopkins, Albert's and his mother's names may have been recorded. A quick check revealed that a census had been taken of people living on campus (U.S. Bureau of the Census, 1920).

Albert and the Missing Pearl

My co-author Sharman Levinson and I met in the refreshment line at the 2005 conference of the European Congress of Psychology in Granada, Spain. We discovered a mutual interest in Watson's career. Soon we were discussing Watson's views of psychoanalysis (Rilling, 2000), Adolf Meyer's role in Watson's dismissal, rumors that Watson made physiological recordings during intercourse (Benjamin, Whitaker, & Ramsey, 2007; Magoun, 1981) and, of course, the fate of Albert. Levinson expressed interest in the materials my students and I had collected, so after the

conference I sent her digitized files of these documents. Among them was a copy of the Johns Hopkins census of 1920.

The Hopkins census was taken on January 2, 1920, between the baseline and conditioning phases of the study. Of 379 persons listed as living in Enumeration District 82 (U.S. Bureau of the Census, 1920), only one, the superintendent of the hospital, was designated as the head of a household. Everyone else, save the superintendent's wife, was listed as an "inmate." These inmates were not patients; they were employees or students.

According to Watson's writings and the film's subtitles, Albert lived almost his entire first year at Johns Hopkins. Hopes that his name would be recorded on the census were unfounded; no one younger than 14 years of age was listed. Evidence would later show that some employees living on the Johns Hopkins campus were parents of young children. Why then were no family members included in the census?

A likely explanation is that the census taker did not go to the residences, where she may have encountered children. Instead, she may have set up a desk in a central location and waited for the employees to come to her. Almost everyone she recorded was unmarried or widowed. Quite likely, the census taker never asked about children or spouses because she assumed that no families lived on campus.

A close examination of the census itself furnishes some support for this analysis. Most census records include an exact address, such as a street and house number. The Johns Hopkins census is unusual in that all the respondents are simply listed as living at "Johns Hopkins Hospital"; no attempt was made to specify the particular building or room where they resided.

The occupation of the employees provided the key to locating the woman that we believe to be Albert's mother. "Wet nurse" was not one of the occupations included in the census. Levinson, however, noticed that three women, Pearl Barger, Ethel Carter, and Arvilla Merritte, were listed as "foster mothers." Of all occupations reported for Enumeration District 82, this was the only one that could include wet nurses. *Foster mother* is a term encompassing a variety of activities involving maternal care for someone else's child. To advance our investigation, we needed to determine if these foster mothers were lactating during the winter of 1919–1920.

We were particularly interested in Pearl because she was Caucasian and her last name began with "B." Could Albert B. be Albert Barger? Several hundred hours of examining birth, death, census, marriage, and other records yielded no evidence of Pearl's motherhood. We remained open to the possibility that Pearl was a wet nurse. Still, all we had determined was that she lived on campus at the time of the Watson and Rayner (1920) study and probably worked with children.

After failing to find an association between Pearl Barger and Albert, we shifted our attention to the remaining foster mothers. Ethel Carter could have been a wet nurse; she had a baby on August 26, 1919 ("Johns Hopkins Hospital Records of Births," 1919). Ethel probably knew Albert, but she was not his mother. Ethel Carter was a Black woman, the only Black residing in Enumeration District 82.

The third foster mother, Arvilla Merritte, was White, 22 years old, and literate. Hospital records and documents from the

Maryland State Archives revealed that Arvilla gave birth to an unnamed male Caucasian on March 9, 1919, at Johns Hopkins (Department of Health and Mental Hygiene, 1919; "Johns Hopkins Hospital Records of Births," 1919). These documents identify the father as William Merritte, age 25, born in Maryland. Mother and child were released from the hospital on March 21. Today, a hospitalization of 12 days would be indicative of a medical problem. Such lengthy stays, however, were commonplace at Johns Hopkins in 1919.

Further searching revealed no traces of Arvilla Merritte. Like Pearl Barger and Albert, she disappeared. Once more we were without direction. Despite these setbacks, we remained optimistic that somewhere there was a thread that would lead us to Albert. That thread turned up on Baby Merritte's birth record.

Arvilla resided on the Johns Hopkins campus, presumably with her son. If mother and son were living together, where was William Merritte? Father, mother, and son shared the same last name, but the relationship between the husband and wife seemed distal. Or, perhaps the marriage was fictitious.

The motivation for feigning marriage was obvious. In 1919, unwed mothers faced severe censure. A marriage, even an imaginary one, might protect the dignity of mother and child. The birth certificate listed Irons as Arvilla's maiden name. I asked one of my most trusted research assistants to begin looking for Arvilla Irons.

A Johns Hopkins Foster Mother Introduces Her Family

A genealogical search revealed that Arvilla was the mother of Maurice Irons, who was the father of Larry and Gary Irons. Arvilla was an unusual name, and Larry and Gary Irons were currently living in Maryland. Most likely, we had found the family of the foster mother listed in the 1920 Johns Hopkins census.

Larry left an e-mail address on the genealogical website so that relatives might contact him. His invitation presented an opportunity laced with a problem. How does one explain to strangers one's interest in their grandmother's personal life? I composed a message describing the significance of Albert to psychology and requesting permission for further contact.

It was an exhilarating moment when I received a phone call from Gary Irons. Gary was more interested in family history than was his brother Larry, so it fell to him to call me. He confirmed that his grandmother worked at the Harriet Lane Home and gave birth to a son on March 9, 1919. She named the baby Douglas Merritte.

After speaking with Gary, I pondered the possibility that Douglas might be Albert. Arvilla was working at Johns Hopkins on January 2, 1920. The census placed her on campus when Watson and Rayner were conducting their investigation. If Douglas was born on March 9, Arvilla was probably lactating at the time of the Watson and Rayner study. Douglas shared three other Albert attributes; he was male, Caucasian, and born between March 2 and March 16.

How likely was it that a child born to a Johns Hopkins wet nurse would meet these three criteria? Rather than informally perform the computations, I made the necessary assumptions

explicit. It seemed reasonable to estimate that half the wet nurses' children would be male, that half would be Caucasian, and that their births would be randomly distributed throughout the year. If these assumptions were correct, then the odds were 1 in 104 ($1/2 \times 1/2 \times 1/26$) that a child of a 1920 Johns Hopkins wet nurse would be male, Caucasian, and born between March 2 and March 16. Even if my assumptions lacked precision, the calculations demonstrated that it would be unusual for two individuals to have as much in common as Douglas and Albert.

The likelihood that Douglas was Albert also depended on the number of wet nurses living in the Harriet Lane Home. We identified two potential in-residence wet nurses from the 1920 census, but could there have been more? Initial plans called for as many as 10 wet nurses to be housed in the Harriet Lane Home (Park, 1957). However, blueprints (Wyatt and Nolting Architects, 1909), an early description of the facilities (Howland, 1912–1913), and the recollections of one of the original staff physicians (Park, n.d.) suggest that there were never 10, and probably no more than four, wet nurses concurrently living in the Harriet Lane Home.

If, as we suspect, Arvilla was a wet nurse, then Douglas is one of a very few children who could be Albert. But were Douglas and Albert the same person or nursery mates? The strongest argument against Douglas's being Albert was his name. In the following section we first make the case for Albert B. being the actual name of the baby in the Watson and Rayner (1920) study. Then we consider why, if the baby in the study was Douglas, Watson and Rayner may not have called him Douglas when writing their article.

What's in a Name?

The main reason to believe that Albert was the baby's name is that in 1920 psychologists were not obligated to conceal the identity of their participants. The American Psychological Association did not adopt a formal ethics code until 1953 (American Psychological Association, 1953). Although Watson and Rayner (1920) have been castigated for not removing Albert's conditioned fear (Cornwell & Hobbs, 1976; Harris, 1979), we are not aware that they have been criticized for breeching confidentiality.

The lack of a formal ethics code does not mean that Watson or other psychologists were insensitive to confidentiality issues. Watson's other writings do little to clarify his views on confidentiality. In *Psychology From the Standpoint of a Behaviorist,* Watson (1919e) described assessments of babies Thorne, Nixon, and Lee. These names could be pseudonyms, but they could also be actual last names. In the same text, at least 18 babies are identified only by their initials. These initials may reflect a desire to maintain confidentiality, but they may simply be abbreviations.

To our knowledge, Albert is the only baby that Watson refers to by first name. Whether intentional or not, using the first name was a publicity-generating masterstroke. Giving the baby a name made him easier to relate to. Calling him "Baby A" or assigning him a number would have stolen his warmth, psychologically distancing him from readers. Watson may have realized early on a negative side effect of psychologists' later ethical practices. Confidentiality transforms people into faceless data points, often making it difficult for the general public to identify with participants and to fully appreciate the importance of psychologists' work.

The impetus for confidentiality may have come from Arvilla herself. As her grandchildren reported, she sometimes refused to share important parts of her life with her immediate family. It would have been within character for Arvilla to ask Watson to conceal her son's name.

Apart from confidentiality, there may be another reason why Watson did not write about Baby Douglas. He may never have known or cared what Arvilla named her child. Johns Hopkins had a rigid social system, and wet nurses were near the bottom of that hierarchy (Park, n.d.). Professors did not socialize with wet nurses. The information Watson and Rayner (1920) furnished about Albert is the type of data that would be expected in a case study and does not necessarily demonstrate a personal interest in the baby or his mother.

If Watson used a pseudonym, why did he choose Albert B.? Charles Brewer may have the answer to that question. At the 2008 meeting of the Southeastern Psychological Association, Brewer entertained my students and me with fascinating Watson stories. Between tales, I asked if Watson might have coined the name Albert B. Brewer reminded me that Watson's mother and maternal grandmother were very religious. Watson was named John Broadus in honor of a prominent Baptist minister, John Albert Broadus (Robertson, 1901; Watson, 1936).

If Brewer's inference is correct, then Albert B. may not have been the only instance of Watson's playful use of names. Shortly after his divorce was finalized, John and Rosalie married. They had two sons, William, born in 1921, and James, born in 1924. Brewer (1991) questioned whether "the combination of their sons' first names into 'William James' was fortuitous" (p. 180). Although Watson and William James advocated very different systems of psychology, Watson was a great admirer of his predecessor. There is no way to determine if these combinations are due to chance or were the product of a clever and verbally facile mind. My guess is that Albert B. derives from John Albert Broadus.

Our investigation would have ended at this point if not for the discovery of an old trunk. Inside were contents private and precious, the milestones of Arvilla Irons Merritte's life. Unless otherwise referenced, the following account was supplied by co-author Gary Irons, Arvilla's grandson.

Arvilla's Story

Arvilla was born in 1898 in New Jersey, the youngest of John and Lizzie Irons's eight children. The family moved to rural Amelia, Virginia, around 1910. Arvilla's father was a carpenter and painter. Her mother was well educated and served as her church's pianist. Arvilla was an attractive teenager but possessed a volatile temper. Her family's nickname for her, "Cyclone Bill," suggests a less than tranquil disposition.

On December 18, 1915, Arvilla gave birth to Maurice Albert Irons, father unknown. All accounts agree that she was a devoted mother. Nevertheless, in 1918 or early 1919, Arvilla

left Maurice to be raised by his grandparents and moved to Baltimore. Her departure was precipitated by another pregnancy. According to an 89-year-old niece, two friends told Arvilla that she could give birth at Johns Hopkins and then get a job at the hospital. Our first record of Arvilla in Maryland is the birth of her son Douglas on March 9, 1919.

No specific details of Arvilla's life at Johns Hopkins are known. Early in the early 1920s, Arvilla and Douglas left Johns Hopkins and moved near Mt. Airy, Maryland. There, Arvilla obtained employment with a farmer, Raymond Brashears. Raymond's wife, Flora Hood Brashears, was sickly and needed help caring for her home and young daughter.

Mrs. Brashears ("Deaths: Mrs. Flora Belle Brashears," 1924) succumbed to meningitis on May 15, 1924. In 1926, Arvilla married Wilbur Hood, known to the Irons family as Hoody. After 13 years of marriage, a daughter, Gwendolyn, was born to Arvilla and Hoody. Following Gwendolyn's birth, Arvilla's attention centered on home and daughter, but Hoody was more interested in socializing with his friends. The two grew apart and divorced about 1945. Arvilla remained healthy and vigorous throughout most of her senior years, dying in 1988 at the age of 89.

Gwendolyn came across her mother's trunk as she was preparing for the funeral. Inside were two colorized photographic portraits; one of Maurice when he was 4 or 5 years old and the second of an infant she did not recognize. The baby may have remained unidentified if not for a fortuitous event many years before. As a child, Gary inadvertently came across the open trunk. He questioned his mother about the pictures. She told him that the photographs were of Maurice and Douglas. The discovery of Douglas was understandably upsetting to Gwendolyn. Her mother had never told her that she had a second brother.

Gwendolyn gave the two portraits to Gary and his wife Helen. A short time later, their oldest daughter, Dana, found Gwendolyn still examining the contents of the trunk. Dana was given a small mitten, a baby's shoe similar to the one Douglas was wearing in his picture, and a black and white photograph from which Douglas's colorized portrait was produced. On the back of the photograph was written "Vincent Mitchell Studios, 111 W. Lexington Street, Baltimore." The studio was less than two miles from the Harriet Lane Home.

Comparisons of the Portrait and Film

Gary agreed to mail me a photograph of Douglas's portrait. As I awaited the picture of Douglas, I made stills from Watson's (1923) movie. Regrettably, there were no close-ups of Albert, so enlargements were made to better observe the baby's features. Multiple stills were developed, because there was no single "best" shot. One frame revealed a distinctive eyebrow, another yielded a good look at the nose, and so on.

After the photograph of Douglas arrived, several colleagues and I scrutinized the images. We agreed that both boys had long arching eyebrows, an upturned nose, and a "Cupid's bow mouth." Several stills showed a dark vertical area near the

Finding Little Albert: A Journey to John B. Watson's Infant Laboratory by Hall P. Beck, Sharman Levinson, and Gary Irons

83

center of Albert's chin. This could be the distinct dimple seen in Douglas's portrait. Alternatively, the low resolution of the old film leaves open the possibility that this area is a shadow.

Examinations of the eyes, eye sockets, and ears were less informative. In the stills, Albert's eyes look like black dots. The eye sockets lacked definition; we could not determine their lengths or the space between them. Also, in his portrait, Douglas was wearing a bonnet that obscured his ears. Although the photographic data were not ideal, neither I nor my colleagues saw any evidence to indicate that Douglas was not Albert. Thus, I deemed that a more thorough and expert biometric analysis was warranted.

An argument can be made that the shortcomings of the photographic evidence precluded meaningful biometric comparisons. The quality of Watson's (1923) movie limited the precision with which Albert's facial features could be measured. The enlargements of Albert's face were of such low resolution that they would not reproduce well in a journal.

An even greater problem was that we did not know Douglas's age when his portrait was taken. Infant facial features change rapidly, making it difficult or impossible to determine if photographs of babies of different ages show the same person (Wilkinson, 2004). I recognized that we could not conduct a confirmatory test, but a disconfirmatory evaluation might be possible. That is, the difference between Albert and Douglas might be so great that a biometric assessment could establish that the two boys could not be the same individual.

When in need, I have always relied on the kindness of scientists. Alan Brantley, formerly of the Federal Bureau of Investigation, and Randy Palmer, retired from the North Carolina Department of Corrections, began calling their contacts for me. Eventually they put me in touch with William Rodriguez of the Armed Forces Institute of Pathology. He graciously consented to compare the photograph of Douglas with stills of Albert taken from the Watson film.

As expected, Rodriguez (personal communication, June 13, 2008) pointed out that the fast rate of tissue growth during infancy ruled out a definitive identification of Albert. He then addressed the question: Did the photographic evidence reveal that Douglas and Albert were different people?

My examination using a simplified cross-sectional ratio comparison appears to suggest that one cannot exclude the subject in question as possibly being baby Albert. There are certainly facial similarities based upon my observations, even taking into account the differential chronological age of the subjects depicted. In conclusion, the two photographs could be the same individual. (W. Rodriguez, personal communication, June 13, 2008)

The visual and biometric comparisons revealed a resemblance between the two boys. Nevertheless, if we possessed only the photographic data, we could not say with confidence that Douglas was Albert. Thankfully, the photographic evidence does not need to be considered in isolation. The photographic data can be examined in conjunction with our other findings to determine the likelihood that Douglas and Albert are the same person.

Conclusion

This article describes our search for Little Albert. First, we sought to learn as much as possible about Albert. Then we tried to find a child who matched these attributes. After seven years, we discovered an individual, Douglas Merritte, who shared many characteristics with Albert. The findings are summarized below.

1. Watson and Rayner (1920) tested Albert during the winter of 1919–1920. At the time of the study, Albert and his mother were living on the Johns Hopkins campus. Census data show that Douglas's mother, Arvilla, resided on the Johns Hopkins campus on January 2, 1920.
2. Watson and Rayner (1920) stated that Albert's mother was a wet nurse in the Harriet Lane Home. According to family history, Arvilla worked in the Harriet Lane Home.
3. Douglas was born on March 9, 1919, so Arvilla was probably lactating at the time of the investigation. She could then have served as a wet nurse.
4. Documents suggest that there were never many, probably no more than four, wet nurses concurrently residing in the Harriet Lane Home.
5. Douglas was born at Johns Hopkins and was cared for by his mother after she left the hospital. Thus, it is highly probable that Douglas lived on campus with his mother during the winter of 1919–1920.
6. Assuming that Douglas lived with Arvilla, he, like Albert, spent almost his entire first year at Johns Hopkins.
7. Like Albert, Douglas left the institution during the early 1920s.
8. Albert's baseline was assessed when he was 8 months 26 days of age. By jointly considering Watson and Rayner's (1920) article, the film (Watson, 1923), and Watson's correspondence with Goodnow (1919; Watson, 1919b), we determined that baseline was recorded on or around December 5, 1919. Douglas was 8 months 26 days old on December 5, 1919.
9. Albert and Douglas were Caucasian males.
10. There are physical resemblances between the two boys. Visual inspection and biometric analyses of the Douglas portrait and the Little Albert film stills revealed "facial similarities." No features were so different as to indicate that Douglas and Albert could not be the same individual.

It is possible, but improbable, that these commonalities are happenstance. Although some of these attributes apply to more than one person, the likelihood that the entire set applies to anyone other than Albert is very small. The available evidence strongly supports the hypothesis that Douglas Merritte is Little Albert. After 89 years, psychology's lost boy has come home.

Epilogue to a Quest

Gary Irons, his wife Helen, and I drove to the Prospect Cemetery where Arvilla is buried. Then we traveled several miles to the Locust Grove Church. Beside the church is a small well-kept cemetery. The heading on Douglas's gravestone reads, "Douglas, Son of Arvilla Merritte, March 9, 1919 to May 10, 1925." Below is an inscription, taken from Felicia Hemans's (189-?, p. 331) *Dirge of a Child:*

> The sunbeam's smile, the zephyr's breath,
> All that it knew from birth to death.

As I watched Gary and Helen put flowers on the grave, I recalled a daydream in which I had envisioned showing a puzzled old man Watson's film of him as a baby. My small fantasy was among the dozens of misconceptions and myths inspired by Douglas.

None of the folktales we encountered during our inquiry had a factual basis. There is no evidence that the baby's mother was "outraged" at her son's treatment (Rathus, 1987) or that Douglas's phobia proved resistant to extinction (Blum, 2002; Kleinmuntz, 1974). Douglas was never deconditioned (Prytula, Oster, & Davis, 1977), and he was not adopted by a family north of Baltimore (Cohen, 1979).

Nor was he ever an old man. Our search of seven years was longer than the little boy's life. I laid flowers on the grave of my longtime "companion," turned, and simultaneously felt a great peace and profound loneliness.

We will probably never know if Douglas experienced any long-term effects from Watson and Rayner's (1920) attempts to condition him. No family stories suggest that Douglas was afraid of furry objects or loud noises. Of course, a lack of evidence does not necessarily mean that the conditioning procedure had no ill effects or that Douglas's treatment was ethical.

Whatever happened to Douglas, better known as Little Albert? After leaving the Harriet Lane Home, the robust child shown in Watson's (1923) film became sickly. According to his death certificate (Department of Health, Bureau of Vital Statistics, 1925), Douglas developed hydrocephalus in 1922. Acquired hydrocephalus is often caused by a disease or condition such as encephalitis, meningitis, or a brain tumor (Turkington, 2002). We were unable to determine the source of Douglas's illness, but a reasonable conjecture is that he contracted meningitis from Flora Brashears.

The Albert saga did not end in a rural Maryland graveyard. It is still being written in his legacy to psychology. Although his conditioning apparently did not produce an outcry at the time the study was published (Buckley, 1989; Simpson, 2000), his treatment has come to exemplify the need for an ethical code to protect the rights of participants.

For all its methodological limitations, the Little Albert study (Watson & Rayner, 1920) became a landmark in behavioral psychology. Albert's conditioning helped stimulate a movement that reshaped the conduct and practice of our discipline (Benjamin, 2007). All behavior therapies trace their lineage to Mary Cover Jones's (1924) counter-conditioning of Peter, a follow-up to the Albert investigation. Watson and Rayner's simple study of fear acquisition and generalization

initiated the development of effective treatments for phobias (Field & Nightingale, 2009; Wolpe, 1958) and an array of other behavioral problems (Masters & Rimm, 1987; Rachman, 1997).

Albert's fame now transcends the Watson and Rayner (1920) study. As much as Pavlov's dogs, Skinner's pigeons, and Milgram's obedience experiments, the conditioning of Albert is the face of psychology. To many, Little Albert embodies the promise and, to some, the dangers inherent in the scientific study of behavior.

References

American Psychological Association. (1953). *Ethical standards of psychologists.* Washington, DC: Author.

Beck, L. F. (1938). A review of sixteen-millimeter films in psychology and allied sciences. *Psychological Bulletin, 35,* 127–169.

Benjamin, L. T., Jr. (2007). *A brief history of modern psychology.* Malden, MA: Blackwell.

Benjamin, L. T., Jr., Whitaker, J. L., & Ramsey, R. M. (2007). John B. Watson's alleged sex research: An appraisal of the evidence. *American Psychologist, 62,* 131–139.

Blair-Broeker, C. T., Ernst, R. M., & Myers, D. G. (2003). *Thinking about psychology. The science of mind and behavior.* New York: Worth.

Blum, D. (2002). *Love at Goon Park: Harry Harlow and the science of affection.* Cambridge, MA: Perseus.

Boring, E. G. (1937). The lag of publication in journals of psychology. *The American Journal of Psychology, 49,* 137–139.

Brewer, C. L. (1991). Perspectives on John B. Watson. In G. A. Kimble, M. Wertheimer, & C. L. White (Eds.), *Portraits of pioneers in psychology* (pp. 171–186). Washington, DC: American Psychological Association.

Buckley, K. W. (1989). *Mechanical man: John Broadus Watson and the beginnings of behaviorism.* New York: Guilford Press.

Bureau of Labor Statistics, U.S. Department of Labor. (2009). *CPI inflation calculator.* Retrieved June 29, 2009, from www.bls.gov/data/inflation_calculator.htm

Cohen, D. (1979). *J. B. Watson—The founder of behaviourism: A biography.* London: Routledge & Kegan Paul.

Cornwell, D., & Hobbs, S. (1976, March 18). The strange saga of little Albert. *New Society,* pp. 602–604.

Deaths: Mrs. Flora Belle Brashears. (1924, May 24). *The Frederick Post,* p. 5.

Department of Health and Mental Hygiene, Division of Vital Records (Birth Record, BC). (1919). *Baby Merritte, 70288, 02/25/04/006.* In the Maryland State Archives (MSA T310–230), Annapolis, MD.

Department of Health, Bureau of Vital Statistics (Death Record Counties). (1925). *Douglas Merritte, Carroll County, 10 May 1925.* In the Maryland State Archives (MSA S1179, MdHR 50, 259–375, 2/56/62)(1), Annapolis, MD.

Field, A. P., & Nightingale, Z. C. (2009). Test of time: What if Little Albert had escaped? *Clinical Child Psychology and Psychiatry, 14,* 311–319.

Goodnow, F. J. (1919). Letter to John B. Watson, October 28, 1919. In the Ferdinand Hamburger, Jr., Archives of The Johns Hopkins University (Record Group 02.001/Office of the President/Series 1/File 115, Department of Psychology, 1913–1919), Baltimore, MD.

Finding Little Albert: A Journey to John B. Watson's Infant Laboratory by Hall P. Beck, Sharman Levinson, and Gary Irons

85

Griggs, R. A. (2009). *Psychology: A concise introduction*. New York: Worth.

Harris, B. (1979). Whatever happened to little Albert? *American Psychologist, 34,* 151–160.

Hemans, F. (189-?). *The poetical works of Mrs. Hemans*. New York: Thomas Y. Crowell.

Howland, J. (1912–1913). The Harriet Lane Home for Invalid Children. *Johns Hopkins Alumni Magazine, 1,* 115–121.

Johns Hopkins Hospital Records of Births March 11, 1916 to October 28, 1919. (1919). In the Alan Mason Chesney Medical Archives of The Johns Hopkins Medical Institutions (Box 504923), Baltimore, MD.

Jones, M. C. (1924). A laboratory study of fear: The case of Peter. *Pedagogical Seminary, 31,* 308–315.

Jones, M. C. (1974). Albert, Peter, and John B. Watson. *American Psychologist, 29,* 581–583.

Jones, M. C. (1975). A 1924 pioneer looks at behavior therapy. *Journal of Behavior Therapy and Experimental Psychiatry, 6,* 181–187.

Jones, M. C. (1976). Letter to Cedric A. Larson, July 28, 1976. In the Cedric Larson Papers, Archives of the History of American Psychology, University of Akron, Akron, OH.

Kleinmuntz, B. (1974). *Essentials of abnormal psychology*. New York: Harper & Row.

LeUnes, A. (1983). Little Albert from the viewpoint of abnormal psychology textbook authors. *Teaching of Psychology, 10,* 230–231.

Magoun, H. W. (1981). John B. Watson and the study of human sexual behavior. *Journal of Sex Research, 17,* 368–378.

Masters, J. C. & Rimm, D. C. (1987). *Behavior therapy: Techniques and empirical findings*. San Diego, CA: Harcourt Brace Jovanovich.

Murray, F. S. (1973). In search of Albert. *Professional Psychology, 4,* 5–6.

Park, E. A. (1957). [Description of the Harriet Lane Home]. In the Alan Mason Chesney Medical Archives of The Johns Hopkins Medical Institutions (Records of the Harriet Lane Home, Collection Harriet Lane Home, Series 4b), Baltimore, MD.

Park, E. A. (n.d.). *The Howland period from 1912 to 1926*. In the Alan Mason Chesney Medical Archives of The Johns Hopkins Medical Institutions (Records of the Harriet Lane Home, Collection Harriet Lane Home, Series 4b), Baltimore, MD.

Park, E. A., Littlefield, J. W., Seidel, H. M., & Wissow, L. S. (2006). *The Harriet Lane Home: A model and a gem*. Baltimore: Johns Hopkins University, Department of Pediatrics.

Paul, D. B., & Blumenthal, A. L. (1989). On the trail of Little Albert. *Psychological Record, 39,* 547–553.

Prytula, R. E., Oster, G. D., & Davis, S. F. (1977). The "rat-rabbit" problem: What did John B. Watson really do? *Teaching of Psychology, 4,* 44–46.

Rachman, S. (1997). The evolution of cognitive behaviour therapy. In D. M. Clark & C. G. Fairburn (Eds.), *Science and practice of cognitive behavior therapy* (pp. 1–26). New York: Oxford University Press.

Rathus, S. A. (1987). *Psychology*. New York: Holt, Rinehart & Winston.

Resnick, J. H. (1974). In pursuit of Albert. *Professional Psychology, 5,* 112–113.

Rilling, M. (2000). John Watson's paradoxical struggle to explain Freud. *American Psychologist, 55,* 301–312.

Robertson, A. T. (1901). *Life and letters of John Albert Broadus*. Philadelphia: American Baptist Publication Society.

Samelson, F. (1980). J. B. Watson's Little Albert, Cyril Burt's twins, and the need for a critical science. *American Psychologist, 35,* 619–625.

Simpson, J. C. (2000, April). It's all in the upbringing. *Johns Hopkins Magazine, 52,* 62–65.

Turkington, C. (2002). Hydrocephalus. In *The encyclopedia of the brain and brain disorders* (2nd ed., pp. 134–135). New York: Facts on File.

University Register 1919–20. (1919, November). *Johns Hopkins University Circular, 38*(9, Whole No. 319, New Series).

U.S. Bureau of the Census. (1920). Johns Hopkins Hospital, Baltimore City, Maryland. In *Fourteenth Census of the United States, 1920* (Enumeration District 82, Sheet 4A; Roll: T625_661). Retrieved June 29, 2009 from Ancestry Library database.

[Vassar College transcript of Rosalie Alberta Rayner]. (1919). In the Cedric Larson Papers, Archives of the History of American Psychology, University of Akron, Akron, OH.

Watson, J. B. (1918). Letter to Frank J. Goodnow, December 31, 1918. In the Ferdinand Hamburger, Jr., Archives of The Johns Hopkins University (Record Group 02.001/Office of the President/Series 1/File 115, Department of Psychology, 1913–1919), Baltimore, MD.

Watson, J. B. (1919a). Letter to Bertrand Russell, October 4, 1919. In the Cedric Larson Papers, Archives of the History of American Psychology, University of Akron, Akron, OH.

Watson, J. B. (1919b). Letter to Frank J. Goodnow, December 5, 1919. In the Ferdinand Hamburger, Jr., Archives of The Johns Hopkins University (Record Group 02.001/Office of the President/Series 1/File 115, Department of Psychology, 1913–1919), Baltimore, MD.

Watson, J. B. (1919c). Letter to Frank J. Goodnow, November 13, 1919. In the Ferdinand Hamburger, Jr., Archives of The Johns Hopkins University (Record Group 02.001/Office of the President/Series 1/File 115, Department of Psychology, 1913–1919), Baltimore, MD.

Watson, J. B. (1919d). Letter to Frank J. Goodnow, October 27, 1919. In the Ferdinand Hamburger, Jr., Archives of The Johns Hopkins University (Record Group 02.001/Office of the President/Series 1/File 115, Department of Psychology, 1913–1919), Baltimore, MD.

Watson, J. B. (1919e). *Psychology from the standpoint of a behaviorist* (1st ed.). Philadelphia: J. B. Lippincott.

Watson, J. B. (1919f). A schematic outline of the emotions. *Psychological Review, 26,* 165–196.

Watson, J. B. (1920a). Letter to E. L. Thorndike, May 13, 1920. In the Ferdinand Hamburger, Jr., Archives of The Johns Hopkins University (Record Group 02.001/Office of the President/Series 1/File 115, Department of Psychology, 1920–1921), Baltimore, MD.

Watson, J. B. (1920b). Letter to Frank J. Goodnow, January 12, 1920. In the Ferdinand Hamburger, Jr., Archives of The Johns Hopkins University (Record Group 02.001/Office of the President/Series 1/File 115, Department of Psychology, 1920–1921), Baltimore, MD.

Watson, J. B. (1922). Letter to Adolf Meyer, December 14, 1922. In the Adolf Meyer Papers (Unit I/3974/21), Alan Mason Chesney Medical Archives of The Johns Hopkins Medical Institutions, Baltimore, MD.

Watson, J. B. (Writer/Director). (1923). *Experimental investigation of babies* [motion picture]. (Distributed by C. H. Stoelting Co., 424 N. Homan Ave, Chicago, IL).

Watson, J. B. (1924a). *Behaviorism*. New York: Norton.

Watson, J. B. (1924b). *Psychology from the standpoint of a behaviorist* (2nd ed.). Philadelphia: J. B. Lippincott.

Watson, J. B. (1925). Experimental studies on the growth of the emotions. *Pedagogical Seminary, 32,* 328–348.

Watson, J. B. (1928a, February). The heart or the intellect? *Harper's Magazine,* pp. 345–352.

Watson, J. B. (1928b). *Psychological care of infant and child.* New York: Norton.

Watson, J. B. (1936). Letter to Thomas W. Harrell and Ross Harrison, June 16, 1936. In the Cedric Larson Papers, Archives of the History of American Psychology, University of Akron, Akron, OH.

Watson, J. B., & Lashley, K. S. (1920). A consensus of medical opinion upon questions relating to sex education and venereal disease campaigns. *Mental Hygiene, 4,* 769–847.

Watson, J. B., & Rayner, R. (1920). Conditioned emotional reactions. *Journal of Experimental Psychology, 3,* 1–14.

Watson, J. B., & Watson, R. R. (1921). Studies in infant psychology. *Scientific Monthly, 13,* 493–515.

Wilkinson, C. (2004). *Forensic facial recognition.* Cambridge, England: Cambridge University Press.

Wolpe, J. (1958). *Psychotherapy by reciprocal inhibition.* Stanford, CA: Stanford University.

Wyatt and Nolting Architects. (1909). [Fourth floor plan, Harriet Lane Home]. In the Architectural Drawing Collection Harriet Lane Home (HLH 004A), Alan Mason Chesney Medical Archives of The Johns Hopkins Medical Institutions, Baltimore, MD.

Critical Thinking

1. Who was "Little Albert"?
2. What were the research steps involved in discovering his true identity?
3. Was the "Little Albert" study ethical?

Create Central

www.mhhe.com/createcentral

Internet References

'Little Albert' regains his identity
www.apa.org/monitor/2010/01/little-albert.aspx

A new twist in the sad saga of Little Albert
http://chronicle.com/blogs/percolator/a-new-twist-in-the-sad-saga-of-little-albert/28423

HALL P. BECK, Department of Psychology, Appalachian State University; **SHARMAN LEVINSON,** Department of Psychology, The American University of Paris, Paris France; **GARY IRONS,** Finksburg, Maryland.

Beck et al., Hall P. From *American Psychologist,* October 2009, pp. 605–614. Copyright © 2009 by American Psychological Association. Reprinted by permission via Rightslink.

Article   Prepared by: Eric Landrum, *Boise State University*

Psychological Science and Safety: Large-Scale Success at Preventing Occupational Injuries and Fatalities

E. SCOTT GELLER

Learning Outcomes

After reading this article, you will be able to:

- Discuss the origins of behavior-based safety initiatives.

- Explain the key elements of behavior-based safety programs and their effectiveness in reducing injuries and fatalities in the workplace.

At the time of this writing, the eyes of the world are on the oil crisis in the Gulf of Mexico—an ongoing, massive environmental catastrophe resulting from an April 20, 2010, oil-well blowout and explosion that killed 11 platform workers and injured 17 others. Most of these eyes are sympathetic, realizing the severe devastation to marine and wildlife habitats and the fishing and tourism industries. Many are also empathic, because they themselves have experienced similar disastrous consequences to humanity and its milieu as the result of a sudden unforeseen calamity.

However, many are also accusatory, attempting to find a "root cause" of this tragedy by assigning blame to the leader or CEO of one of the organizations involved. For example, the chief executive of British Petroleum, who had leased the oil rig from Transocean Ltd., condemned Transocean because it was their equipment and operating system that failed. But British Petroleum shareholders and the United States government criticize British Petroleum for insufficient oversight of its contractors. Other fault-finding parties hold Halliburton responsible because the rig explosion occurred about 20 hours after Halliburton workers cemented the production lines in the well casing to seal off the oil reservoir from the well bore. Plus, some accuse the United States government for allowing deep-well drilling in the first place and not imposing sufficient safety standards, supervision, and enforcement.

Many of these condemning eyes are looking for ways to punish the individuals who caused this horrific event. With substantial media attention, they seemingly believe large fines and incarceration will prevent such disasters in the future. Others appear convinced the only answer is to stop all off-shore oil drilling completely.

With 40 years of research and scholarship related to industrial and community safety, I see a missing link in all of these viewpoints. Here I explain how psychological science has been applied in organizations worldwide to turn human dynamics into an asset rather than a liability for preventing occupational injuries, fatalities, and calamities like the Deepwater Horizon oil spill.

The Vision of a Total Safety Culture

Imagine a workplace in which everyone feels responsible for safety and does something about it on a daily basis. Top managers, supervisors, and line workers frequently go beyond the call of duty to identify hazards and at-risk behaviors, and they intervene to correct them as soon as possible. Safety is not considered a priority that can be conveniently shifted depending on the demands of the situation; rather, safety is a value linked to every priority of a given situation (Geller, 2001a).

In this Total Safety Culture, "accident investigations" are not conducted to find the "root cause" of an injury. In fact, the popular term *accident* is not used at all to refer to unintentional property damage or an injury that could have been prevented with the proper execution of a safety-related process or procedure. The terms *investigation* and *root cause* are also eliminated because these reflect a blame game and the unwarranted assumption the "accident" was caused by one independent variable.

Advocates for the Total Safety Culture realize severe punitive consequences following an undesirable behavior can cause more harm than good, by activating negative attitudes and instilling fear into the organizational culture, thereby stifling the reporting of close calls and minor injuries and discouraging the kinds of safety-related conversations needed to learn from mistakes and prevent more serious casualties.

An injury or close-call analysis replaces the accident investigation, and contributing factors are identified, rather than a root cause, in a fact-finding process that involves every relevant employee. The Total Safety Culture participants realize many behavioral, environmental, and person (e.g., attitudinal and cognitive) factors potentially contribute to a close call, injury, or fatality. This vision of a Total Safety Culture is actually a reality at numerous companies worldwide. How was this cultural shift attained? These corporations implemented an employee-driven behavior-based safety process (e.g., Grindle, Dickinson, & Boettcher, 2000; Sulzer-Azaroff & Austin, 2000).

The Beginning of Behavior-Based Safety

In 1983, the Corporate Safety Director of Ford Motor Company asked me to help his safety management team increase safety-belt use among Ford employees at approximately 110 facilities. In brief, I developed training materials that explicated the basics of applying principles of behavior analysis to *define* the target behavior (in this case, vehicle safety-belt use), *observe* its frequency of occurrence, *intervene* to increase the frequency of the target behavior, and subsequently *test* the impact of the intervention by comparing frequencies of the target behavior during baseline, intervention, and follow-up phases. The process was labeled "DO IT," and the overall approach was termed *behavior-based safety*—a label I had been using since 1979 to refer to field research evaluating the impact of interventions designed to decrease risky behavior and/or increase safe behavior.

Besides teaching and implementing the evidence-based principles of applied behavior analysis (Baer, Wolf, & Risley, 1968), this large-scale program included the following components, which facilitate the sustained success of current behavior-based safety programs: (a) Safety leaders selected from each site attended a 2-day education/training session to learn behavior-based safety principles and customize practical applications for their work culture; (b) with a teaching manual, discussion, and practice workbooks,[1] the leaders were held accountable to select and train a behavior-based safety-steering committee at their site with the mission to develop and coordinate a DO IT process for increasing employee safety-belt use; (c) directed to follow the basic principles of behavior-based safety and report pre- and postintervention data (i.e., the weekly use of vehicle safety belts at their site), each behavior-based safety team designed an observation schedule and intervention plan to fit their situation; (d) behavior-based safety facilitators attended follow-up information-sharing sessions off site to learn from the successes and failures of other behavior-based safety teams and receive refresher instruction from me; and (e) the corporate safety office periodically distributed a newsletter that reported site-specific and overall results of the corporate-wide behavior-based safety program designed to increase safety-belt use, and it also described various innovative interventions developed by certain behavior-based-safety steering teams.

Following the success of this corporate-wide behavior-based safety program, which increased vehicle safety-belt use among all Ford employees from 9% to 54% in 1984,[2] the Corporate Safety Director asked me to help him expand the

1. Focus intervention on observable behavior.
2. Look for external factors to understand and improve behavior.
3. Direct with activators and motivate with consequences.
4. Focus on positive consequences to motivate behavior.
5. Apply a DO IT process to improve intervention.
6. Use theory to integrate information, not to bias observation or limit exploration.
7. Design interventions with consideration of internal feelings and attitudes.

Figure 1   The seven principles of behavior-based safety.

behavior-based safety process to address the human side of safety within Ford plants. This led to me teaching the principles of behavior-based safety at the facilities of several automobile-manufacturing companies, including Ford, General Motors, and Chrysler. After learning the seven basic principles of behavior-based safety (see Figure 1), representatives of work teams at an industrial site learned how to expand the DO IT process beyond one behavior. More specifically, they were shown how to develop and apply a critical behavior checklist to help achieve an injury-free workplace.

Interpersonal Coaching

Employee teams used the worksheet shown in Figure 2 to develop a critical behavior checklist to fit their work process. Through interactive discussions, each work team defined safe and risky behaviors in their work areas relevant to each operating procedure shown in Figure 2. Some categories were irrelevant for a particular work group, and many behavior-based safety teams added another operating process to cover a distinct set of relevant work behaviors.

Workers used the specific critical behavior checklist designed for their work area to observe a coworker (always with the employee's permission) and then to offer behavior-based feedback by revealing the critical behavior checklist results. Percent-safe scores were calculated per one-on-one coaching sessions (with only the observer's name reported on the critical behavior checklist). These achievement percentages were then averaged across individual critical behavior checklists to obtain percent-safe averages per behavior, per work team, per department, and per plant. Work teams changed their critical behavior checklists regularly to target behaviors with the lowest percent-safe scores. This behavior-based safety coaching process was also used to assess barriers to safe behavior and facilitators of risky behavior, as well as environmental hazards.

Worldwide Dissemination of Behavior-Based Safety

Starting in the mid-1980s, behavior-based safety became increasingly popular in industrial settings nationwide and subsequently, throughout the world. Several books detail the principles and procedures of behavior-based safety (e.g., Cooper, 2009; Geller, 1998, 2001a, 2001b; Krause, Hidley, & Hodson, 1996; McSween, 1995), and a number of systematic reviews

Operating Procedures	Safe Observation	Risky Observation
BODY POSITIONING/PROTECTING		
Positioning/protecting body parts (e.g., avoiding line of fire by using personal protective equipment, equipment guards, barricades)		
VISUAL FOCUSING		
Eyes and attention devoted to ongoing task(s)		
COMMUNICATING		
Verbal or nonverbal interaction that affects safety		
PACING OF WORK		
Rate of ongoing work (e.g., spacing breaks appropriately, rushing)		
MOVING OBJECTS		
Body mechanics while lifting, pushing/pulling		
COMPLYING WITH LOCKOUT/TAGOUT		
Following procedures for lockout/tagout		
COMPLYING WITH PERMITS		
Obtaining, then complying with permit(s) (e.g., confined space entry, hot work, excavation, open line, hot tap)		

Figure 2   A worksheet for developing a critical behavior checklist.

of the literature provide solid evidence for the success of this approach to injury prevention (e.g., Grindle et al., 2000; McAfee & Winn, 1989; Sulzer-Azaroff & Austin, 2000).

Since the early 1990s, an annual "Behavioral Safety Now" convention, sponsored in part by the Cambridge Center for Behavioral Studies, has enabled several hundred employees from organizations around the world to share their behavior-based safety innovations and learn more about the human dynamics of injury prevention from leading consultants and researchers. In addition, several behavior-based safety consulting firms host their own annual "Behavior-Based Safety Users" conference to provide continuous learning and momentum for their clients.

The Behavior-Based Safety Principles

Some labor unions have rejected behavior-based safety because they believe the process puts improper blame on the injured worker (Hoyle, 1998), perhaps because of the fault-finding bias referred to at the start of this article. In fact, when presented correctly, behavior-based safety targets employee behavior as only one dimension of an injury-prevention system while also engaging the wage worker in the discovery and improvement of environmental, engineering, and cultural factors related to hazard removal and injury prevention.

How does behavior-based safety facilitate open conversation about safety-related issues and ways to address them? When the principles and procedure of behavior-based safety are understood and followed by both managers and wage workers (as explained and explicated elsewhere; Geller, 1998, 2001a, 2001b), employees perceive increased choice and personal

control over the safety and health of themselves and others. Their paradigm for attaining and sustaining an injury-free workplace is transformed from reactive, failure-oriented, and individualistic to proactive, achievement-focused, and collectivistic.

The behavior-based safety principles listed in Figure 1 are founded on behavioral science as conceptualized and researched by B.F. Skinner (1953). The focus is on examining external factors (Principle 2) to explain and improve behavior and then applying the ABC model—A for activator, B for behavior, and C for consequence (Principle 3)—to design interventions for improving behavior at individual, group, and organizational levels (Cooper, 2009; Geller, 1998, 2001a, 2001b). Continuous learning and improvement occurs with a DO IT process (Principle 5) that monitors the impact of a behavior-change intervention and then uses process and outcome data to refine the intervention. The systematic evaluation of a number of DO IT processes can lead to a body of knowledge worthy of integrating into a theory (Principle 6).

Principles 4 and 7 reflect Skinner's concern for people's feelings and attitudes, even though he rejected unobservable constructs from scientific study as causes or outcomes of behavior. In Skinner's words, "the problem is to free men, not from control, but from certain kinds of control" (Skinner, 1971, p. 41). He goes on to explain why control by negative consequences must be reduced in order to increase perceptions of personal freedom. Similarly, subsequent researchers have demonstrated the detrimental motivational effects of contingencies that restrict an individual's perception of autonomy (e.g., Deci & Ryan, 1995).

Organizations that have implemented a behavior-based safety observation and feedback process have made great strides in achieving an injury-free workplace. However, the typical behavior-based safety approach does not address the person domain of safety reflected in Principle 7, including perceptions, attitudes, beliefs, expectancies, and cognitions of employees. Indeed, since the mid-1990s, several consultant groups have been marketing their services for industrial safety as more comprehensive or holistic than those providing behavior-based safety training and consultation.

Actually, many of the behavior-based safety trainers present a rather narrow view of the human element in injury prevention, with some of their teaching being potentially detrimental to safety. For example, it is common for a consultant to teach the ABC model as if antecedent stimuli "trigger" or cause behavior to occur, as when a conditioned stimulus elicits a conditioned response in classical conditioning. In other words, the critical role of choice is left out of the explanation of the three-term contingency, thus missing an opportunity to explain the impact of perceived autonomy on self-determinism (Deci & Ryan, 1995).

Furthermore, behavior-based safety consultants often state the ultimate goal is to make safe behavior habitual whereby individuals perform safely without thinking. While there are certainly circumstances when it is beneficial to respond automatically (as in emergencies and some sports activities), in most safety-related situations it is better to accompany the behavior with cognition. Self-talk before, during, and after a safe behavior enables the participant to anticipate and perform slight variations in a certain response as a function of situational changes while also providing personal affirmation and self-persuasion for the behavior, which in turn enhances self-accountability (Aronson, 1999) and self-motivation (Geller, 2005).

Moreover, almost every consulting firm targeting the human dynamics of industrial safety (and there are many such firms) includes a perception survey as an initial diagnostic tool. Subsequently, they purport to use the results of this survey to customize an intervention program for the organization. This approach clearly reflects a consideration of factors beyond overt behavior as contributors to hazard recognition and injury prevention.

These perspectives, especially the narrow and incomplete presentations by the army of behavior-based safety consultants worldwide, led me to develop an expanded version of behavior-based safety. The approach is called people-based safety and is described in books (Geller, 2005, 2008; Geller & Veazie, 2009), as well as in DVDs and accompanying workbooks I have developed and that have been disseminated by a leading training and consulting corporation.[3] This approach was also customized for application among health care professionals to reduce medical error and keep patients safe (Geller & Johnson, 2007) and is called people-based patient safety.[3]

The people-based safety and people-based patient safety approaches are not marketed as an alternative to behavior-based safety but rather as an evolution that integrates the best of behavior-based and person-based safety, as signified by the acronym ACTS: acting, coaching, thinking, and seeing.[3] The Acting and Coaching components are essentially behavior-based safety, except self-coaching and self-management techniques are incorporated. These added processes are supported through self-talk, which involves the Thinking component of people-based safety and people-based patient safety.

The Seeing dimension of people-based safety and people-based patient safety takes into consideration the divergent views of safety-related issues, which should be assessed with a perception survey and considered when designing and evaluating interventions to improve safety performance. Person factors are addressed in this domain of people-based safety, including five person states shown to increase one's propensity to go beyond the call of duty to help another person (i.e., self-esteem, self-efficacy, personal control, optimism, and belongingness; Geller, 2001a, 2001b; Geller, Roberts, & Gilmore, 1996). After workshop participants learn the psychological definitions of these five states and take a survey to assess their current score per each state, they entertain practical ways to enhance these states in themselves and others, thereby increasing the likelihood workers will actively care for each other's safety.

Conclusion

The example of the British Petroleum Deepwater Horizon tragedy illustrates a potential outcome of a worksite that does not report hazards, close calls, and minor injuries on a regular basis, thereby missing opportunities to correct environmental and behavioral factors that could contribute to a serious injury or even a fatality. These worksites, common in industries worldwide, measure their safety success exclusively by counting injuries per work hours (e.g., total recordable injury rate). By prioritizing such after-the-fact numbers over leading indicators of possible injuries, these industries cultivate a loss-control or failure-avoiding culture wherein workers are reluctant to report and discuss their safety-related mistakes.

News reports have suggested the oil-rig employees on the Deepwater Horizon worked in a culture that discouraged the reporting of hazards, close calls, minor injuries, and other factors that could have led to a serious injury if not corrected. While such a work culture is not unusual, it is inappropriate to claim such a culture existed on that Transocean oil rig without a systematic and objective analysis. Furthermore, it is unfair to assume a direct cause-and-effect connection between such a culture (if it existed) and the oil-well blowout and explosion.

However, it is intuitive that a work culture that attends to leading indicators of occupational injuries by encouraging the report and correction of factors that contributed to a close call or minor injury would prevent major injuries and fatalities. Here I have reviewed an ongoing approach in industries worldwide that successfully cultivates such a work culture by engaging workers in creating, applying, and evaluating a peer-to-peer behavior-based coaching process. Evidence-based reviews in books and journal articles support this kind of beneficial culture change accompanying behavior-based and people-based safety.

Nevertheless, the behavior-based and people-based safety procedures reviewed here may not be the only or most cost-effective way to develop a work culture that activates and reinforces proactive reporting and follow-up correcting of behavioral and environmental factors that might predict a serious injury or fatality. While the existing evidence gives a deciding edge to behavior-based and people-based safety in this regard, follow-up research is needed to explore alternative intervention paradigms

Psychological Science and Safety: Large-Scale Success at Preventing Occupational Injuries and Fatalities by E. Scott Geller

91

and reveal procedures for enhancing the impact and durability of behavior-based and people-based safety programs, as well as to demonstrate the advantages (if any) of people-based safety over behavior-based safety.

Notes

1. These original materials (including a manual, discussion guide, and practice workbook), expanded to address all safety-related behavior, are available from the author upon request at esgeller@vt.edu.

2. In personal communication, the corporate safety director (Dale A. Gray) estimated this program enabled Ford Motor Company to realize "a savings of over $22 million" and it "saved at least 20 lives and reduced injuries to more than 800 others."

3. In addition to the referenced books on people-based safety and people-based patient safety, more details about this approach to industrial and health care safety are available from Safety Performance Solutions, Inc., Suite 228, 610 N. Main St., Blacksburg, VA 24060; Tel: 540 951 7233; e-mail: safety@safetyperformance.com. Log on to www.safetyperformance.com for more information and links to obtain numerous behavior-based safety, people-based safety, and people-based patient safety articles at no cost.

Recommended Reading

Deci, E.L., & Flaste, R. (1995). *Why we do what we do: Understanding self-motivation.* New York, NY: Penguin Books. An easy-to-read review of the evidence-based determinants of self-motivation: competence, choice, and connections with others.

Geller, E.S. (2001). *Working safe: How to help people actively care for health and safety* (2nd ed.). New York, NY: Lewis Publishers. A step-by-step practical look at how to use behavioral science to improve health and safety in organizations and throughout communities.

Geller, E.S., & Johnson, D. (2007). (See References). Addresses the human dynamics of error prevention in health care by improving communication, teamwork, and the proactive examination of leading indicators of potential harm to patients.

Geller, E.S., & Veazie, B. (2010). *When no one's watching: Living and leading self-motivation.* Newport, VA: Make-A-Difference, LLC. An engaging, fast-paced, and true-to-life narrative, laced with leadership lessons, that teaches evidence-based ways to increase self-motivation in yourself and others.

Williams, J. (2010). *Keeping people safe: The human dynamics of injury prevention.* Lanham, MD: The Rowman & Littlefield Publishing Group, Inc. An easy-to-read procedural text providing the tools for developing an effective organizational safety culture, based on the principles of psychological science.

Declaration of Conflicting Interests

The author declared he had no conflicts of interest with respect to his authorship or the publication of this article.

References

Aronson, E. (1999). The power of self-persuasion. *American Psychologist, 54,* 875–884.

Baer, D.M., Wolf, M.M., & Risley, T.R. (1968). Some current dimensions of applied behavior analysis. *Journal of Applied Behavior Analysis, 1,* 91–97.

Cooper, D. (2009). *Behavioral safety: A framework for success.* Franklin, IN: B-Safe Management Solutions.

Deci, E.L., & Ryan, R.M. (1995). *Intrinsic motivation and self-determinism in human behavior.* New York, NY: Plenum.

Geller, E.S. (1998). *Understanding behavior-based safety: Step-by-step methods to improve your workplace.* (2nd ed.). Neenah, WI: J.J. Keller & Associates.

Geller, E.S. (2001a). Behavior-based safety in industry: Realizing the large-scale potential of psychology to promote human welfare. *Applied & Preventive Psychology, 10,* 87–105.

Geller, E.S. (2001b). *The psychology of safety handbook.* Boca Raton, FL: CRC Press.

Geller, E.S. (2005). *People-based safety: The source.* Virginia Beach, VA: Coastal Training Technologies Corporation.

Geller, E.S. (2008). *Leading people-based safety: Enriching our culture.* Virginia Beach, VA: Coastal Training Technologies Corporation.

Geller, E.S., & Johnson, D. (2007). *People-based patient safety: Enriching your culture to prevent medical error.* Virginia Beach, VA: Coastal Training Technologies Corporation.

Geller, E.S., Roberts, D.S., & Gilmore, M.R. (1996). Predicting propensity to actively care for occupational safety. *Journal of Safety Research, 27,* 1–8.

Geller, E.S., & Veazie, B. (2009). *The courage factor: Leading people-based culture change.* Virginia Beach, VA: Coastal Training Technologies Corporation.

Grindle, A.C., Dickinson, A.M., & Boettcher, W. (2000). Behavioral safety research in manufacturing settings: A review of the literature. *Journal of Organizational Behavior Management, 20,* 29–68.

Hoyle, B. (1998). *Fixing the workplace, not the worker: A workers' guide to accident prevention.* Lakewood, CO: Oil, Chemical and Atomic Workers International Union.

Krause, T.R., Hidley, J.H., & Hodson, S.J. (1996). *The behavior-based safety process: Managing improvement for an injury-free culture.* (2nd ed.). New York, NY: Van Nostrand Reinhold.

McAfee, R.B., & Winn, A.R. (1989). The use of incentives/feedback to enhance workplace safety: A critique of the literature. *Journal of Safety Research, 20,* 7–19.

McSween, T.E. (1995). *The values-based safety process: Improving your safety culture with a behavioral approach.* New York, NY: Van Nostrand Reinhold.

Skinner, B.F. (1953). *Science and human behavior.* New York, NY: Macmillan.

Skinner, B.F. (1971). *Beyond freedom and dignity.* New York, NY: Alfred A. Knopf.

Sulzer-Azaroff, B., & Austin, J. (2000). Does BBS work? Behavior-based safety and injury reduction: A survey of the evidence. *Professional Safety, 45*(7): 19–24.

Critical Thinking

1. Describe how psychological scientists are applying behavior-analytic methods to reduce injury and death in the workplace.

2. Describe in detail the specific aspects of safety training in the workplace that seem to be particularly effective in reducing injury and death.
3. What is a 'total safety culture,' and how are accidents regarded?

Create Central

www.mhhe.com/createcentral

Internet References

Science of behavioral safety

www.behavioral-safety.com/free-behavioral-safety-resource-center/free-behavior-based-safety-articles/scientific-articles-on-bbs

Physical and psychological health and safety

http://ohsonline.com/blogs/the-ohs-wire/2013/08/psychological-injuries.aspx

Geller, E. Scott. From *Current Directions in Psychological Science*, vol. 20, no. 2, April 2011, pp. 109–114. Copyright © 2011 by the Association for Psychological Science. Reprinted by permission of Sage Publications via Rightslink.

Article   Prepared by: Eric Landrum, *Boise State University*

The Perils and Promises of Praise

**The wrong kind of praise creates self-defeating behavior.
The right kind motivates students to learn.**

CAROL S. DWECK

Learning Outcomes

After reading this article, you will be able to:

- Describe the various ways that praise may motivate students to learn and the ways in which praise may impair learning.

- Distinguish between a "fixed mindset" and a "growth mindset."

We often hear these days that we've produced a generation of young people who can't get through the day without an award. They expect success because they're special, not because they've worked hard.

Is this true? Have we inadvertently done something to hold back our students?

I think educators commonly hold two beliefs that do just that. Many believe that (1) praising students' intelligence builds their confidence and motivation to learn, and (2) students' inherent intelligence is the major cause of their achievement in school. Our research has shown that the first belief is false and that the second can be harmful—even for the most competent students.

As a psychologist, I have studied student motivation for more than 35 years. My graduate students and I have looked at thousands of children, asking why some enjoy learning, even when it's hard, and why they are resilient in the face of obstacles. We have learned a great deal. Research shows us how to praise students in ways that yield motivation and resilience. In addition, specific interventions can reverse a student's slide into failure during the vulnerable period of adolescence.

Fixed or Malleable?

Praise is intricately connected to how students view their intelligence. Some students believe that their intellectual ability is a fixed trait. They have a certain amount of intelligence, and that's that. Students with this fixed mind-set become excessively concerned with how smart they are, seeking tasks that will prove their intelligence and avoiding ones that might not (Dweck, 1999, 2006). The desire to learn takes a backseat.

Other students believe that their intellectual ability is something they can develop through effort and education. They don't necessarily believe that anyone can become an Einstein or a Mozart, but they do understand that even Einstein and Mozart had to put in years of effort to become who they were. When students believe that they can develop their intelligence, they focus on doing just that. Not worrying about how smart they will appear, they take on challenges and stick to them (Dweck, 1999, 2006).

> **When students believe that they can develop their intelligence, they focus on doing just that.**

More and more research in psychology and neuroscience supports the growth mind-set. We are discovering that the brain has more plasticity over time than we ever imagined (Doidge, 2007); that fundamental aspects of intelligence can be enhanced through learning (Sternberg, 2005); and that dedication and persistence in the face of obstacles are key ingredients in outstanding achievement (Ericsson, Charness, Feltovich, & Hoffman, 2006).

Alfred Binet (1909/1973), the inventor of the IQ test, had a strong growth mind-set. He believed that education could transform the basic capacity to learn. Far from intending to measure fixed intelligence, he meant his test to be a tool for identifying students who were not profiting from the public school curriculum so that other courses of study could be devised to foster their intellectual growth.

The Two Faces of Effort

The fixed and growth mind-sets create two different psychological worlds. In the fixed mind-set, students care first and foremost about how they'll be judged: smart or not smart. Repeatedly, students with this mind-set reject opportunities to learn if they might make mistakes (Hong, Chiu, Dweck, Lin, & Wan, 1999; Mueller & Dweck, 1998). When they do make mistakes or reveal deficiencies, rather than correct them, they try to hide them (Nussbaum & Dweck, 2007).

They are also afraid of effort because effort makes them feel dumb. They believe that if you have the ability, you shouldn't need effort (Blackwell, Trzesniewski, & Dweck, 2007), that ability should bring success all by itself. This is one of the worst beliefs that students can hold. It can cause many bright students to stop working in school when the curriculum becomes challenging.

Finally, students in the fixed mind-set don't recover well from setbacks. When they hit a setback in school, they *decrease* their efforts and consider cheating (Blackwell et al., 2007). The idea of fixed intelligence does not offer them viable ways to improve.

Let's get inside the head of a student with a fixed mind-set as he sits in his classroom, confronted with algebra for the first time. Up until then, he has breezed through math. Even when he barely paid attention in class and skimped on his homework, he always got *A*s. But this is different. It's hard. The student feels anxious and thinks, "What if I'm not as good at math as I thought? What if other kids understand it and I don't?" At some level, he realizes that he has two choices: try hard, or turn off. His interest in math begins to wane, and his attention wanders. He tells himself, "Who cares about this stuff? It's for nerds. I could do it if I wanted to, but it's so boring. You don't see CEOs and sports stars solving for *x* and *y*."

By contrast, in the growth mind-set, students care about learning. When they make a mistake or exhibit a deficiency, they correct it (Blackwell et al., 2007; Nussbaum & Dweck, 2007). For them, effort is a *positive* thing: It ignites their intelligence and causes it to grow. In the face of failure, these students escalate their efforts and look for new learning strategies.

Let's look at another student—one who has a growth mind-set—having her first encounter with algebra. She finds it new, hard, and confusing, unlike anything else she has ever learned. But she's determined to understand it. She listens to everything the teacher says, asks the teacher questions after class, and takes her textbook home and reads the chapter over twice. As she begins to get it, she feels exhilarated. A new world of math opens up for her.

It is not surprising, then, that when we have followed students over challenging school transitions or courses, we find that those with growth mind-sets outperform their classmates with fixed mind-sets—even when they entered with equal skills and knowledge. A growth mind-set fosters the growth of ability over time (Blackwell et al., 2007; Mangels, Butterfield, Lamb, Good, & Dweck, 2006; see also Grant & Dweck, 2003).

The Effects of Praise

Many educators have hoped to maximize students' confidence in their abilities, their enjoyment of learning, and their ability to thrive in school by praising their intelligence. We've studied the effects of this kind of praise in children as young as 4 years old and as old as adolescence, in students in inner-city and rural settings, and in students of different ethnicities—and we've consistently found the same thing (Cimpian, Arce, Markman, & Dweck, 2007; Kamins & Dweck, 1999; Mueller & Dweck, 1998): Praising students' intelligence gives them a short burst of pride, followed by a long string of negative consequences.

In many of our studies (see Mueller & Dweck, 1998), 5th grade students worked on a task, and after the first set of problems, the teacher praised some of them for their intelligence ("You must be smart at these problems") and others for their effort ("You must have worked hard at these problems"). We then assessed the students' mind-sets. In one study, we asked students to agree or disagree with mind-set statements, such as, "Your intelligence is something basic about you that you can't really change." Students praised for intelligence agreed with statements like these more than students praised for effort did. In another study, we asked students to define intelligence. Students praised for intelligence made significantly more references to innate, fixed capacity, whereas the students praised for effort made more references to skills, knowledge, and areas they could change through effort and learning. Thus, we found that praise for intelligence tended to put students in a fixed mind-set (intelligence is fixed, and you have it), whereas praise for effort tended to put them in a growth mind-set (you're developing these skills because you're working hard).

We then offered students a chance to work on either a challenging task that they could learn from or an easy one that ensured error-free performance. Most of those praised for intelligence wanted the easy task, whereas most of those praised for effort wanted the challenging task and the opportunity to learn.

Next, the students worked on some challenging problems. As a group, students who had been praised for their intelligence *lost* their confidence in their ability and their enjoyment of the task as soon as they began to struggle with the problem. If success meant they were smart, then struggling meant they were not. The whole point of intelligence praise is to boost confidence and motivation, but both were gone in a flash. Only the effort-praised kids remained, on the whole, confident and eager.

When the problems were made somewhat easier again, students praised for intelligence did poorly, having lost their confidence and motivation. As a group, they did worse than they had done initially on these same types of problems. The students praised for effort showed excellent performance and continued to improve.

Finally, when asked to report their scores (anonymously), almost 40 percent of the intelligence-praised students lied. Apparently, their egos were so wrapped up in their performance that they couldn't admit mistakes. Only about 10 percent of the effort-praised students saw fit to falsify their results.

Praising students for their intelligence, then, hands them not motivation and resilience but a fixed mind-set with all its vulnerability. In contrast, effort or "process" praise (praise for engagement, perseverance, strategies, improvement, and the like) fosters hardy motivation. It tells students what they've done to be successful and what they need to do to be successful again in the future. Process praise sounds like this:

- You really studied for your English test, and your improvement shows it. You read the material over several times, outlined it, and tested yourself on it. That really worked!

- I like the way you tried all kinds of strategies on that math problem until you finally got it.
- It was a long, hard assignment, but you stuck to it and got it done. You stayed at your desk, kept up your concentration, and kept working. That's great!
- I like that you took on that challenging project for your science class. It will take a lot of work—doing the research, designing the machine, buying the parts, and building it. You're going to learn a lot of great things.

What about a student who gets an *A* without trying? I would say, "All right, that was too easy for you. Let's do something more challenging that you can learn from." We don't want to make something done quickly and easily the basis for our admiration.

What about a student who works hard and *doesn't* do well? I would say, "I liked the effort you put in. Let's work together some more and figure out what you don't understand." Process praise keeps students focused, not on something called ability that they may or may not have and that magically creates success or failure, but on processes they can all engage in to learn.

Motivated to Learn

Finding that a growth mind-set creates motivation and resilience—and leads to higher achievement—we sought to develop an intervention that would teach this mind-set to students. We decided to aim our intervention at students who were making the transition to 7th grade because this is a time of great vulnerability. School often gets more difficult in 7th grade, grading becomes more stringent, and the environment becomes more impersonal. Many students take stock of themselves and their intellectual abilities at this time and decide whether they want to be involved with school. Not surprisingly, it is often a time of disengagement and plunging achievement.

We performed our intervention in a New York City junior high school in which many students were struggling with the transition and were showing plummeting grades. If students learned a growth mind-set, we reasoned, they might be able to meet this challenge with increased, rather than decreased, effort. We therefore developed an eight-session workshop in which both the control group and the growth-mind-set group learned study skills, time management techniques, and memory strategies (Blackwell et al., 2007). However, in the growth-mind-set intervention, students also learned about their brains and what they could do to make their intelligence grow.

They learned that the brain is like a muscle—the more they exercise it, the stronger it becomes. They learned that every time they try hard and learn something new, their brain forms new connections that, over time, make them smarter. They learned that intellectual development is not the natural unfolding of intelligence, but rather the formation of new connections brought about through effort and learning.

Students were riveted by this information. The idea that their intellectual growth was largely in their hands fascinated them. In fact, even the most disruptive students suddenly sat still and took notice, with the most unruly boy of the lot looking up at us and saying, "You mean I don't have to be dumb?"

Indeed, the growth-mind-set message appeared to unleash students' motivation. Although both groups had experienced a steep decline in their math grades during their first months of junior high, those receiving the growth-mind-set intervention showed a significant rebound. Their math grades improved. Those in the control group, despite their excellent study skills intervention, continued their decline.

What's more, the teachers—who were unaware that the intervention workshops differed—singled out three times as many students in the growth-mindset intervention as showing marked changes in motivation. These students had a heightened desire to work hard and learn. One striking example was the boy who thought he was dumb. Before this experience, he had never put in any extra effort and often didn't turn his homework in on time. As a result of the training, he worked for hours one evening to finish an assignment early so that his teacher could review it and give him a chance to revise it. He earned a *B+* on the assignment (he had been getting *C*s and lower previously).

Other researchers have obtained similar findings with a growth-mind-set intervention. Working with junior high school students, Good, Aronson, and Inzlicht (2003) found an increase in math and English achievement test scores; working with college students, Aronson, Fried, and Good (2002) found an increase in students' valuing of academics, their enjoyment of schoolwork, and their grade point averages.

To facilitate delivery of the growth-mind-set workshop to students, we developed an interactive computer-based version of the intervention called *Brainology.* Students work through six modules, learning about the brain, visiting virtual brain labs, doing virtual brain experiments, seeing how the brain changes with learning, and learning how they can make their brains work better and grow smarter.

We tested our initial version in 20 New York City schools, with encouraging results. Almost all students (anonymously polled) reported changes in their study habits and motivation to learn resulting directly from their learning of the growth mind-set. One student noted that as a result of the animation she had seen about the brain, she could actually "picture the neurons growing bigger as they make more connections." One student referred to the value of effort: "If you do not give up and you keep studying, you can find your way through."

Adolescents often see school as a place where they perform for teachers who then judge them. The growth mind-set changes that perspective and makes school a place where students vigorously engage in learning for their own benefit.

Going Forward

Our research shows that educators cannot hand students confidence on a silver platter by praising their intelligence. Instead, we can help them gain the tools they need to maintain their confidence in learning by keeping them focused on the *process* of achievement.

Maybe we have produced a generation of students who are more dependent, fragile, and entitled than previous generations. If so, it's time for us to adopt a growth mind-set and learn from our mistakes. It's time to deliver interventions that will truly boost students' motivation, resilience, and learning.

References

Aronson, J., Fried, C., & Good, C. (2002). Reducing the effects of stereotype threat on African American college students by shaping theories of intelligence. *Journal of Experimental Social Psychology, 38,* 113–125.

Binet, A. (1909/1973). *Les idées modernes sur les enfants* [Modern ideas on children]. Paris: Flamarion. (Original work published 1909)

Blackwell, L., Trzesniewski, K., & Dweck, C. S. (2007). Implicit theories of intelligence predict achievement across an adolescent transition: A longitudinal study and an intervention. *Child Development, 78,* 246–263.

Cimpian, A., Arce, H., Markman, E. M., & Dweck, C. S. (2007). Subtle linguistic cues impact children's motivation. *Psychological Science, 18,* 314–316.

Doidge, N. (2007). *The brain that changes itself: Stories of personal triumph from the frontiers of brain science.* New York: Viking.

Dweck, C. S. (1999). *Self-theories: Their role in motivation, personality and development.* Philadelphia: Taylor and Francis/ Psychology Press.

Dweck, C. S. (2006). *Mindset: The new psychology of success.* New York: Random House.

Ericsson, K. A., Charness, N., Feltovich, P. J., & Hoffman, R. R. (Eds.). (2006). *The Cambridge handbook of expertise and expert performance.* New York: Cambridge University Press.

Good, C., Aronson, J., & Inzlicht, M. (2003). Improving adolescents' standardized test performance: An intervention to reduce the effects of stereotype threat. *Journal of Applied Developmental Psychology, 24,* 645–662.

Grant, H., & Dweck, C. S. (2003). Clarifying achievement goals and their impact. *Journal of Personality and Social Psychology, 85,* 541–553.

Hong, Y. Y., Chiu, C., Dweck, C. S., Lin, D., & Wan, W. (1999). Implicit theories, attributions, and coping: A meaning system approach. *Journal of Personality and Social Psychology, 77,* 588–599.

Kamins, M., & Dweck, C. S. (1999). Person vs. process praise and criticism: Implications for contingent self-worth and coping. *Developmental Psychology, 35,* 835–847.

Mangels, J. A., Butterfield, B., Lamb, J., Good, C. D., & Dweck, C. S. (2006). Why do beliefs about intelligence influence learning success? A social-cognitive-neuroscience model. *Social, Cognitive, and Affective Neuroscience, 1,* 75–86.

Mueller, C. M., & Dweck, C. S. (1998). Intelligence praise can undermine motivation and performance. *Journal of Personality and Social Psychology, 75,* 33–52.

Nussbaum, A. D., & Dweck, C. S. (2007). Defensiveness vs. remediation: Self-theories and modes of self-esteem maintenance. *Personality and Social Psychology Bulletin.*

Sternberg, R. (2005). Intelligence, competence, and expertise. In A. Elliot & C. S. Dweck (Eds.), *The handbook of competence and motivation* (pp. 15–30). New York: Guilford Press.

Critical Thinking

1. How does praise motivate students to learn?

2. In what ways might praise impair learning?

3. What is the difference between a "fixed mind-set" and a "growth mind-set"?

Create Central

www.mhhe.com/createcentral

Internet References

Children and praise: Why certain types of praise may backfire
www.psychologytoday.com/blog/parenting-news-you-can-use/201302/ children-praise-why-certain-types-praise-may-backfire

Why praising your child may do more harm than good
www.dailymail.co.uk/health/article-2261903/Why-praising-child-harm -good-Psychologist-claims-comments-makes-unhappy.html

CAROL S. DWECK is the Lewis and Virginia Eaton Professor of Psychology at Stanford University and the author of *Mindset: The New Psychology of Success* (Random House, 2006).

Dweck, Carol S. From *Educational Leadership*, October 2007, pp. 34–39. Copyright © 2007 by ASCD. Reprinted by permission. The Association for Supervision and Curriculum Development is a worldwide community of educators advocating sound policies and sharing best practices to achieve the success of each learner. To learn more, visit ASCD at www. ascd.org.

Article   Prepared by: Eric Landrum, *Boise State University*

Will Behave for Money

Contingency management—sometimes in the form of simply paying people to quit drugs or exercise more—is making the jump from small-scale studies to populationwide programs.

SADIE F. DINGFELDER

Learning Outcomes

After reading this article, you will be able to:

- Describe what is meant by a contingency management intervention.

- Explain the challenge of having positive behaviors continue after the termination of successful contingency management programs.

It was a chilly February day in Concord, N.H., and the audience of a hundred judges, prosecutors and probation officers facing psychologist Douglas Marlowe, JD, PhD, was perhaps even chillier. They'd invited him to speak because newly enacted legislation made it tough to incarcerate nonviolent addicted and mentally ill offenders. Instead, the criminal justice system would provide alternative programs, including drug courts that reward good behavior and punish missteps—a system that many of Marlowe's audience members viewed skeptically.

"I know what a lot of you are thinking right now: 'You want me to take these high-risk antisocial, addicted individuals and give them,'"—Marlowe switches to a mocking voice—*"positive reinforcement."* You're thinking, 'Why should I give them rewards for doing what the rest of us are legally, ethically and morally required to do anyway? Who rewards me for not breaking the law? Who rewards me for not doing drugs?' "But you have to remember there was a time in all your lives when people *did* reward you for doing simple, basic things. People applauded when you went poopie in the potty. . . . Your families did an extraordinarily good job of socializing you, and that is why you are all judges and lawyers and corrections officers today."

It's a talk Marlowe has given many times as chief of science, policy and law for the National Association of Drug Court Professionals. And it works, he says. If you remind people of their own learning histories, they become more receptive to the idea that even hardened criminals can change. Then, he tells them how to use psychology's fundamental laws of reinforcement to help drug-addicted offenders quit—the technique psychologists call contingency management.

For example, some judges send offenders to jail the first time they fail a urine test. But research shows that it's more effective to have gradually escalating penalties. Positive reinforcement —in the form of token gifts and pep-talks from judges—also improves abstinence and recidivism rates. But perhaps the most important quality of a good drug court is regular drug testing and swift consequences, Marlowe says.

"The courtroom is the perfect place to deliver a contingency management intervention," says Marlowe. "I think Skinner himself would have loved a courtroom where punishment and reward were delivered systematically."

The courtroom, however, is just one of many venues where psychologists are applying contingency management on a larger scale than ever before. After spending the better part of a century germinating in psychology labs, psychologist-designed programs are finally taking root in the wider world, especially in drug treatment programs and company wellness initiatives. The results, so far, are nothing short of staggering: Homeless people with HIV are remembering to take their medications, cocaine addicts are showing up to work on time and drug-free, and already healthy workers are becoming even healthier, by increasing their gym attendance and refilling prescriptions on time. As for drug courts, those that faithfully apply principles pioneered by B.F. Skinner are reducing recidivism by upward of 35 percent, according to a research review by Marlowe (in the *Chapman Journal of Criminal Justice*). That success has spurred a huge uptick in drug court participation nationwide, to the point that every state now offers drug courts, says Marlowe.

In essence, Skinner is scaling up.

"We're on the cusp of a new generation of contingency management," says Joshua Klapow, PhD, a public health professor and contingency management researcher at the University of Alabama at Birmingham. "We're taking mom-and-pop projects, designed for a few hundred people at most, and learning how to apply them to whole populations."

Pay to Play

Contingency management programs are often deceptively simple. Most reinforce good behavior by giving people cash or vouchers. For example, a program developed by James

Sorensen, PhD, a University of California, San Francisco, psychology professor, paid HIV-positive methadone patients for taking their antiretroviral medication. By giving 66 participants vouchers worth an average of $5 per day, Sorensen and his colleagues increased pill taking from 56 percent to 78 percent, according to a study published in *Drug and Alcohol Dependence* (Vol. 88, No. 1).

Getting people to take lifesaving medications may not seem like a major accomplishment, but many of the study's participants were homeless, which makes keeping track of medications—not to mention refrigerating them—difficult, Sorensen says. Previous attempts to increase medication compliance by getting people into housing and providing counseling were popular with patients, but didn't improve their medication taking.

"HIV is not the highest thing on your priority list when you are hungry and living without shelter," Sorensen says.

It may seem obvious that paying people will encourage them to do what you want—that is, after all, how all jobs work—but the details are critically important, Sorensen says. For instance, you can't just ask people if they took their medications; you have to objectively verify it and provide reinforcement as quickly as possible. To do that, Sorensen uses MEMS caps, medication bottles that record the time and date of every opening. Also, you don't just want to pay a flat rate—escalating payments for consecutive instances of good behavior are far more effective, according to more than a decade of research by Stephen Higgins, PhD, a psychology professor at the University of Vermont.

"You want people to be more invested as time goes on," Higgins says. That technique worked well in a 2010 study published in *Addiction*. In the study, 166 pregnant smokers provided a urine sample twice a week. If that sample showed no evidence of smoking, the woman earned a shopping voucher worth $6.25, a sum that grew by $1.25 for each consecutive clean sample. If a participant slipped, that reset the payments to $6.25, though participants could get back to their highest-previous payout for returning two more consecutive clean samples.

This payment system may seem complicated, but it helped 34 percent of the women quit smoking, compared with 7.4 percent in the control condition. It also resulted in healthier babies, with women in the incentive program having low-birth-weight infants only 6 percent of the time, compared with 19 percent in the control condition.

So, if contingency management is so effective, even with people who have otherwise intractable problems, what's the catch? They can be more expensive than treatment-as-usual, and many people worry about the ethics of paying some people to do what everyone else does for free. However, such qualms are lessening in the face of the growing health-care crisis, Higgins says.

"There is some resistance or discomfort with the concept of economic incentives, but people are beginning to see that we all pay for unhealthy behaviors anyway," he says. "If somebody is engaging in cigarette smoking, or not managing any chronic illness, or engaging in a sedentary lifestyle, we all end up paying for it through insurance pools, Medicaid or Medicare."

Secrets of Sustainability

Another criticism of contingency management programs is that, like most interventions, effects tend to fade after the program ends. For example, HIV-positive participants in Sorenson's study returned to taking their medications only half the time as soon as the study ended. One solution is to continue the program indefinitely—a tack which, while expensive, would save the health-care system money by reducing the spread of AIDS, Sorenson says.

Another solution is to have contingency management programs pay for themselves. That's the tack Kenneth Silverman, PhD, a psychology professor at Johns Hopkins School of Medicine, is taking. In his lab, drug-free urine samples are the price of admission to a data-entry workplace that pays an average of $10 an hour. The company, Johns Hopkins Data Services, provides its employees—all of whom have drug problems—with a higher base pay rate for workers for each consecutive clean urine sample and gives bonuses for good job performance.

Corporate and university clients defray the cost of the program, but it still requires grant money to run. As a result, people can only work at Johns Hopkins Data Services for the duration of a study—a few years, at most. However, three Maryland employers have expressed a willingness to hire program graduates, who would continue to take random drug tests as a condition of employment, says Anthony DeFulio, PhD, associate director of the program.

"We are harnessing the power of wages to maintain drug abstinence," DeFulio says.

Another way to fund contingency management programs is to have people pay for them themselves. That's the business model of the website www.stickK.com, where you set a goal for yourself and put a price on that goal—say, to lose a pound a week for $5 a week. If you meet your goal, you keep the money. If you don't, that $5 goes to what stickK.com founder Jordan Goldberg calls an "anti-charity," a group that you have identified that you strongly disagree with.

"If you're for gun control, you'll be extra-motivated to keep us from sending your money to the National Rifle Association," says Goldberg, adding that you can choose other consequences, such as betting against friends or sending money to causes you support. (The company makes money through advertising and corporate partnerships.)

These kinds of automated systems are driving the movement of contingency management from small-scale studies to major population-level applications, says Joe Schumacher, PhD, a professor of medicine and contingency management researcher at the University of Alabama at Birmingham.

"Incentive systems are going high-tech," he says.

Schumacher is best known for his work using contingency management to get homeless people with crack addictions to quit, but he's now extending that work to larger populations through a Birmingham-based company called ChipRewards.

ChipRewards recently collaborated with Chattanooga, Tenn., to create a program for 3,200 of the city's workers. They adapted software originally created for business loyalty programs to monitor how often employees, for example, go to the gym, refill prescriptions or attend preventative health screenings. The program automatically issues employees good-behavior points, which can be exchanged online for a variety of products.

That means the same computer program that encourages you to eat nine burritos to get one free may soon help you lose the weight you gained eating all those burritos.

ChipRewards has been hired by several large companies and is being used by more than 100,000 employees, says Klapow, ChipRewards' chief behavioral scientist. In the future, programs like his could create large-scale medication adherence programs for pharmacetical companies, since they stand to earn money if people remember to refill their prescriptions. Adherence also helps people better manage chronic illness and reduces the nation's health-care costs, Klapow says.

Of course, not everyone is enthusiastic about the idea of having companies electronically monitor and reward healthy behaviors. It's one thing to use contingency management to help people with drug addictions, but it's quite another to apply these programs to the wider population, says George Loewenstein, PhD, a behavioral economics professor at Carnegie Mellon University.

A case in point, he says, is weight loss. We can pay people to eat more healthfully—in fact, he did just that in a randomized controlled trial in the June *Journal of General Internal Medicine*. In the study, participants in the contingency management condition lost an average of eight more pounds than people in the control condition. But to address widespread obesity, it's better to lower the cost of fresh fruits and vegetables and raise the cost of processed food, he says.

"Contingency management tackles the problem at the individual level, but we risk losing sight of the real underlying causes of the problem and possibly even blaming the victim," he says.

Then, there's the larger issue of free will. As contingency management systems spread, will we begin to see ourselves as nothing more than rats in Skinner boxes?

"There's the potential of going overboard," Loewenstein says. "Ending up in a 'Walden Two'-type society doesn't seem like such a great outcome to me."

Critical Thinking

1. What is positive reinforcement, and what is the ultimate intended effect of positive reinforcement on a particular behavior of interest?

2. How are drug courts using the principles of contingency management to change the behavior of drug offenders?

3. To what extent are the roots of behavioral problems explored within contingency management scenarios?

Create Central

www.mhhe.com/createcentral

Internet References

Game-based contingency management for smoking cessation
www.c4tbh.org/the-center/what-we-re-up-to/active-projects/game-based-contingency-management-for-smoking-cessation.html

Reward programs help smokers quit, research shows
www.rti.org/newsroom/news.cfm?obj=F63D3E6B-5056-B100-0C72F10915811617

Article Prepared by: Eric Landrum, *Boise State University*

Phobias: The Rationale behind Irrational Fears

DEAN BURNETT

Learning Outcomes

After reading this article, you will be able to:

- Identify some of the basic types of phobias and their formal names.
- Consider the difficulty in diagnosing phobias.

Recently, this section featured an article about the tarantula *Typhochlaena costae*. While the piece was very interesting, this was likely lost on some readers, as it's difficult to focus on details while distracted by the sound of your own screaming.

Arachnophobia is one of the more well-known phobias and can be very potent. Searching the science section for some lunchtime reading is not the sort of activity that typically includes spiders, so to be suddenly confronted, apropos of nothing, by an image of a humungous tarantula probably caught many unawares. How many tablets/phones/laptops were ruined due to being hurled across the room in a panic?

Most would consider this an overreaction. Granted, there are many dangerous species of spider (I'd link to examples but can't find any without pictures, and I'm not a hypocrite) but the odds of encountering one are, in the UK at least, vanishingly small. And even then, the biggest spider is physically no match for a person; a rolled up newspaper is not considered a lethal weapon among humans. Arachnophobes substantially outnumber people who have been genuinely injured by spiders, and yet the irrational fear of spiders is commonplace.

What scares people often makes little logical sense. As I do stand-up comedy on occasion, I'm regularly told I'm "incredibly brave," yet all I'm doing is saying words in front of people. The people who tell me I'm brave think nothing of driving, an often fatal practice. But when you do genuinely fear something for no rational reason, then you may have a phobia.

Phobias are psychologically interesting. There are three possible types: specific phobias, social phobias and agoraphobia. Agoraphobia isn't just a fear of open spaces; it describes a fear of any situation where escape would be difficult and/or help wouldn't be forthcoming. The fact that most such situations occur outside the sufferer's home results in them not going out much, which is probably where the "open spaces" confusion comes from.

Specific phobias are probably the most recognised. Specific phobias are an irrational fear of a specific thing or situation. Specific phobias can be further subdivided into situational (eg claustrophobia), natural environment (eg acrophobia), animal (eg the aforementioned arachnophobia) or blood-injection-injury types (eg ... blood and injections, I guess). You could still have a phobia which doesn't fit any of these descriptors though. Maybe you've got an irrational fear of being categorised? If so, sorry.

Social phobias are where you have an irrational fear of how people will react to you in a situation. The fear of rejection or judgement from others is a powerful force for humans; much of how we think and behave is calibrated around the views and behaviours of others. There's a whole discipline about it. People value the views of others differently of course. One way to reduce the value you place on the opinions of strangers is to read the comments on the internet. Any comments, anywhere.

How do we even develop a fear that is by definition irrational? One explanation is classical conditioning; you experience something bad involving a thing, you associate the bad experience with that thing, then you become afraid of that thing. But clever humans can also learn by observation; you see your mother panicking frantically in response to a wasp when you're a child, you'll likely be afraid of wasps too.

If we are given enough (possibly inaccurate) information, we may just "figure out" things are scary via instructional fear acquisition. Certain horror films are particularly good at this, presenting everyday things like birds as things to be feared, associations which stay with people for a long time. The Final Destination series is particularly cruel in that it tries to make people terrified of "not dying". We may even have evolved to acquire some phobias. Research has shown that primates tend to learn to fear snakes very quickly when compared to other stimuli. If you're evolving in an environment where snakes are a genuine but subtle threat, this tendency would help no doubt. It might explain the spider thing too.

Not so sure about aerophobia though, we probably didn't need to worry about that on the African Savannah.

What can you do about this? It's not like those with phobias aren't aware of them. One of the criteria in the DSM-IV for diagnosing phobias is that the sufferer is aware of the irrational nature of their fear. There are a lot of brain regions involved, like the insular cortex and amygdala. And you can't simply make someone encounter the thing they're afraid of to show them it's harmless. As far as the brain is concerned, the fear response IS a negative physical consequence, so on a subconscious level the phobia is self-fulfilling.

There are methods of treating phobias if they're genuinely debilitating. Systematic desensitisation is one approach (where the source of the phobia is introduced in easily-managed stages), cognitive behavioural therapy, even antidepressants if all else fails.

It's different if you're talking about things like homophobia or Islamophobia, as often these are more likely to be misleadingly named prejudices than genuine phobias. There are fewer options for treating these though; science has tackled many psychological conditions, but there's still no known cure for being a dick.

Critical Thinking

1. How do you think psychologists distinguish between a rational fear and an irrational fear? Think about snakes—could there be both rational fears and irrational fears? Explain.

2. How do different social phobias impact how a person acts around others? Are there sometimes hidden benefits to phobias? Explain.

Create Central

www.mhhe.com/createcentral

Internet References

The rationale behind the irrational
www.smh.com.au/lifestyle/life/the-rationale-behind-the-irrational-20130730-2qw5h.html

Why do people have phobias?
http://io9.com/5881188/why-do-people-have-phobias

Unit 5

UNIT

Prepared by: Eric Landrum, *Boise State University*

Cognitive Processes

As Reggie watches his 4-month-old child, he is convinced that his baby possesses some degree of understanding of the world around her. In fact, Reggie is sure he has one of the smartest babies in the neighborhood. Although he is a proud father, he keeps his thoughts to himself so as not to alienate the parents of less capable babies.

George lives in the same neighborhood as Reggie. George doesn't have any children, but he does own two golden retrievers. Despite George's most concerted efforts, the dogs never come to him when he calls them. In fact, they have been known to run in the opposite direction on occasion. Instead of being furious, George accepts his dogs' disobedience because he is sure the dogs are just not all that bright.

Both of these scenarios illustrate important and interesting ideas about cognition or thought processes. In the first vignette, Reggie ascribes cognitive abilities and high intelligence to his child; in fact, Reggie perhaps ascribes too much cognitive ability to his 4-month-old. On the other hand, George assumes that his dogs are not intelligent—more specifically, that the dogs are incapable of premeditated disobedience—and therefore forgives the dogs.

As you read about Reggie and his child and George and his dogs, you used many well-researched cognitive resources. You deciphered the marks on the page that we call letters and words and made sense of them. As you go through this process of comprehension, you are forming thoughts—effortlessly and automatically—about the meaning of what you are reading. You may think to yourself, "Reggie is really biased about his baby's intellectual abilities" or that "It's not George's dogs who lack intelligence, it is George". As you are processing this information, you are also drawing on your memories of any experiences you may have had with babies or with golden retrievers or both—although before you started reading this scenario, you probably were not thinking about babies or golden retrievers. The story tapped your long-term memory story, and your previous experiences were brought to mind.

What you are experiencing firsthand is cognition, which psychologists like to define as the mental abilities involved in the acquisition, maintenance, and use of knowledge. Cognition is critical to our survival as adults. Of course, people think differently from one another, and psychologists report on interesting differences in cognitive development and in adult cognition.

Psychologists have also studied, and continue to study, nonhuman (animal) cognition and how it helps these creatures adapt to their unique environmental demands. New research presented in this unit even points to the influence of one's environment—such as how clean or messy a room can be—as influencing our attitudes and behaviors. These and other related phenomena form the heart and soul of cognitive science, which is showcased in this unit.

You may be doing many other tasks while reading this unit, such as listening to music in the background, checking your cell phone for text messages, and chatting with your roommate. While it may feel like you are being productive, dividing your attention to complete many tasks at one time may not be as efficient as you think!

Article   Prepared by: Eric Landrum, *Boise State University*

Dangerous Distraction

Psychologists' research shows how cell phones, iPods, and other technologies make us more accident prone and are laying the foundation to make using these gadgets less dangerous.

AMY NOVOTNEY

Learning Outcomes

After reading this article, you will be able to:

- Describe the ways that our use of advanced technology is sometimes dangerous.

- Summarize the suggestions that psychologists offer for using advanced technology more safely.

On a Tuesday evening two years ago, avid cyclists Christy Kirkwood and Debbie Brown were finishing a 13-mile bike ride in Orange County, Calif., when a driver talking on a cell phone swerved into their bike path, knocking Kirkwood off her bike and throwing her 227 feet. The motorist—who had been travelling at 55 mph—continued a short distance before stopping to see what had happened, says University of Utah psychology professor David Strayer, PhD, who served as a consultant on the case.

"The driver thought he'd hit a deer," Strayer recalls.

Kirkwood died from her injuries. Unfortunately, such tragedies have become all too common. In fact, two epidemiological studies—one published in 1997 in *The New England Journal of Medicine* (Vol. 336, No. 7), and another published online in 2005 in the British medical journal *BMJ*—report that talking on the cell phone while driving increases your risk of being in an accident fourfold—an alarming statistic given that 84 percent of Americans own cell phones, according to the Cellular Telecommunications and Internet Association.

In addition, a new report from the AAA Foundation for Traffic Safety finds that more than half of U.S. drivers admit to using a cell phone while driving, at least occasionally. The Human Factors and Ergonomics Society estimates that 2,600 deaths and 330,000 injuries in the United States result each year from driver cell phone use.

Of course, Americans are increasingly using personal digital assistants and other devices that undermine their attention, as well. Last fall, 25 people died and 113 were injured when a commuter train collided head-on with a freight train outside Los Angeles. A National Transportation Safety Board investigation found that text messaging may have played a role: Cell phone records showed the train's engineer had sent a text message 22 seconds before the crash. Last year, Americans sent more than 600 billion text messages—10 times the number they sent three years ago. And 41 percent of us have logged onto the Internet outside our homes or offices, either with a wireless laptop connection or a handheld device, finds a 2007 Pew Internet Project survey.

The problem doesn't just rest with drivers: A 2007 study in *Accident Analysis and Prevention* (Vol. 39, No. 1) by University of South Wales psychologist Julie Hatfield, PhD, found that female pedestrians talking on mobile phones were less likely to look for traffic before stepping into the street and crossed the road more slowly, increasing their risk of colliding with a vehicle.

"As technology and interruption become more and more prevalent, the negative consequences of not paying attention become more pronounced," says Strayer.

With their knowledge of human behavior and cognition, Strayer and other psychologists are exploring the causes of distraction and working to raise awareness of its danger. At the same time, scientists are designing technology that isn't as mentally demanding.

Limited Capacity

Most people have no problem watching television as they jog on a treadmill or chewing gum while they walk. These are largely effortless tasks that require little sustained attention or thinking. And that may be why many believe they can drive and do any number of secondary tasks as well—from eating or applying makeup to scanning for a song on their MP3 players or talking on cell phones.

But cognitive scientists' research shows the brain has limited bandwidth. Research by psychologists Marcel Just, PhD, and Tim Keller, PhD, of the Center for Cognitive Brain Imaging at Carnegie Mellon University, examined brain activity while participants performed two high-level tasks—responding whether auditorily presented sentences were true or false and mentally rotating three-dimensional objects—both separately and then concurrently. Their findings, published in 2001 in *NeuroImage* (Vol. 14, No. 2), suggest when performing the actions together, brain activation, primarily in the temporal and parietal areas of the cortex, was substantially less than the sum of the activation when participants performed the two tasks alone, even though the tasks drew on different brain regions.

This suggests, Just says, that dual-tasking compels the brain to pull from some shared, limited resource, slowing reaction time.

Another new study he led, published last year in *Brain Research* (Vol. 1, No. 205), examines how this central bottleneck plays out when we're driving. Researchers collected fMRI images of 29 undergraduates as they simulated steering a vehicle along a curving road, either undisturbed or while listening to spoken sentences that they judged as true or false. They found that the listening task reduced driving-related brain activity—the spatial processing that takes place in the parietal lobe—by almost 40 percent.

Just says he expects that such reduction in brain activity occurs no matter where the speech comes from, be it a cell phone, fellow passenger or even a talk radio show.

"Processing spoken language is especially insidious in cars because it's automatic," Just says. "When we ask subjects to ignore what's being said, you can still see the activation associated with the processing of that language."

Meanwhile, new research in the December *Journal of Experimental Psychology: Applied* (Vol. 14, No. 4) shows that cell phone conversations are especially detrimental to driving. The researchers found that cell phone users are more likely to drift out of their lanes and miss their exits than people having in-person conversations. Interestingly, conversations with passengers barely affected any of these three measures. In fact, most passengers took an active role in supporting the driver, often by discussing surrounding traffic. This shared situational awareness may help drivers synchronize an in-vehicle conversation with the processing demands of driving, says study author Frank Drews, PhD, a University of Utah psychology professor.

"If you look at the crash risk, you're actually somewhat less likely to be involved in an accident if you have a passenger than if you're driving by yourself," says Strayer, who collaborated with Drews and colleague Monisha Pasupathi, PhD, on the study.

Human factors experts at the Virginia Tech Transportation Institute (VTTI) have gone a step further to explore how driver inattention leads to collisions. With support from the National Highway Traffic Safety Administration, Virginia Tech researchers tracked driver behavior in 100 vehicles equipped with video and sensor devices for one year. During that time, the vehicles traveled nearly 2 million miles and were involved in 69 crashes and 761 near-crashes. Researchers found that nearly 80 percent of crashes and 65 percent of near-crashes involved driver inattention up to three seconds before the event.

"We were actually able to physically see drivers who were talking on their cell phones, dialing, applying makeup and all the other secondary tasks, and there was no question when it was a contributing factor in the occurrence of a crash," says Charlie Klauer, PhD, a senior research associate at VTTI.

The group recently completed a similar study with 40 teen drivers, who are often the most inexperienced and the earliest adopters of new technologies. Klauer expects the results will show that teens have trouble adapting their behaviors in hazardous driving situations and that distractive devices play an even larger role in teen accidents.

New research also establishes the risks of other technologies:

- Drews's as-yet-unpublished research on text messaging suggests the activity may make motorists even more inattentive: A driver's chance of getting into an accident increases sixfold when he is texting.
- Research by Susan Chisholm, PhD, of the Cognitive Ergonomics Research Lab at the University of Calgary, shows the dangers of mixing digital music players and driving. Her study of 19 drivers age 18 to 22 shows that collisions nearly doubled while people performed such iPod tasks as scanning to find a particular song (*Accident Analysis and Prevention,* Vol. 40, No. 2).
- Research by Hatfield and colleague Timothy Chamberlain reveals that in-car TV screens distract drivers of neighboring cars, resulting in reduced reaction times and impaired lane-keeping.
- There's even concern that car navigation systems may distract the very drivers they are trying to help. In a simulated-driving study published in *Human Factors* (Vol. 46, No. 4), researchers found that when motorists entered information into a touch-screen navigation system, they drove outside lane boundaries 21 percent of the time, as compared with undistracted drivers who strayed only 1.5 percent of the time. Even those providing an address to a speech-recognition system left their lanes 6 percent of the time.

Psychology's Solutions

Among the ways psychologists are seeking to improve driver safety is developing technological interventions that reduce a driver's workload. Backed by his own research (*Accident Analysis and Prevention,* Vol. 40, No. 2), John D. Lee, PhD, director of human factors research at the University of Iowa's National Advanced Driving Simulator, has found that providing real-time and post-drive feedback to drivers on how well they're doing behind the wheel will help mitigate distraction. With the help of eye-tracking technology, Lee's team has designed an alert system that monitors what motorists are looking at and warns them when their eyes veer away from the road for more than two seconds.

Meanwhile, at the University of Michigan's Transportation Research Institute, scientists have developed a tool to measure traffic conditions, road surface and visibility. Taking into account the driver's experience level, the equipment prevents the driver from receiving phone calls or entering an address into a navigation system when conditions get dangerous.

Early versions of both devices are already in place in some Saabs and Volvos. University of Michigan psychologist Paul Green, PhD, is hopeful that these types of countermeasures will help get motorists' attention back on the road.

"It isn't the solution, it's just a piece of the solution, but it's an interesting one," Green says.

Psychologists are also working to raise awareness about the dangers of distracted driving.

The VTTI researchers, for example, are working with non-profit organizations, including the Bedford County Combined Accident Reduction Effort, to get the word out about the effects of distracted driving. Thanks to their efforts, the Bedford County driver's education program encourages parents and teens to use driving contracts that limit cell phone and MP3 player use while driving.

In a national effort, in April the National Highway Traffic Safety Administration published "Driver Distraction: A Review of the Current State of Knowledge," which summarizes research on inattentive driving and examines ways to address the problem through public awareness and legislation. In response to the report, APA Chief Executive Officer Norman B. Anderson, PhD, sent a letter to NHTSA urging the organization to identify areas in need of further research and make recommendations for public outreach efforts.

"Distracted driving is a public health hazard without age barriers that is often misunderstood by not only the public but also by both state and local policymakers," Anderson wrote.

Just agrees, noting that a deeper appreciation for the cognitive strain secondary tasks put on our ability to drive or cross the road might help reduce fatalities.

"I think people are unaware of the fact that using a cell phone has such a massive impact on their performance," he says.

Research that compares and quantifies driver distraction could help. One such study, published in *Human Factors* (Vol. 48, No. 2), suggests that a driver talking on a cell phone is more impaired than one with a blood alcohol level exceeding 0.08.

"Most people wouldn't think of getting in a car with someone who's been drinking, but they don't have a big problem getting into a car with someone who's using their cell phone," Just says.

"Most people wouldn't think of getting in a car with someone who's been drinking, but they don't have a big problem getting into a car with someone who's using their cell phone."

—Marcel Just
Center for Cognitive Brain Imaging
at Carnegie Mellon University

Yet efforts to reduce driving while intoxicated went beyond public awareness and increasingly included hefty fines, says Anne McCartt, PhD, vice president of research at the Insurance Institute for Highway Safety. In the case of inattentive drivers, legislation limiting cell phone use may prove effective, she notes. At *Monitor* press time, no state had yet banned all cell phone use by every driver, but 17 states and the District of Columbia do prohibit novice drivers from using cell phones,

and six states and D.C. have outlawed drivers from using handheld phones. Seven states bar text messaging, and nine prohibit teens from the activity.

McCartt admits, however, that these laws either are often not enforced enough to change driver behavior, or they exempt hands-free devices without taking into account the research that shows hands-free devices are just as dangerous as hand-held ones. In fact, some psychologists say hands-free exemptions may encourage motorists originally disinclined to use a cell phone while driving to view the activity as safe.

"To some extent, these laws that didn't pay attention to the science may end up actually making the roads a little less safe," Strayer says.

William C. Howell, PhD, chair of the Human Factors and Ergonomics Society's government relations committee, agrees, noting that policymakers may be passing laws to assure the public that they're curing the problem while they are actually misdiagnosing it.

"Not only do we have a bunch of virtually unenforceable and uninformed laws but a false sense that they represent a fix," he says. "Sure, we need to keep up the pressure for more research, but we know enough about how attention works already to guide strategies for addressing the problem in much more promising directions. In other words, our society should be using what's already known more judiciously in dealing with this problem while doing the research necessary to find even more effective approaches."

One way to do this may be to target driver distraction campaigns toward those on the other end of the phone line, says Drews.

"Cell phone conversations take two people," he says. "We need to convince those callers who know that the person they're talking to is driving to ask the driver to pull over or to call them back later."

He says disseminating this message more broadly to the public might help solve the problem more effectively—and may be more economical—than new vehicle technologies or additional legislation.

"It doesn't cost anything," he notes. "They just have to hang up."

Safety First

Psychologists' research is also informing legislation on the hazards of using these technological devices even when people are not behind the wheel. In 2007, when two pedestrians were killed after being hit while listening to iPods, New York state senator Carl Kruger proposed legislation that would ban the use of handheld devices such as BlackBerrys, iPods and portable video games while crossing streets in major New York cities. Under the bill, pedestrians and bicyclists caught using any kind of electronic device while crossing a street would be hit with a $100 fine. In July, Illinois became the first state to consider a ban on using a cell phone while crossing a street. Neither bill has passed, but several organizations have moved to make pedestrians more aware of the dangers of technologies that divert our attention.

In July, the American College of Emergency Physicians Foundation warned against cell phone use while driving, bicycling, rollerblading or walking, saying they'd noticed a rise in injuries and deaths related to sending texts while engaging in these activities. Also last year, the nonprofit London-based organization Living Streets installed padded lampposts on a busy street in London as part of a safety campaign targeting distracted pedestrians. The move was prompted by a United Kingdom phone survey of 68,000 that found that one in 10 have been injured while walking and texting on their cell phone.

Just says he's not surprised that the use of cell phones while walking has prompted concern.

"Our research extends to other tasks besides driving," Just says. "The reason walking is different, though, is because when you're driving, the person you're most likely to hurt is someone other than yourself."

Psychologists say they hope work like this leads to increased motorist and pedestrian safety, just as campaigns and laws to encourage seat belt use—which has increased every year since NHTSA began collecting data in 1994—led to a steady decrease in passenger fatalities.

Critical Thinking

1. Can technology be dangerous? If so, how so?

2. What can increase the safety of using advanced technology?

3. Why do you think so much of the research on distractions is focus on the drivers of automobiles? What are some other examples of common life situations where a distraction could be potentially dangerous?

Create Central

www.mhhe.com/createcentral

Internet References

Distracted driving: Has technology lead to more dangerous roadways?
www.theoaklandpress.com/general-news/20130815/distracted-driving-has-technology-led-to-more-dangerous-roadways

Drivers and legislators dismiss cellphone risks
www.nytimes.com/2009/07/19/technology/19distracted.html

Novotney, Amy. From *Monitor on Psychology*, February 2009, pp. 32–36. Copyright © 2009 by American Psychological Association. Reproduced with permission. No further reproduction or distribution without written permission from the American Psychological Association.

Article   Prepared by: Eric Landrum, *Boise State University*

The Secret Life of Pronouns by James Pennebaker: What Do "I" and "We" Reveal about Us?

Are There Hidden Messages in Pronouns?
James Pennebaker says computers reveal secret patterns.

JULIET LAPIDOS

Learning Outcomes

After reading this article, you will be able to:

- Explain how the use of function words could be valuable in a situation where lie detection was the goal.

- Describe how frequent users of I-words may be different from others on additional psychological variables.

Some 110 years after the publication of the *Psychopathology of Everyday Life*, in which Sigmund Freud analyzed seemingly trivial slips of the tongue, it's become common knowledge that we disclose more about ourselves in conversation—about our true feelings, or our unconscious feelings—than we strictly intend. Freud focused on errors, but correct sentences can betray us, too. We all have our signature tics. We may describe boring people as "nice" or those we dislike as "weird." We may use archaisms if we're trying to seem smart, or slang if we'd prefer to seem cool. Every time we open our mouths we send out coded, supplementary messages about our frame of mind.

Although much of this information is easy to decode ("nice" for "boring" won't fool anyone), linguistic psychologist James Pennebaker suggests in *The Secret Life of Pronouns* that lots of data remain hidden from even the most astute human observers. "Nice" and "weird" are both content words; he's concerned with function words such as pronouns (I, you, they), articles (a, an, the), prepositions (to, for, of), and auxiliary verbs (is, am, have). We hardly notice these bolts of speech because we encounter them so frequently.

With the help of computer programs to count and scrutinize them, however, patterns emerge.

Sounds enticing; sounds, in fact, rather like a publisher's fantasy pitch, combining the strangely long-lasting craze for language books laced with pop psychology, and the added hook, the modern touch, of a computer that observes and catalogs beyond measly human capacity: a Watson for the psychiatric establishment. To Pennebaker's credit, his claims are fairly modest, especially when compared with those of Deborah Tannen and other practitioners of the word-sleuth genre. (He doesn't promise that if we change our pronoun usage we'll see tangible improvements in our social lives.) The problem is that much of what he turns up is even more modest than he seems to notice. Counting function words as they're used in ordinary life often yields the opposite of what Freud detected in confessions from the couch: confirmation of the obvious.

The most ingenious application Pennebaker proposes for function-word analysis is lie-detection, something of a dark art. Several years ago, Pennebaker and a couple of colleagues recruited 200 students and asked them to write two essays about abortion, one espousing a true belief, the other a falsehood. They asked another group to state their true and false takes in front of a video camera. When judges were called in to figure out which was which, they were accurate 52 percent of the time. (50 percent is chance.) A computer, programmed to look for specific "markers of honesty" gleaned from previous studies, performed much better, with a 67 percent accuracy rate. Truth-tellers, Pennebaker explains, tend to use more words, bigger words, more complex sentences, more exclusive words (except, but, without, as in the sentence "I think this but not that"), and more I-words (I, me, my, etc.). Liars, apparently, trade in simple, straightforward statements lacking in specificity because—Pennebaker posits—it's actually pretty difficult to make stuff up. They avoid self-reference because they don't feel ownership of their expressed views.

When Pennebaker dips into the more general field of "emotion detection" (he calls it that), his word-counting feels a bit Rube Goldberg-ish. After Sept. 11, 2001, Pennebaker and a colleague saved the LiveJournal.com postings of over a thousand amateur bloggers. They found that "bloggers immediately dropped in their use of I-words" following the attacks, and that their use of we-words almost doubled. Pennebaker takes these fluctuations to mean that "shared traumas bring people together," "shared traumas deflect attention away from the self," and that "shared traumas, in many ways, are positive experiences" (because people feel more socially connected). The brute fact that Sept. 11 influenced pronoun usage may interest readers, but Pennebaker's analysis merely reiterates long-held psychological dogma. (Try Googling "shared traumas bring people together.") I can't help but wonder if Pennebaker—albeit unconsciously—interpreted his results to match the conventional wisdom.

Perhaps that's harsh: Certainly there's nothing wrong with devising yet another way to elucidate common human responses, and Pennebaker's experiments are always imaginative. Yet it's often the case that his conclusions, especially the ones he draws from I-word usage, are heavily dependent on context and prior knowledge.

In one chapter, Pennebaker notes that Rudolph Giuliani demonstrated a dramatic increase in I-words during the late spring of 2000, when he was still mayor of New York. Pennebaker fills us in that "Giuliani's life [was] turned upside down . . . . He was diagnosed with prostate cancer, withdrew from the senate race against Hillary Clinton, separated from his wife on national television . . . and, a few days later, acknowledged his 'special friendship' with Judith Nathan." Pennebaker adds that "by early June, friends, acquaintances, old enemies, and members of the press all noticed that Giuliani seemed more genuine, humble, and warm." So it's reasonable to conclude that Giuliani's ascending I-word usage reflected a "personality switch from cold and distanced to someone who [due to a few significant setbacks] was more warm and immediate."

But we already knew that. If we didn't, where would Pennebaker's method leave us? He argues, at various points, that the following groups use I-words at higher rates:

1. Women
2. Followers (not leaders)
3. Truth-tellers (not liars)
4. Young
5. Poor
6. Depressed
7. Afraid (but not angry)
8. Sick

The common thread unifying these seemingly random clusters is, roughly, an enhanced focus on personal experience. Sick and depressed people dwell on their conditions and are thus more likely than their healthy counterparts to talk about themselves. Followers, in conversation with leaders, might be after something: "I was wondering if I could have a raise." That's pretty close to a tautology, though, and does nothing to solve the problem that, without insider information, it's impossible to know which condition or attribute I-usage reflects. A word-count-wannabe presented with Giuliani's speeches might deduce, erroneously, that the mayor had become more truthful, or less leaderly, or had lost money.

For obvious reasons, I'm unusually attuned to my pronoun usage at the moment, and I've noticed a thing or two. I start off this essay with lots of we-words (16 in the introduction), and sprinkle them throughout. With the exception of the section you're currently reading, I drop only one self-referencing I (in the fifth paragraph). I don't deny that this imbalance might mean something. Perhaps it indicates that, like politicians who drone on about what "we" expect from the president, or how "we" want a return to old-fashioned American values, I'm trying to imply audience agreement when, in truth, I have no clue what the audience thinks. But you don't need to count pronouns to figure that out. You only need to know that you're reading a book review.

Critical Thinking

1. What is the difference between content words and function words?

2. What is the pattern of word use differences between truth-tellers and liars?

3. What does the research indicate when one person uses a high frequency of I-words compared to someone else who uses I-words infrequently?

Create Central

www.mhhe.com/createcentral

Internet References

The secret language code
   www.scientificamerican.com/article.cfm?id=the-secret-language-code

It's all about "me": What pronouns reveal about us
   www.pri.org/stories/arts-entertainment/books/how-you-use-pronouns-lie-detectors-personality-projectors5676.html

Article   Prepared by: Eric Landrum, *Boise State University*

The Epidemic of Media Multitasking While Learning

ANNIE MURPHY PAUL

Learning Outcomes

After reading this article, you will be able to:

- Define multitasking, including what actually happens when students think they are multitasking.

- Understand mental fatigue and the impact it has on student performance.

Living rooms, dens, kitchens, even bedrooms: Investigators followed students into the spaces where homework gets done. Pens poised over their "study observation forms," the observers watched intently as the students—in middle school, high school, and college, 263 in all—opened their books and turned on their computers.

For a quarter of an hour, the investigators from the lab of Larry Rosen, a psychology professor at California State University-Dominguez Hills, marked down once a minute what the students were doing as they studied. A checklist on the form included: reading a book, writing on paper, typing on the computer—and also using email, looking at Facebook, engaging in instant messaging, texting, talking on the phone, watching television, listening to music, surfing the web. Sitting unobtrusively at the back of the room, the observers counted the number of windows open on the students' screens and noted whether the students were wearing ear-buds.

Although the students had been told at the outset that they should "study something important, including homework, an upcoming examination or project, or reading a book for a course," it wasn't long before their attention drifted: Students' "on-task behavior" started declining around the two-minute mark as they began responding to arriving texts or checking their Facebook feeds. By the time the 15 minutes were up, they had spent only about 65 percent of the observation period actually doing their schoolwork.

"We were amazed at how frequently they multitasked, even though they knew someone was watching," Rosen says. "It really seems that they could not go for 15 minutes without engaging their devices," adding, "It was kind of scary, actually."

Concern about young people's use of technology is nothing new, of course. But Rosen's study, published in the May issue of *Computers in Human Behavior,* is part of a growing body of research focused on a very particular use of technology: media multitasking while learning. Attending to multiple streams of information and entertainment while studying, doing homework, or even sitting in class has become common behavior among young people—so common that many of them rarely write a paper or complete a problem set any other way.

But evidence from psychology, cognitive science, and neuroscience suggests that when students multitask while doing schoolwork, their learning is far spottier and shallower than if the work had their full attention. They understand and remember less, and they have greater difficulty transferring their learning to new contexts. So detrimental is this practice that some researchers are proposing that a new prerequisite for academic and even professional success—the new marshmallow test of self-discipline—is the ability to resist a blinking inbox or a buzzing phone.

The media multitasking habit starts early. In "Generation M2: Media in the Lives of 8- to 18-Year-Olds," a survey conducted by the Kaiser Family Foundation and published in 2010, almost a third of those surveyed said that when they were doing homework, "most of the time" they were also watching TV, texting, listening to music, or using some other medium. The lead author of the study was Victoria Rideout, then a vice president at Kaiser and now an independent research and policy consultant. Although the study looked at all aspects of kids' media use, Rideout told me she was particularly troubled by its findings regarding media multitasking while doing schoolwork.

"This is a concern we should have distinct from worrying about how much kids are online or how much kids are media multitasking overall. It's multitasking while learning that has the biggest potential downside," she says. "I don't care if a kid wants to tweet while she's watching American Idol, or have music on while he plays a video game. But when students are doing serious work with their minds, they have to have focus."

For older students, the media multitasking habit extends into the classroom. While most middle and high school students don't have the opportunity to text, email, and surf the

Internet during class, studies show the practice is nearly universal among students in college and professional school. One large survey found that 80 percent of college students admit to texting during class; 15 percent say they send 11 or more texts in a single class period.

During the first meeting of his courses, Rosen makes a practice of calling on a student who is busy with his phone. "I ask him, 'What was on the slide I just showed to the class?' The student always pulls a blank," Rosen reports. "Young people have a wildly inflated idea of how many things they can attend to at once, and this demonstration helps drive the point home: If you're paying attention to your phone, you're not paying attention to what's going on in class." Other professors have taken a more surreptitious approach, installing electronic spyware or planting human observers to record whether students are taking notes on their laptops or using them for other, unauthorized purposes.

Such steps may seem excessive, even paranoid: After all, isn't technology increasingly becoming an intentional part of classroom activities and homework assignments? Educators are using social media sites like Facebook and Twitter as well as social sites created just for schools, such as Edmodo, to communicate with students, take class polls, assign homework, and have students collaborate on projects. But researchers are concerned about the use of laptops, tablets, cellphones, and other technology for purposes quite apart from schoolwork. Now that these devices have been admitted into classrooms and study spaces, it has proven difficult to police the line between their approved and illicit uses by students.

In the study involving spyware, for example, two professors of business administration at the University of Vermont found that "students engage in substantial multitasking behavior with their laptops and have non-course-related software applications open and active about 42 percent of the time." The professors, James Kraushaar and David Novak, obtained students' permission before installing the monitoring software on their computers—so, as in Rosen's study, the students were engaging in flagrant multitasking even though they knew their actions were being recorded.

Another study, carried out at St. John's University in New York, used human observers stationed at the back of the classroom to record the technological activities of law students. The spies reported that 58 percent of second- and third-year law students who had laptops in class were using them for "non-class purposes" more than half the time. (First-year students were far more likely to use their computers for taking notes, although an observer did note one first-year student texting just 17 minutes into her very first class—the beginning of her law school career.)

Texting, emailing, and posting on Facebook and other social media sites are by far the most common digital activities students undertake while learning, according to Rosen. That's a problem, because these operations are actually quite mentally complex, and they draw on the same mental resources—using language, parsing meaning—demanded by schoolwork.

David Meyer, a psychology professor at the University of Michigan who's studied the effects of divided attention on learning, takes a firm line on the brain's ability to multitask: "Under most conditions, the brain simply cannot do two complex tasks at the same time. It can happen only when the two tasks are both very simple and when they don't compete with each other for the same mental resources. An example would be folding laundry and listening to the weather report on the radio. That's fine. But listening to a lecture while texting, or doing homework and being on Facebook—each of these tasks is very demanding, and each of them uses the same area of the brain, the prefrontal cortex."

Young people think they can perform two challenging tasks at once, Meyer acknowledges, but "they are deluded," he declares. It's difficult for anyone to properly evaluate how well his or her own mental processes are operating, he points out, because most of these processes are unconscious. And, Meyer adds, "there's nothing magical about the brains of so-called 'digital natives' that keeps them from suffering the inefficiencies of multitasking. They may like to do it, they may even be addicted to it, but there's no getting around the fact that it's far better to focus on one task from start to finish."

Researchers have documented a cascade of negative outcomes that occurs when students multitask while doing schoolwork. First, the assignment takes longer to complete, because of the time spent on distracting activities and because, upon returning to the assignment, the student has to refamiliarize himself with the material.

Second, the mental fatigue caused by repeatedly dropping and picking up a mental thread leads to more mistakes. The cognitive cost of such task-switching is especially high when students alternate between tasks that call for different sets of expressive "rules"—the formal, precise language required for an English essay, for example, and the casual, friendly tone of an email to a friend.

Third, students' subsequent memory of what they're working on will be impaired if their attention is divided. Although we often assume that our memories fail at the moment we can't recall a fact or concept, the failure may actually have occurred earlier, at the time we originally saved, or encoded, the memory. The moment of encoding is what matters most for retention, and dozens of laboratory studies have demonstrated that when our attention is divided during encoding, we remember that piece of information less well—or not at all. As the unlucky student spotlighted by Rosen can attest, we can't remember something that never really entered our consciousness in the first place. And a study last month showed that students who multitask on laptops in class distract not just themselves but also their peers who see what they're doing.

Fourth, some research has suggested that when we're distracted, our brains actually process and store information in different, less useful ways. In a 2006 study in the *Proceedings of the National Academy of Sciences,* Russell Poldrack of the University of Texas–Austin and two colleagues asked participants to engage in a learning activity on a computer while also carrying out a second task, counting musical tones that sounded while they worked. Study subjects who did both tasks at once appeared to learn just as well as subjects who did the first task by itself. But upon further probing, the former group proved much less adept at extending and extrapolating their new knowledge to novel contexts—a key capacity that psychologists call transfer.

Brain scans taken during Poldrack's experiment revealed that different regions of the brain were active under the two conditions, indicating that the brain engages in a different form of memory when forced to pay attention to two streams of information at once. The results suggest, the scientists wrote, that "even if distraction does not decrease the overall level of learning, it can result in the acquisition of knowledge that can be applied less flexibly in new situations."

Finally, researchers are beginning to demonstrate that media multitasking while learning is negatively associated with students' grades. In Rosen's study, students who used Facebook during the 15-minute observation period had lower grade-point averages than those who didn't go on the site. And two recent studies by Reynol Junco, a faculty associate at Harvard's Berkman Center for Internet & Society, found that texting and using Facebook—in class and while doing homework—were negatively correlated with college students' GPAs. "Engaging in Facebook use or texting while trying to complete schoolwork may tax students' capacity for cognitive processing and preclude deeper learning," write Junco and a co-author. (Of course, it's also plausible that the texting and Facebooking students are those with less willpower or motivation, and thus likely to have lower GPAs even aside from their use of technology.)

Meyer, of the University of Michigan, worries that the problem goes beyond poor grades. "There's a definite possibility that we are raising a generation that is learning more shallowly than young people in the past," he says. "The depth of their processing of information is considerably less, because of all the distractions available to them as they learn."

Given that these distractions aren't going away, academic and even professional achievement may depend on the ability to ignore digital temptations while learning—a feat akin to the famous marshmallow test. In a series of experiments conducted more than 40 years ago, psychologist Walter Mischel tempted young children with a marshmallow, telling them they could have two of the treats if they put off eating one right away. Follow-up studies performed years later found that the kids who were better able to delay gratification not only achieved higher grades and test scores but were also more likely to succeed in school and their careers.

Two years ago, Rosen and his colleagues conducted an information-age version of the marshmallow test. College students who participated in the study were asked to watch a 30-minute videotaped lecture, during which some were sent eight text messages while others were sent four or zero text messages. Those who were interrupted more often scored worse on a test of the lecture's content; more interestingly, those who responded to the experimenters' texts right away scored significantly worse than those participants who waited to reply until the lecture was over.

This ability to resist the lure of technology can be consciously cultivated, Rosen maintains. He advises students to take "tech breaks" to satisfy their cravings for electronic communication: After they've labored on their schoolwork uninterrupted for 15 minutes, they can allow themselves two minutes to text, check websites, and post to their hearts' content. Then the devices get turned off for another 15 minutes of academics.

Over time, Rosen says, students are able extend their working time to 20, 30, even 45 minutes, as long as they know that an opportunity to get online awaits. "Young people's technology use is really about quelling anxiety," he contends. "They don't want to miss out. They don't want to be the last person to hear some news, or the ninth person to 'like' someone's post." Device-checking is a compulsive behavior that must be managed, he says, if young people are to learn and perform at their best.

Rideout, director of the Kaiser study on kids and media use, sees an upside for parents in the new focus on multitasking while learning. "The good thing about this phenomenon is that it's a relatively discrete behavior that parents actually can do something about," she says. "It would be hard to enforce a total ban on media multitasking, but parents can draw a line when it comes to homework and studying—telling their kids, 'This is a time when you will concentrate on just one thing.' "

Parents shouldn't feel like ogres when they do so, she adds. "It's important to remember that while a lot of kids do media multitask while doing homework, a lot of them don't. One out of five kids in our study said they 'never' engage in other media while doing homework, and another one in five said they do so only 'a little bit.' This is not some universal norm that students and parents can't buck. This is not an unreasonable thing to ask of your kid."

So here's the takeaway for parents of Generation M: Stop fretting about how much they're on Facebook. Don't harass them about how much they play video games. The digital native boosters are right that this is the social and emotional world in which young people live. Just make sure when they're doing schoolwork, the cellphones are silent, the video screens are dark, and that every last window is closed but one.

Critical Thinking

1. What is the impact of multitasking on grades? If a student wanted to improve his or her grades, what would be the optimum strategy regarding schoolwork and study?

2. Think about the modern day version of the marshmallow test. If a student has to check for text messages 8 times in 30 minutes, what do you think this means for his or her ability to deeply process and learn?

Create Central

www.mhhe.com/createcentral

Internet References

Media multitasking: The new marshmallow test
   http://blogs.edweek.org/teachers/teaching_now/2013/05/media_
   multitasking_the_new_marshmallow_test.html

Expert advice: Kids and multitasking
   www.commonsensemedia.org/educators/blog/expert-article-kids
   -and-multitasking

Article   Prepared by: Eric Landrum, *Boise State University*

Pigeons, Like Humans, Can Behave Irrationally

SANDRA UPSON

Learning Outcomes

After reading this article, you will be able to:

- Understand the types of behaviors that pigeons participate in.

- Appreciate some of the parallels between human and animal behavior.

Gambling may seem like a uniquely human activity. Twinkling slot machines and croupiers in starched white shirts may be about as far from the natural world as we can get. Yet one team of researchers, led by psychologist Thomas Zentall at the University of Kentucky, has taken a particular interest in how animals gamble. The group reasons that if we can identify irrational behaviors in animals, such as gambling, we might discover common brain mechanisms related to such seemingly complex behaviors.

According to behavioral ecologists, Zentall recounts, animals should never gamble because evolution has honed them over many thousands of years into optimal foragers. That is, animals should expend the least amount of energy and time to consume the greatest number of calories. Yet this is not always the case.

In a recent series of experiments Zentall and his colleagues have found that pigeons make some of the same common reasoning mistakes as humans do. For example, they exhibit a strong tendency to select a riskier option over a smaller, safer reward. In one avian version of a casino, pigeons had to choose between a low-probability payoff of 10 food pellets (versus zero) and a high-probability payoff of three pellets. (The expected value is two pieces of kibble in the first case and three in the second.) Although at first the birds chose the more profitable three-pellet option, over time they switched strategies and went for the suboptimal 10-pellet gamble again and again. Research on human gamblers reveals a complementary trend. Compulsive gamblers pay little attention to their losses, tending to remember when they won but not the frequency of winning.

Other studies have shown that pigeons fall prey to the sunk cost fallacy, just as humans do. We might sit through a disappointing movie on the off chance it improves and thus redeems our ticket purchase, or we might stick with a failing business because we hope that our fortunes will change. Similarly, pigeons will continue working on a challenging task to earn a snack rather than switching mid-task to a much easier activity with the same reward. "There's something fundamental about this tendency," Zentall says. "It's not just something cultural for us, such as a belief that we should finish what we've started."

At the annual meeting of the *American Psychological Association* this past weekend, Zentall presented new research on the pigeon version of yet another cognitive bias, the "less is more" heuristic. When making rapid judgments between two things, we tend to give greater weight to the average quality of our options rather than the overall quantity. For example, in one famous experiment done by behavioral scientist Christopher Hsee, participants were asked to rate two collections of dinnerware. One set consisted of 24 pristine plates. The other set contained 31 perfect pieces plus nine broken ones. The participants tended to place a higher value on the smaller set—even though the second option contained more flawless dishes.

Rhesus macaques display similar behavior. They like but do not love to eat a slice of cucumber as a snack. Yet if you let a monkey choose between a grape plus a cucumber or just a grape, the monkey will choose just the grape. Like humans, these monkeys appear to judge their choices by the average quality of the offer, rather than the quantity, suggesting that this cognitive shortcut has deep evolutionary roots.

Now for the pigeons. Instead of grapes or plates, the pigeons were presented with peas, which they find delicious. They consider milo seeds, also known as sorghum, less appealing but still palatable. When given the option of either a sole pea or a pea and a milo seed, however, the birds chose the pea and the milo seed. They appeared to behave more rationally than either humans or monkeys.

To look more closely at this surprising behavior, the team divided the pigeons into two groups to see if the birds' level of hunger might play a role. When the pigeons were hungrier, they made the optimal choice, going for the pea and the milo seed. When the pigeons were only somewhat hungry, they suddenly behaved like humans and chose just the pea. "If it's really important to them they go for quantity," Zentall explains. "If they're not so hungry they go for quality."

Zentall suggests that across species, quality may be easier—that is, faster—to judge than quantity. In the wild pigeons typically face competition from their fellow birds, so the bird that reacts the fastest to the sight of food is most likely to snag the morsel. Our ancestors likely faced similar pressures.

As for why pigeons seem to outperform us some of the time? Zentall suggests that motivation may be the answer. Our biases are not inviolable rules of behavior—they are tendencies we reveal when making quick decisions. When humans are tested in the lab, the stakes are typically very low. Given sufficient motivation, we, too, become more likely to think through a scenario and make the better choice.

Critical Thinking

1. What is the sunk cost fallacy, and how does that phenomenon influence how humans make decisions over time?

2. Decision-making biases tend to emerge more when humans are in a hurry to make a decision rather than when deliberation is possible. Why do you think this is so? Explain.

Create Central

www.mhhe.com/createcentral

Internet References

Are animals as irrational as humans?
www.plosbiology.org/article/info%3Adoi%2F10.1371%2Fjournal.pbio.0020434

Are we rational animals?
http://psychcentral.com/blog/archives/2011/01/31/are-we-rational-animal

Article Prepared by: Eric Landrum, *Boise State University*

Physical Order Produces Healthy Choices, Generosity, and Conventionality, Whereas Disorder Produces Creativity

KATHLEEN D. VOHS, JOSEPH P. REDDEN, AND RYAN RAHINEL

Learning Outcomes

After reading this article, you will be able to:

- Understand how the organization or disorganization of one's environment can influence other attitudes and decisions made in that environment.

- Observe the basic elements of research method designs and how comparisons between groups can yield interesting and important outcomes.

The human mind likes order, rules, and tradition. Yet disorder, unruliness, and unconventionality also hold appeal. In fact, both order and disorder are prevalent in nature (Koole & Van den Berg, 2005) and in culture (Baumeister, 2005). Order and disorder, therefore, might be functional, particularly insofar as they could activate different psychological states and benefit different kinds of outcomes.

Past work suggests that feelings and inferences about order and disorder exist across a range of cultures and constructs. At the trait level, preference for order is associated with valuing tradition, convention, and conservatism. In contrast, individuals at ease with disorder can tolerate ambiguity and place a high value on freedom (Dollinger, 2007; Feather, 1971; Kaplan & Kaplan, 1989). At a cultural level, the anthropologist Mary Douglas (1966) noted that physical order often is linked to morality, patterns, and correctness, whereas disorder is linked to deviations and taboo.

We reasoned that such dispositional differences in reactions to order versus disorder might translate to the situational level. We hypothesized that orderly environments would encourage adherence to social convention and overall conservatism, whereas disorderly environments would encourage people to seek novelty and unconventional routes. Three experiments supported these hypotheses.

Scholarship on the behavioral effects of physical orderliness largely comes from sociology's broken-windows theory (Keizer, Lindenberg, & Steg, 2008; Wilson & Kelling, 1982), which posits that minor signs of disorder can cause much bigger consequences, such as delinquency and criminality. Psychology has shown that a related dimension, cleanliness (e.g., exposure to cleaning-related scents), leads to morally good behaviors, such as reciprocity (Liljenquist, Zhong, & Galinsky, 2010; Mazar & Zhong, 2010; Zhong, Strejcek, & Sivanathan, 2010). The broad conclusion from both fields is that environmental disorder impels bad or even destructive behavior, whereas cleanliness supports normatively good and moral outcomes.

Our point of departure from prior work was our reasoning that order and disorder are common states of the environment that activate different mind-sets, which in turn might benefit different outcomes. Little work has investigated whether physical orderliness influences behaviors that are not decidedly moral. Furthermore, to our knowledge, no work has shown positive consequences of a disorderly environment. The current work explored both possibilities, and in doing so established that variations in physical orderliness produce effects that are wider ranging than those currently known. Our findings imply that varying the environment can be an effective way to shape behavior.

We tested outcomes that have been linked to tradition and convention, namely, healthy food choices (Roberts, Jackson, Fayard, Edmonds, & Meints, 2009), financial generosity (Schweizer, 2008), creativity (Simonton, 1999), and preference for tradition (Eidelman, Crandall, & Pattershall, 2009). We predicted that physical order, more than relative disorder, would lead to the desirable behaviors of healthy eating and charitable giving (Experiment 1). We also hypothesized that there would be positive outcomes from physical disorder. This novel hypothesis took the form of expecting that a disorderly room, compared with an orderly one, would enhance the desirable behavior of creativity (Experiment 2). Last, Experiment 3 tested the normatively neutral outcome of preference for tradition versus novelty; we predicted that this preference would depend on the physical environment (i.e., a cross-over effect).

Experiment 1: Environmental Order Encourages Healthy Choices and Charitable Donations

Experiment 1 tested whether physical order would promote healthy choices and charitable behavior. On the basis of hints in the literature that convention is associated with healthy eating (Roberts et al., 2009) and cleanliness with giving (Liljenquist et al., 2010), we predicted that people placed in an orderly environment would be more likely to choose a healthy snack over an unhealthy snack than would people placed in a disorderly environment and that they would also donate more money to charity.

Method
Participants and Design

Thirty-four Dutch students participated. They were randomly assigned to an orderly or a disorderly condition.

Procedure

We manipulated environmental orderliness by having participants complete the study in an orderly or disorderly room. The rooms were adjacent (and therefore had the same sunlight exposure and view), and they had the same size and configuration. The main difference was their orderliness. The disorderly room had papers and common office items scattered throughout the work space. The orderly room had no clutter.

Participants first were told that they would receive €3 for participating. Then they completed unrelated filler questionnaires intended to ensure that all participants spent the same amount of time (10 min) in the orderly or disorderly environment.

Next, participants were presented with an opportunity to donate to a charity. They learned that the department in which the study was being conducted supports a charity that supplies children with toys and books (Fennis, Janssen, & Vohs, 2009). Participants wrote the amount, if any, they chose to donate on a sheet of paper, which they placed into a sealed envelope (so that self-presentation concerns would be dispelled).

The researcher then discussed the concepts measured in the filler questionnaires as a partial debriefing. Upon exiting, participants were allowed to take an apple or chocolate bar, which constituted the measure of healthy food choice. Participants then were fully debriefed.

Results and Discussion

The results supported our predictions. Participants who completed the study in the orderly room donated more than twice as much as those who completed the study in the disorderly room ($M = €3.19$, $SD = 3.01$, vs. $M = €1.29$, $SD = 1.76$), $t(32) = 2.24$, $p = .03$, $d = 0.73$. Fully 82% of participants in the orderly room donated some money, versus 47% in the disorderly room, $\chi^2(1, N = 34) = 4.64$, $p < .04$, $\varphi = .37$. Also as predicted, participants in the orderly room chose the apple (over the chocolate) more often than those in the disorderly room ($M = 67\%$ vs. $M = 20\%$), $\chi^2(1, N = 30) = 6.65$, $p < .05$, $\varphi = .44$.

The results confirmed the prediction that an orderly (vs. disorderly) environment leads to more desirable, normatively good behaviors. Sitting in a tidy room led to healthier food choices and greater financial support of a charitable institution, relative to sitting in a cluttered room.

Experiment 2: Environmental Disorder Stimulates Creativity

Experiment 1 demonstrated that environmental order, more than disorder, encourages healthy choices and charitable behavior. Experiment 2 took a different tack and investigated a context in which a disorderly environment could produce normatively desirable behavior. Given that orderliness is paired with valuing convention, a disorderly state should encourage breaking with convention, which is needed to be creative (Simonton, 1999). Therefore, we predicted that being in a disorderly environment would have the desirable effect of stimulating creativity.

Experiment 2 improved upon Experiment 1 in using two identical rooms. That is, for Experiment 2, we simply altered each room to be either orderly or disorderly. These changes helped to assuage concerns that differences other than variations in orderliness could account for any observed differences in results between conditions.

Method
Participants and Design

Forty-eight American students participated in a two-condition (orderly vs. disorderly environment) design.

Procedure

Participants completed tasks in a room arranged to be either orderly or disorderly. To measure creativity, we adapted the Alternative Uses Task (Guilford, 1967). Participants imagined that a company wanted to create new uses for the ping-pong balls that it manufactured. They were instructed to list up to 10 new uses for ping-pong balls.

Scoring Creativity

Participants' ideas were scored for their creativity. Two coders, blind to condition, rated each idea on a 3-point scale (1 = *not at all creative*, 3 = *very creative*; $\kappa = .81$, $p < .01$); disagreements were resolved through discussion.

Creative output was operationalized in three ways. One method was to average the creativity scores for each participant.

The second method was to sum each participant's scores (overall creativity). The third method was to count each participant's highly creative ideas (Friedman & Förster, 2001), that is, those that the coders rated a 3 on the scoring metric.

Results

We predicted that participants in the disorderly room would generate more creative solutions than would participants in the orderly room. This prediction was supported by the measure of average creativity, which differed by condition (disorderly: $M = 1.80$, $SD = 0.47$; orderly: $M = 1.41$, $SD = 0.48$), $t(46) = 2.82$, $p < .01$, $d = 0.83$. Likewise, analyses of overall creativity showed that participants in the disorderly room were more creative ($M = 7.9$, $SD = 4.40$) than those in the orderly room ($M = 5.6$, $SD = 3.10$), $t(46) = 2.08$, $p < .05$, $d = 0.61$. Analyses of the number of highly creative ideas also supported our hypothesis. As expected, participants in the disorderly room generated more highly creative ideas ($M = 1.00$, $SD = 1.35$) than did participants in the orderly room ($M = 0.21$, $SD = 0.41$), $t(46) = 2.74$, $p < .01$, $d = 0.81$.

Finally, to rule out the alternate explanation that effort rather than creativity drove the results, we tested whether the number of ideas produced differed by condition. It did not, $t < 1$.

Discussion

Being creative is aided by breaking away from tradition, order, and convention (Dollinger, 2007; Simonton, 1999), and a disorderly environment seems to help people do just that. Three operationalizations of creativity supported our prediction that sitting in a messy, disorderly room would stimulate more creative ideas than sitting in a tidy, orderly room. It could be that our disorderly laboratory violated participants' expectations, which can aid creativity (Ritter et al., 2012). Our preferred explanation, though, is that cues of disorder can produce creativity because they inspire breaking free of convention. What is more, we observed a previously undocumented effect—that cues of disorder can produce highly desirable outcomes.

Experiment 3: Environmental Effects on Preference for Traditional versus Novel Options

The prior experiments' outcomes had a normative slant to them, in that donating money to help needy children, eating healthy foods, and being creative are esteemed and widely valued behaviors. Experiment 3 tested whether orderly and disorderly environments can influence outcomes that are devoid of a normative interpretation (see the Pretest section in Results).

We measured preference for a new versus a classic option. Participants completed a task that ostensibly would help local restaurateurs create new menus. One of the options was labeled differently in the two conditions. That option was framed as either classic, the established choice, or new, an unexplored option (Eidelman et al., 2009). We predicted that participants would choose the option framed as classic more when seated in an orderly (vs. disorderly) room, and, conversely, that they would choose the option framed as new more when seated in a disorderly (vs. orderly) room.

The physical location of the rooms was changed from the locations used in Experiments 1 and 2. As in Experiment 2, two rooms were made up to be orderly or disorderly, depending on condition. These changes helped to reduce concerns that features particular to the rooms, rather than the rooms' orderliness, drove any difference in results between the conditions.

Method
Participants and Design

One hundred eighty-eight American adults participated in a 2 (environmental orderliness: orderly vs. disorderly) $\times$ 2 (label: classic vs. new) between-subjects design.

Procedure

We manipulated environmental orderliness by randomly assigning participants to complete the study in a room arranged to be orderly or disorderly.

Participants were told that the study concerned preferences for menu items at a nearby snack shop. Participants imagined that they were getting a fruit smoothie with a "boost" (i.e., additional ingredients). Three types of boosts were available: health, wellness, or vitamin. We varied the framing of the health-boost option so that it cued the concept of convention or novelty. To cue novelty, we added a star with the word *new* superimposed. To cue convention, we added a star with the word *classic* super-imposed. The dependent measure was choice of the health-boost option.

Pretest

We conducted a pretest to confirm whether the choice of the classic or new option was indeed devoid of normative overtones. As in the main experiment, participants ($n = 28$) read about the local snack shop and its fruit smoothies. They read that the menu display showed a boost option with a "new" sign next to it, whereas another boost had a "classic" sign. Participants rated which option, if either, was the "correct" option, the "right" option, and the "better" option, using a sliding scale ($0 = new$, $50 = neither$, $100 = classic$).

Results
Pretest

As expected, the overwhelming reaction in the pretest was that neither the classic nor the new option was normatively correct. For all three judgments of normativeness, the average rating was not statistically different from 50, the numerical rating corresponding to *neither* (correct option: $M = 52.50$, $SD = 21.90$; right option: $M = 50.29$, $SD = 21.18$; better option: $M = 48.04$, $SD = 22.19$), $ts < 1$. These data confirm our claim that this experiment tested the effects of physical orderliness on outcomes that do not reflect what is normatively good or correct—a novel contribution to the literature.

Main Experiment

We predicted an interaction between label and environmental orderliness, such that being in the orderly room would make the classic option more appealing, whereas being in the disorderly room would make the new option more appealing. We performed a logistic regression with choice of the health boost as the dependent measure, and environmental orderliness and label as between-subject factors. The main effects were not significant (χ^2s < 0.5), whereas the expected interaction was, $\chi^2(1, N = 188) = 7.59$, $p < .01$, $\varphi = .20$.

Planned contrasts supported our predictions. When the health boost was framed as classic, participants were more likely to choose it if they were in the orderly room ($M = 35\%$) than if they were in the disorderly room ($M = 18\%$), $\chi^2(1, N = 188) = 3.73$, $p = .05$, $\varphi = .20$. In contrast, when the health boost was framed as novel, participants showed the reverse pattern (disorderly room: $M = 36\%$; orderly room: $M = 17\%$), $\chi^2(1, N = 188) = 4.53$, $p < .04$, $\varphi = .22$.

Discussion

Experiment 3 showed that environmental order affected preferences for established versus novel outcomes. The results supported our prediction that an orderly environment would activate a mind-set of following convention whereas a disorderly environment would promote exploring new avenues. Highlighting the novelty of these results were the conclusions from a pretest, which confirmed that there was no normatively correct option in this context. Rather, orderliness seemed to encourage a general mind-set for conservatism and tradition, and disorder had the effect of stimulating the desire for the unknown.

General Discussion

Order and disorder are concepts as old as the physical objects that create them. Considering that neither order nor disorder has won out (i.e., humans have not sought to eliminate either one), we reasoned that each environment suits different outcomes. Drawing on work from personality psychology, moral psychology, and even sociology, we hypothesized that physical order would promote a mind-set of tradition and convention, which would encourage healthy behavior, charitable donations, and upholding the status quo. We also hypothesized that physical disorder would promote a mind-set of unconventionality, leading to enhanced creativity and an appreciation for novelty. Three experiments supported our predictions.

The results were robust across a range of methodological and conceptual changes. We used a total of six rooms, which suggests that the results were not due to the particulars of specific places. The findings obtained among diverse samples of participants—European students, American students, and American community adults. The experiments took a multimethod, multimeasure approach, for example, by measuring conventionality as both reduced creativity and preference for established routes. Our investigation included choice measures, and we measured behavior (healthy-snack choice, donations, and creativity) three times. The consistency of results across methodological, sample, and physical changes speaks to the effect's robustness.

Prior work has tended to characterize disorderly environments as capable of producing wild, harmful, or bad behavior, and orderly environments as evoking honesty, prosociality, and goodness. The results of our experiments suggest that the effects of physical orderliness are broader and more nuanced than that. Disorderly environments seem to inspire breaking free of tradition, which can produce fresh insights. Orderly environments, in contrast, encourage convention and playing it safe. Such tendencies can imply good, bad, or simply neutral consequences depending on the context. In short, our work demonstrates that understanding the psychological consequences of physical orderliness requires a broad perspective that includes a range of normative and nonnormative outcomes.

Conclusion

There exists a large and growing industry centered on instilling environmental orderliness. Proponents claim that people see measurable life improvements from becoming neat and tidy, and the industry can point to multiple billions of dollars in annual revenue as evidence of success. In contrast, many creative individuals with Nobel prizes and other ultra-prestigious awards prefer—and in fact cultivate—messy environments as an aid to their work (Abrahamson & Freedman, 2007). One such person was Einstein, who is widely reported to have observed, "If a cluttered desk is a sign of a cluttered mind, of what, then, is an empty desk a sign?" (e.g., www.goodreads.com).

As is the case with many vociferous debates, it seems that both sides have a point. Orderly environments promote convention and healthy choices, which could improve life by helping people follow social norms and boosting well-being. Disorderly environments stimulate creativity, which has widespread importance for culture, business, and the arts. Our systematic investigations revealed that both kinds of settings can enable people to harness the power of these environments to achieve their goals.

References

Abrahamson, E., & Freedman, D. H. (2007). *A perfect mess: The hidden benefits of disorder.* New York, NY: Little, Brown.

Baumeister, R. F. (2005). *The cultural animal: Human nature, meaning, and social life.* New York, NY: Oxford University Press.

Dollinger, S. J. (2007). Creativity and conservatism. *Personality and Individual Differences, 43,* 1025–1035.

Douglas, M. (1966). *Purity and danger.* London, England: Routledge.

Eidelman, S., Crandall, C. S., & Pattershall, J. (2009). The existence bias. *Journal of Personality and Social Psychology, 97,* 765–775.

Feather, N. T. (1971). Organization and discrepancy in cognitive structures. *Psychological Review, 78,* 355–379.

Fennis, B. M., Janssen, L., & Vohs, K. D. (2009). Acts of benevolence: A limited-resource account of compliance with charitable requests. *Journal of Consumer Research, 35,* 906–924.

Friedman, R., & Förster, J. (2001). The effects of promotion and prevention cues on creativity. *Journal of Personality and Social Psychology, 81,* 1001–1013.

Guilford, J. P. (1967). *The nature of human intelligence.* New York, NY: McGraw-Hill.

Kaplan, R., & Kaplan, S. (1989). *The experience of nature: A psychological perspective.* New York, NY: Cambridge University Press.

Keizer, K., Lindenberg, S., & Steg, L. (2008). The spreading of disorder. *Science, 322,* 1681–1685.

Koole, S. L., & Van den Berg, A. E. (2005). Lost in the wilderness: Terror management, action orientation, and nature evaluation. *Journal of Personality and Social Psychology, 88,* 1014–1028.

Liljenquist, K., Zhong, C.-B., & Galinsky, A. D. (2010). The smell of virtue: Clean scents promote reciprocity and charity. *Psychological Science, 21,* 381–383.

Mazar, N., & Zhong, C.-B. (2010). Do green products make us better people? *Psychological Science, 21,* 494–498.

Ritter, S. M., Damian, R. I., Simonton, D. K., van Baaren, R., Strick, M., Derks, J., & Dijksterhuis, A. (2012). Diversifying experiences enhance cognitive flexibility. *Journal of Experimental Social Psychology, 48,* 961–964.

Roberts, B. W., Jackson, J. J., Fayard, J. V., Edmonds, G., & Meints, J. (2009). Conscientiousness. In M. R. Leary & R. H. Hoyle (Eds.), *Handbook of individual differences in social behavior* (pp. 369–381). New York, NY: Guilford Press.

Schweizer, P. (2008). *Makers and takers: Why conservatives work harder, feel happier, have closer families, take fewer drugs, give more generously, value honesty more, are less materialistic and envious, whine less and even hug their children more than liberals.* New York, NY: Random House.

Simonton, D. K. (1999). Creativity as blind variation and selective retention: Is the creative process Darwinian? *Psychological Inquiry, 10,* 309–328.

Wilson, J. Q., & Kelling, G. (1982, March). Broken windows. *The Atlantic Monthly,* pp. 29–38.

Zhong, C.-B., Strejcek, B., & Sivanathan, N. (2010). A clean self can render harsh moral judgment. *Journal of Experimental Social Psychology, 46,* 859–862.

Critical Thinking

1. Do you tend to prefer an organized personal environment or a disorganized personal environment? Why? Do you think that may influence how others see you? Explain.

2. Thinking about creativity, which environment lead to greater perceptions of creativity? Why do you think this is so? Explain.

Create Central

www.mhhe.com/createcentral

Internet References

Does your office betray your personality?
www.apa.org/monitor/mar02/officebetray.aspx

The personality of personal spaces
www.utexas.edu/features/archive/2002/spaces.html

Vohs, Kathleen D.; Redden, Joseph P.; Rahinel, Ryan. From *Psychological Science*, vol. 24, no.8, August 2013. Copyright © 2013 by Sage Publications—JOURNALS. Reprinted by permission via Rightslink.

Unit 6

UNIT

Prepared by: Eric Landrum, *Boise State University*

Emotion and Motivation

Jasmine's sister was a working mother who always reminded Jasmine about how exciting life on the road was as a sales representative. Jasmine stayed home because she wanted to take care of her children, 2-year-old Jessica, 4-year-old Kristen, and newborn Jade. One day, Jasmine was having a difficult time with the children. The baby, Jade, had been crying all day from colic. The other two children had been bickering over their toys. Jasmine, realizing that it was already 5:15 pm and her husband would be home any minute, frantically started preparing dinner. She wanted to fix a nice dinner so that she and her husband could eat after the children went to bed, then relax together.

This particular evening, however, did not turn out as expected. Jasmine sat waiting for her no-show husband. When he finally walked in the door at 10:15 pm, Jasmine was furious. His excuse, that his boss had invited the whole office for dinner, didn't help Jasmine feel better. Jasmine reasoned that her husband could have called to say that he wouldn't be home for dinner; he could have taken 5 minutes to do that. He said he did but the phone was busy. Her face was red with rage. She screamed at her husband. Suddenly, bursting into tears, she ran into the living room. Her husband retreated to the safety of their bedroom. Exhausted and disappointed, Jasmine sat alone and pondered why she was so angry with her husband. Was she just tired? Was she frustrated by dealing with young children all day and simply wanted to be around another adult? Was she secretly worried and jealous that

her husband was seeing another woman and he had lied about his whereabouts? Was she combative because her husband's and her sister's lives seemed so much more rewarding than her own? Jasmine was unsure of how she felt and why she exploded in such rage at her husband, whom she loved dearly.

This story, although sad and gender stereotypical, is not necessarily unrealistic when it comes to emotions. There are times when we are moved by strong emotions. On other occasions, when we expect to cry, we find that our eyes are dry. What are these strange feelings we call emotions? What motivates us to become angry at someone we love? How is it sometimes when we need certain motivations (such as completing an assignment before a deadline), the motivation to do the work is absent until right before the deadline? How can we become more efficient (both at home and in the workplace) in understanding how our emotions influence our behavioral choices?

These questions and others have inspired psychologists to study motivation and emotion. Jasmine's story, besides introducing these topics to you, also illustrates why these two topics are usually interrelated in psychology. Some emotions are pleasant, so pleasant that we are motivated to keep experiencing them. Pleasant emotions are exemplified by love, pride, and joy. Other emotions are terribly draining and oppressive—so negative that we hope they will be over as soon as possible. Negative emotions are exemplified by anger, grief, and jealousy. Motivation, emotion, and their relationship to one another are the focus of this unit.

Women at the Top: Powerful Leaders Define Success as Work + Family in a Culture of Gender by Fanny M. Cheung and Diane F. Halpern

123

Article

Prepared by: Eric Landrum, *Boise State University*

Women at the Top

Powerful Leaders Define Success as Work + Family in a Culture of Gender

How do women rise to the top of their professions when they also have significant family care responsibilities? This critical question has not been addressed by existing models of leadership. In a review of recent research, we explore an alternative model to the usual notion of a Western male as the prototypical leader. The model includes (a) relationship-oriented leadership traits, (b) the importance of teamwork and consensus building, and (c) an effective work–family interface that women with family care responsibilities create and use to break through the glass ceiling. We adopted a cross-cultural perspective to highlight the importance of relational orientation and work–family integration in collectivistic cultures, which supplements models of leadership based on Western men. Our expanded model of leadership operates in the context of a "culture of gender" that defines expectations for women and men as leaders. This complex model includes women in diverse global contexts and enriches our understanding of the interplay among personal attributes, processes, and environments in leadership.

FANNY M. CHEUNG AND DIANE F. HALPERN

Learning Outcomes

After reading this article, you will be able to:

- Understand and explain the factors that contribute to how women with families achieve success as leaders.

- Describe the role of the "culture of gender" in how women in different cultures achieve success as leaders.

There are two very different stories about women's leadership around the world, and depending on which one you choose to tell, and your attitudes toward women in leadership positions, the news is either very good or very bad. Despite the endless blogging and newspaper headlines to the contrary, women are not "opting out" of the workforce to stay home with their babies. The workforce participation of mothers did drop by 2% since its peak in 2000, but as economist Boushey (2005) demonstrated, there was a similar drop in employment for women without children and for all men, which was caused by a general recession from 2001 to 2004. For the first time in U.S. history, women are close to surpassing men in their employment rate, largely because most of the jobs lost in the recent recession have occurred in manufacturing, construction, and finance, where the jobs are largely held by men. The most recently available data show that women now hold 49.1% of jobs in the United States (Rampell, 2009). On the other side of the globe is China,

where economic development and culture differ from those in the Western industrialized world but the figure for women's employment is quite similar (45%; "Women Take 45%," 2007). Women are better educated than ever before; they comprise the majority of undergraduate college enrollments in industrialized countries and are catching up in the developing countries (57% in the United States: Peter & Horn, 2005; 44% in China: Department of Population, Social, Science and Technology Statistics, National Bureau of Statistics, 2004). As might be expected from the growing trend of women's higher educational achievement, there are more women than men in mid-level management positions, which has created an overflowing "pipeline" of managers ready for advancement to top-level executive positions in the United States.

Now for the bad news: Despite women's success in education and mid-level management, few women make it to the "O" level—CEO, CFO (chief financial officer), CIO (chief information officer), or CTO (chief technology officer)—in the corporate world or to comparable top levels in noncorporate settings, such as the highest levels of political office or the top rungs of the academic ladder. In the United States, women hold approximately 50% of all management and professional positions, outnumbering "men in such occupations as financial managers; human resource managers; education administrators; medical and health services managers; accountants and auditors; budget analysts; property, real estate, and social and community service managers" (U.S. Department of Labor, Women's Bureau, 2006, para. 12). Despite their middle-management success, only 2% of the Fortune 500 CEOs and 2% of the Fortune 1000 CEOs are women ("Fortune 500 2006: Women CEOs," 2006). Comparable data from the FTSE (Financial Times Stock Exchange) 250 (Singh & Vinnicombe, 2006) show that 2.8% of CEOs for the top 250 companies listed on the London Stock Exchange are women.

A half century after the women's movement, women have only moved to the halfway mark in the corporate world and other organizations in the industrialized Western societies; most are stuck in middle management. Women in other parts of the world are still far from that halfway mark. For example, in China, women make up 16.8% of the heads of government departments and the Communist Party, social organizations, enterprises, and institutions (Department of Population, Social, Science and Technology Statistics, National Bureau of Statistics, 2004). Even in Hong Kong, which continues to be a more westernized and economically affluent special administrative region after its reunification with China in 1997, women constitute 29.1% of persons employed as managers and administrators (Census and Statistics Department, Government of the Hong Kong Special Administrative Region, 2007). A bevy of commentators have suggested that women are better suited for the "New Economy," with its emphasis on communication and interpersonal skills and the rapid loss of jobs in manufacturing, agriculture, and other job sectors in which physical strength is an asset. Although this may seem like a logical conclusion, there are very few women who have made it to the top leadership positions.

Why are there so few women at the top of the leading organizations given the large numbers that are stalled at middle management? An important clue can be found by taking a closer look at the women who have made it into the rarified atmosphere of life at the top. Almost half of these top executives have no children, and almost half of all women in the United States with salaries greater than $100,000 have no children (Dye, 2005; Hewlett, 2002). Similar data have been found for women who achieve at the highest ranks at research universities, where there have been extensive and eye-opening analyses of the success of women with children. Only one third of all women who began their jobs at research universities without children ever become mothers, and among those who attain tenure, women are twice as likely as their male counterparts to be single 12 years after obtaining their doctorates (Mason & Goulden, 2004). The double standard is alive and well in the workplace. The presence of children signals stability and responsibility for men, who are assumed to be better workers because of their roles as breadwinners. The identical situation for women has the opposite effect.

Recent studies have confirmed the *motherhood wage penalty,* a term that describes the consistent finding that mothers earn less than comparable women without children and less than men in general. By contrast, married men enjoy a *marriage premium,* which refers to one of the most reliable findings in the labor economics literature—the economic advantage that fathers enjoy in the workplace (Hersch & Stratton, 2000). In an experimental investigation of this phenomenon, Correll, Benard, and Paik (2007) responded to a variety of employment advertisements with applications from women that varied

according to whether the women had children or were childless. The applications were carefully matched on work-relevant dimensions. Only 3.1% of the mothers were invited for an interview, compared with 6.6% of the identically qualified women who had no children. Discriminatory practices against women were further documented by these researchers when paid undergraduates rated fictitious applicants for employment. Mothers were rated as less competent and were offered a lower starting salary than comparable women without children. The choice for highly successful women has been clear: Choose either a baby or a briefcase.

But what about those women who refused to make such a choice and succeeded at the top of their professions with children and other family care responsibilities? What can we learn from these women who are leading dually successful lives with (by their own description) happy, thriving families and occupational success at the highest levels? While there have been many studies on work–family conflicts for women workers or managers in general, there are few such studies on women leaders in the literature and none that specifically compared women with and without family care responsibilities.

Given the small number of women at the top, most studies on women leaders have relied on in-depth and qualitative interviews. Studies of these exceptional women are not representative of the norm, but they highlight gaps in our understanding of leadership from a gender-sensitive perspective. These studies do not have representative samples, as the population is small, but generally rely on personal networks and snowball techniques in reaching these exceptional targets. For example, Cantor and Bernay (1992) interviewed 25 American women politicians holding high federal, state, and local elected offices; they used structured questions to investigate how these women developed the leadership qualities that enable them to succeed in politics. Cantor and Bernay identified three critical elements in the leadership equation for these women politicians: competent self, creative aggression, and woman-power. Instead of attempting to behave like men in a male environment, these women leaders embraced and integrated typically female qualities, such as tenderness and caring, with assertiveness and achievement orientation. White, Cox, and Cooper (1992) interviewed 48 women executives, entrepreneurs, politicians, and senior professionals in the United Kingdom on their childhoods, education, and work and family histories to examine their career trajectories. Walton's (1997) study of 11 women heads of colleges in the United Kingdom also adopted an interview method to cover a range of themes, including the women's academic career paths, family influences, self-worth, and job satisfaction.

Qualitative studies of women leaders from other ethnic backgrounds have also been conducted in recent years. Gomez and her colleagues (2001) conducted semi-structured, in-depth interviews to investigate the career development of 20 notable Latinas in the United States whose contributions on the local, national, or international level were recognized in their communities. Their study included contextual and cultural variables in addition to personal variables and the family–work interface. The contextual and cultural factors included social movements, economic trends, public policies, and discrimination at the macro level. At the more personal or interpersonal level, the individual's socioeconomic and educational background, social support, availability of mentors, and role models were important factors.

Richie and her colleagues (1997) also used semistructured, in-depth interviews to compare nine high-achieving African women and nine European American women across eight occupational fields in the United States. The interviews covered the participants' work behaviors and attitudes, their sociocultural and personal backgrounds, and the current contextual conditions that led to particular career actions and consequences. The stories told by their participants showed that they achieved career success on their own terms. Their leadership styles were characterized by interconnectedness. Social support provided an important means for them to balance their personal and professional lives. The authors concluded that women's career development differed from men's, and they confirmed "the inappropriateness of applying career theories written by and based on White men to White women and people of color" (Richie et al., 1997, p. 145).

Kawahara, Esnil, and Hsu (2007) interviewed 12 Asian American women leaders who were considered to be high achievers. The themes that were covered in the interviews included the women's personal attributes, leadership styles, support systems, self-worth, and cultural competence. The comments collected from the interviews demonstrated the emphasis on relating to others and creating a harmonious environment, both of which are reflective of collectivistic values. Family and partner support were recognized as playing an important role in these women's achievement.

Studies with women leaders from different ethnic backgrounds highlight the additional context of culture in which women navigate through the *labyrinth,* a term preferred by Eagly and Carli (2007) to the *glass ceiling* metaphor. Culture defines the expectations for women's and men's roles in society and sets the norms and values in social behavior. Cross-cultural studies of top women leaders could provide a richer understanding of the convergent and divergent contextual factors that characterize women's leadership.

Using semi-structured open-ended interviews, we studied 62 women at the top of their professions who either were or had been married and who had significant family care responsibilities (usually children, but we also included care for other family members such as a disabled sibling or parent). Top-level positions included legislators, government ministers, business executives, college presidents, chiefs of police, and other senior-level professionals from China, Hong Kong, and the United States (Halpern & Cheung, 2008). These three societies provide a comparison in terms of cultural context and socioeconomic milieu. Hong Kong is more similar to China in cultural background but at the same time is more similar to the United States in terms of socioeconomic environment, whereas China and the United States are more distinct from one another in both culture and socioeconomic milieu (Watkins, 2006). In addition to describing their career development and leadership styles, these top women leaders in American and Chinese societies described how they created and negotiated a work–family interface. These highly successful women shared their strategies for leading dually successful lives. This study provides a cross-cultural perspective on the key issues for studying women's leadership. We use the lessons we learned from our study to structure the framework of the following review of the research literature on women leaders.

Integrating Work and Family

Previous research on women in employment has highlighted work–family balance as a major concern (Allen, Herst, Bruck, & Sutton, 2000; Byron, 2005). Working mothers everywhere are known to be short on time, always working a "second shift" after they finish a day at their hectic jobs (Hochschild, 1989). Many countries across the world have conducted time use surveys (United Nations Statistics Division, n.d.). The common finding is that women in paid employment generally spend more hours per day on household duties than do their male counterparts (e.g. Galinsky, 2005). Early studies of work–family balance adopted a scarcity perspective (Greenhaus & Beutell, 1985). It was assumed that the demands of family and work were competing for a finite amount of time, resulting in conflict and stress.

By studying women leaders who managed to maintain their family lives while they advanced in their careers, we identified personal characteristics and strategies that women used to overcome these barriers. As workers in "extreme jobs" that require "24/7" commitment (Hewlett & Luce, 2006), the dually successful top women leaders we interviewed employed many strategies to "make more time." As revealed in our study and other studies of women leaders, these women considered themselves to be experts in multitasking. Because they each lived one life rather than two separate lives at work and at home, they created links between family and work, although they kept their role identities distinct. For example, children went to work with them and often accompanied them on business trips, not only because it allowed the women to spend more time with their children but also because it helped the children understand where their mommies went when they left the house. The women worked from home at least part of the time, often setting rules for switching activities, such as working on Sunday night rather than during the day when they spent the weekend with family, or always being at home for dinner and then working after the children went to bed.

Beyond Work–Family Balance

Recent research on the work–family interface has taken a more balanced view and considered more complex interactions between the work and family domains, which include both negative and positive spillovers in the work–family interface (Rapoport, Bailyn, Fletcher, & Pruitt, 2002). From their meta-analysis reviewing 178 studies on the work–family interface, Ford, Heinen, and Langkamer (2007) found that support from family and work domains was positively related to cross-domain satisfaction. Friedman and Greenhaus (2000) found that when work and family were integrated, the two roles could enhance each other. In integrating these two roles, managing role boundaries was more important than just reducing time at work. Particularly for women, the work–family boundary is more permeable. Thus, we propose that the metaphor of work–family balance be replaced with a metaphor that recognizes the gains that can be achieved by combining or integrating work and family roles (Halpern & Murphy, 2005).

Baltes and Heydens-Gahir (2003) extended a general model of life management strategy to study work–family conflict. They classified the repertoire of adaptive behavior strategies as SOC: selection, optimization, and compensation. The primary focus of *selection* is on the articulation and setting of goals, which give direction to behavior. In our study (Halpern & Cheung, 2008), the top women leaders were very clear about their goals and their priorities. Family and work were both important, and day-to-day decisions were based on family and work needs. They also excelled in the *optimization* strategies through scheduling of time and multitasking. They were flexible in adopting the *compensation* strategy by using alternative means such as outsourcing when time and material resources were limited.

In order to accept the alternative means of fulfilling the demands of a role, many women leaders redefine the structural and personal roles that the workplace and the society have imposed on women (Frone, 2003). In the studies reviewed, most of the women leaders who are married and have families embrace both their family and work roles. However, instead of being superwomen who hold themselves to the highest standards for all of the role-related tasks of being wives and mothers, they adopt different internal and external strategies to redefine their roles. They learn to let go and outsource household tasks just as they would outsource work in a busy office. They recognize that they do not have to do it all by themselves. They alter their internal conceptions of the demands of their work and family roles and define these roles in ways that are meaningful and helpful to them.

Research on work–family balance in Chinese societies suggests a different cultural perspective in understanding the definition of work and family roles. These studies show that work and family are viewed as interdependent domains, unlike the distinct segregation of these two domains in Western concepts of work and family. In individualistic societies, overwork would be considered as taking time away from the family and sacrificing the family for the advancement of one's own career. In collectivistic societies, overwork is likely to be seen as sacrificing oneself for the family, since commitment to work is viewed as a means to ensuring financial security for the family (Yang, Chen, Choi, & Zou, 2000). The needs of the self are subsumed under the needs of the collective. As such, the work–family boundary is more permeable in Chinese societies (Francesco & Shaffer, 2009).

A cross-national comparative study (Spector et al., 2004) involving 15 samples of managers across three culturally distinct regions—Anglo-majority countries (Australia, Canada, England, New Zealand, and the United States), China (Hong Kong, mainland China, and Taiwan), and seven Latin American countries—showed that for the Anglo culture, working long hours was related to work–family stress. For the Chinese and Latin cultures, this was not the case. For the Chinese managers, being married and having children were associated with higher job satisfaction and psychological well-being. A series of studies conducted by Aryee and his colleagues on the work–family interface in Hong Kong (Aryee, Field, & Luk, 1999; Aryee, Luk, Leung, & Lo, 1999) also showed that work and family involvement per se did not lead to work–family conflict. Time conflict did not necessarily lead to strain.

A recent study of working adults in the United States found that women and men with an egalitarian outlook on life, which means they were committed to both their work and their families, reported feeling less guilty when family life interfered with their work than traditional women and men whose commitment was to only one of these spheres of life (Livingston & Judge, 2008). It is interesting to note that these researchers did not find much guilt when work interfered with family life, although one possible explanation for this asymmetry is that few of their participants had partners (36%) or young children (25%). The successful combination of family and work will depend on the obligations people have in both of these spheres.

Past studies of work–life balance rarely included leaders at the top with substantial family care responsibilities and have not considered their responses as a distinct group. Partly it is because this is not an issue that is considered important to men as leaders; partly it is because there are very few top women leaders to be studied. In studies of women leaders, however, we found that the dually successful Western women leaders tended to integrate their work and family roles in the collective unit of the family. Many also regarded family as their priority, and the motivation to succeed at work was to contribute to the well-being of their families and children. In reframing their work as an ally instead of an enemy of the family (Friedman & Greenhaus, 2000), the women leaders in many of the qualitative studies we reviewed reported satisfaction in both domains.

Redefining Roles

In order to integrate their family roles and work roles, the women leaders in the studies we reviewed redefined their own norms for being a good mother and being a leader, making these roles more compatible than they were under the norms prescribed by the larger society. According to their own definitions, a good mother is highly involved in her children's lives and activities, but she does not need to spend all of her time with them. Typically, the women leaders in these studies described their devotion to their children and their families. But because they considered family their highest priority, they dedicated themselves to finding solutions to make it work. These solutions included self-enforced standards to ensure that they always had dinner with their families, took the children on any business trip that lasted more than three days, never missed an important event such as a school play or soccer game, and helped with homework every night. For example, in our study (Halpern & Cheung, 2008), one Hong Kong woman executive made a long-distance telephone call to her children every night when she was posted overseas (before Internet communication was widely accessible) and had them fax their homework to her hotel room, which she then faxed back to them after she reviewed it. Several Chinese women leaders talked about going home to eat dinner with their families before leaving for a business dinner or an evening meeting in order to maintain family togetherness. U.S. women leaders talked with pride about never or rarely missing an important event in their children's lives, which they achieved by arranging their work around these events.

These highly successful women also redefined their roles as successful leaders, which included work + family. They worked long hours, but they also managed to leave work for family time. They counted performance and outcome rather than the actual hours at work. Earlier in their careers, some of the women "flew below the radar" and just left work without announcing why to be at after-school events, completing their work later in the evening. Their employers learned that it was their performance that counted. Once they were in positions of leadership, the women leaders had more control over their work schedules, which allowed them to handle dual demands more openly.

Women's dual roles may be viewed as two circles, one representing family and one work. When the demands of a two-circle life are too much for anyone to manage, the total area for both circles needs to be reduced. One way to reduce the total area is to overlap the circles when possible, symbolically blending work and family (see Figure 1). The portion of the family circle that extends beyond the overlap can be reduced with practical strategies such as hiring help to clean the house, prepare meals, and even shop for presents—by outsourcing anything that does not directly contribute to spending time with one's family. In addition, the portion of the circle representing work that is not overlapping with family can also be reduced. Employees can be empowered to do their work without the direct involvement of the women leaders. Many of these high-powered mothers created work-related expectations that also reduced the size of the "work" circle, such as always leaving work at 7:00 or whatever time they routinely set for themselves and scheduling luncheon meetings instead of evening dinners with clients so as to eat dinner with their families.

Family and Spousal Support

Inevitably, the women leaders interviewed in the various studies all cited the importance of their family support in making it to the top. Having collective identities that emphasized family loyalty, they also fell back on their families to provide support. They relied on some combination of supportive husbands, extended families, and hired help in societies where domestic help was accessible.

The extended family provided much needed help with household chores and child care. Particularly for women from collectivistic societies, proximity to the extended family facilitated their support networks. Part-time and live-in home help supplemented this network. Even in the United States, home help is not as economically inaccessible to professional women as many people believe. The difficulty lies more in getting reliable and stable home help, as well as in women's personal belief that they have to do everything themselves. In interviews with women leaders, they would talk about child-care arrangements,

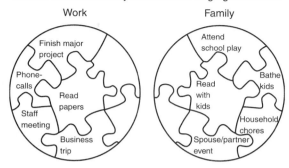

Distinct Work and Family Domains in a Segregated Model

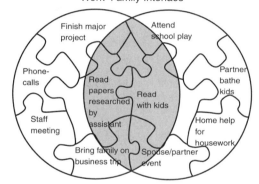

Overlapping Work–Family Domains in an Integrated Model

Figure 1   Segregated versus Integrated Models of Work–Family Interface

supervision of domestic helpers, and maintaining emotional labor with the extended family. In studies of male leadership, these arrangements are assumed to be taken care of by someone and are rarely explicitly discussed.

Another distinctive concern for women leaders is their spousal relationships. Studies of marital relationships show that one of the biggest problems for working women is their husbands' lack of support for their careers (Gilbert, 1988; Vannoy-Hiller & Philliber, 1991). In Western studies of mate selection, men prefer to marry down, which usually includes marrying women who are shorter, weigh less, have less education, and earn less than they do (Schoen & Weinick, 1993). So the superior social status of women leaders may pose a threat to their marriages if their husbands are uncomfortable breaking with traditional sex role norms.

The married women leaders in the various studies converged in their appreciation of their husbands' support. Otherwise, their marriages might not have lasted. The supportive husbands were reported to take on a substantial share in housework. More important, they provided emotional support and encouragement. In our study (Halpern & Cheung, 2008), we specifically addressed the women leaders' relationships with their husbands. Under the strong patriarchal norms in Chinese families, the success of women leaders might have posed a stronger threat to their husbands. However, in this selective sample of women leaders who had stayed married, many described their husbands as their biggest fans, cheerleaders, coaches, and mentors. These husbands were self-assured and confident of themselves. They endorsed egalitarian values toward women. They did not endorse the hierarchical patriarchal norms of marriage and did not feel threatened by the reversed normative roles that put their wives in the limelight and gave them "superior" status.

It is particularly difficult when a family moves for the advancement of the wife's career and the husband takes up the role of the trailing spouse, often with uncertain career prospects at the new location and the loss of a good job at the old location. However, the couples who moved repeatedly to accommodate the wife's promotions considered the sacrifices made by the trailing spouse to be worthwhile. For these couples, the wife's accomplishments and the resources she brought to the marriage were redefined as collective assets to the family instead of threats in a power struggle.

The women leaders who stayed happily married emphasized that they and their husbands grew together in the marriage. They exhibited what marital counselors would call healthy couple behaviors—responsibility, alignment of goals, mutual encouragement and acceptance, commitment to equality in the relationship, empathic listening and open communication, willingness to discuss their relationship, and willingness to engage in joint conflict resolution (Blume, 2006). There was a great deal of give and take, discussion, and negotiation in these marriages. Amidst their busy schedules, our interviewees created the time and space to share their lives with their marital partners. Many of the women mentioned how they designated evenings or weekends for the family or for special dates with their husbands.

Women's Style of Leadership

Do women lead differently from men? Eagly and Carli (2007) observed that while leadership roles promote similarities in male and female leaders, women generally have a more democratic, participative, and collaborative style of leading. Stern (2008) reviewed studies of high-achieving women and concurred that these women tend to adopt a relational leadership style. They also demonstrate a strong sense of conviction and self-worth. Femininity and leadership are no longer considered incompatible. Virtually all of the women we interviewed believed that their style of leadership as women was better suited for the contemporary workplace. They did not reject femininity or shy away from including family roles as metaphors for their leadership roles. Some of the Chinese women talked about leading like grandmothers or mothers, which included being firm when necessary but always supportive, similar to what Cantor and Bernay (1992) described as "maternal strengths" in the American women politicians. These women were not advocating for a "mushy" or feel-good notion of what a "feminine" approach to leadership might be. Instead, the usual definition they provided included being serious about their work, maintaining the highest personal standards, promoting communication, and being considerate and respectful of their staffs. They

also strongly emphasized the notion of a leader as a person of moral character and a role model, which together with a relational orientation have been found to be defining characteristics of leadership in Chinese culture (Smith & Wang, 1996). In Stern's (2008) review of women leaders, making a social contribution and being of service to others were also featured in the women's narratives about their leadership. In Cantor and Bernay's (1992) description of the "womanpower" of women politicians, advancing an agenda of helping others was one of the key motives for their entering politics. Women leaders are particularly conscious of their role in promoting gender equality in their organizations.

In the narratives of women leaders, competition and power are rarely featured. Few of the women leaders in the studies we reviewed mentioned their own power in their narratives about their leadership style or goals. Instead, they emphasized empowering others and creating consensus. They demonstrated what Chin (2007) described as the collaborative process in feminist leadership. Almost all of the women talked about creating flatter organizations and sharing information widely throughout the organization. What emerged is a definition of what is known in the leadership literature as a *transformational* leadership style. Burns (1978) defined transformational leaders as those who "*engage* with others in such a way that leaders and followers raise one another to higher levels of motivation and morality" (p. 20). Over the past 30 years, the concept of transformational leadership has evolved to include leaders who are inspiring, optimistic, moral, and equitable. Judge and Piccolo (2004) built on earlier work in their study of transformational leadership and extended the concept to include charismatic individuals who provide others with inspirational motivation, intellectual stimulation, individual consideration, and a higher purpose in life. This style of leadership is most often contrasted with the more traditional and hierarchically organized transactional style. Transformational leaders transform others by pushing them to assume new points of view and to question their prior assumptions (Goethals, 2005). The perception that women tend to use transformational styles of leadership to a greater extent than do men was confirmed in a meta-analytic review by Eagly, Johannesen-Schmidt, and van Engen (2003) of 45 separate studies. These researchers also found that women leaders tended to engage in more reward-contingency behaviors than men leaders. In other words, the women leaders linked employee rewards to their behaviors in appropriate ways that allowed employees to see the link between their efforts and outcomes at work and the rewards they received. Although the size of the effect that differentiated women from men leaders was small, the meta-analysis showed consistent findings that favored women leaders.

The definition of transformational leadership is more congruent with the interpersonal characteristics associated with women leaders than with the aggressive and hierarchical characteristics associated with male leaders. Women leaders across different studies converge in stressing the importance of communication and team building. In a meta-analytic review of the literature, Lowe, Kroeck, and Sivasubramaniam (1996) found that transformational leadership has a greater association with effective outcomes than does transactional leadership. Logically, then, it might be expected that women, in general, would be more effective leaders because they are more likely to use the style that is associated with better outcomes. The few studies that have examined the effect of having women in top corporate positions confirm this prediction. In one study, researchers sampled over 700 businesses listed in a *Fortune* magazine list of 1,000 businesses (Krishnan & Park, 2005). They found that women constituted 6.7% of the "top management teams" and 2.8% of the line positions on these teams. (Line positions are those directly related to the profitability of the corporation, as opposed to positions in human resources or communications, which are more likely to be filled by women.) The main finding was a significant positive relationship between the number of women in top management and the financial performance of the company. This is a powerful and important finding. In explaining their results, these researchers noted that differences between female and male leadership styles were crucial, especially women's greater willingness to share information, which can drive better performance throughout the company. It is good for business to keep everyone in the know so they can act with fuller knowledge about the entire company.

Climbing One Rung at a Time

As Cantor and Bernay (1992) pointed out, most women leaders did not have sandbox dreams of greatness in their childhoods. The women leaders in our study (Halpern & Cheung, 2008) created successful lives for themselves by working hard and working smart. As in Gomez et al.'s (2001) study of Latina leaders, mothers and mentors figured prominently in the women's tales of how they got where they are today. Their mothers played an important role in inspiring them to try their best and in building their self-confidence early in life, and mentors provided an insider's guide to what they needed to know and provided networking opportunities. We note here that although the idea of mentoring is not as well recognized in Asian cultures as it is in the West, the Asian women often acknowledged informal mentoring relationships, without using this particular label.

An important path toward success for most of the contemporary women leaders was through education. The women achieved a high educational level, which built their self-efficacy and provided them upward mobility. Notwithstanding the sociocultural barriers to women's higher education during their lifetimes, the women in the various studies were either encouraged by their families to pursue education as a key to a better life or strived on their own at a later stage in life to get the preparation they needed for advancement. As Fassinger (2005) suggested, high self-efficacy is a key to women's career success.

In Madsen's (2007) study of 10 American women who served as college or university presidents, a pattern of ongoing personal and professional development was identified. These women leaders demonstrated a continuous process of self-monitoring and self-empowerment in taking on challenging responsibilities while inspiring and supporting the people around them.

In Gomez et al.'s (2001) study of 20 Latina leaders, the career–life path of the participants was characterized as an implementation of the self within an immediate context, influenced by their family background, sociopolitical conditions, and cultural environment. Equipped with an ardent sense of self, the participants used social support networks and cognitive reframing to maintain a balanced perspective or to open new doors when confronting challenges.

As in Gomez et al.'s (2001) study, the women we interviewed concurred in acknowledging a pattern of unintended leadership development. In the early stages of their careers, none of the women planned on making it to the top of their professions or, to use Eagly and Carli's (2007) metaphor, making career moves within a labyrinth. They did not strategically plan their routes or attempt to identify the blind alleys at that stage. As many of the women leaders told us, they never thought it would be possible. They found meaningful work that they loved and climbed one rung at a time as they rose to meet new challenges. Few of the women took career breaks or used any family-friendly policies such as part-time employment or flexible scheduling as they moved through the ranks, in part because these options were not generally available at the time. Their stories reflect that they used a blend of "whatever works."

It would be misleading to label circuitous and unplanned routes to the top as serendipity because the opportunities opened for women who were prepared for the uphill climb. The choices the women leaders made earlier in their careers were considered assets rather than losses. Take the example of Sarah Weddington, the former presidential advisor who did not get a job at a high powered law firm when she got out of law school because she was a woman. She ended up with the opportunity to argue the landmark *Roe v. Wade* case in the U.S. Supreme Court and then went on to find jobs in the higher rungs of politics and government. She called it the "step-by-step method of leadership" (Halpern & Cheung, 2008, p. 219). This is similar to the description by Cantor and Bernay (1992) of how women politicians turned what others perceived to be obstacles into possibilities for themselves.

Our sample included two women who became a chief of police and a chief of one of the largest sheriff's departments in the United States, positions that epitomize male leadership. The police chief told us that as she was being promoted within the department, she realized that she would need to have a college degree and a master's degree to make it anywhere near the top, and she had neither. What she did have at the time was a full-time-plus job as a detective with irregular work hours (homicides do not happen within a 9 to 5 day) and young children. She took her time and waited until her children were in high school and then went to college at night, earning both of the necessary degrees and, ultimately, promotion to the top of the force. A number of the women entrepreneurs from China served previously in the People's Liberation Army, a choice that becomes more understandable when one considers that the only alternative they might have had at the time was to be educated by peasants in the countryside, an educational experience that was in accord with the ideology of the Cultural Revolution. Their military training prepared them well for taking the risks they had to take in starting their own businesses later during the new economic reforms in China.

Now that they are in positions of leadership, the successful women leaders are making it easier for the mothers (and others) who are behind them to handle the often competing demands of running a corporation and going home to change diapers and read bedtime stories. As leaders and policymakers, they are competent professionals who overtly demonstrate their care for their employees and clients in their official policies and everyday interactions, thus creating a model of leadership that takes the best parts of both of the traditional roles of leader and mother.

Cultural Differences and Convergence

The field of cross-cultural leadership has underscored the importance of examining contextual factors when defining leadership (Avolio, 2007). Studies of ethnic women leaders have also highlighted how sociocultural context and cultural identity shape the interpretive lens with which women view the career–life paths they steer (Gomez et al., 2001; Richie et al., 1997).

In cross-cultural psychology, national cultures have been compared in terms of different dimensions of societal norms (Hofstede, 1980). Anglo cultures, like that of the United States, are considered to be individualistic. In these cultures, identity is based in the individual, and emphasis is placed on autonomy and independence. Individuals are supposed to take care of themselves and their immediate families, which consist of the nuclear unit of a couple and their children. In contrast, Asian cultures, like that of the Chinese, are considered to be collectivistic in orientation. Identity is embedded in the social system, an organization, or a group to which the individual belongs. People are born into extended families that take care of them in exchange for their loyalty. Interdependence and harmony among group members are emphasized. As in other societies that emphasize family orientation, the Chinese and the African American women leaders in our study as well as the Latina leaders in Gomez et al.'s (2001) study were more likely to receive social support from their extended families than were the Anglo women leaders.

Culture also defines the social expectations for women's and men's roles. In traditional Chinese culture, women's roles are defined by their different family roles throughout the life stages: daughter, wife, and mother, who should obey, respectively, their father, husband, and son. However, cultural ideologies change with historical events, although there is some lag time before normative attitudes and behaviors change. Socioeconomic and political developments in contemporary China have expanded women's roles. The Communist Party ideology has emphasized liberating Chinese women from their feudalistic oppression as one of the goals of class struggle, and the late Chairman Mao's motto that "women can hold up half the sky" during the 1960s encouraged women to participate in all walks of life. Global campaigns of the women's movement have raised consciousness on gender equality and women's empowerment. There are now legal instruments in China, Hong Kong, and the United States to protect women's rights in employment. However, the structure of the patriarchal family role ascribed to women has moved relatively little despite large changes in the everyday lives of women and men.

Despite great differences in the sociopolitical context during their childhoods, there were striking similarities among the women from China, Hong Kong, and the United States. Many of the mainland Chinese women experienced hardship as they grew up during the Japanese incursion, the Second World War in the 1940s, and the establishment of the People's Republic of China, which was followed by the horrific conditions during the Cultural Revolution, a time when education was denigrated and families were torn apart. The women leaders from Hong Kong had a "foot in two cultures," living first under British rule and, since 1997, under a special administrative region of China which continued to flourish as an international financial center. The leaders from the United States grew up just as opportunities for women opened up as a result of affirmative action and increased legal protection against overt discrimination, although the Equal Rights Amendment failed to gain sufficient support to become national law. Despite the vast sociopolitical differences among these three societies, the culture of gender, with its prescription of appropriate gender roles, exerted a stronger impact on women.

The narratives of the women leaders whom we interviewed (Halpern & Cheung, 2008) highlighted themes that reflected their cultural ideologies. Although all of the women leaders featured their family roles prominently in describing their personal identities, what they considered to be the essential tasks of these roles differed. The American women leaders prided themselves on never missing their children's school plays or soccer games; mothers in Hong Kong put more emphasis on helping their children with their schoolwork. A dominant feature in the Chinese mother's role is overseeing their children's education, with heavy emphasis on supervision of homework and preparation for examinations. Food is another cultural theme that is prominent in the Chinese family. The Chinese mothers from mainland China, Hong Kong, and the United States alike emphasized family dinners as a symbol of family togetherness, describing how they ate with their children before they went out to their own business dinners or went back to work at the office at night. When the hierarchical norms of husband and wife were reversed, the Chinese women leaders were sensitive to how their husbands might lose "face" and took measures to protect against such situations.

Although culture prescribes the expectations for gender roles and behaviors, there are differences within the culture in the way in which individuals play out these roles. We recognize that there are also ethnic, regional, and class differences within the larger cultural group. For example, some of the American women leaders relied on live-in helpers, with fewer of them relying on their extended families for help with child care than the women in mainland China and Hong Kong. The physical distance for the U.S. women from their extended families may have been a barrier that made using this resource a rare occurrence.

The Culture of Gender

When we began our study, we thought there would be many differences between the Chinese and American women leaders in how they managed the combination of top-level work and a successful family life. We expected that the American women leaders would segregate their work and family roles more distinctly, as suggested by Western theories and research on work–family conflict. However, the cultural differences we found relate more to the contents rather than the structure of the role ideology. There was more convergence in the way that these women leaders interwove work and family roles on their paths to the top. Even though they subscribed to gender roles, the Chinese and the American women leaders alike defied the constraints of sexism, which is pervasive across culture. They embraced the multifaceted roles involved in being women. With their growing confidence in their own identities, they did not need to conform to the roles and behaviors of men in order to become leaders. Unlike Western men, they did not segregate their work roles and family roles into distinct domains that could result in conflict. Instead, they integrated their work and family roles in ways that enabled them to harmonize both. Their successful strategies can inform our understanding of the work–family interface. A recent study of working adults in the Netherlands also found that women were more likely to use strategies that facilitated the combination of work and family than were men (van Steenbergen, Ellemers, & Mooijaart, 2007). Instead of viewing the combination of these two spheres of life as necessarily negative, the women found ways to benefit from combining their dual roles, which was a consistent theme among our sample of women leaders and other studies of women leaders with families.

In hindsight, one reason for the cross-cultural similarities is that all of the women share what we are calling "the culture of gender." Notwithstanding the cultural differences found according to the usual understanding of culture, there are pancultural gender role norms that create opportunities and constraints for all women leaders (Inglehart & Norris, 2003). In every society, gender norms prescribe the roles and behaviors that differentiate the experiences of women and men. There are restrictions inherent in the roles of women that make it difficult for them to achieve at high levels in demanding careers. Across national boundaries, women leaders are exposed to similar stereotypes that form sexist prejudice in organizations and to the same media that scrutinize their physical appearance, clothing, and family responsibilities with a magnifying glass while portraying their male counterparts as dealing with substantive issues. Reviewing the culture of gender helps us to expand our understanding of leadership, which includes not only individual traits and behaviors but also the process of integrating work and family as two major domains in a leader's life.

An Alternative Model of Leadership

Leadership studies have moved beyond the "trait" and "situation" approaches to more integrated theories of leadership that include the contributions of relationships, contexts, and culture (Avolio, 2007). We note here that in all the qualitative studies of women leaders, researchers relied on the women's tales of their success and how they perceived the interplay among their life roles. The use of semi-structured interviews led the participants to respond to particular aspects of their careers in ways they chose to recall. Families, employers, and employees may have perceived the lives of these women very differently, but we were more concerned with how the women explained their own choices and actions. They were (mostly) pleased with their success at work and at home, which led us to label them as dually successful.

The success stories of the women leaders in various studies show us not only a fuller picture of how women can attain leadership but also how gender can inform leadership research. The study of women's leadership styles and their integration of work and family roles have enriched our understanding of the interplay of personal attributes, processes, and environment in a complex model of leadership that includes women in diverse global contexts. Their exceptional experiences guide us to consider an alternative model to the usual notion of a Western male as the prototypical leader in an organizational setting. This alternative model encompasses a fuller picture of leaders as human beings who steer their lives successfully (Figure 2). It includes the multiple roles of leaders in a complex world. It shows the developmental steps taken by the leaders navigating through their life courses, which are shaped by sociopolitical conditions and current contexts. These contexts may facilitate greater access to education and mentoring for women, which in turn build up their self-efficacy. Flexible working conditions and social support make it possible for women to combine work and family. These steps are not meant to be rigid sequences but are intended to illustrate the incremental and interactional nature of leadership development. The model strengthens the consideration of the interpersonal and relational dimensions of leadership. The transformational leadership style creates a flatter organization in a global work context. This model also recognizes the importance of the integration of different domains of a leader's life. The interplay of these domains varies during different developmental stages of the leader's life course. We suggest that filling family roles such as those of mothers and caregivers, becoming leaders at work, and making these roles compatible have helped women to cultivate the transformational style of leadership.

We base our suggestions on the lessons we learned from the successful women leaders who have families, which is an unusual group. We do not intend to paint an overly rosy picture of these women's lives. They had their share of hardship and strain at work and at home. But they have managed to steer through the labyrinth despite the barriers. We did not speak to their family members and get their perspectives. That will be a direction for future studies. We also recognize that women leaders without families may face convergent and divergent issues, and so do men leaders with and without families. What we are suggesting is that a more comprehensive and inclusive model takes into account the gaps in existing models. Future research could compare how women at different stages of the career

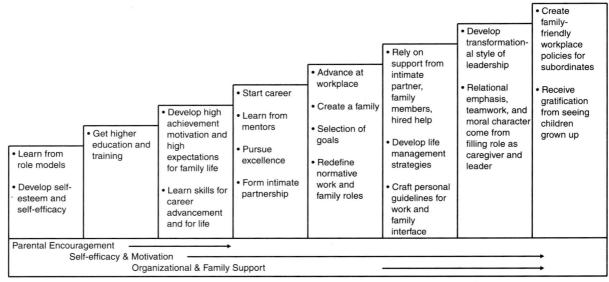

Figure 2   Step-by-Step Model of Leadership Development Incorporating Work and Family Roles

development and family life cycles construe their life purposes in incremental steps, and how powerful men and women define their success as work + family in a model of transformational leadership.

References

Allen, T. D., Herst, D. E. L., Bruck, C. S., & Sutton, M. (2000). Consequences associated with work-to-family conflict: A review and agenda for future research. *Journal of Occupational Health Psychology, 5,* 278–308, doi:101037/1076-8998.5.2.278

Aryee, S., Field, D., & Luk, V. (1999). A cross-cultural test of a model of work–family interface. *Journal of Management, 25,* 491–511. doi: 10.1177/014920639902500402

Aryee, S., Luk, V., Leung, A., & Lo, S. (1999). Role stressors, interrole conflict, and well-being: The moderating effect of spousal support and coping behaviors among employed parents in Hong Kong. *Journal of Vocational Behavior, 54,* 259–278. doi:10.1006/jvbe. 1998.1667

Avolio, B. J. (2007). Promoting more integrative strategies for leadership theory-building. *American Psychologist, 62,* 25–33. doi:10.1037/0003-066X.62.1.25

Baltes, B. B., & Heydens-Gahir, H. A. (2003). Reduction of work–family conflict through the use of selection, optimization, and compensation behaviors. *Journal of Applied Psychology, 88,* 1005–1018. doi:10.1037/0021-9010.88.6.1005

Blume, R. (2006). *Becoming a family counselor: A bridge to family therapy theory and practice.* Hoboken, NJ: Wiley.

Boushey, H. (2005, November). *Are women opting out? Debunking the myth* [Briefing paper]. Retrieved from the Center for Economic and Policy Research website: www.cepr.net/documents/publications/opt_out_2005_11_2.pdf

Burns, J. M. (1978). *Leadership.* New York, NY: Harper & Row.

Byron, K. (2005). A meta-analytic review of work–family conflict and its antecedents. *Journal of Vocational Behavior, 67,* 169–198. doi:10.1016/j.jvb.2004.08.009

Cantor, D. W., & Bernay, T. (1992). *Women in power: The secrets of leadership.* Boston, MA: Houghton Mifflin.

Census and Statistics Department, Government of the Hong Kong Special Administrative Region. (2007). *Women and men in Hong Kong: Key statistics.* Hong Kong, China: Author. Retrieved from www.censtatd.gov.hk/products_and_services/products/publications/statistical_report/social_2007_data/index_cd_B1130303_dt_back_yr_2007.jsp

Chin, J. L. (2007). Overview: Women and leadership: Transforming visions and diverse voices. In J. L. Chin, B. Lott, J. K. Rice, & J. Sanchez-Hucles (Eds.), *Women and leadership: Transforming visions and diverse voices* (pp. 1–17). Oxford, England: Blackwell.

Correll, S. J., Benard, S., & Paik, I. (2007). Getting a job: Is there a motherhood penalty? *American Journal of Sociology, 112,* 1297–1338. doi:10.1086/511799

Department of Population, Social, Science and Technology Statistics, National Bureau of Statistics. (2004). *Women and men in China: Facts and figures 2004.* Beijing, China: Author. Retrieved from www.stats.gov.cn/english/statisticaldata/otherdata/men&women_en.pdf

Dye, J. L. (2005, December). *Fertility of American women: June 2004* (Current Population Reports, P20–555). Retrieved from U.S. Census Bureau website: www.census.gov/prod/2005pubs/p20–555.pdf

Eagly, A. H., & Carli, L. L. (2007). *Through the labyrinth: The truth about how women become leaders.* Boston, MA: Harvard Business School Press.

Eagly, A. H., Johannesen-Schmidt, M. C., & van Engen, M. (2003). Transformational, transactional, and laissez-faire leadership styles: A meta-analysis comparing women and men. *Psychological Bulletin, 95,* 569–591. doi:10.1037/0033-2909.129.4.569

Fassinger, R. (2005). Theoretical issues in the study of women's career development: Building bridges in a brave new world. In W. B. Walsh & M. L. Savickas (Eds.), *Handbook of vocational psychology: Theory, research, and practice* (3rd ed., pp. 85–126). Mahwah, NJ: Erlbaum.

Ford, M. T., Heinen, B. A., & Langkamer, K. L. (2007). Work and family satisfaction and conflict: A meta-analysis of cross-domain relations. *Journal of Applied Psychology, 92,* 57–80. doi:10.1037/0021-9010.92.1.57

Fortune 500 2006: Women CEOs for Fortune 500 companies. (2006, April 17). *Fortune, 153*(7). Retrieved from http://money.cnn.com/magazines/fortune/fortune500/womenceos/

Francesco, A. M., & Shaffer, M. A. (2009). Working women in Hong Kong: *Neuih keuhng yahn* or oppressed class? In F. M. Cheung & E. Holroyd (Eds.), *Mainstreaming gender in Hong Kong society* (pp. 311–334). Hong Kong, China: Chinese University Press.

Friedman, S. D., & Greenhaus, J. H. (2000). *Work and family—Allies or enemies? What happens when business professionals confront life choices.* New York, NY: Oxford University Press.

Frone, M. R. (2003). Work–family balance. In J. C. Quick & L. E. Tetrick (Eds.), *Handbook of occupational health psychology* (pp. 143–162). Washington DC: American Psychological Association.

Galinsky, E. (2005). *Overwork in America: When the way we work becomes too much.* New York, NY: Families and Work Institute.

Gilbert, L. A. (1988). *Sharing it all: The rewards and struggles of two-career families.* New York, NY: Plenum Press.

Goethals, G. R. (2005). Presidential leadership. *Annual Review of Psychology, 56,* 545–570. doi:10.1146/annurev.psych.55.090902.141918

Gomez, M. J., Fassinger, R. E., Prosser, J., Cooke, K., Mejia, B., & Luna, J. (2001). Voces abriendo caminos (Voices forging paths): A qualitative study of the career development of notable Latinas. *Journal of Counseling Psychology, 48,* 286–300. doi:10.1037/0022-0167.48.3.286

Greenhaus, J. H., & Beutell, N. J. (1985). Sources of conflict between work and family roles. *Academy of Management Review, 10,* 76–88.

Halpern, D. F., & Cheung, F. M. (2008). *Women at the top: Powerful leaders tell us how to combine work and family.* New York, NY: Wiley/Blackwell.

Halpern, D. F., & Murphy, S. E. (Eds.). (2005). *From work–family balance to work–family interaction: Changing the metaphor.* Mahwah, NJ: Erlbaum.

Hersch, J., & Stratton, L. S. (2000). Household specialization and the male marriage wage premium. *Industrial and Labor Relations Review, 54,* 78–94. doi:10.2139/ssrn.241067

Hewlett, S. A. (2002). Executive women and the myth of having it all. *Harvard Business Review, 80,* 66–73.

Hewlett, S. A., & Luce, C. B. (2006). Extreme jobs: The dangerous allure of the 70-hour work week. *Harvard Business Review, 84,* 49–59.

Hochschild, A. R. (1989). *The second shift.* London, England: Penguin.

Hofstede, G. (1980). *Culture's consequences: International differences in work-related values.* Beverly Hill, CA: Sage.

Inglehart, R., & Norris, P. (2003). *Rising tide: Gender equality and cultural change around the world.* New York, NY: Cambridge University Press.

Judge, T. A., & Piccolo, R. F. (2004). Transformational and transactional leadership: A meta-analytic test of their relative validity. *Journal of Applied Psychology, 89,* 901–910. doi:10.1037/0021-9010.89.5.755

Kawahara, D. M., Esnil, E. M., & Hsu, J. (2007). Asian American women leaders: The intersection of race, gender, and leadership. In J. L. Chin, B. Lott, J. K. Rice, & J. Sanchez-Hucles (Eds.), *Women and leadership: Transforming visions and diverse voices* (pp. 297–313). Malden, MA: Blackwell.

Krishnan, H. A., & Park, D. (2005). A few good women—on top management teams. *Journal of Business Research, 58,* 1712–1720. doi:10.1016/j.jbusres.2004.09.003

Livingston, B. A., & Judge, T. A. (2008). Emotional responses to work–family conflict: An examination of gender role orientation among working men and women. *Journal of Applied Psychology, 93,* 207–211. doi:10.1037/0021-9010.93.1.207

Lowe, K. B., Kroeck, K. G., & Sivasubramaniam, N. (1996). Effectiveness correlates of transformational and transactional leadership: A meta-analytic review of the MLQ literature. *The Leadership Quarterly, 7,* 385–425. doi:10.1016/S1048-9843(96)90027-2

Madsen, S. R. (2007). Women university presidents: Career paths and educational backgrounds. *Academic Leadership, 5,* 11–16.

Mason, M. A., & Goulden, M. (2004, November–December). Do babies matter (Part II)?: Closing the baby gap. *Academe, 90*(6) 10–15. Retrieved from http://ucfamilyedge.berkeley.edu/babies%20matterII.pdf

Peter, K., & Horn, L. (2005). *Gender differences in participation and completion of undergraduate education and how they changed over time* (NCES 2005–169). Retrieved from National Center for Education Statistics website: http://nces.ed.gov/pubs2005/2005169.pdf

Rampell, C. (2009, February 5). As layoffs surge, women may pass men in job force. *New York Times.* Retrieved from www.nytimes.com/2009/02/06/business/06women.html

Rapoport, R., Bailyn, L., Fletcher, J. K., & Pruitt, B. H. (2002). *Beyond work–family balance: Advancing gender equity and workplace performance.* San Francisco, CA: Jossey-Bass.

Richie, B. S., Fassinger, R. E., Linn, S. G., Johnson, J., Prosser, J., & Robinson, S. (1997). Persistence, connection, and passion: A qualitative study of the career development of highly achieving African American–Black and White women. *Journal of Counseling Psychology, 44,* 133–148. doi:10.1037/0022-0167.44.2.133

Schoen, R., & Weinick, R. M. (1993). Partner choice in marriage and cohabitations. *Journal of Marriage and the Family, 55,* 408–414. doi:10.2307/352811

Singh, V., & Vinnicombe, S. (2006). *The Female FTSE Report 2006: Identifying the new generation of women directors.* Retrieved from www.som.cranfield.ac.uk/som/dinamic-content/research/documents/ftse2006full.pdf

Smith, P. B., & Wang, Z. M. (1996). Chinese leadership and organizational structures. In M. B. Bond (Ed.), *The handbook of Chinese psychology* (pp. 322–337). Hong Kong, China: Oxford University Press.

Spector, P. E., Cooper, C. L., Poelmans, S., Allen, T. D., O'Driscoll, M., Sanchez, J. I., . . . Lu. L. (2004). A cross-national comparative study of work–family stressors, working hours, and well-being: China and Latin America versus the Anglo world. *Personnel Psychology, 57,* 119–142. doi:10.1111/j.1744-6570.2004.tb02486.x

Stern, T. (2008). Self-esteem and high-achieving women. In M. A. Paludi (Ed.), *The psychology of women at work: Challenges and solutions for our female workforce. Vol. 3. Self, family and social affects* (pp. 25–53). Westport, CT: Praeger.

United Nations Statistics Division. (n.d.). Allocation of time and time use. Retrieved from http://unstats.un.org/unsd/demographic/sconcerns/tuse/

U.S. Department of Labor, Women's Bureau. (2006). *Quick facts on women in the labor force in 2006.* Retrieved from www.dol.gov/wb/factsheets/Qf-laborforce-06.htm

Vannoy-Hiller, D., & Philliber, W. W. (1991). *Equal partners: Successful women in marriage.* Newbury Park, CA: Sage.

van Steenbergen, E. F., Ellemers, N., & Mooijaart, A. (2007). How work and family can facilitate each other: Distinct types of work–family facilitation and outcomes for women and men. *Journal of Occupational Health Psychology, 12,* 279–300. doi:10.1037/1076-8998.12.3.279

Walton, K. D. (1997). UK women at the very top: An American assessment. In H. Eggins (Ed.), *Women as leaders and managers in higher education* (pp. 70–90). Bristol, PA: Open University Press.

Watkins, K. (2006). *Human development report 2006. Beyond scarcity: Power, poverty and the global water crisis.* New York, NY: United Nations Development Programme. Retrieved from http://hdr.undp.org/en/media/HDR06-complete.pdf

White, B., Cox, C., & Cooper, C. (1992). *Women's career development: A study of high flyers.* Cambridge, MA: Blackwell.

Women take 45% workforce in China. (2007, May 18). *People's Daily Online.* Retrieved from http://english.people.com.cn/200705/18/eng20070518_375703.html

Yang, N., Chen, C. C., Choi, J., & Zou, Y. (2000). Sources of work–family conflict: A Sino-U.S. comparison of the effects of work and family demands. *Academy of Management Journal, 43,* 113–123. doi:10.2307/1556390

Critical Thinking

1. What appear to be the key factors related to how women with families achieve success as leaders?

2. What is the "culture of gender" and how does it influence women in different culture to achieve success in leadership?

3. How have older theories of leadership (such as trait and situation-based theories) yielded to new theories of leadership that incorporate culture and gender?

Create Central

www.mhhe.com/createcentral

Internet References

Gender neutral flexibility

www.nlcstrategies.com/home/topics-in-flexibility/gender-neutral-flexibility

The competitive agenda of family-friendly policies

http://pwc.blogs.com/gender_agenda

FANNY M. CHEUNG, Department of Psychology, The Chinese University of Hong Kong; **DIANE F. HALPERN,** Department of Psychology Claremont McKenna College.

Article — Prepared by: Eric Landrum, *Boise State University*

Resisting Temptation

Eric Wargo

Learning Outcomes

After reading this article, you will be able to:

- Define self-control within the context of everyday life.
- Summarize the key elements of a person's ability to exercise self-control.

Every year the holidays put us grownups through the same wringer. Sometime late in December, we remember that the "holiday spirit" is really not about eager anticipation and indulgence; it is about controlling ourselves, resisting temptations, mastering our urges. All that food, occasions to drink a little or a lot too much, the pressure cooker of families and relatives . . . so many opportunities to say, do, or consume things we might regret.

And now comes January, that cold month when we all lay in our warm beds and reconsider our resolutions. Get up early and go to the gym before work? I must have been drunk when I resolved to do that.

The problem of how we master our impulses and follow through on our goals is not new, of course—it has engaged philosophers for as long as there have been people in togas. Controlling our passions and cravings was emphasized by the ancient Stoics and Buddhists, for example, and virtue derived from self-restraint is a cornerstone of the Judeo-Christian tradition. In one way or another, all cultures have regarded the ability to discipline ourselves as central to what defines us as human. Animals appear to obey their appetites in the moment; people—at least, adult people—can say "no" to what may be immediately tempting, for the sake of the greater material rewards or moral virtue that come from reining ourselves in.

Yet most of us fail to rein ourselves in as much as we would like, at least in some part of our lives. In one way or another, failures of willpower are at the root of countless problems in our society—obesity, addictions, violence, relationship problems, consumer debt, to name just a few. For this reason, the science of willpower—as a subset of the larger domain of self-regulation (see Baumeister & Vohs, 2004)—is emerging as a major priority in the psychological sciences. Where does willpower come from? Why do some people have more of it than others? How can it be strengthened?

Hot Marshmallows

The litmus test of how much willpower you have is whether you can resist a marshmallow. At least, this is the paradigm in the classic deferral-of-gratification studies conducted at Stanford in the early 1970s by current APS President Walter Mischel (see Mischel, 1996). In one version of his famous experiment, four-year-olds were left in a room with a bell, with which they could summon an experimenter who, they were promised, would give them a single marshmallow. But they were also told that if they could hold out and wait for the experimenter to return on his own, they would receive two marshmallows. In other variants, the children had the first marshmallow in front of them from the start and had to resist this immediate temptation if they were to reap the larger reward. In such studies, some kids managed to wait up to 20 minutes for the grand prize of two marshmallows, and some caved early for the lesser reward.

The principle underlying the challenge faced by those four-year-olds is sometimes called *temporal discounting:* To a small child, one marshmallow right away may seem more valuable than two marshmallows in some indefinite future. Transposed to adult behavior, it is easy to see how temporal discounting leads otherwise rational people to compromise their long-term health and happiness for short-term gains. That big-screen TV on sale in Best Buy might seem more tangibly rewarding as you stand gazing at it than some vague future free of credit card payments. Or tonight's dessert special—chocolate mousse cake—may seem more important (as you observe another lucky diner savor it) than a slimmer waistline down the road.

A single marshmallow, like a single trip to the gym or a single impulse purchase, may seem trivial, but over the course of life, our successes and failures in the area of self-mastery add up to predict a lot about our success and failure in many areas. People high in self-control are healthier, have better relationships, and are more successful in school and work than those low in the trait. The children in Mischel's marshmallow study, for example, were tracked through adolescence, and the researchers found that the four-year-olds who successfully delayed gratification to reap a larger reward were better adjusted later and scored higher on their SATs than did those who hadn't been able to hold out (Mischel, 1996).

Sigmund Freud thought that young children developed the capacity for deferring gratification by forming mental images of desired stimuli (the mother's breast was Freud's exemplar, but you could think in terms of marshmallows too); they endured frustration and laid the foundations for later self-mastery by enjoying their mental pictures in place of the real objects they represented. Mischel used his sweet-treat paradigm to test Freud's theory and found that the Viennese psychoanalyst was only partly right. Keeping a reward in mind, and thereby maintaining an expectation of it, did seem to be important. But some mental marshmallows worked considerably better than others.

Specifically, encouraging kids to create vivid, highly arousing mental images of the sweet, gooey treat led them quickly unto temptation, whereas encouraging them to form abstract, non-arousing (or "cold") cognitive representations (thinking of the marshmallows as "puffy clouds," for instance) facilitated waiting. Children who were able to wait for two marshmallows did so by distracting themselves from the aversive wait by thinking about something else instead—or, in some versions of the experiment, by forming arousing, or "hot," mental images of alternative, unavailable rewards, such as a warm fresh pretzel.

Mischel's discovery leads to real-life strategies for self-control: Viewing temptations abstractly—"cooling" immediate stimuli—helps redress the here-and-now bias produced by temporal discounting, enabling us to take a longer-term perspective. By the same token, making long-term priorities "hot" adds weight to those goals, helping them defeat our short-term impulses.

Many psychologists view self-control in terms of the interplay of two distinct self-regulation systems, one that is planful and takes more mental effort, and one that is quick and impulsive and responsive to stimuli in the moment. In the model proposed by Mischel and APS Fellow Janet Metcalfe (Columbia), the more emotional "hot" system dukes it out with the reasoned and rational "cool" system (Metcalfe & Mischel, 1999). These systems are part of a larger cognitive-affective processing system—a constellation of goal representations, expectations about our self-efficacy and competence (i.e., it matters for our willpower if we believe we have it), and situational appraisals that interact and moderate each other (Mischel & Ayduk, 2004). Research in neuroscience is lending support to such dual-process theories by showing the brain systems involved in both impulsivity and self-control.

Willpower in the Brain

Most Psychology 101 students know the story of Phineas Gage, the Vermont railroad worker who received the first known prefrontal lobotomy when an explosively propelled iron rod passed clear through the front of his head, destroying parts of his frontal lobe. That Gage survived this freak accident at all is miraculous, particularly considering it happened in 1848. But it was the dramatic change in his behavior after his accident that earned Gage his permanent place in psychology textbooks. Once an "efficient and capable" foreman, his accident rendered him, according to his physician, irreverent, profane, impatient, obstinate, vacillating, and unable to follow through with his plans. He became an impulsive and ineffectual shadow of his former self–in short, "no longer Gage."

Gage's accident was hardly a controlled experiment, and some of the anecdotal evidence in the case is now viewed with a critical eye by scientists. But the take-home point has held for over a century and a half: Be careful when tamping dynamite with an iron rod. The other take-home point has been pretty much just as durable, at least in psychology: Willpower and other executive faculties like decision making have a lot to do with the *prefrontal cortex,* or PFC.

Neuroimaging and other tools are rapidly adding to our understanding of the various executive processes that unfold in the human forebrain. The front-most or anterior portion of the PFC, which is implicated in working memory capacity, is linked to the kinds of deferral of gratification tasks studied by Mischel. This may be because overriding temporal discounting requires keeping long-term goals in mind (see Shamosh et al., 2008). Other major structures within the PFC include the dorsolateral PFC, associated with forethought and inhibition of impulses, and the ventromedial PFC, involved in regulating emotions and sensitivity to punishment and reward. The latter area is what was probably damaged in Gage's case (see Wagar & Thagard, 2004).

Information about punishment and reward is vital to making sound decisions. Patients with damage to the ventromedial PFC have trouble taking the long view and considering the future consequences of immediate payoffs—what University of Iowa neurologist Antoine Bechara and his colleagues have called "myopia for the future" (Bechara, Tranel, & Damasio, 2000). This is shown in a risk-decision paradigm known as the Iowa Gambling Task, in which participants overturn cards from an array of decks that vary in the size of the monetary rewards offered. Some of the decks appear highly rewarding at first but also contain catastrophic losses that ultimately bankrupt players who preferentially choose them. People with ventromedial PFC damage tend to persist in picking from these high-payout but ultimately treacherous bad decks. Bechara (2005) suggests that failures of willpower such as drug addiction can be understood as a failure of the prefrontal, long-term reward/punishment system to suppress an impulsive, short-term reward/punishment system involving the brain's limbic system, particularly the amygdala.

Whether the cool-headed prefrontal system is able to override our emotional, amygdala-based impulses depends on various factors. Age is one of them: The ventromedial PFC matures later than other brain systems (it is still developing in early adulthood); as a result, children and adolescents also perform poorly on the Iowa Gambling Task (Hooper, Luciana, Conklin, & Yarger, 2004), and generally make poorer decisions than adults do (see Reyna & Farley, 2006). Stress is another factor: Exposure to stressors such as loud noises, crowds, bureaucratic frustrations, or being discriminated against has been found to reduce people's performance in subsequent self-control tasks (see Muraven & Baumeister, 2000).

Flex Your Muscles

One of the main limits on willpower, though, turns out to be . . . willpower. Exerting self-control in one domain makes it harder to exert self-control in another, at least right away. Over the past decade and a half, a large number of studies have shown that executive processes by which we control our impulses behave a lot like muscles that get tired through use.

In a study led by APS Fellow Roy Baumeister (Florida State University), a group of hungry participants was forbidden from eating freshly baked cookies sitting on a plate in front of them and made to eat radishes instead. These participants gave up faster on a subsequent frustrating task than did a control group who had been freely allowed to indulge their sweet tooth (Baumeister, Bratslavsky, Muraven, & Tice, 1998). And in a study led by Mark Muraven (SUNY-Albany), participants made to suppress all thoughts of a white beer for five minutes consumed more beer afterwards in a "taste test" than did those in a control group, even though they knew they would subsequently be taking a driving test (Muraven, Collins, & Neinhaus, 2002).

Numerous variants of this paradigm—making a group of participants exercise restraint in one situation and then comparing their performance with that of a control group in a subsequent self-control task—have shown the same pattern: Self-control is a limited resource that can be drained through exertion (Baumeister, Vohs, & Tice, 2007). Baumeister and colleagues call this fatigued state "ego-depletion," and it is a significant discovery because it explains why many of our specific willpower failures occur when our strength has been taxed by other self-control demands. Refraining from blowing up at one's boss during the day may make it hard to resist a big meal of comfort food that evening. The constant effort of sticking to a diet may cause us to make more impulsive purchases at the mall.

The muscle that controls willpower does much more than just keep our impulses in check. It is part of a larger set of executive functions involved in self-monitoring, coping with stressors, weighing alternatives, and making decisions, all of which draw on the same limited energy source. In a recent series of studies led by Kathleen Vohs (University of Minnesota), participants who were asked to choose among various consumer products subsequently showed diminished pain tolerance and consumed less of a nasty-tasting vinegar drink (even though they were paid a nickel per ounce consumed); college students asked to choose among various college courses subsequently studied less for a math test, opting to play video games or read magazines instead (Vohs et al., 2008). Non-ego-depleted persons are also better at logical reasoning and intelligent thought (see Baumeister, Vohs, & Tice, 2007) and at dealing with setbacks that are unexpected (see Baumeister, 2008).

It is even possible to become ego-depleted by watching *other people* exert willpower. In a new study by psychologists at Yale and UCLA, participants were asked to put themselves in the shoes of a fictional hungry waiter or waitress in a gourmet restaurant who was forbidden from eating on the job. They then viewed pictures of various products like watches, cars, and appliances and rated how much they would be willing to spend for them. Exercising vicarious self-control led people to be willing to spend more on the consumer goods, as compared with a control group (Ackerman, Goldstein, Shapiro, & Bargh, in press).

Impulse purchases and eating binges may let us know our willpower is tired, yet until recently psychologists have not known how to assess self-control effort independently of such behavioral indicators. But based on the fact that self-regulation overlaps with brain systems governing the autonomic, "fight-or-flight" stress response, University of Kentucky psychologist Suzanne Segerstrom hypothesized that physiological responses shared with stress might also work as a measure of effort at self-regulation. In 2007, she and her collaborator Lise Solberg Nes published the results of a study showing that participants' heart-rate variability (speeding and slowing of heartbeats), a common stress response, also increased when participants resisted cookies in favor of carrots and when they worked at solving tough anagrams (Segerstrom & Solberg Nes, 2007). Although people often know it when they are stressed, they generally aren't directly aware of exerting self-regulatory exertion, especially for such trivial stakes as a cookie. The new finding points to one way future researchers may directly measure flexing and fatigue of the willpower muscle.

But the $64,000 question is this: If willpower acts like a muscle, can we strengthen it through exercise? Evidence so far suggests the answer is yes: Using self-control in specific areas such as spending or exercise can gradually increase one's resistance to ego-depletion, even in unrelated self-control tasks (Baumeister, Gailliot, DeWall, & Oaten, 2006). For example, in one study, participants suppressed all thoughts of a white beer during an initial task subsequently gave up sooner on a strenuous handgrip task. They all then returned to the lab two weeks later to undergo the same two ordeals; however, in the intervening time, one group engaged in some form of self-regulatory exercise—tracking their food consumption, controlling their mood, or working on their posture. On their second lab visit, those who had exercised in the interim were not as worn out by not thinking of a white beer. Other studies have shown the same benefit of doing daily exercises like using one's nondominant hand for routine tasks or working to improve one's language (such as trying not to curse).

Free Will Hunting

Psychological scientists have often shied away from using terms like "will" or "willpower," preferring the less philosophically or morally loaded "self-control" or the broader "self-regulation." Since the Enlightenment, science has generally accepted that our bodies, and our brains, are machines, subject to the laws of mechanistic causality. If mental processes unfold like clockwork, where could will—that is, free personal choice—enter in?

Attempts to reconcile free will with mechanistic determinism tend to result in the *homuncular fallacy:* Medieval physicians blamed certain mental and physical ailments on homunculi, miniature people working mischief inside our heads and bodies; such a "mini-me" has served psychologists and logicians as an apt metaphor for the hall of mirrors that often results when attempting to explain unconstrained choice in a deterministic universe: If I'm not the one consciously deciding my destiny, something inside of me is. But if I'm just the vehicle for an inner decider, then how does the decider decide? And how is that decided? Simply, how can you account for free will without endlessly deferring the question to a homunculus inside a homunculus inside a homunculus, on to infinity? Just thinking about it is enough to make your homunculus spin.

Twentieth-century psychology tended to deal with the homunculus problem by severely restricting the scope of free will. Freud, for example, argued that much of what we think of as willed behavior is actually governed by instincts and drives that we are unaware of. But to many of his critics, an unconscious self (especially one that expresses not-ready-for-prime-time desires through dreams, symptoms, and slips of the tongue) sounds like just another homunculus, not a real solution to the problem of personal agency. The more empirically grounded Behaviorists of the 1950s, such as B.F. Skinner, advocated that we stoically banish the notion of freedom altogether: Human behavior was purely mechanistic, as obedient to discernible causal laws as any other physical process, and we would create a better world if we gave up our childish belief in free will.

Findings in the neurosciences and cognitive science have lent considerable tacit support to this position. The neurobiologist Benjamin Libet found that motor actions subjects experienced as being consciously willed were actually initiated in the brain as much as a half second prior to subjects' awareness of their own intention (Libet, 1985). APS Fellow and Charter Member John Bargh (Yale) has conducted numerous studies showing the degree to which our actions are governed by automatic, nonconscious processes (see Bargh & Chartrand, 1999; Bargh & Williams, 2006). In light of these kinds of findings, some researchers, like APS Fellow Daniel M. Wegner (Harvard), argue that the feeling of conscious will is an illusion that arises when our automatically guided actions happen to coincide with our internal monitoring of them (Wegner, 2002).

One problem with eliminating free will from the picture is that with it goes the concept of personal responsibility, the philosophical underpinning of modern societies and the root of all ethics. For medieval theologians, human freedom was what makes humans capable of salvation—we can choose rightly and wrongly, and thereby help determine our fate not only here on earth but also in the hereafter. Jean-Paul Sartre went so far as to maintain that every second of our lives we are "radically free" to choose our destiny, fully responsible for every single thing we do, say, or think. (The French philosopher would have little patience for my excuses for not going to the gym.) In 2006, an anonymous editorial-writer in *The Economist* worried what would happen if neuroscience, by exposing the mechanisms of decision making, caused the ideas of free will and responsibility to disappear (Free to Choose?, 2006).

Bearing out such fears, recent research suggests that a world that disbelieved in free will would be a worse place, not better. In a study by Vohs and APS Fellow Jonathan W. Schooler (University of California, Santa Barbara) participants who read a passage about free will's nonexistence by the biologist Francis Crick (the discoverer of DNA) were more likely to cheat on a subsequent arithmetic task than were controls who read a neutral essay (Vohs & Schooler, 2008). In another study, participants read a series of passages that either affirmed or denied the existence of free will and then answered a set of GRE questions; they checked their own answers and rewarded themselves monetarily for their number correct. Again, there was a significant effect: Belief in determinism promoted cheating.

Are the notions of free will—and by extension willpower—simply convenient illusions that somehow keep us from misbehaving?

Sweet Freedom

Ironically, it may be the empirical mindset of psychology that rescues free will from oblivion. Complete determinism is just as unproven and scientifically unprovable as complete freedom is, Baumeister (2008) points out. Moreover, the fact that belief in and desire for freedom are enduring and universal features of human societies makes little sense if there is not some way in which free will is a relevant and useful construct. Baumeister argues that it is most productive to think of it as a continuum: Some people have it more than others, sometimes we are able to hold out for two marshmallows and sometimes we aren't, and it's the difference that is revealing and informative in a science of mind.

The ability to exercise conscious will over our impulses, Baumeister argues, was a late-evolving system that conferred enormous advantages on our ancestors by enabling them to live in complex cultural groups. The executive gray matter occupying the proud position over our eyes expanded rapidly after our hominid ancestors rose up on two feet and began making tools, communicating, and cooperating for the common good. Other social animals exert self-control too, but submitting that control to conscious, reasoned guidance—what most people mean by free will—seems to be a hallmark of humans, whose intricate, rule-bound societies far surpass in complexity those of other species. Yet free action was, and remains, limited by its high energetic costs, as revealed by the ego-depletion research already mentioned.

Recent research by one of Baumeister's students, Matt Gailliot (University of Amsterdam), has revealed just how apt the term *willpower*—once regarded by psychologists as merely a metaphor or folk concept—really is. The brain is powered by glucose, the same thing that powers your muscles. And though the brain makes up only 2 percent of the body's mass, it consumes an amazing 75 percent of the glucose in the blood; executive functions like reasoning, decision making, and impulse control may be especially demanding (Gailliot, 2008). Increased blood glucose has been linked to improved executive processing, working memory, and reaction time; low blood glucose or problems utilizing it have been linked to such self-control problems as aggression and criminality, impulsivity, poor attentional and emotional control, trouble coping with stress, and difficulty quitting smoking.

While working with Baumeister at Florida State University, Gailliot conducted a series of studies showing just what a glucose guzzler willpower can be (Gailliot et al., 2007). Participants in ego-depletion experiments were found to have significantly lower blood sugar following willpower-demanding tasks. And those who replenished their blood sugar with a sweetened drink after exercising self-control in an initial task were better able to master temptation in a subsequent task than a control group of subjects who instead quenched their thirst with an artificially sweetened beverage. Gailliot has also gone on to examine the role of glycogen, the chemical form in which glucose is stored in the body and brain for future use (Gailliot, 2008). The brain's glycogen stores become recharged during sleep and gradually become depleted over the course of the day. It is likely that this pattern partly accounts for the diminished willpower (and other aspects of executive functioning) commonly experienced in the evening. (Other factors that can drain glycogen stores are stress, alcohol, and possibly even high summer temperatures.)

The seeming irony for dieters in the willpower–blood glucose link is not lost on Gailliot and his colleagues: Future research will need to examine if there is a Catch-22 effect whereby limiting sugar intake through dieting could actually impede our ability to resist, say, sugary food (there's something else to make your homunculus spin). In any case, the authors emphasize that the lesson in their research is *not* to start sucking down soda or candy bars in an effort to boost willpower: Such foods give a quick, temporary boost to blood sugar, which is why the researchers used sweet drinks for their laboratory studies, but the effect is short lived. Over time, high sugar consumption can lead to insulin resistance or even diabetes, conditions in which the ability to metabolize glucose is seriously impaired (Taubes, 2007), with all the willpower problems that may entail. Fortunately, the glucose fuel needed for the body and brain are metabolized from many other, better food sources; protein and complex carbohydrates (e.g., vegetables and fruit) maintain a steady supply of glucose throughout the day and are surely a better bet for optimal brainpower and willpower (Gailliot et al, 2007).

Saving Gas

Willpower is a highly energy-demanding process in an already energy-hungry organ, so it makes sense that we only use it when we have to (Baumeister, 2008). Most of the time, for many of our daily-life activities, relatively automatic processes and reflexive responses to situational cues are good enough to guide us.

Given willpower's scarcity, an effective strategy for following through on your New Year's resolutions may be to circumvent it altogether. APS Fellow and Charter Member Peter M. Gollwitzer (NYU) has studied the difference between mere goals (such as "I want to lose weight") and *implementation intentions,* which actually specify a plan of action ("When the waiter comes, I'm going to order a salad"; Gollwitzer, Fujita, & Oettingen, 2004). The latter prove to be much more effective in helping us keep our promises to ourselves. Implementation intentions help us notice opportunities for working toward our objectives (e.g., the waiter taking my order) and even anticipate likely obstacles, prescribing ways of dealing with them. In a number of experiments, Gollwitzer has found that creating mental links between situational cues and predecided courses of action—"if–then plans"—helps enlist the force of habit to alleviate willpower's brain burden, allowing a predetermined behavior to unfold without too much effortful deliberation.

Whether we view willpower in terms of its muscle-like qualities or in terms of competing (e.g., hot vs. cold) circuits in a complex cognitive control system, a positive message in the psychological science of willpower is that self-mastery, however limited, is also responsive to intervention and improvement. By adjusting how we think of the things that tempt us in the short term and the goals we are striving for in the long, we can alter the balance of these influences. We can also build self-control the same way we build our biceps, not only improving its strength but also intelligently allocating it to high-priority challenges rather than wasting it on things that are less important. Future research may show that we can even optimize our willpower through diet. And knowing willpower's limitations helps point us in the direction of strategies that can help our goals run off as planned even if our inner decider is fatigued.

This leaves us with no more excuses. I'm off to the gym.

References

Ackerman, J.M., Goldstein, N.J., Shapiro, J.R., & Bargh, J.A. (in press). You wear me out: The vicarious depletion of self-control. *Psychological Science.*

Bargh, J.A., & Chartrand, T.L. (1999). The unbearable automaticity of being. *American Psychologist, 54,* 462–479.

Bargh, J.A., & Williams, E.L. (2006). The automaticity of social life. *Current Directions in Psychological Science, 15,* 1–4.

Baumeister, R.F. (2008). Free will in scientific psychology. *Perspectives on Psychological Science, 3,* 14–19.

Baumeister, R.F., & Vohs, K.D. (2004). *Handbook of self-regulation: Research, theory, and applications.* New York: Guilford.

Baumeister, R.F., Vohs, K.D., & Tice, D.M. (2007). The strength model of self-control. *Current Directions in Psychological Science, 16,* 351–355.

Bechara, A. (2005). Decision making, impulse control and loss of willpower to resist drugs: A neurocognitive perspective. *Nature Neuroscience, 8,* 1458–1463.

Bechara, A., Tranel, D., & Damasio, H. (2000). Characterization of the decision-making deficit of patients with ventromedial prefrontal cortex lesions. *Brain, 123,* 2189–2202.

Free to choose? Modern neuroscience is eroding the idea of free will. (2006, December 19). *The Economist, 381,* 16–18.

Gailliot, M.T. (2008). Unlocking the energy dynamics of executive functioning: Linking executive functioning to brain glycogen. *Perspectives on Psychological Science, 3,* 245–263.

Gailliot, M.T., Baumeister, R.F. DeWall, C.N., Maner, J.K., Plant, E.A., Tice, D.M., et al. (2007). Self-control relies on glucose as a limited energy source: Willpower is more than a metaphor. *Journal of Personality and Social Psychology, 92,* 325–336.

Gollwitzer, P.M., Fujita, K., & Oettingen, G. (2004). Planning and the implementation of goals. In R.F. Baumeister & K.D. Vohs (Eds.), *Handbook of self-regulation: Research, theory, and applications* (pp. 211–228). New York: Guilford.

Hooper, C.J., Luciana, M., Conklin, H.M., & Yarger, R.S. (2004). Adolescents' performance on the Iowa Gambling Task: Implications for the development of decision-making and ventromedial prefrontal cortex. *Developmental Psychology, 40,* 1148–1158.

Libet, B. (1985). Unconscious cerebral initiative and the role of conscious will in voluntary action. *Behavioral and Brain Sciences, 8,* 529–566.

Metcalfe, J., & Mischel, W. (1999). A hot/cool system analysis of delay of gratification: Dynamics of willpower. *Psychological Review, 106,* 3–19.

Mischel, W. (1996). From good intentions to willpower. In P.M. Gollwitzer and J.A. Bargh (Eds.), *The psychology of action.* (pp. 197–218). New York: Guilford.

Mischel, W., & Ayduk, O. (2004). Willpower in a cognitive-affective processing system: The dynamics of delay of gratification. In R.F. Baumeister & K.D. Vohs (Eds.), *Handbook of self-regulation: Research, theory, and applications* (99–129). New York: Guilford.

Muraven, M., & Baumeister, R.F. (2000). Self-regulation and depletion of limited resources: Does self-control resemble a muscle? *Psychological Bulletin, 126,* 247–259.

Muraven, M., Collins, R. L., Neinhaus, K. (2002). Self-control and alcohol restraint: An initial application of the self-control strength model. *Psychology of Addictive Behaviors, 16,* 113–120.

Reyna, V.F., & Farley, F. (2006). Risk and rationality in adolescent decision making: Implications for theory, practice, and public policy. *Psychological Science in the Public Interest, 7,* 1–44.

Segerstrom, S.C., & Solberg Nes, L. (2007). Heart rate variability reflects self-regulatory strength, effort, and fatigue. *Psychological Science, 18,* 275–281.

Shamosh, N.A., DeYoung, C.G., Green, A.E., Reis, D.L., Johnson, M.R., Conway, A.R.A., et al. (2008). Individual differences in delay discounting: Relation to intelligence, working memory, and anterior prefrontal cortex. *Psychological Science, 19,* 904–911.

Taubes, G. (2007). *Good calories, bad calories.* New York: Knopf.

Vohs, K.D., Baumeister, R.F., Schmeichel, B.J., Twenge, J.M., Nelson, N.M., & Tice, D.M. (2008). Making choices impairs subsequent self-control: A limited-resource account of decision making, self-regulation, and active initiative. *Journal of Personality and Social Psychology, 94,* 883–898.

Vohs, K.D., & Schooler, J.W. (2008). The value of believing in free will: Encouraging a belief in determinism increases cheating. *Psychological Science, 19,* 49–54.

Wagar, B.M., & Thagard, P. (2004). Spiking Phineas Gage: A neurocomputational theory of cognitive–affective integration in decision making. *Psychological Review, 111,* 67–79.

Wegner, D.M. (2002). *The illusion of conscious will.* Cambridge, MA: MIT Press.

Critical Thinking

1. How does self-control work?
2. How does self-control operate in the context of everyday life?
3. What are the key elements of a person's ability to exercise self-control?

Create Central

www.mhhe.com/createcentral

Internet References

Trying to resist temptation? Think about God

www.scientificamerican.com/article.cfm?id=trying-to-resist-tempation-think-about-god

Avoiding temptation: Self-control requires a good night of sleep

www.huffingtonpost.com/christopher-m-barnes/self-control-and-sleep_b_3327960.html

Article   Prepared by: Eric Landrum, *Boise State University*

What Does Guilt Do?

ART MARKMAN

Learning Outcomes

After reading this article, you will be able to:

- List the different methods by which guilt can be used to facilitate the repair of damaged interactions.

- Differentiate between guilt and other emotions, such as feeling badly; describe how are they similar and different.

If you do something wrong that hurts someone else, you feel *guilty*. Guilt is a valuable emotion, because it helps to maintain your ties to the people in your community. It provides a painful consequence for actions that would weaken the groups that you belong to.

Because guilt is painful, people often find ways to soothe their feelings by making up for their actions in some way. These repairs are also useful, because they help to re-strengthen people's ties to the community that they have damaged.

A paper in the May, 2012 issue of *Personality and Social Psychology Bulletin* by Cynthia Cryder, Stephen Springer, and Carey Morewedge explored the way that people make these repairs. They contrasted two possibilities. One possibility is that when you do something wrong, you try to make it up to the specific people you hurt. A second possibility is that a guilty person will try to do something for other people to help them feel better.

One set of studies explored a hypothetical situation described by a story. In this case, college students read that they were part of a group project. In a control condition, they were responsible for giving a presentation about the results of the project, and they gave the presentation. In an experimental condition, they were responsible for giving a presentation, but overslept.

Later that day, participants read that they were having dinner at a restaurant with a group. Some people were told that they were having dinner with their project *team*. The dinner was BYOB (bring your own bottle), and so participants had to select how much they would pay for a bottle of wine. They were allowed to select from a set of wines ranging in price (and quality) from $8 to $20. In addition, they were told that after dinner when everyone had paid what they thought they owed, the table was $9 short on the bill. Participants were asked how much additional money they would contribute toward the shortfall.

Participants who were made to feel guilty were willing to pay more for a bottle of wine, and they contributed more toward the bill than people who were not made to feel guilty.

So far, this result just indicates that guilty people want to do something to help people. In another condition, people made to feel guilty were told that they were having dinner with a different group of people. In this case, people spent about the same amount on the wine and the bill as those in the control condition. So, people want to make repairs specifically to the people they harmed.

Two other results from this set of studies are also interesting.

One is that guilt is a specific emotion that is different from just feeling bad about an action. In another study, the researchers compared feeling guilty (using the oversleeping scenario just described) to a case where someone cheated on the project by using slides prepared by a group who did a similar project the previous year. In this case, the dinner scenario only included the need to add money to the dinner bill. Participants who felt guilty added more money to the bill than those who cheated.

The second is that guilt also affected real decisions of participants. In a clever study, research participants were made to feel guilty toward another participant. They were given an elaborate description of the experiment written in small print. Few participants read the whole set of instructions. Then, they were given the choice of eating either some fruit flavored jellybeans or some vomit flavored jellybeans. Unsurprisingly, most people chose the fruit flavored jellybeans. After making their choice, participants were told that "as they read in the description of the study," another participant was going to have to eat the jellybeans they did not select. This made people feel guilty that they made someone else eat vomit flavored jellybeans. In a control condition, participants were told that their partner would eat the same flavor jellybeans they selected.

After eating the fruit flavored candy, participants played a *dictator game*. The dictator game comes from *behavioral economics*. Participants are given money (in this case $5) and are told that they can keep as much of it as they want, but they can choose how much they would like to give to a partner. Participants were told that their partner in this game was the same participant who would eat the jellybeans based on their initial selection. Participants whose initial choice forced their partner to eat vomit flavored beans gave about three times as much money to their partner as those whose initial choice forced their partner to eat fruit flavored beans.

These results show the positive power that guilt can have. Whenever you do something that could hurt another person, you run the risk of damaging your relationship with them. Your feelings of guilt lead you to be more generous to that person in a way that can demonstrate clearly that your relationship is valuable.

One thing that further research needs to explore is how people who have been hurt by someone else react to these gestures. It would be interesting to know whether you are more likely to *forgive* people who take actions to show that they value their relationship with you.

Critical Thinking

1. What is the value of guilt?

2. In an experimental situation where guilt is being studied, how does being made to feel guilty influence other feelings and behaviors?

3. What, if any, are some of the positive outcomes of guilt?

Create Central

www.mhhe.com/createcentral

Internet References

Guilt and shame
www.beyondintractability.org/essay/guilt-shame

5 tips for dealing with guilt
http://psychcentral.com/blog/archives/2007/11/27/5-tips-for-dealing-with-guilt

Markman, Art. Excerpted from *Ulterior Motives* and reprinted in *Psychology Today*, May 8, 2012. http://www.psychologytoday.com/blog/ulterior-motives/201205/what-does-guilt-do

Article   Prepared by: Eric Landrum, *Boise State University*

Need Motivation? Declare a Deadline

PHYLLIS KORKKI

Learning Outcomes

After reading this article, you will be able to:

- Distinguish between the relative pressures of working under a deadline and working without a deadline.

- Articulate the original meaning of the word "deadline."

At a meeting last Tuesday, I told my colleagues that I would finish this column—which is about deadlines—by noon on Thursday. I spent part of Tuesday afternoon searching the word "deadlines" on Google, but didn't make much progress. By late afternoon, I felt a tiny knot of fear in my stomach. What if I let my co-workers down? So I wrote something silly just to get started. This paragraph.

During my Googling I found out that Dan Ariely is an expert on deadlines, and I forced myself to contact him because I had promised to get this work done.

Making that declaration was a good move, as it turns out. Publicly committing to meeting a deadline is a powerful motivator because it puts your reputation on the line, said Mr. Ariely, a professor of psychology and behavioral economics at Duke University and the author of *Predictably Irrational.*

Workers who fail to meet deadlines risk the disapproval—and sometimes the wrath—of their managers and colleagues. Still, some people will blow a deadline, rationalizing that there is both a "deadline" and a "real deadline." They will use whatever devices and excuses they can muster to buy more time.

But what about assignments that don't have clear deadlines? Or projects that are so large that they must be done in increments, so that pulling an all-nighter isn't an option? Or creative goals that no one much cares about, except you?

I know people who, through boundless narcissism, single-minded obsession or unfathomable self-discipline can complete big projects without deadlines. Many of us, though, need a looming threat to finish major work.

People respond well to deadlines because meeting them provides a distinct feeling of having achieved something within a time frame. "It's a good way to keep score," Professor Ariely said.

It is possible to motivate yourself, he said, by announcing a deadline to others—perhaps on Facebook or on Twitter. Not meeting the deadline would then feel like breaking a promise, he said: "It does say something about your character."

A mere announcement on Twitter, though, would hardly be enough for die-hard procrastinators. If you are one of them, consider creating a situation that has real consequences, Professor Ariely said. Give a friend $100 and say, "If I don't meet my deadline you can keep this." Or, he said, try the prospect of public humiliation. Make a bet with your friends: if you don't meet the deadline, you must run through the streets naked.

Perhaps Professor Ariely has friends who really would force him to run naked through the streets of Durham, N.C. My friends are warm and supportive and would say "that's O.K." if I didn't meet my self-imposed deadline, which, of course, makes them wonderful friends but not good enforcers.

I have always wanted to write a book, however, and it occurs to me: Why not hire someone to hector me? Services like TaskRabbit have sprung up to help people with all manner of tasks, including fixing their computers and doing their laundry. Surely a stranger would be willing, for a small fee, to call or text me and say: "Have you written those 500 words you said you would write by 8 a.m.?" It's worth a try. A shaming e-mail if I don't do my assignment should be included in the price.

Here may be the secret to meeting a big self-imposed deadline: First, divide the work into smaller tasks and set deadlines for every one of them. Then find a tough and reliable person to hold you accountable for meeting each one. Make meeting the big deadline—not achieving perfection—the ultimate goal. Voilà. You're making no guarantees of quality, but perhaps your work can be improved later.

THIS column, for example, is nowhere near as good as it was as a vague idea in my mind's eye. There's so much more I wanted to cover, including the etymology of the word "deadline." (O.K., I'll throw it in: It was formerly "a boundary around a military prison beyond which a prisoner could not venture without risk of being shot by the guards," according to Dictionary.com.)

I wanted to discuss the link between death and deadlines, and whether death awareness affects people at work, a topic that has been explored by Prof. Adam Grant, an organizational psychologist at the Wharton School of the University of Pennsylvania.

But I ran out of time, and that's the point. This column—inferior though it is to what I had imagined—is done, and it's done because I had a deadline.

Critical Thinking

1. Think about deadlines and your own work. Do you work best without the pressure of a deadline, or do you prefer a deadline? Do you work far in advance of the deadline, or start work just before its due date? Explore and explain.

2. Do you (or others you know) utilize self-imposed deadlines? Is that more or less effective for you than other-imposed deadlines? Explain.

Create Central

www.mhhe.com/createcentral

Internet References

Motivating employees to reach deadlines

http://work.chron.com/motivating-employees-reach-deadlines-3145.html

How the most successful people motivate themselves (and stay motivated)

http://work.chron.com/motivating-employees-reach-deadlines-3145.html

Article

Prepared by: Eric Landrum, *Boise State University*

Self-Efficacy in the Workplace: Implications for Motivation and Performance

FRED C. LUNENBURG

Learning Outcomes

After reading this article, you will be able to:

- Articulate the definition of self-efficacy and understand how it applies to the workplace.

- Identify the four major factors thought to influence self-efficacy as presented by the author.

Mainly due to the work of Albert Bandura, self-efficacy has a widely acclaimed theoretical foundation (Bandura, 1986), an extensive knowledge base (Bandura, 1997; Maddux, 1995, 2002), and a proven record of application in the workplace (Bandura, 1997, 2004; Stajkovic & Luthans, 1998). Nine large-scale meta-analyses consistently demonstrate that the efficacy beliefs of organization members contribute significantly to their level of motivation and performance (Bandura & Locke, 2003).

Self-Efficacy Defined

Self-efficacy (also known as *social cognitive theory* or *social learning theory*) is a person's belief that she is capable of performing a particular task successfully (Bandura, 1977, 1997). Think of self-efficacy as a kind of self-confidence (Kanter, 2006) or a task-specific version of self-esteem (Brockner, 1988). Self-efficacy has three dimensions: *magnitude,* the level of task difficulty a person believes she can attain; *strength,* the conviction regarding magnitude as strong or weak; and *generality,* the degree to which the expectation is generalized across situations. An employee's sense of capability influences his perception, motivation, and performance (Bandura, 1997). We rarely attempt to perform a task when we expect to be unsuccessful.

Following is an example. One professor may believe that she can learn how to teach graduate courses online on her own. Another professor may have strong doubts about his ability to learn how to teach graduate courses online without taking some

formal training. Self-efficacy has powerful effects on learning, motivation, and performance, because people try to learn and perform only those tasks that they believe they will be able to perform successfully. Self-efficacy affects learning and performance in three ways (Bandura, 1982):

1. *Self-efficacy influences the goals that employees choose for themselves.* Employees with low levels of self-efficacy tend to set relatively low goals for themselves. Conversely, an individual with high self-efficacy is likely to set high personal goals. Research indicates that people not only learn but also perform at levels consistent with their self-efficacy beliefs.

2. *Self-efficacy influences learning as well as the effort that people exert on the job.* Employees with high self-efficacy generally work hard to learn how to perform new tasks, because they are confident that their efforts will be successful. Employees with low self-efficacy may exert less effort when learning and performing complex tasks, because they are not sure the effort will lead to success.

3. *Self-efficacy influences the persistence with which people attempt new and difficult tasks.* Employees with high self-efficacy are confident that they can learn and perform a specific task. Thus, they are likely to persist in their efforts even when problems surface. Conversely, employees with low self-efficacy who believe they are incapable of learning and performing a difficult task are likely to give up when problems surface. In an extensive literature review on self-efficacy, Albert Bandura and Edwin Locke (2003) concluded that self-efficacy is a powerful determinant of job performance.

Sources of Self-Efficacy

Since self-efficacy can have powerful effects on organizations, it is important to identify its origin. Bandura (1997) has identified four principal sources of self-efficacy: past performance, vicarious experience, verbal persuasion, and emotional cues.

Past Performance

According to Bandura, the most important source of self-efficacy is past performance. Employees who have succeeded on job-related tasks are likely to have more confidence to complete similar tasks in the future (high self-efficacy) than employees who have been unsuccessful (low self-efficacy). Managers or supervisors can boost self-efficacy through careful hiring, providing challenging assignments, professional development and coaching, goal setting, supportive leadership, and rewards for improvement.

Vicarious Experience

A second source of self-efficacy is through vicarious experience. Seeing a co-worker succeed at a particular task may boost your self-efficacy. For example, if your co-worker loses weight, this may increase your confidence that you can lose weight as well. Vicarious experience is most effective when you see yourself as similar to the person you are modeling. Watching LeBron James dunk a basketball might not increase your confidence in being able to dunk the basketball yourself if you are 5 feet, 6 inches tall. But if you observe a basketball player with physical characteristics similar to yourself, it can be persuasive.

Verbal Persuasion

The third source of self-efficacy is through verbal persuasion. Essentially this involves convincing people that they have the ability to succeed at a particular task. The best way for a leader to use verbal persuasion is through the *Pygmalion effect*. The Pygmalion effect is a form of a self-fulfilling prophesy in which believing something to be true can make it true.

Rosenthal and Jacobson's (1968) classic study is a good example of the Pygmalion effect. Teachers were told by their supervisor that one group of students had very high IQ scores (when in fact they had average to low IQ scores), and the same teacher was told that another group of students had low IQ scores (when in fact they had high IQ scores). Consistent with the Pygmalion effect, the teachers spent more time with the students they *thought* were smart, gave them more challenging assignments, and expected more of them—all of which led to higher student self-efficacy and better student grades. A more recent experiment conducted by Harvard researchers in a ghetto community produced similar results (Rist, 2000). The Pygmalion effect also has been used in the workplace. Research has indicated that when managers are confident that their subordinates can successfully perform a task, the subordinates perform at a higher level. However, the power of the persuasion would be contingent on the leader's credibility, previous relationship with the employees, and the leader's influence in the organization (Eden, 2003).

Emotional Cues

Finally, Bandura argues that emotional cues dictate self-efficacy. A person who expects to fail at some task or finds something too demanding is likely to experience certain physiological symptoms: a pounding heart, feeling flushed, sweaty palms, headaches, and so on. The symptoms vary from individual to individual, but if they persist may become associated with poor performance.

Self-efficacy has been related to other motivation theories. Edwin Locke and Gary Latham suggest that goal-setting theory and self-efficacy theory complement each other. When a leader sets difficult goals for employees, this leads employees to have a higher level of self-efficacy and also leads them to set higher goals for their own performance. Why does this happen? Research has shown that setting difficult goals for people communicates confidence (Locke & Latham, 2002). For example, suppose that your supervisor sets a high goal for you. You learn that it is higher than the goal she has set for your colleagues. How would you interpret this? You would probably think that your supervisor believes you are capable of performing better than others. This sets in motion a psychological process in which you are more confident in yourself (higher self-efficacy) and then you set higher personal goals for yourself causing you to perform better. Self-efficacy also may be related to effort-performance relationships in expectancy theory (Vroom, 1964).

Implications of Self-Efficacy in the Workplace

Bandura devotes considerable attention to the workplace in his groundbreaking book, *Self-Efficacy: The Exercise of Control*. More recently, he provided an extensive review of the growing body of research dealing with the direct and indirect influence of self-efficacy on work-related personal and organizational effectiveness (Bandura, 2004). This research review of the impact of self-efficacy includes a wide range of topics such as training and development, teaming (i.e., collective efficacy), change and innovation, leadership, and stress. From this considerable body of theory and research on self-efficacy, the following managerial and organizational implications are provided (Ivancevich, Konopaske, & Matteson, 2011; Luthans, Yuussef, & Avolio, 2007):

Selection/Promotion Decisions

Organizations should select individuals who have high levels of self-efficacy. These people will be motivated to engage in the behaviors that will help them perform well in the workplace. A measure of self-efficacy can be administered during the hiring/promotion process.

Training and Development

Organizations should consider employee levels of self-efficacy when choosing among candidates for training and development programs. If the training budget is limited, then greater return (i.e., job performance) on training investment can be realized by sending only those employees high in self-efficacy. These people will tend to learn more from the training and, ultimately, will be more likely to use that learning to enhance their job performance.

Goal Setting and Performance

Organizations can encourage higher performance goals from employees who have high levels of self-efficacy. This will lead to higher levels of job performance from employees, which is critical for many organizations in an era of high competition.

Conclusion

Self-efficacy (beliefs about one's ability to accomplish specific tasks) influences the tasks employees choose to learn and the goals they set for themselves. Self-efficacy also affects employees' level of effort and persistence when learning difficult tasks. Four sources of self-efficacy are past performance, vicarious experience, verbal persuasion, and emotional cues. Managerial and organizational implications of self-efficacy in the workplace include hiring and promotion decisions, training and development, and goal setting.

References

Bandura, A. (1977). *Social learning theory.* Englewood Cliffs, NJ: Prentice Hall.

Bandura, A. (1982). Self-efficacy mechanism in human agency. *American Psychologist, 37,* 122–147.

Bandura, A. (1986). *Social foundations of thought and action.* Upper Saddle River, NJ: Prentice Hall.

Bandura, A. (1997). *Self-Efficacy: The exercise of control.* New York, NY: W.H. Freeman.

Bandura, A. (2004). Cultivate self-efficacy for personal and organizational effectiveness. In E. A. Locke (Ed.), *Handbook of principles of organizational behavior* (pp. 120–136). Malden, MA: Blackwell.

Bandura, A., & Locke, E. A. (2003). Negative self-efficacy and goal effects revisited. *Journal of Applied Psychology, 88*(1), 87–99.

Brockner, J. (1988). Self-esteem at work. Lexington, MA: Lexington Books.

Eden, D. (2003). Self-fulfilling prophecies in organizations. In J. Greenberg (Ed.), *Organizational behavior: The state of the science* (2nd ed.) (pp. 91–122). Mahwah, NJ: Erlbaum.

Ivancevich, J. M., Konopaske, R., & Matteson, M. T. (2011). *Organizational behavior and management* (9th ed.). New York, NY: McGraw-Hill.

Kanter, R. M. (2006). *Confidence: How winning and losing streaks begin and end.* New York, NY: Crown Publishing.

Locke, E. A., & Latham, G. P. (2002). Building a practically useful theory of goal setting and task motivation: A 35-year odyssey. *American Psychologist, 57*(9), 707–717.

Luthans, F., Youssef, C. M., & Avolio, B. J. (2007). *Psychological capital.* New York, NY: Oxford University Press.

Maddux, J. E. (1995). *Self-efficacy, adaptation and adjustment: Theory, research, and application.* New York, NY: Plenum Press.

Maddux, J. E. (2002). Self-efficacy. In C. R. Snyder & S. J. Lopez (Eds.), *Handbook of positive psychology* (pp. 277–287). New York, NY: Oxford University Press.

Rist, R. C. (2000). Student social class and teacher expectations: The self-fulfilling prophesy in ghetto education. *Harvard Educational Review, 70*(3), 266–301.

Rosenthal, R., & Jacobson, L. (1968). *Pygmalion in the classroom.* New York, NY: Holt, Rinehart, and Winston.

Stajkovic, A. D., & Luthans, F. (1988). Self-efficacy and work-related performance: A meta-analysis. *Psychological Bulletin, 124*(2), 240–261.

Vroom, V. H. (1994). *Work and motivation.* New York, NY: Wiley.

Critical Thinking

1. Thinking about your own work history—or the work you hope to have someday—what would be some of the factors or variables that will influence your self-efficacy (your belief that you can perform certain tasks successfully)?

2. Thinking about past performance, vicarious experience, verbal persuasion, and emotional cues, which of those do you think will influence you the most in a future job or career? Explain your answer.

Create Central

www.mhhe.com/createcentral

Internet References

Assessing the importance of building self-efficacy to impact motivation, performance levels, and team effectiveness

http://thesportdigest.com/archive/article/assessing-importance-building
-self-efficacy-impact-motivation-performance-levels-and-team-e-0

Employee self-efficacy: How to identify, how to help

http://psychlearningjournal.wordpress.com/2012/03/26/employee-self
-efficacy-how-to-identify-how-to-help

Lunenburg, Fred C. From *International Journal of Management, Business, and Administration,* vol. 14, no. 1, 2011, pp. 1–6. Copyright © 2011 by The International Journal of Business and Management Research. Reprinted by permission.

Unit 7

UNIT

Prepared by: Eric Landrum, *Boise State University*

Development

Two families—the Garcias and the Smiths—are brand new parents; in fact, they are still at the hospital with their newborns. When the babies are not in their mothers' rooms, both sets of parents wander down to the hospital's neonatal nursery where pediatric nurses care for both babies—José Garcia and Kimberly Smith. Kimberly is alert, active, and often cries and squirms when her parents watch her. On the other hand, José is quiet, often asleep, and less attentive to external commotion when his parents view him in the nursery.

Why are these babies so different? Are the differences gender related? Will these differences disappear as these children develop, or will they be expressed even more prominently? What role will parenting choices play in the development of each child? Will Kimberly excel at sports and José excel at art? Can Kimberly overcome her parents' poverty and succeed in a professional career? Will José become a doctor like his mother or a pharmacist like his father? Will both of these children avoid childhood disease, maltreatment, and the other misfortunes that sometimes occur with children? Developmental psychologists are concerned with all of the Kimberlys and Josés of our world. Developmental psychologists study age-related changes in language, motor and social skills, cognition, and physical health. Developmental psychologists are interested in the common skills shared by all children, as well as the differences among children, and the events that create these differences. And developmental psychologists are not only interested in child development, but our development over the lifespan from birth to death.

For just a moment, think back over your developmental path. What kind of person are you? What sorts of skills do you possess? Are you artistic? Are you athletic? Do you enjoy reading? Do you speak more than one language? Are you outgoing or shy? Do you have higher levels of self-control or lower levels of self-control? What about your personal values such as integrity and honor—how did you acquire these values? Did you have to work hard at becoming the person you are now, or did you just sort of become who you are naturally? Think now about the present and the future. How are you changing as a college student—is college shaping the way you think and challenging your values and beliefs? Will you ever stop developing or changing or growing or looking at the world in new ways?

In general, developmental psychologists are concerned with the forces that guide and direct development over the course of a lifetime. Some developmental theorists argue that the major forces that shape a child are found in the environment, such as social class, quality of available stimulation, parenting style, and so on. Other theorists insist that genetics and related physiological/ biological factors such as hormones are the major forces that underlie human development. A third set of psychologists believe that a combination or interaction of both sets of factors (nature and nurture) are responsible for development. In this unit, we explore what developmental psychologists can tell us about human growth and change over the lifespan.

Article   Prepared by: Eric Landrum, *Boise State University*

The Mind at Midlife

Longstanding beliefs say the adult brain is best in its youth, but research now suggests otherwise. The middle-aged mind preserves many of its youthful skills and even develops some new strengths.

MELISSA LEE PHILLIPS

Learning Outcome

After reading this article, you will be able to:

- Explain the nature of the human mind in middle-aged people.

Ask those who've entered the thick of middle age what they think about their mental capacities and you're likely to hear a slew of complaints—their brains don't work as quickly as they used to, they're distractable and unfocused, and they can never remember anyone's name.

While some of these complaints reflect real declines in brain function in our middle years, the deficiencies of a middle-aged brain have likely been overstated by anecdotal evidence and even by some scientific studies.

Contrary to its reputation as a slower, duller version of a youthful brain, it seems that the middle-aged mind not only maintains many of the abilities of youth but actually acquires some new ones. The adult brain seems to be capable of rewiring itself well into middle age, incorporating decades of experiences and behaviors. Research suggests, for example, the middle-aged mind is calmer, less neurotic and better able to sort through social situations. Some middle-agers even have improved cognitive abilities.

"There is an enduring potential for plasticity, reorganization and preservation of capacities," says cognitive neuroscientist Patricia Reuter-Lorenz, PhD, of the University of Michigan in Ann Arbor.

Researchers now have an unprecedented wealth of data on the aging brain from the Seattle Longitudinal Study, which has tracked the cognitive abilities of thousands of adults over the past 50 years. These results show that middle-aged adults perform better on four out of six cognitive tests than those same individuals did as young adults, says study leader Sherry Willis, PhD, of the University of Washington in Seattle.

While memorization skills and perceptual speed both start to decline in young adulthood, verbal abilities, spatial reasoning, simple math abilities and abstract reasoning skills all improve in middle age.

Cognitive skills in the aging brain have also been studied extensively in pilots and air-traffic controllers. Again, older pilots show declines in processing speed and memory capacity, but their overall performance seems to remain intact. In a study published in *Neurology* (Vol. 68, No. 9) in 2007, researchers tested pilots age 40 to 69 as they performed on flight simulators. Older pilots took longer to learn to use the simulators but did a better job than their younger colleagues at achieving their objective: avoiding collisions.

Many middle-aged people are convinced that they're just not as mentally skilled or even as intelligent as they used to be, Willis says. But it's possible that's an illusion arising from the aspects of cognition that do suffer in middle age.

"They may get the sense they're cognitively slow just because they're perceptually slow or slow with psychomotor skills," she says, when in reality their brains are performing most tasks remarkably well.

"This time of life brings so many new opportunities to invest in your own cognitive and physical resources, so you can buffer against the effects of older age."

—Patricia Reuter-Lorenz
University of Michigan in Ann Arbor

Changing Strategies

Researchers used to believe that brain activity would slow down with aging so that older brains would show less activity overall than younger ones. But functional neuroimaging studies have overturned that assumption.

For example, psychologist Cheryl Grady, PhD, of the University of Toronto, and her colleagues have found that older adults use more of their brains than young adults to accomplish certain tasks. In a study published in the *Journal of Neuroscience* (Vol. 3, No. 2) in 1994, Grady reported that performing a face-matching task activates mainly the occipital visual areas in younger adults, but older adults use these areas as well as the prefrontal cortex. (Both groups of adults are equally skilled at the task.)

Several groups, including Grady's, have also found that older adults tend to use both brain hemispheres for tasks that only activate one hemisphere in younger adults. Younger adults show similar bilateralization of brain activity if the task is difficult enough, Reuter-Lorenz says, but older adults use both hemispheres at lower levels of difficulty.

The strategy seems to work. According to work published in *Neuroimage* (Vol. 17, No. 3) in 2002, the best-performing older adults are the most likely to show this bilateralization. Older adults who continue to use only one hemisphere don't perform as well.

Reuter-Lorenz finds these changes with age encouraging, as they show that the middle-aged brain is capable of altering how it does things in order to accomplish the task at hand. "Compensation through some brain mechanisms may make up for losses in others," she says.

Grady cautions that many studies on the middle-aged brain are preliminary, as this age group "hasn't been studied very much. It certainly hasn't been studied enough." Most functional imaging studies, for example, tend to recruit college students and retirees as study subjects, Grady says. Cognitive characteristics of in-between ages are often simply extrapolated from the two ends of the spectrum.

While a linear continuum may be accurate for many traits, it may not always be a valid assumption. Grady's own work on brain activation during memory tasks, for example, suggests that the middle-aged pattern does fall between those of a young adult and an elderly person.

For example, the amount of white matter in the brain, which forms the connections among nerve cells, seems to increase until age 40 or 50 and then falls off again. "So that suggests that there are some developmental changes that really don't hit their peak until somewhere in middle age," Grady says.

At Least the Glasses Are Rose-Colored

Emotions and social interactions—even personality—may systematically change as people enter middle age. Many studies have found that people become calmer and less neurotic as they age. "There's a quieting of emotional storms," Reuter-Lorenz says.

Work by cognitive psychologist Mara Mather, PhD, of the University of Southern California in Los Angeles, has found that older adults tend to focus more on positive information and less on negative information than their younger counterparts. In 2004, she and her colleagues reported in *Psychological Science* (Vol. 15, No. 4) that the amygdala in older adults actually responds less to negative stimuli (such as unpleasant pictures) than it does in young adults. Starting around age 40, people also show a better memory for positive images than for negative ones, and this trend continues until at least age 80.

This "positivity effect" is seen even more strongly in people who are doing exceptionally well cognitively, Mather says, "so it doesn't seem to be something that just goes along with cognitive decline; it seems to be something that's an active process."

These findings fit with many self-reports from middle-aged and older individuals, Mather says. Older adults rank emotional stability and positive affect as more important than younger adults do, and they say that they're better at regulating their own emotions than they were in their youth.

Although scientifically analyzing such qualities as judgment and wisdom is considerably more difficult than measuring psychomotor speed or memory storage capacity, some researchers are trying to do just that. Research over the past several years has reported that middle-aged people are much more expert at many social interactions—such as judging the true intentions of other human beings—than are those either younger or older.

And work by David Laibson, PhD, at Harvard University, found that adults in midlife show better economic understanding and make better financial decisions than either younger or older adults. In fact, the average person's financial judgment seems to peak at 53.

Variability and Influences

One of the middle-aged mind's most striking features may not be any one feature or ability, but rather the variation in cognitive skills that's found in this age group. Although differences in cognition obviously exist among individuals at all ages, these differences seem to increase in middle age.

For example, memory and attention frequently suffer in middle age, but some individuals' abilities actually improve in midlife. In Willis's Seattle study, most participants' ability to remember lists of words declined in middle age, but about 15 percent performed better on this task than they did as young adults.

"If you study a wide range of abilities, you begin to realize how very complex cognitive decline is and how many individual differences there are," Willis says.

This variation in behavioral performance is also reflected in expression of genes related to learning and memory. In a study published in *Nature* in 2004 (Vol. 429, No. 6,994), the brains of adults under age 40 consistently showed little damage and high levels of expression of these genes, while brains from those over 73 showed lots of damage and low gene expression. But in the middle-aged group, results varied widely. Some middle-aged brains were already shutting down, whereas others were indistinguishable from a 30-year-old brain.

"It's a very interesting and heterogeneous group," Grady says. With more study of middle age in general—especially of those who seem to glide through those years with cognitive abilities intact or even improving—scientists hope to enable many more people to preserve cognitive health into old age.

So far, research suggests that remaining cognitively impressive with age comes from adopting certain behaviors as well as possessing some genetic luck, Willis says. For example, researchers have identified several gene variants that are risk factors for early memory problems. But people who show cognitive improvement in midlife also tend to be more physically, cognitively and socially active than those who don't fare as well.

"Instead of a crisis, middle age should be thought of as a time for a new form of self-investment," Reuter-Lorenz says. "This time of life brings so many new opportunities to invest in your own cognitive and physical resources, so you can buffer against the effects of older age."

Critical Thinking

1. What are the characteristics of mental life during middle age?
2. Describe the ways in which modern research is shedding new light on our beliefs about cognitive functioning during middle age.
3. What are some of the research findings regarding being calm and neuroticism as people age?

Create Central

www.mhhe.com/createcentral

Internet References

Half dead: Men and the "midlife crisis"
http://blogs.scientificamerican.com/bering-in-mind/2011/10/03/half-dead-men-and-the-mid-life-crisis

Fighting depression and the midlife crisis
http://healthymidlife.com/fight-midlife-depression-crisis

The midlife crisis: An opportunity in disguise?
http://psychcentral.com/lib/the-mid-life-crisis-an-opportunity-in-disguise/00010442

Article | Prepared by: Eric Landrum, *Boise State University*

Blessed Are Those Who Mourn— and Those Who Comfort Them

In our death-denying society, all too often the message is: Get over it and get back to normal. The fact is, the bereaved's "normal" never will be the same.

DOLORES PUTERBAUGH

Learning Outcomes

After reading this article, you will be able to:

- Assess the theory that the United States is a "death-denying society."
- Explain the most effective approach to interacting with a person who has recently experienced death of a friend or significant other.

Disbelief is the first thing you feel. The news does not make any sense. There is some mental scrambling around for an anchor. Is this real? How could this be? There is sadness and surprise and, perhaps hidden in the back of your mind, a sense of relief that it did not happen to you.

A friend, coworker, or extended family member has lost a loved one. Perhaps it was after a long illness, or maybe it was sudden and even violent: a crime, an accident, or suicide. The deceased may have been very old or an infant, perhaps not even yet born. Your friend's life has been irreparably changed, and you have an important role to play—even if you are "just" a coworker.

We live in a death-denying society. Most companies offer little time off for survivors, with many people using vacation days or even unpaid leave to accommodate vigils, funeral, and initial recovery. The physically and emotionally wounded survivors return to school or work within days, and often the expectation is that they will be "back to normal." The fact is, their "normal" has changed forever. Bereavement is a ripping away of part of one's heart. A hospice nurse told me the thing that strikes her most about bereavement counseling is that people always are taken by surprise at how powerful it is; the societal message of "getting over it" has infected most individuals.

Since we all will go through this—not once, but many times—it makes sense to figure out what to do to be helpful.

Perhaps this will come back around to us, or perhaps we will just have the satisfaction of knowing that we tried to be supportive of a friend in need.

In *Healing Grief at Work: 100 Practical Ideas After Your Workplace Is Touched by a Loss,* clinician Alan Wolfelt reveals the experience of a client whose coworkers announced, one year after her child's death, that it was time to put away the picture on her desk and move on with her life. Knowing that this is shockingly inappropriate still does not provide guidance on how to behave. Of course, you would like to think you are more compassionate than that, but how can one act on that compassion? Some simple aspects to being appropriately supportive are: be physically present; do not assume the "expert's" position; be a friend.

If a coworker has lost a loved one, you might not think it appropriate to go to the vigil or the funeral. Go! The vigil, visitation, and funerals, as well as the meal afterwards, not only are for the deceased—they are for the mourners, who need affirmation of their loss, recognition of their status as mourners, and support in their time of pain. Make sure you sign the guest book, greet the family, and participate in the rites whenever appropriate. Religious rites exist to help honor the deceased person and to provide comfort to the bereaved; every faith has developed rites to be celebrated in community, not alone. As part of the community of survivors, your role is to offer support.

In the weeks after the loss, continue to provide a physical presence. You may be rebuffed; deal with it and keep trying. This is not a time to keep score over whose turn it is to call whom, or who is next to invite whom to lunch. Prepare meals; invite the mourners over for food or call and invite yourself (with a prepared meal) over to their house. Show up with cleaning supplies or with a box of tissues. It can mean a lot to someone if you are able to help with the tasks that the deceased used to do. The survivor may be too upset or physically incapable of taking over the deceased's chores. Asking for help is difficult for most people, so volunteer your services.

Losing someone we love creates a tremendous void inside. The mourner may feel completely without anchor. This individual cannot be expected to hold up his or her end of the relationship with you at present. Saying, "Call me if you want to talk," is not good enough; be the one who calls and says, "How are you?" or "What about going out for breakfast on Saturday?" Evenings and weekends usually are hardest for those in mourning; make yourself available and be specific with your invitations.

Mourners often complain to me that friends, coworkers, and extended family analyze their (the mourners') grief process and mental health. This is not useful feedback. A common intervention by nonmourners is to provide unsolicited instruction on what stage of grief the mourner is experiencing. Some friends attempt to provide comfort by trying to put the loss into perspective. Another common error is to give mental health diagnoses and recommendations. Not only is this presumptuous, but it is self-aggrandizing on the friends', coworkers', or extended family's part. It is as if to say, "Let's look at you as a case study."

In a similar vein, more misused than any other expert is Elisabeth Kubler-Ross, whose 1969 work, *On Death and Dying,* was based on intensive interviews with the terminally ill and their families. She identified specific stages that occurred between the terminal diagnosis and death: denial and isolation; anger; bargaining; depression; acceptance; and hope. In the first stage, the reality is not accepted; the patient believes this is not happening. In the second stage, the reality begins to set in, but there is anger. From a psychological standpoint, anger is the emotion that accompanies the desire to change a situation; the dying person wants to fight the terminal condition. Next comes bargaining, generally with God: if you cure me, I'll never ———— or I'll always ————. This normal reaction can become paralyzing if the ill person is burdened with an ill-formed theology that believes in a higher power who doles out earthly experiences based on behavior. When bargaining fails, a depressed state of helplessness often ensues. It is beneficial if the dying are able to reach a stage of acceptance and hope. With all due respect to Kubler-Ross and her landmark work with the dying, many researchers and clinicians believe we cannot transfer her stages of dying on those in grief.

These normal reactions to terrible news often have been used to provide a template for grief. However, other researchers and specialists in the field offer different structures for making sense of the mourning process. J.W. Worden identified four primary tasks of grieving that assure a healthy outcome: accepting the fact of the death; working through the pain of the grief; adjusting to a world without the deceased; and renegotiating the internal relationship with the deceased so that the survivor can move forward with life.

Friends and coworkers should—at all costs —avoid announcing to the bereaved what stage, phase, or task they believe the mourner is experiencing at present, or should be. There are not very many "shoulds," if any, in grieving. Each person's experience of grief is unique and even experienced counselors are hesitant to assess any judgment on where someone "should" be at a given point in their grief. There are some specific things that

must happen for a grief to become integrated into the person, but these happen gradually, with some overlapping, regressing, patience, and considerable pain.

Gaining Perspective

Another error often made by those trying to comfort grieving persons is attempting to put things into perspective. Survivors have been told to be grateful that someone who died unexpectedly "went quickly without suffering," while those whose loved ones died in hospice care are informed that they are fortunate that there was an opportunity to "say goodbye." Others who nursed dying loved ones for weeks, months, or even years have confided that friends are less sympathetic because they presume they "had a chance to prepare and could do their grieving in advance." Each person's experience of grief is unique, shaped by the relationship as well as their history, spirituality, and physical, emotional, and mental resources. Friends and family should refrain from rating someone else's grief.

This also is not a time to diagnose. As a mental health professional, I sometimes am asked about this: When is grieving "depression"? This question most often comes from friends of a survivor. My response is that it is normal to feel depressed after a tremendous loss. For some months, the bereaved can expect to have disruptions in sleep, appetite, and energy. Some people will sleep often; a bereavement counselor with more than 20 years in the field describes the experience of grief like recovering from major surgery: sleep and healthy foods are imperative parts of healing; take naps every day, she recommends. Others may suffer lack of sleep. They feel exhausted and crave the escape of sleep, but are restless. Some lose their appetite while others may gain weight by eating for comfort. Concentration may be very poor, and short-term memory temporarily may become impaired. Most mourners can benefit from carrying a small notebook and writing down all tasks, even the simplest, for a few months after the death.

Some mourners will suffer a terrifying inertia. Taking the initiative to call you will be overwhelming. Simple tasks often take twice as long as usual. Doing any chores around the house will feel exhausting, and it especially can be difficult to take over the things that the deceased used to do. Others may fly into a frenetic pace, using busyness as a kind of drug to keep the emotional darkness at bay.

It is important to take some kind of action if the person shows signs of suicidal planning, such as talking about "when I'm gone," giving away personal items, and suddenly seeming upbeat (a sign that he or she has come to a decision about how to handle things—by dying). In this case, immediately go to other family members, clergy, or consult a mental health professional on what to do.

This is not a time to preach. Even ordained clergy assert that it is not recommended at this juncture to teach the mourning about your particular theology of life and death. Accept them where they are and help them find comfort within their own tradition. Encourage and let yourself be part of the rituals of grieving: prayer services, memorial Masses, candles, planting trees, or otherwise offering memorial are important means to express formally the process of separation and loss.

Being a good friend, coworker, or family member to someone who is mourning is simple, but not always easy. In many ways, you should continue whatever your relationship was before the death. If you had lunch together, continue to have lunch together; if you rotated card games at one another's home, keep up the routine.

Do not be afraid to say the deceased person's name. If tears come, it is not because you reminded the mourner of the dead person. He or she was in no danger of forgetting! Most people want to hear people talk about the person they love. They want to hear the funny stories and warm memories you may have, or be given the opportunity to share some of their own. Let them tell you the same stories over and over. This narration of the life they shared is part of the healing process. Ask to see photo albums and to hear the tales of times past. Listen to the story of the death and surrounding experiences as often as you have to. They are integrating the story of the person they love and have lost into their life in the present.

Mourners may ask if they are "going crazy" based on poor concentration, edginess, thinking they see or hear the deceased, and either great tearfulness or an inability to cry. It would help if friends and coworkers were patient and accepting of these aspects to grief.

Keep in mind the anniversaries of the death and, if you were close to the people, any significant dates such as birthdays or wedding anniversaries. Monthly anniversaries of the death are very difficult and mourners are well aware of these dates. Send a card, bring in flowers, or invite your friend over for a meal.

Holidays will be terribly difficult: Do not wait until the last minute to invite someone in mourning over for Thanksgiving, a concert, and other holiday (or nonholiday) religious or social activities. If the person is "taken" for Thanksgiving, ask them for the next day. That typical four-day holiday weekend can be torture if it seems like everyone else is with people they love.

Let's Talk—Or Not

For many, talking about their feelings is difficult. Our voyeuristic television shows may indicate otherwise, but it often is hard to discuss one's innermost feelings. Activities done side-by-side, rather than face-to-face, may encourage gradual conversation and sharing of thoughts, feelings, and memories surrounding the deceased's life, death, and the survivor's life since the death. Fishing, walking, and long drives are great ways to let someone have an opportunity for private conversation.

When conversation can occur, hold back trite sayings such as "He's in a better place," or "She's your guardian angel," or (perhaps worst of all), "It was God's will." Without intimate familiarity with the mourner's theology, you risk hurting that individual terribly. People in mourning do not need fortune telling about their future prospects ("You'll have other children" or "You're young . . . you'll find someone else"). They do not need to be advised about having a "stiff upper lip" or "toughing it out."

Do not singlehandedly take on responsibility to spare this person from grief. If you are very close with the individual in mourning, be sure you have a support system of your own. Spending a lot of time with someone who is grieving can be upsetting. You may find yourself recalling your own grief experiences and feelings of loss. Share these, at first, with someone else in your circle rather than with the bereaved. They are not ready to commiserate until later in the process.

Most important, do not take a grieving person's anger, tears, rebuffs, or rejection personally. It will be healthier for you and more helpful for your friend if you bear in mind that terrible pain sometimes interferes with polite behavior. Respect people's desire for some time and privacy but do not give up, walk away, or leave them alone.

Critical Thinking

1. Is it true that the United States is a "death-denying society"? Please explain.
2. What is the most effective approach to interacting with a person who has recently experienced the death of a friend or significant other?
3. How do researchers define a harmonious relationship?

Create Central

www.mhhe.com/createcentral

Internet References

The death of a child: The grief of the parents—a lifetime journey
www.athealth.com/consumer/disorders/parentalgrief.html

Funeral etiquette: What to say and not to say to those who have just lost a loved one
www.remembranceprocess.com/remembrance-process/step-two/funeral
-etiquette/65-funeral-etiquette-what-to-say-and-what-not-to-say-to-those
-who-have-just-lost-a-loved-one

DOLORES PUTERBAUGH is a psychotherapist in private practice in Largo, Fla.

Article   Prepared by: Eric Landrum, *Boise State University*

Harnessing the Wisdom of the Ages

A volunteer program seeks to enhance minds young and old.

Amy Maxmen

Learning Outcomes

After reading this article, you will be able to:

- Describe the preliminary findings of the relationship observed between elderly individuals who volunteer and their cognitive capabilities.

- Understand the impact of continued executive functioning in later adulthood and its impact on physiological brain systems.

At age 63, Joyce Lawrence found that for the first time in her life, she had time on her hands. Her children had left her Baltimore home to raise their own families and she had retired from her job as a correction officer in prisons. Her duties were over, but she felt a growing urge to contribute to society in some other way.

"At our age, you're left alone a lot of the time and it's easy to just watch TV or watch cars go by because you feel no one needs you anymore," she says. "But that's not true. After you have that pity party, you need to find out how you're needed and go make yourself useful."

For Lawrence, the opportunity to be useful came through the Experience Corps, a nonprofit organization that brings retired volunteers as mentors to struggling students in needy schools. The program was the brainchild of psychologist and social reformer John Gardner, PhD, remembered for his push to improve education, eliminate poverty and promote equality. As Secretary of Health, Education and Welfare under President Lyndon Johnson in the 1960s, he launched Medicare and oversaw the passage of the Elementary and Secondary Education Act, which aimed to ensure quality education for poor and rich students alike. At 76 years old, he wrote a concept paper that served as the blueprint for the Experience Corps (http://www .experiencecorps.org/about_us/john_gardners_vision.cfm). In it, he argues that sending seniors out to pasture does a disservice to them as well as to society, and that a program like Experience Corps could capitalize on the wisdom of the elderly.

"We believe," he wrote, "that the large numbers of us over age 65 constitute a rich reservoir of talent, experience and commitment potentially available to society."

The Experience Corps now include about 2,000 seniors nationwide, who mentor elementary school students for at least 15 hours each week, especially in low-income neighborhoods where class sizes swell. Student attendance and reading comprehension appear to improve in classes supported by volunteers. And based on testimonials, the volunteers enjoy the program.

However, anecdotes may not be enough to keep the program afloat when education and public health budgets are strained. At the moment, the program relies on federal funding through AmeriCorps (the Corporation for National and Community Service), as well as state and local public and private funds, and foundations including the Atlantic Philanthropies. To examine whether the cost of the program is justified, Linda Fried, MD, MPH, the dean of Columbia's Mailman School of Public Health, has solicited help from an interdisciplinary group of colleagues to assess its impact on the students and elderly volunteers. Together with the Johns Hopkins Center on Aging and Health, she's developed a research-community partnership with the Greater Homewood Community Corporation to conduct trials assessing the program.

Quantifying Cognition

Michelle Carlson, PhD, an associate professor of psychology at Johns Hopkins, says her preliminary findings suggest that the cognitive capabilities of elderly volunteers in the Experience Corps improve. Small teams of Experience Corps volunteers cooperate with teachers to help children who struggle with reading and learning. Beyond aiding kids with their studies, the volunteers provide the individual encouragement often lacking in crowded classrooms.

"Every child has different needs, so that means the volunteers must solve problems, multitask and exercise their executive abilities on a broad level," says Carlson. After 32 hours of training, participants volunteer for at least 15 hours per week within schools, where they assist classroom teachers and librarians by helping students read, recommending books, and providing one-on-one encouragement to children who've struggled with their lessons.

Those executive abilities—planning, abstract thinking and filtering relevant sensory information—are also crucial for driving, shopping, cooking and other activities necessary for independent living, and so strengthening those abilities can help seniors stay independent longer. Carlson says the intellectual and social engagement, and the physical activity, which volunteering in schools requires, might have that effect, but it's difficult to prove causation. After all, seniors who retain their cognitive faculties longer might volunteer more often—and might fare equally well if they didn't.

To demonstrate causality, Carlson and her colleagues analyzed functional magnetic resonance imaging (fMRI) data for signs of improvement or at least maintenance in the prefrontal brain region that supports executive function, in Experience Corps volunteers and in elderly people not involved in the program. In two pilot studies published in 2008 and 2009 in *The Gerontologist* and the *Journal of Gerontology,* the team reported gains in executive function, according to cognitive tests and increased activity in the prefrontal regions of volunteers compared with controls. She and her colleagues have increased the number of participants to 702 in a trial that began in 2005. If participants who have been active in the program for two years show cognitive benefits or cognitive stability that accrues beyond one year of exposure or less, Carlson and colleagues can check off a critical element in proving causality—a dose-dependent effect.

"Even if the program simply maintains brain function over two years, that implies we can delay an individual's progression to dementia, and that has huge personal and public health implications," says Carlson.

Importantly, the Experience Corps reaches a population of senior citizens who are at high risk for cognitive impairment—often those from lower economic classes with no college education. The majority of participants are African American. Carlson says that in her trials, she intentionally tries to reach this at-risk population, who traditionally do not volunteer for health promotion programs, but are willing to serve the community.

"These volunteers are not the 'worried well,'" says Carlson. They don't usually leap at treatments and tasks marketed as cognitive-enhancing, such as ginkgo biloba and Sudoku, she says, but many respond to "calls to service" to help youth in need.

Nonetheless, the program in Baltimore, with 292 volunteers, costs about $1.5 million a year. That cost includes stipends for the volunteers' food and travel expenses, yearly salaries for the directors, program administrator, entry personnel, a volunteer coordinator and the cost of the training sessions. So, the Experience Corps is far more expensive than Sudoku and ginkgo. But Carlson argues that quick fixes like these haven't been shown to translate into broad improvements in cognition, particularly in real-world measures of executive functioning, while her preliminary analyses suggest the Experience Corps does. The way in which the program's activities improve executive functioning, however, may be tough to untangle.

"The Experience Corps can't tell us the nitty-gritty details on mechanism," says Arthur Kramer, PhD, a professor of psychology at the University of Illinois at Urbana-Champaign, "but from a practical point of view, it doesn't matter a whole heck of a lot."

A Boost for Students

To complement the neuroscience research, Johns Hopkins health economist Kevin Frick, PhD, is leading an effort to compute the program's financial and health effects by looking at its impact on teachers, tutored students and elderly participants. In a 2004 pilot study in the Journal of Urban Health, Frick's team found that the immediate improvements in health gained by participants over two years don't balance out the program's cost. However, this equation might change if long-term studies find that the program staves off dementia, Frick says.

Moreover, it's too soon to tell if the program increases children's chances of graduating high school. If it does, the program would be well worth its price tag. The team determined that the annual cost of the Baltimore program would be offset by the higher salaries earned by people with high school diplomas, if graduation rates increase by just 0.5 percent, or 1 in 200, because of Experience Corps interventions early on. However, filling in variables like the rate of high school graduation and the time to dementia, which would decrease medical costs, may take up to a decade. "The biggest threat to an economic argument is people's impatience in waiting for a benefit," Frick says.

Finances aside, preliminary results support the notion that the program provides a meaningful ray of light for people in their golden years and in their dawn. And testimony from volunteers doesn't hurt the case. "I go for the mental stimulation, and I go because physically it's good to move around," says Barbara, a 77-year-old participant. "It's emotional, and I must say it's awfully spiritual to know I'm making a difference."

Critical Thinking

1. What is the Experience Corps program, and what are its goals?
2. What are some examples of executive abilities that are necessary for independent living?
3. What region of the brain is linked to the enhanced development of executive function and abilities?

Create Central

www.mhhe.com/createcentral

Internet References

Do we really get wiser with age?
http://science.howstuffworks.com/life/inside-the-mind/human-brain/wiser-with-age.htm

Researchers find that wisdom and happiness increase as people grow older
www.washingtonpost.com/wp-dyn/content/article/2010/08/09/AR2010080904177.html

AMY MAXMEN, is a writer in New York City.

Article   Prepared by: Eric Landrum, *Boise State University*

The Benefits of Positive Parenting

DAVID BORNSTEIN

Learning Outcomes

After reading this article, you will be able to:

- Understand the research outcomes between physical discipline and noncoercive methods of parenting.

- Identify the different community influences and partners that work in collaboration to help the Triple P parenting program experience positive outcomes.

I s there a science to parenting?

For all the current discussion in the United States about gun violence and mental illness, there has been little attention paid to root causes. Any effort aiming to reduce gun violence—or child abuse, intimate partner violence, suicide or sexual abuse—must include a serious discussion about how society can improve the quality of parenting.

In 2010, children's protective service agencies investigated 1.8 million referrals of child abuse and neglect pertaining to 3 million children. Although only 20 percent of these were substantiated, researchers report that physical abuse, including harsh physical discipline that is equivalent to abuse, is vastly underreported and may be 20 times more prevalent than is reflected in official statistics. (In other countries, including Spain, India and Egypt, harsh punishment is even more prevalent.) In Philadelphia, this behavior has recently been linked to the recession and the rate of mortgage foreclosures. When lenders put people out of their homes, one unforeseen consequence is that more kids end up with traumatic brain injuries.

It is now well accepted that physical discipline is not only less effective than other non-coercive methods, it is more harmful than has often been understood—and not just to children. A review of two decades worth of studies has shown that corporal punishment is associated with antisocial behavior and aggression in children, and later in life is linked to depression, unhappiness, anxiety, drug and alcohol use and psychological maladjustment. Beyond beating, parents can also hurt children by humiliating them, labeling them in harmful ways ("Why are you so stupid?"), or continually criticizing their behavior.

Improving the way people parent might seem an impossible challenge, given the competing views about what constitutes good parenting. Can we influence a behavior that is rooted in upbringing and culture, affected by stress, and occurs mainly in private? And even if we could reach large populations with evidence-based messages the way public health officials got people to quit smoking, wear seat belts or apply sunscreen, would it have an impact?

That's what was explored in South Carolina in recent years, and the answer appears to be yes. With funding from the Centers for Disease Control and Prevention, a parenting system called the Triple P—Positive Parenting Program, which was developed at the University of Queensland, Australia, was tested in nine counties across the state. Eighteen counties were randomly selected to receive either a broad dissemination of Triple P's program or services as usual. The results were both highly promising and troubling.

The good news was that, in contrast to the control counties, over two years, the nine counties that received the Triple P Program had a 35 percent reduction in hospitalizations and emergency room visits for child injuries, a 44 percent reduction in out-of-home placements, and a 28 percent reduction in substantiated cases of abuse. The bad news was that the Triple P counties mainly held their ground, while abuse increased elsewhere in the state, possibly because of the recession and the concomitant budget cuts in children's protective services.

The Triple P Program has evolved over the past 35 years. It focuses on families with children under age 12 and has shown efficacy in numerous studies. It started as a home visiting program, but researchers found it too expensive to deliver more widely, so they looked for ways to broaden its reach—to get good parenting into the water supply. "You know how vast Australia is," explains Matthew Sanders, Triple P's founder. "Our question was how do we ensure that all families, regardless of where they lived, could access good quality evidence-based parenting interventions." Sanders experimented with different dissemination techniques, including telephone consultations, and found that they could do just as well as face-to-face meetings.

What's notable about Triple P is that it pursues a community-wide, preventive approach. Sanders believes that all parents would benefit from some education—though some need a light touch while others need significant help. And why would it be otherwise? Unlike driving a truck or teaching, no one needs a permit to become a parent. We copy others and make it up as we go. Without a "reflective awareness" and the benefit of information, says Sanders, parents are apt to struggle with strategies that don't work—or that work for some children, but not others. He has seen a great deal of conflict and unhappiness and violence-begetting rage and humiliation that could have been averted with manageable changes.

Triple P works at multiple levels, ranging from media and communication strategies (TV, Web, radio, newspapers) to brief individual consultations and group sessions to intensive parenting and family interventions for serious difficulties. "You need to get lots of practitioners from different sectors—education, day care, mental health, health, social services, pastoral counseling—who are trained to work with parents and families and give them an added skill," explained Ron Prinz, the director of the Parenting and Family Research Center at the University of South Carolina, who led the Triple P study. "Parents need different ways to get exposed to it." In the nine counties in South Carolina, 649 people received training (three to six days on average) to deliver the program.

For parents, exposures can range from watching a video to participating in two 20-minute phone calls to attending 14 group sessions. "We follow the principle of 'minimal sufficiency,' " says Sanders. "Use the smallest possible intervention to solve or prevent a problem."

There are dozens of strategies and variations for parents—those who have children with disabilities, chronic illnesses, obesity or emotional difficulties, as well as those going through separation or divorce or at risk of maltreating their children. Parents discover techniques like "planned ignoring" (good for low-level misbehavior like whining or minor tantrums where the goal is attention) or learn how to escape the "escalation trap," which occurs when parents get exasperated.

The essence of the research is that children do best when they receive calm and consistent feedback and assertive discipline that's based on reasonable expectations—with significantly more encouragement and positive feedback than criticism. "The main mistake parents make is forgetting the importance of catching kids doing the right thing," says Sanders.

Stephanie Romney, director of the Parent Training Institute at the San Francisco Department of Public Health, agrees. Romney and her colleagues deliver higher level Triple P interventions to 1,000 families, many of whom are involved with children's services. "Typically, the children have been on the receiving end of a lot of negative attention from adults," she said. "Even if the child has misbehaved all day, their parents try to catch them for that brief window when they are behaving well and praise them." Parents are sometimes amazed by the changes. "I've had parents tearing up talking about how their relationship with their child has improved," she added. "They went for a walk together and held hands for the first time. And parents report that they try it out on their spouses and coworkers and it works with them, too."

Triple P is one of several evidence-based parenting programs that have demonstrated how society can reduce behaviors that put children at risk. Some others include SafeCare, Parent Management Training—the Oregon Model, The Incredible Years and Nurse Family Partnership. What is different here is the idea that parenting education could be broadly disseminated.

This is important, because parenting training needs to be destigmatized. It's not just about reducing abuse.

Romney notes that one of Triple P's strengths is that it presents a multiplicity of strategies and leaves it to parents to decide which ones to use. The community approach comes with limitations, however. It's difficult to get parents to come in if they aren't required to and it involves training numerous people to deliver the program—so start-up costs can be a barrier. But a lot of Triple P's teachings are available online. And unlike many parenting blogs, the advice is supported by research.

Parenting doesn't get much attention in policy circles. "We don't have mechanisms that help people to understand that parent education and training can be very effective," explains Richard Barth, dean of the University of Maryland School of Social Work, who has studied parenting programs for 30 years. "The Triple P study showed that if you engage people *before* things go awry, they can avoid problems that we might have predicted for them, or they might have predicted for themselves. There should be a significant investment in understanding how to implement some of the elements of Triple P—so every family and clinician in the United States knows the basics of parenting and the things we can do if things get more difficult."

It's not just for children. "It really influences adult well-being, too" Sanders said. "Parents become less stressed, less angry, less depressed, and have less conflict with their partners. We now have research that shows that parenting interventions improve your capacity to function at work, too."

Critical Thinking

1. Thinking about the parenting you received as a child, would your parents' parenting choices fit within the styles described in this article?

2. Currently, how much of a role do you think community plays in the raising of children? Is your community more active or passive in supporting child development? Describe your answer and why you think this is so.

Create Central

www.mhhe.com/createcentral

Internet References

Promoting positive parenting: Unique parenting program uses cell phones to help families
www.cdcfoundation.org/why/success/promoting-positive-parenting

Learn the benefits of positive parenting
www.selfgrowth.com/articles/learn-the-benefits-of-positive-parenting

---

DAVID BORNSTEIN is the author of *How to Change the World,* which has been published in 20 languages, and *The Price of a Dream: The Story of the Grameen Bank,* and is co-author of *Social Entrepreneurship: What Everyone Needs to Know.* He is a co-founder of the Solutions Journalism Network, which supports rigorous reporting about responses to social problems.

Article   Prepared by: Eric Landrum, *Boise State University*

For Kids, Self-Control Factors into Future Success

NANCY SHUTE

Learning Outcomes

After reading this article, you will be able to:

- Understand the relationship between self-control and health problems.

- Articulate the different ways and environments in which self-control can be taught.

Self-control keeps us from eating a whole bag of chips or from running up the credit card. A new study says that self-control makes the difference between getting a good job or going to jail—and we learn it in preschool.

"Children who had the greatest self-control in primary school and preschool ages were most likely to have fewer health problems when they reached their 30s," says Terrie Moffitt, a professor of psychology at Duke University and King's College London.

Moffitt and a team of researchers studied a group of 1,000 people born in New Zealand in 1972 and 1973, tracking them from birth to age 32. The new study, published in the *Proceedings of the National Academy of Sciences,* is the best evidence yet on the payoff for learning self-discipline early on.

The researchers define self-control as having skills like conscientiousness, self-discipline and perseverance, as well as being able to consider the consequences of actions in making decisions.

The children who struggled with self-control as preschoolers were three times as likely to have problems as young adults. They were more prone to have a criminal record; more likely to be poor or have financial problems; and they were more likely to be single parents.

This study doesn't prove that the lack of self-control in childhood caused these problems, but the large size of the study, and the fact that it followed one group of people over many years, makes a good case for an effect.

Teaching Control

Economists and public health officials want to know whether teaching self-control could improve a population's physical and financial health and reduce crime. Three factors appear to be key to a person's success in life: intelligence, family's socioeconomic status and self-control. Moffitt's study found that self-control predicted adult success, even after accounting for the participants' differences in social status and IQ.

IQ and social status are hard to change. But Moffitt says there is evidence that self-control can be learned.

"Identical twins are not identical on self-control," she says. "That tells us that it is something they have learned, not something they have inherited."

Teaching self-control has become a big focus for early childhood education. At the Clara Barton Center for Children in Cabin John, Md., it starts with expecting a 4-year-old to hang up her coat without being asked.

Director Linda Owen says the children are expected to be responsible for a series of actions when they arrive at school each morning, without help from Mom and Dad. The children sign in, put away their lunches, hang up their own clothes, wash their hands before they can play, and then choose activities in the classroom.

"All those things help with self-management," Owen says.

Mediating Conflict

Of course, not all 4-year-olds are ready to manage that, so the classroom is loaded with cues and clues to help the preschoolers make their own decisions and be responsible.

A series of seven photos over the sink shows the correct sequence for hand washing. A "solutions kit" poster shows techniques the children can use to resolve disagreements themselves, like sharing or playing with another toy. The two teachers give the children multiple cues when it's time to clean up: Lights flash, a bell rings and the children clap and count to 100. That makes it easier to switch gears without a meltdown.

If a child has problems with self-management, the teachers make a customized "visual cue" card, with photos of the four play choices in the room, to make the decision easier.

And teachers Cathie Morton and Daniela Capbert don't just supervise—they're in the thick of the children's play so that when the inevitable conflicts arise, they can redirect the children into other activities or help them talk through their feelings.

When things do go wrong, there are consequences. Timeouts and apologies don't mean much to children at this age, Owen says, so the teachers try to match consequences to the deed. When one of the children accidentally knocks over a 2-foot-tall tower of blocks that several children had spent half the morning building, the teachers ask the builders what should happen next. "Help fix it," one boy says. And, with a little prompting from the adults, they all pitch in and rebuild.

Self-Control at Home

Parents can help their children learn self-control. Mary Alvord is a clinical psychologist in Silver Spring, Md., whose new book, *Resilience Builder Program for Children and Adolescents,* teaches self-control strategies. Take small steps, she says. For example, preschoolers can learn that they don't always get what they want immediately; they may need to wait for that treat.

"I call it Grandma's rule," Alvord says. "No dessert until you finish your dinner."

Parents can help teenagers learn self-control by making sure the family has clear rules for things like curfew or finishing homework before they have screen time. Teenagers who have problems with impulsivity may benefit from special driving classes that let them practice controlling the car in difficult conditions on a racetrack. For all teens, clear rules such as curfews help them regulate themselves.

Though self-control can be improved throughout life, Moffitt says the earlier children can learn these skills of self-discipline and perseverance, the better. "The later you wait in life to try to learn self-control skills, the more problems you have to reverse and overcome."

All the more reason to start picking up blocks when you're very young.

Critical Thinking

1. Think about your own levels of self-control and your current level of control as an adult—do you think the two are related? Can you remember specific incidents in your childhood when you lost control? Did that happen frequently or infrequently? Explore and explain.

2. Let's say that a parent came to you and wanted advice on how to teach her son or daughter self-control. Where would you recommend that she start to look for research-based resources?

Create Central

www.mhhe.com/createcentral

Internet References

Self-control in childhood predicts future success
www.boston.com/bostonglobe/editorial_opinion/oped/articles/2011/06/12/self_control_in_childhood_predicts_future_success

Shute, Nancy. From *NPR*, February 12, 2011, Online. Copyright © 2011 by NPR. www.npr.org.

Unit 8

UNIT

Prepared by: Eric Landrum, *Boise State University*

Personality Processes

Sabrina and Sadie are identical twins. When the girls were young, their parents tried very hard to treat them equally. They dressed them the same, fed them same meals, and allowed them to play with the same toys. Each had a kitten from the same litter. Whenever Sabrina received a present, Sadie received one, too, and vice versa. Both girls attended dance school and completed early classes in ballet and tap dance. For elementary school, the twins were both placed in the same class with the same teacher. The teacher also tried to treat them the same. In junior high school, Sadie became a tomboy. She loved to play rough-and-tumble sports with the neighborhood boys. On the other hand, Sabrina remained indoors and practiced the piano. Sabrina was keenly interested in hobbies such as painting, needlepoint, and sewing. Sadie was more interested in reading novels, especially science fiction, and watching action movies on television.

As the twins matured, they decided it would be best to attend different colleges. Sabrina went to a small, quiet college in a rural setting, and Sadie entered a large public university. Sabrina majored in English, with a specialty in poetry; Sadie switched majors several times and finally decided on a psychology major. Why, when these twins were exposed to the same childhood environment, did their interests, personalities, and paths diverge later? What makes people—even identical twins—so unique

and so different from one another? The study of individual differences resides in the domain of personality psychology.

The psychological study of personality includes two major thrusts. The first has focused on the search for the commonalties of human behavior and personality. Its major question is "How are humans, especially their personalities, affected by specific events or activities?" The second has focused on discovering the bases on which individuals differ in their responses to events, such as the self-control exhibited by Sadie and Sabrina as they went off to college. In its early history, this specialty was called genetic psychology because most people assumed that individual differences resulted from differences in inheritance. By the 1950s, the term *genetic psychology* had given way to the more current terminology: the psychology of individual differences.

Today, most psychologists accept the principle that both genes and the environment are important determinants of any type of behavior, whether it be watching adventure movies or sitting quietly and reading or caring for the elderly. Modern researchers devote much of their efforts to discovering how the two sources of influence (nature and nurture) interact to produce a unique individual. Thus, the focus of this unit is on personality characteristics and the differences and similarities among individuals, with these fascinating differences ranging from cultural expectations and stereotypes to the development of political attitudes.

Article   Prepared by: Eric Landrum, *Boise State University*

Evolutionary Psychology and Intelligence Research

SATOSHI KANAZAWA

Learning Outcomes

After reading this article, you will be able to:

- Evaluate the contribution of evolutionary psychology to the study of intelligence.

- Define and explain the Savanna Principle and how it relates to intelligence research.

Evolutionary psychology and intelligence research have largely stood separately despite the fact that both of these subfields of psychology take biological and genetic influences on human behavior and cognition seriously. In some sense, this is understandable. Evolutionary psychology focuses on universal human nature, which is shared by all humans, or on sex-specific male human nature and female human nature, which are shared by all men and all women, respectively. In contrast, intelligence research (psychometrics) is part of differential psychology, which focuses on what makes individuals different from each other. Psychometrics is concerned with accurate measurement of intelligence precisely because individuals vary in their level of intelligence largely (though not entirely) because of their different genetic makeup.

Yet, as Tooby and Cosmides (1990a) articulated, the concept of universal human nature is not inimical to or incompatible with individual differences (in intelligence or other traits). Although individual differences have yet to be fully integrated into evolutionary psychology (Buss, 1995; Nettle, 2006), some evolutionary psychologists have incorporated heritable or reactively heritable (Tooby & Cosmides, 1990a) individual differences in personality (Buss, 1991; MacDonald, 1995; Nettle, 2005), sociosexuality (Gangestad & Simpson, 1990, 2000), and attachment and reproductive strategies (Belsky, Steinberg, & Draper, 1991; Buss & Greiling, 1999). Scarr (1995), and J. M. Bailey (1998) called for the incorporation of behavior genetics into evolutionary psychology in order to emphasize heritable individual and group differences and provide a fuller explanation of human behavior.

In this article, I follow the lead of earlier evolutionary psychologists who have attempted to incorporate individual differences. I seek to integrate evolutionary psychology, on the one hand, and intelligence research in particular and differential psychology in general, on the other. I aim to incorporate individual differences in general intelligence and other traits into universal human nature. I suggest how and when evolutionary constraints on the human brain, universally shared by all humans, may interact with general intelligence, such that more intelligent individuals have fewer such constraints than less intelligent individuals. I suggest that general intelligence is both a domain-specific evolved psychological mechanism *and* an individual-difference variable. I derive a novel hypothesis, called the Savanna–IQ Interaction Hypothesis, from the intersection of evolutionary psychology and intelligence research and discuss its implications. Among other things, this hypothesis suggests one possible explanation for why general intelligence is correlated with the Big Five personality factor Openness to Experience; at the same time, it calls for a refinement of the concept of novelty. I conclude with several illustrations of how and when more intelligent individuals are more likely than less intelligent individuals to acquire and espouse evolutionarily novel values.

The Savanna Principle

Adaptations, physical or psychological, are designed for and adapted to the conditions of the environment of evolutionary adaptedness, not necessarily to the current environment (Tooby & Cosmides, 1990b). This is easiest to see in the case of physical adaptations, such as the vision and color recognition system.

What color is a banana? A banana is yellow in the sunlight and in the moonlight. It is yellow on a sunny day, on a cloudy day, and on a rainy day. It is yellow at dawn and at dusk. The color of a banana appears constant to the human eye under all these conditions despite the fact that the actual wavelengths of the light reflected by the surface of the banana under these varied conditions are different. Objectively, bananas are not the same color all the time. However, the human eye and color recognition system can compensate for these varied conditions because they all occurred during the course of the evolution of the human vision system, and humans can perceive the objectively varied colors as constantly yellow (Cosmides & Tooby, 1999, pp. 17–19; Shepard, 1994).

So a banana looks yellow under all conditions *except in a parking lot at night.* Under the sodium vapor lights commonly used to illuminate parking lots, a banana does not appear natural yellow. This is because the sodium vapor lights did not exist in the ancestral environment, during the course of the evolution of the human vision system, and the visual cortex is therefore incapable of compensating for them.

The same principle holds for psychological adaptations. Pioneers of evolutionary psychology (Crawford, 1993; Symons, 1990; Tooby & Cosmides, 1990b) all recognized that the evolved psychological mechanisms are designed for and adapted to the conditions of the environment of evolutionary adaptedness, not necessarily to the conditions of the current environment. I systematized these observations into what I called the *Savanna Principle* (Kanazawa, 2004a): The human brain has difficulty comprehending and dealing with entities and situations that did not exist in the ancestral environment. Burnham and Johnson (2005, pp. 130–131) referred to the same observation as the *evolutionary legacy hypothesis,* whereas Hagen and Hammerstein (2006, pp. 341–343) called it the *mismatch hypothesis.*

The Savanna Principle can explain why some otherwise elegant scientific theories of human behavior, such as the subjective expected utility maximization theory or game theory in microeconomics, often fail empirically, because they posit entities and situations that did not exist in the ancestral environment. For example, nearly half the players of one-shot Prisoner's Dilemma games make the theoretically irrational choice to cooperate with their partner (Sally, 1995). The Savanna Principle suggests that this may possibly be because the human brain has difficulty comprehending completely anonymous social exchange and absolutely no possibility of knowing future interactions (which together make the game truly one-shot; Kanazawa, 2004a, pp. 44–45). Neither of these situations existed in the ancestral environment; however, they are crucial for the game-theoretic prediction of universal defection.

Fehr and Henrich (2003) suggested that one-shot encounters and exchanges might have been common in the ancestral environment. In their response to Fehr and Henrich, Hagen and Hammerstein (2006) pointed out that even if one-shot encounters were common in the ancestral environment, anonymous encounters could not have been common, and the game-theoretic prediction of defection in one-shot games requires both noniteration and anonymity. A lack of anonymity can lead to reputational concerns even in nonrepeated exchanges.

As another illustration of the Savanna Principle, individuals who watch certain types of TV shows are more satisfied with their friendships, just as they would be if they had more friends or socialized with them more frequently (Derrick, Gabriel, & Hugenberg, 2009; Kanazawa, 2002). This may possibly be because realistic images of other humans, such as found in television, movies, videos, and photographs, did not exist in the ancestral environment, where all realistic images of other humans *were* other humans. As a result, the human brain may have implicit difficulty distinguishing "TV friends" (the characters repeatedly seen on TV shows) and real friends.

Most evolutionary psychologists and biologists concur that humans have not undergone significant evolutionary changes in the last 10,000 years, since the end of the Pleistocene Epoch, because the environment during this period has not provided a stable background against which natural and sexual selection can operate over many generations (A. S. Miller & Kanazawa, 2007, pp. 25–28). This is the assumption behind the Savanna Principle. More recently, however, some scientists have voiced opinions that human evolution has continued and even accelerated during the Holocene Epoch (Cochran & Harpending, 2009; Evans et al., 2005). Although these studies conclusively demonstrate that new alleles have indeed emerged in the human genome since the end of the Pleistocene Epoch, the implication and importance of such new alleles for evolutionary psychology are not immediately obvious. In particular, with the sole exception of lactose tolerance, it is not clear whether these new alleles have led to the emergence of new evolved psychological mechanisms in the last 10,000 years.

The Evolution of General Intelligence

General intelligence refers to the ability to reason deductively or inductively, think abstractly, use analogies, synthesize information, and apply it to new domains (Gottfredson, 1997; Neisser et al., 1996). The *g* factor, which is often used synonymously with general intelligence, is a latent variable that emerges in a factor analysis of various cognitive (IQ) tests. They are not exactly the same thing. *g* is an *indicator* or *measure* of general intelligence; it is not general intelligence itself. As a measure of reasoning ability, general intelligence is what Cattell (1971) called "fluid intelligence" (*Gf*), not what he called "crystallized intelligence" (*Gc*), which, while influenced by general intelligence, is a measure of acquired knowledge.

The concept of general intelligence poses a problem for evolutionary psychology (Chiappe & MacDonald, 2005; Cosmides & Tooby, 2002; G. F. Miller, 2000a). Evolutionary psychologists contend that the human brain consists of domain-specific evolved psychological mechanisms, which evolved to solve specific adaptive problems (problems of survival and reproduction) in specific domains. If the contents of the human brain are domain specific, how can evolutionary psychology explain general intelligence?

In contrast to views expressed by G. F. Miller (2000b); Cosmides and Tooby (2002), and Chiappe and MacDonald (2005), I proposed that what is now known as general intelligence may have originally evolved as a domain-specific adaptation to deal with evolutionarily novel, nonrecurrent problems (Kanazawa, 2004b). The human brain consists of a large number of domain-specific evolved psychological mechanisms to solve recurrent adaptive problems. In this sense, our ancestors did not really have to *think* in order to solve such recurrent problems. Evolution has already done all the thinking, so to speak, and equipped the human brain with the appropriate psychological mechanisms, which engender preferences, desires, cognitions, and emotions and motivate adaptive behavior in the context of the ancestral environment.

Even in the extreme continuity and constancy of the ancestral environment, however, there were likely occasional problems that were evolutionarily novel and nonrecurrent, problems that required our ancestors to think and reason in order to solve. Such problems may have included, for example, the following:

1. Lightning has struck a tree near the camp and set it on fire. The fire is now spreading to the dry underbrush. What should I do? How can I stop the spread of the fire? How can I and my family escape it? (Since lightning never strikes the same place twice, this is guaranteed to be a nonrecurrent problem.)

2. We are in the middle of the severest drought in a hundred years. Nuts and berries at our normal places of gathering, which are usually plentiful, are not growing at all, and animals are scarce as well. We are running out of food because none of our normal sources of food are working. What else can we eat? What else is safe to eat? How else can we procure food?

3. A flash flood has caused the river to swell to several times its normal width, and I am trapped on one side of it while my entire band is on the other side. It is imperative that I rejoin them soon. How can I cross the rapid river? Should I walk across it? Or should I construct some sort of buoyant vehicle to use to get across it? If so, what kind of material should I use? Wood? Stones?

To the extent that these evolutionarily novel, nonrecurrent problems happened frequently enough in the ancestral environment (a different problem each time) and had serious enough consequences for survival and reproduction, then any genetic mutation that allowed its carriers to think and reason would have been selected for, and what we now call "general intelligence" could have evolved as a domain-specific adaptation for the domain of evolutionarily novel, nonrecurrent problems, which did not exist in the ancestral environment and for which there are therefore no dedicated modules.

From this perspective, general intelligence may have become universally important in modern life (Gottfredson, 1997; Herrnstein & Murray, 1994; Jensen, 1998) only because our current environment is almost entirely evolutionarily novel. The new theory suggests, and empirical data confirm, that more intelligent individuals are better than less intelligent individuals at solving problems only if they are evolutionarily novel. More intelligent individuals are not better than less intelligent individuals at solving evolutionarily familiar problems, such as those in the domains of mating, parenting, interpersonal relationships, and wayfinding (Kanazawa, 2004b, 2007), unless the solution involves evolutionarily novel entities. For example, more intelligent individuals are no better than less intelligent individuals in finding and keeping mates, but they may be better at using computer dating services. Three recent studies, employing widely varied methods, have all shown that the average intelligence of a population appears to be a strong function of the evolutionary novelty of its environment (Ash & Gallup, 2007; D. H. Bailey & Geary, 2009; Kanazawa, 2008).

My theory (Kanazawa, 2004b) builds on and shares common themes with earlier evolutionary theories of intelligence, which posit climatic, ecological, and social novelties as the main forces behind the evolution of intelligence. Jerisen (1973) employed the concept of the encephalization quotient (EQ) to explain the evolution of intelligence of species as a function of the novelty of their ecological niches. Dunbar's (1998) and Humphrey's (1976) social brain hypothesis and Byrne and Whiten's (1988) machiavellian intelligence hypothesis both explain the evolution of intelligence as a consequence of having to deal with and potentially deceive a large number of conspecifics in the group. Geary's (2005) motivation-to-control theory explains the expansion of the human brain as a result of the human need to control, first its physical environment and then the social environment of fellow humans. Gottfredson (1997) argued that other humans provide the greatest complexities in social life, which select for greater intelligence. Social relationships, while themselves evolutionarily familiar and recurrent, may occasionally add novelty and complexity that requires general intelligence to deal with.

"Intelligences"

In recent years, psychologists have discussed various forms of intelligence or "intelligences," such as emotional intelligence (Mayer, Salovey, & Caruso, 2008; Salovey & Mayer, 1990), social intelligence (Kihlstrom & Cantor, 2000; Marlowe, 1986), mating intelligence (Geher & Miller, 2007), and Gardner's (1983) notion of multiple intelligences, which include linguistic, logical-mathematical, bodily-kinesthetic, spatial, musical, interpersonal, and intrapersonal intelligences. There is no question that these are all important intrapersonal and interpersonal skills and abilities that individuals need in their daily lives. Further, it seems reasonable to suggest that there are individual differences in such skills and abilities in the realm of interpersonal relations.

However, it is not at all clear what we gain by referring to such skills, competences, and abilities as "intelligences." The concept of intelligence in its historical origin in psychology was purely cognitive (Spearman, 1904). I personally would have preferred to keep it that way; however, the tide appears to have turned against my purist position. Whether to call these intrapersonal and interpersonal competencies "intelligences" or "skills," however, is a purely semantic matter without any necessary substantive implications. At any rate, in this article, I focus exclusively on purely cognitive general intelligence and not on other forms of intelligence, for two reasons. First, this is how most intelligence researchers and psychometricians define the concept of intelligence. Although educational, social, clinical, and industrial/organizational psychologists may refer to other "intelligences" as predictors of individual performance, intelligence researchers are nearly unanimous in their exclusive focus on cognitive general intelligence (Jensen, 1998). Second, as mentioned above, the concept of *general* intelligence presents a particular theoretical problem for evolutionary psychology's modular view of the human brain. Such a modular view can easily accommodate other "intelligences" as separate domain-specific modules, but it has more difficulty incorporating *general* intelligence with its seeming domain generality.

Other people and interactions with them (including mating) are "entities and situations" that we are certain existed during the entire period of human evolution. The theory of the evolution of general intelligence would therefore predict that general intelligence would not increase or correlate with emotional intelligence, social intelligence, or mating intelligence, each of which independently evolved to solve evolutionarily familiar problems in a given domain (Mayer, Salovey, Caruso, & Sitarenios, 2001, pp. 236–237). Several studies demonstrate that general intelligence is uncorrelated (or sometimes even negatively correlated) with measures of emotional, social, and mating intelligence (Davies, Stankov, & Roberts, 1998; Derksen, Kramer, & Katzko, 2002; Ford & Tisak, 1983; Fox & Spector, 2000; Kanazawa, 2007; Marlowe & Bedell, 1982).

There is some contrary evidence, however. Mayer, Roberts, and Barsade (2009) explicitly defined emotional intelligence as an application of general intelligence to the domain of emotions, and Roberts, Zeidner, and Matthews's (2001) study shows that measures of emotional intelligence are significantly and moderately *positively* correlated with general intelligence (as measured by the Air Force Qualifying Test). The question of whether emotional, social, and mating intelligences are "really" intelligences and how cognitive they are is difficult to answer definitively because, as Mayer et al. (2008) noted, there is a very wide spectrum of approaches to these other "intelligences." Some of them take cognitive intelligence seriously, others do not.

Is Evolutionary Novelty a Domain?

The theory of the evolution of general intelligence as a domain-specific adaptation is subject to two contradictory criticisms. The first criticism is that the domain of evolutionary novelty, which encompasses all entities and situations that did not exist in the ancestral environment, is too large and undefined, and thus a set of potentially indefinite evolutionarily novel problems presents the same "frame problem" that inspired Tooby and Cosmides (1992) to advocate the domain-specific view of the human mind. The second criticism is that evolutionarily novel problems in the ancestral environment and throughout human evolutionary history have by definition been few and far between, and thus they could not have exerted sufficient selection pressure to lead to the evolution of general intelligence as a domain-specific adaptation.[1]

Is the Domain of Evolutionary Novelty Too Large?

Evolutionarily novel problems have two characteristics in common: They are unanticipated by evolution (and thus there are no dedicated modules to solve them), and they are solvable by logical reasoning. Technically, all adaptive problems, evolutionarily novel or otherwise, are in principle logically solvable. Given sufficient time and data, for example, men, collectively and over time, can eventually figure out that women with symmetrical facial features are genetically healthier and that those with low waist-to-hip ratios are more fecund, so they should find them more desirable as mates. However, for such evolutionarily familiar and recurrent problems like mate selection, evolution short-circuits the long process of trial and error and

simply equips men with the module that inclines them to find women with symmetrical features and low waist-to-hip ratios sexually attractive without really knowing why. For other, evolutionarily novel, nonrecurrent problems, however, evolution has not had time or opportunity to equip humans with such dedicated modules, and they therefore have to "figure out" the problems anew and on their own by logic and reason.

What defines the domain of evolutionarily novel problems, along with their being novel and unanticipated by evolution, is their logical solvability, and it is therefore no larger nor any less defined than other domains, such as cheater detection, language acquisition, and face recognition. After all, potential cheaters may be any kind of exchange partner, and potential deception may occur in any situation. But cheaters all have one thing in common: violation of social contract. Similarly, potential first language to be acquired by a newborn baby may come in any form; there are a nearly infinite number of natural human languages. Yet they all have key features in common, what Chomsky (1957) calls the deep structure of grammar. Hence a developmentally normal human baby, equipped with the language acquisition device, can acquire any human language as its native language, however diverse and varied on the surface such languages may be. Similarly, all evolutionarily novel problems, infinite though they may be in potential number, have certain features in common that define them, chief among which is their logical solvability.

It is not that evolution can anticipate a whole host of evolutionarily novel problems in the future (any more than it could have anticipated the emergence of new human languages such as English or German). It is just that people who have been able to solve (rare and nonrecurrent) evolutionarily novel problems in the past genetically pass on the same ability to their descendants, who can then use it to solve other evolutionarily novel problems in the future, because all evolutionarily novel problems share the common characteristic of logical solvability.

All evolved psychological mechanisms (or modules) are content rich (Tooby & Cosmides, 1992). The contents of general intelligence as a domain-specific adaptation are a set of tools that allow its possessors to arrive at logical conclusions. Such a set of logical tools may include the principle of transitivity (If A then B, and if B then C, then it follows that if A then C); what is now known as Mills's methods of induction (such as the method of difference and the method of concomitant variation); syllogism and deductive reasoning (although deduction begins with a universally true major premise, which is unlikely to have been available to our ancestors); analogy; abstraction, and so forth. In general, intelligent people are those who can use these logical tools and reason correctly and efficiently.

Is the Domain of Evolutionary Novelty Too Small?

A second criticism of the theory avers that evolutionarily novel, nonrecurrent problems could not have arisen frequently enough in the ancestral environment to exert sufficient selection pressure to lead to the evolution of general intelligence or any other adaptation. Selection pressure, however, is a multiplicative function of the frequency of the problem and the magnitude of the selective force. Even a very weak selective force could lead to an evolved adaptation if the adaptive problem in question happens frequently enough over the course of human evolution to accumulate its small effects. Conversely, even a very infrequent adaptive problem can exert sufficient selection pressure if the magnitude of the selective force (the negative consequences of failing to solve the adaptive problem) is sufficiently great.

To take an extreme example for illustrative purposes, suppose a widespread drought or massive flash flood (of a kind used in the examples of evolutionarily novel problems above) on average happens once a century (roughly five generations), but, every time it happens, it kills everyone below the median in logical thinking and reasoning ability. So the adaptive problem happens very infrequently, but the selective force is very strong. In this scenario, in only one millennium (a blink of an eye on the evolutionary time scale), the average intelligence of the population becomes greater than the top 0.1% of the original population. This is equivalent to the current population of the United States, with the mean IQ of 100, changing to a new population 10 centuries later with a mean IQ of 146. From our current perspective, the average person then will be a genius. Even if the selective force was much weaker (one tenth of the original scenario above) and the adaptive problem only wiped out the bottom 5% in logical reasoning (allowing the top 95% of the population to survive each drought or flood every century), it would still take only 13,500 years to achieve a comparable effect on the average intelligence of the population and shift it upward by more than three standard deviations.

It would therefore appear that even an infrequent adaptive problem can produce sufficient selection pressure if the selective force is sufficiently strong. It would not be unreasonable to speculate that *some* (different) novel and nonrecurrent problem happened once a century during the evolutionary past that required our ancestors to think and reason to solve and that killed off the bottom 5% of the population in such an ability. General intelligence as a domain-specific adaptation would then have evolved relatively rapidly, in less than 15,000 years.

Is General Intelligence a Domain-Specific Adaptation or an Individual-Difference Variable?

Some critics (Borsboom & Dolan, 2006) contend that general intelligence could not be an adaptation because it is an individual-difference variable. Adaptations are universal and constant features of a species shared by all its members; in contrast, there are obviously heritable individual differences in general intelligence, whereby some individuals are more intelligent than others. These critics argue that adaptations and heritable individual differences are mutually exclusive.

These criticisms betray profound misunderstanding of the nature of adaptations. A trait could simultaneously be an evolved adaptation and an individual-difference variable. In fact, *most adaptations exhibit individual differences.* Full-time bipedalism is a uniquely human adaptation, yet some individuals walk and run faster than others. The eye is a complex

adaptation, yet some individuals have better vision than others. Language is an adaptation, yet some individuals learn to speak their native language at earlier ages and have greater linguistic facility than others.

Individual differences in general intelligence and other adaptations are what Tooby and Cosmides (1990a) called random quantitative variation on a monomorphic design. "Because the elaborate functional design of individuals [e.g., general intelligence as a domain-specific adaptation] is largely monomorphic [shared by all members of a species], our adaptations do not vary in their architecture from individual to individual (*except quantitatively* [emphasis added])" (Tooby & Cosmides, 1990a, p. 37).

Intraspecific (interindividual) differences in such traits pale in comparison to interspecific differences. Carl Lewis and I run at a virtually identical speed compared with cheetahs or sloths. Similarly, Einstein and I have virtually identical intelligence compared with cheetahs or sloths. It is therefore possible for a trait to be both universal and species-typical (exhibiting virtually no variation in the architecture in a cross-species comparison) *and* to manifest vast individual differences in quantitative performance among members of a single species. General intelligence may be one such trait.

Tooby and Cosmides (1990a, pp. 38–39) made this exact point, using "a complex psychological mechanism regulating aggression" (p. 38) as their example. They contended that this mechanism is an adaptation, even though there are heritable individual differences in the mechanism's threshold of activation (i.e., whether one has a "short fuse" or not). Tooby and Cosmides suggested that a complex psychological mechanism regulating aggression "is (by hypothesis) universal and therefore has zero heritability" (p. 38) even though "the *variations* in the exact level at which the threshold of activation is set are probably not adaptations" (p. 39).

The ability to run bipedally, faster than a sloth but slower than a cheetah, is a trait that is universally shared by all normally developing humans; it is a species-typical adaptation with zero heritability. But the exact speed at which a human can run is a heritable individual-difference variable and is therefore not an adaptation. Similarly, I propose that general intelligence is an adaptation and has zero heritability (in the sense that all humans have the ability to think and reason), even though the exact level of an individual's general intelligence ("IQ") is not an adaptation and is a highly heritable individual-difference variable. And Tooby and Cosmides (1990a, p. 57) contended that "nonadaptive, random fluctuations in the monomorphic design of a mental organ can give rise to heritable individual differences *in nearly every manifest feature of human psychology* [emphasis added]." One would therefore expect some individual differences in general intelligence as a domain-specific adaptation.

Explicitly recognizing that general intelligence can simultaneously be a domain-specific, species-typical adaptation *and* an individual-difference variable allows us to integrate evolutionary psychology—the study of species-typical evolved psychological mechanisms—and intelligence research—the study and measurement of heritable individual differences in general intelligence. Further, Tooby and Cosmides's (1990a) notion of the random quantitative (but heritable) variations on a monomorphic design would allow us to study individual differences in other evolved psychological mechanisms.

For example, the cheater detection module was among the first evolved psychological mechanisms to be discovered (Cosmides, 1989). It is clearly an adaptation, in that all human beings have the evolutionarily given and innate ability to detect when they might be cheated out of a fair exchange in a social contract. But are there individual differences in how well individuals can detect cheaters? Are some individuals inherently better at it than others? If so, are such individual differences heritable? Are some individuals genetically predisposed to fall victim to cons and scams?

Theory of mind is another evolved psychological mechanism; adult humans have the ability to infer the mental states of others. However, we already know that some individuals with pathological conditions (autism, Asperger's syndrome) have a weakened or absent capacity for theory of mind (Baron-Cohen, 1995). Can developmentally typical individuals also vary in their theory of mind? Dunbar (2005) suggested that there are individual differences in higher order theory of mind ("I think that you think that Sally thinks that Anne thinks that . . .") and that good writers like Shakespeare are rare because great dramas like *Othello* require writers to possess a sixth-order theory of mind. If individuals can vary in their capacity for higher order theory of mind, it seems reasonable to suggest that they might also vary in their capacity for first-order theory of mind, with some being better than others at accurately inferring the mental states of another person. If so, can such individual differences in the evolved psychological mechanism of theory of mind be heritable, since we already know that autism and Asperger's syndrome may be heritable (A. Bailey et al., 1995; Folstein & Rutter, 1988)?

Incorporating individual differences, not only in general intelligence but in other evolved psychological mechanisms, will allow us to pursue these and other questions at the new frontier where evolutionary psychology meets differential psychology.

How General Intelligence Modifies the Evolutionary Limitations of the Human Brain

The logical conjunction of the Savanna Principle and the theory of the evolution of general intelligence suggests a qualification of the Savanna Principle. If general intelligence evolved to deal with evolutionarily novel problems, then the human brain's difficulty in comprehending and dealing with entities and situations that did not exist in the ancestral environment (proposed in the Savanna Principle) should interact with general intelligence such that the Savanna Principle will hold stronger among less intelligent individuals than among more intelligent individuals. More intelligent individuals should be better able than less intelligent individuals to comprehend and deal with evolutionarily novel (but *not* evolutionarily familiar) entities and situations.

Thus, the Savanna–IQ Interaction Hypothesis (Kanazawa, 2010) suggests that less intelligent individuals have greater difficulty than more intelligent individuals with comprehending and dealing with evolutionarily novel entities and situations that did not exist in the ancestral environment; in contrast, general intelligence does not affect individuals' ability to comprehend and deal with evolutionarily familiar entities and situations that existed in the ancestral environment.

Evolutionarily novel entities that more intelligent individuals are better able to comprehend and deal with may include ideas and lifestyles, which form the basis of their values and preferences; it would be difficult for individuals to prefer or value something that they cannot truly comprehend. Hence, applied to the domain of preferences and values, the Savanna–IQ Interaction Hypothesis suggests that more intelligent individuals are more likely than less intelligent individuals to acquire and espouse evolutionarily novel preferences and values that did not exist in the ancestral environment but that general intelligence has no effect on the acquisition and espousal of evolutionarily familiar preferences and values that existed in the ancestral environment (Kanazawa, 2010).

General Intelligence and Openness to Experience

Research in personality psychology has shown that one of the five-factor personality model factors—Openness to Experience—is significantly positively (albeit moderately) correlated with intelligence (Ackerman & Heggestad, 1997). The similarity and overlap between intelligence and openness are apparent from the fact that some researchers call this personality factor "intellect" rather than "openness" (Goldberg, 1992; McRae, 1994). Although it is widely accepted by personality psychologists that intelligence and openness covary across individuals, it is not known why (Chamorro-Premuzic & Furnham, 2006). The Savanna–IQ Interaction Hypothesis can potentially provide one explanation for why more intelligent individuals are more open to new experiences and are therefore more prone to seek novelty. It is instructive to note from this perspective that only the actions, ideas, and values facets of openness to experience are significantly correlated with general intelligence, not the fantasy, esthetics, and feelings facets (Gilles, Stough, & Loukomitis, 2004; Holland, Dollinger, Holland, & MacDonald, 1995).

At the same time, the Savanna–IQ Interaction Hypothesis suggests a possible need to refine the concept of novelty and to distinguish between *evolutionary novelty* (entities and situations that did not exist in the ancestral environment) and *experiential novelty* (entities and situations that individuals have not personally experienced in their own lifetimes). Although the five-factor personality model does not specify the type of novelty that open individuals are more likely to seek, the Savanna–IQ Interaction Hypothesis suggests that more intelligent individuals are more likely to seek only evolutionary novelty, not necessarily experiential novelty.

For example, all those who are alive in the United States today have lived their entire lives in a strictly monogamous society, and despite recent news events, very few contemporary Americans have any personal experiences with polygyny. Therefore monogamy is experientially familiar for most Americans, whereas polygyny is experientially novel. The five-factor model may therefore predict that more intelligent individuals are more likely to be open to polygyny as an experientially novel idea or action.

In contrast, humans have been mildly polygynous throughout their evolutionary history (Alexander, Hoogland, Howard, Noonan, & Sherman, 1979; Leutenegger & Kelly, 1977), and socially imposed monogamy is a relatively recent historical phenomenon (Kanazawa & Still, 1999). Therefore polygyny is evolutionarily familiar, whereas monogamy is evolutionarily novel. The Savanna–IQ Interaction Hypothesis would therefore predict that more intelligent individuals are more likely to be open to monogamy and less open to polygyny. In fact, the evidence suggests that more intelligent men are more likely to value monogamy and sexual exclusivity than are less intelligent men (Kanazawa, 2010).

As another example, for most contemporary Americans, traditional names derived from the Bible, such as John and Mary, are experientially more familiar than untraditional names such as OrangeJello and LemonJello (Levitt & Dubner, 2005). So the five-factor model may predict that more intelligent individuals are more likely to give their children untraditional names such as Orange Jello and LemonJello than are less intelligent individuals. From the perspective of the Savanna–IQ Interaction Hypothesis, however, both John and OrangeJello are equally evolutionarily novel (because the Bible itself and all the traditional names derived from it are evolutionarily novel), so it would not predict that more intelligent individuals are more likely to give their children untraditional names. In fact, there is no evidence at all that more intelligent individuals are more likely to prefer untraditional names for their children (Fryer & Levitt, 2004; Lieberson & Bell, 1992).

The Savanna–IQ Interaction Hypothesis underscores the need to distinguish between evolutionary novelty and experiential novelty. It can potentially explain why more intelligent individuals are more likely to seek evolutionary novelty but not necessarily experiential novelty. It further suggests that the established correlation between openness and intelligence may be limited to the domain of evolutionary novelty, not necessarily experiential novelty, but the current measures of openness do not adequately address this proposal.

Empirical Illustrations

The Savanna–IQ Interaction Hypothesis, derived from the intersection of evolutionary psychology and intelligence research, suggests one potential way to account for some known individual differences. I discuss just a few of them here for illustrative purposes.

TV Friends

Consistent with the Savanna Principle, I (Kanazawa, 2002) and Derrick et al. (2009) showed that individuals who watch certain types of TV shows are more satisfied with their friendships, which suggests that they may possibly have implicit difficulty distinguishing evolutionarily novel realistic images of actors they repeatedly see on TV and their real friends. My reanalysis of the same data from the General Social Surveys shows, however, that this seeming difficulty in distinguishing between "TV friends" and real friends appears to be limited to men and women with below-median intelligence (Kanazawa, 2006). Those who are above the median in intelligence do not report greater satisfaction with friendships as a function of watching more TV; only those below the median in intelligence do. This finding seems to suggest that the evolutionary constraints on the brain suggested by the Savanna Principle, whereby individuals have implicit difficulty recognizing realistic electronic images on TV for what they are, appear to be weaker or altogether absent among more intelligent individuals.

Political Attitudes

It is difficult to define a whole school of political ideology precisely, but one may reasonably define *liberalism* (as opposed to *conservatism*) in the contemporary United States as the genuine concern for the welfare of genetically unrelated others and the willingness to contribute larger proportions of private resources for the welfare of such others. In the modern political and economic context, this willingness usually translates into paying higher proportions of individual incomes in taxes toward the government and its social welfare programs.

Defined as such, liberalism is evolutionarily novel. Humans (like other species) are evolutionarily designed to be altruistic toward their genetic kin (Hamilton, 1964a, 1964b), their repeated exchange partners (Trivers, 1971), and members of their deme (a group of intermarrying individuals) or ethnic group (Whitmeyer, 1997). They are not designed to be altruistic toward an indefinite number of complete strangers whom they are not likely ever to meet or exchange with. This is largely because our ancestors lived in small bands of 50–150 genetically related individuals, and large cities and nations with thousands and millions of people are themselves evolutionarily novel.

An examination of the 10-volume compendium *The Encyclopedia of World Cultures* (Levinson, 1991–1995), which describes *all* human cultures known to anthropology (more than 1,500) in great detail, as well as extensive primary ethnographies of traditional societies (Chagnon, 1992; Cronk, 2004; Hill & Hurtado, 1996; Lee, 1979; Whitten, 1976), reveals that liberalism as defined above is absent in these traditional cultures. Although sharing of resources, especially food, is quite common and often normatively prescribed among hunter-gatherer tribes, and although trade with neighboring tribes often takes place (Ridley, 1996), there is no evidence that people in contemporary hunter-gatherer bands *freely* share resources with *members of other tribes*. Because all members of a hunter-gatherer tribe are genetic kin or at the very least repeated exchange partners (friends and allies for life), sharing of resources among them does not qualify as an expression of liberalism as defined above. Given its absence in the contemporary hunter-gatherer tribes, which are often used as modern-day analogs of our ancestral life, it may be reasonable to infer that sharing of resources with total strangers that one has never met or is not ever likely to meet—liberalism—was not part of our ancestral life. Liberalism may therefore be evolutionarily novel, and the Savanna–IQ Interaction Hypothesis would predict that more intelligent individuals are more likely to espouse liberalism as a value than are less intelligent individuals.

Analyses of large representative American samples from the National Longitudinal Study of Adolescent Health (Add Health) and the General Social Surveys confirm this prediction (Kanazawa, 2010). Net of age, sex, race, education, earnings, and religion, more intelligent individuals are more liberal than their less intelligent counterparts. For example, among the Add Health respondents, those who identify themselves as "very liberal" in early adulthood have a mean childhood IQ of 106.4, whereas those who identify themselves as "very conservative" in early adulthood have a mean childhood IQ of 94.8. Even though past studies show that women are more liberal than men (Lake & Breglio, 1992; Shapiro & Mahajan, 1986; Wirls, 1986), and Blacks are more liberal than Whites (Kluegel & Smith, 1986; Sundquist, 1983), the analyses show that the effect of intelligence on liberalism is twice as large as the effect of sex or race.

Choice within Genetic Constraints: Circadian Rhythms

Choice is not incompatible with or antithetical to genetic influence. As long as heritability (h^2) is less than 1.0, individuals can still exercise some choice within broad genetic constraints. For example, political ideology has been shown to be partially genetically influenced; some individuals are genetically predisposed to be liberal or conservative (Alford, Funk, & Hibbing, 2005; Eaves & Eysenck, 1974). Nonetheless, individuals can still choose to be liberal or conservative within broad genetic constraints, and, as discussed above, more intelligent individuals are more likely to choose to be liberal than are less intelligent individuals.

Another example of choice within genetic constraints is circadian rhythms—whether one is a morning person or a night person. Virtually all species in nature, from single-cell organisms to mammals, including humans, exhibit a daily cycle of activity called circadian rhythm (Vitaterna, Takahashi, & Turek, 2001). The circadian rhythm in mammals is regulated by two clusters of nerve cells called the suprachiasmatic nuclei (SCN) in the anterior hypothalamus (Klein, Moore, & Reppert, 1991). Geneticists have by now identified a set of genes that regulate the SCN and thus the circadian rhythm among mammals (King & Takahashi, 2000). "Humans, however, have the unique ability to cognitively override their internal biological clock and its rhythmic outputs" (Vitaterna et al., 2001, p. 90).

Although there are some individual differences in the circadian rhythm, whereby some individuals are more nocturnal than others, humans are basically a diurnal (as opposed to nocturnal) species. Humans rely very heavily on vision for navigation but, unlike genuinely nocturnal species, cannot see in the dark or under little lighting, and our ancestors did not have artificial lighting during the night until the domestication of fire. Any human in the ancestral environment up and about during

the night would have been at risk of predation by nocturnal predators.

Once again, ethnographic evidence from traditional societies available in *The Encyclopedia of World Cultures* (Levinson, 1991–1995) and extensive ethnographies (Chagnon, 1992; Cronk, 2004; Hill & Hurtado, 1996; Lee, 1979; Whitten, 1976) suggest that people in traditional societies usually rise shortly before dawn and go to sleep shortly after dusk in order to take full advantage of the natural light provided by the sun. There is no indication that there are any sustained nocturnal activities, other than occasional conversations and singing, in these tribes. It is therefore reasonable to infer that our ancestors must also have limited their daily activities to daylight, and sustained nocturnal activities are largely evolutionarily novel. The Savanna–IQ Interaction Hypothesis would therefore predict that more intelligent individuals are more likely to be nocturnal than are less intelligent individuals.

Analysis of a large representative sample from Add Health confirms this prediction (Kanazawa & Perina, 2009). Net of age, sex, race, marital status, parenthood, education, earnings, religion, current status as a student, and number of hours worked in a typical week, more intelligent children grow up to be more nocturnal as adults than do less intelligent children. Compared with their less intelligent counterparts, more intelligent individuals go to bed later on weeknights (when they have to get up at a certain time the next day) and on the weekend (when they do not), and they wake up later on weekdays (but not on the weekend, for which the positive effect of childhood IQ on nocturnality is not statistically significant). For example, those with childhood IQs of less than 75 go to bed around 11:42 p.m. on weeknights in early adulthood, whereas those with childhood IQs of over 125 go to bed around 12:30 a.m.

Conclusion

This article seeks to integrate evolutionary psychology—the study of universal human nature—and intelligence research—the study and measurement of individual differences in intelligence. Tooby and Cosmides's (1990a) notion of random quantitative variation on a monomorphic design allows us to view general intelligence as both a domain-specific evolved adaptation (monomorphic design) and an individual-difference variable (random quantitative variation). Such random quantitative variation can also be highly heritable.

Although I have focused on general intelligence and psychometrics in this article, the proposed approach can integrate evolutionary psychology and any aspect of differential psychology. Aggression, theory of mind, the cheater detection mechanism, and some personality traits could all simultaneously be evolved psychological mechanisms and individual-difference variables.

The Savanna–IQ Interaction Hypothesis, which derives from the intersection of evolutionary psychology and intelligence research, suggests that more intelligent individuals are better able to comprehend and deal with evolutionarily novel entities and situations than are less intelligent individuals, but general intelligence does not affect individuals' ability to comprehend and deal with evolutionarily familiar entities and situations. The hypothesis suggests a new way to view some individual differences, such as the extent to which individuals implicitly confuse "TV friends" and real friends, political attitudes on the liberal–conservative continuum, and circadian rhythms, even when these traits are under some genetic control. As long as heritability (h^2) is less than 1.0, there is room for some individual choice.

The general approach proposed in this article will allow genuine integration of evolutionary psychology, on the one hand, and intelligence research in particular and differential psychology in general, on the other. It would simultaneously allow evolutionary psychologists to study a much wider range of psychological traits than hitherto possible and intelligence researchers and differential psychologists to make use of the theories and concepts of evolutionary psychology.

Note

1. I thank Jeremy Freese and Todd K. Shackelford, respectively, for articulating these views to me.

References

Ackerman, P. L., & Heggestad, E. D. (1997). Intelligence, personality, and interests: Evidence for overlapping traits. *Psychological Bulletin, 121,* 219–245. doi:10.1037/0033–2909.121.2.219

Alexander, R. D., Hoogland, J. L., Howard, R. D., Noonan, K. M., & Sherman, P. W. (1979). Sexual dimorphisms and breeding systems in pinnipeds, ungulates, primates, and humans. In N. A. Chagnon & W. Irons (Eds.), *Evolutionary biology and human social behavior: An anthropological perspective* (pp. 402–435). North Scituate, MA: Duxbury Press.

Alford, J. R., Funk, C. L., & Hibbing, J. R. (2005). Are political orientations genetically transmitted? *American Political Science Review, 99,* 153–167.

Ash, J., & Gallup, G. G., Jr. (2007). Paleoclimatic variation and brain expansion during human evolution. *Human Nature, 18,* 109–124. doi:10.1007/s12110–007–9015-z

Bailey, A., Le Couteur, A., Gottesman, I., Bolton, P., Simonoff, E., Yuzda, E., & Rutter, M. (1995). Autism as a strongly genetic disorder: Evidence from a British twin study. *Psychological Medicine, 25,* 63–77. doi:10.1017/S0033291700028099

Bailey, D. H., & Geary, D. C. (2009). Hominid brain evolution: Testing climatic, ecological, and social competition models. *Human Nature, 20,* 67–79. doi:10.1007/s12110–008–9054–0

Bailey, J. M. (1998). Can behavior genetics contribute to evolutionary behavioral science? In C. Crawford & D. L. Krebs (Eds.), *Handbook of evolutionary psychology: Ideas, issues, and applications* (pp. 211–233). Mahwah, NJ: Erlbaum.

Baron-Cohen, S. (1995). *Mind blindness: An essay on autism and theory of mind.* Cambridge, MA: MIT Press.

Belsky, J., Steinberg, L., & Draper, P. (1991). Childhood experiences, interpersonal development, and reproductive strategy: An evolutionary theory of socialization. *Child Development, 62,* 647–670. doi:10.1111/j.1467–8624.1991.tb01558

Borsboom, D., & Dolan, C. V. (2006). Why g is not an adaptation: A comment on Kanazawa (2004). *Psychological Review, 113,* 433–437. doi:10.1037/0033–295X.113.2.433

Burnham, T. C., & Johnson, D. D. P. (2005). The biological and evolutionary logic of human cooperation. *Analyse & Kritik, 27,* 113–135.

Buss, D. M. (1991). Evolutionary personality psychology. *Annual Review of Psychology, 42,* 459–491. doi:10.1146/annurev.ps.42.020191.002331

Buss, D. M. (1995). Evolutionary psychology: A new paradigm for psychological science. *Psychological Inquiry, 6,* 1–30.

Buss, D. M., & Greiling, H. (1999). Adaptive individual differences. *Journal of Personality, 67,* 209–243. doi:10.1111/1467–6494.00053

Byrne, R., & Whiten, A. (1988). *Machiavellian intelligence: Social expertise and the evolution of intellect in monkeys, apes, and humans.* Oxford, England: Oxford University Press.

Cattell, R. B. (1971). *Abilities: Their structure, growth, and action.* Boston, MA: Houghton Mifflin.

Chagnon, N. (1992). *Yanomamö* (4th ed.). Fort Worth, TX: Harcourt Brace Jovanovich.

Chamorro-Premuzic, T., & Furnham, A. (2006). Intellectual competence and the intelligent personality: A third way in differential psychology. *Review of General Psychology, 10,* 251–267. doi:10.1037/1089–2680.10.3.251

Chiappe, D., & MacDonald, K. (2005). The evolution of domain-general mechanisms in intelligence and learning. *Journal of General Psychology, 132,* 5–40.

Chomsky, N. (1957). *Syntactic structures.* The Hague, The Netherlands: Mouton.

Cochran, G., & Harpending, H. (2009). *The 10,000 year explosion: How civilization accelerated human evolution.* New York, NY: Basic Books.

Cosmides, L. (1989). The logic of social exchange: Has natural selection shaped how humans reason? Studies with the Wason selection task. *Cognition, 31,* 187–276. doi:10.1016/0010–0277(89)90023–1

Cosmides, L., & Tooby, J. (1999). *What is evolutionary psychology?* Unpublished manuscript, Center for Evolutionary Psychology, University of California, Santa Barbara.

Cosmides, L., & Tooby, J. (2002). Unraveling the enigma of human intelligence: Evolutionary psychology and the multimodular mind. In R. J. Sternberg & J. C. Kaufman (Eds.), *The evolution of intelligence* (pp. 145–198). Mahwah, NJ: Erlbaum.

Crawford, C. B. (1993). The future of sociobiology: Counting babies or proximate mechanisms? *Trends in Ecology and Evolution, 8,* 183–186. doi:10.1016/0169–5347(93)90145-F

Cronk, L. (2004). *From Mukogodo to Maasai: Ethnicity and cultural change in Kenya.* Boulder, CO: Westview.

Davies, M., Stankov, L., & Roberts, R. D. (1998). Emotional intelligence: In search of an elusive construct. *Journal of Personality and Social Psychology, 75,* 989–1015. doi:10.1037/0022–3514.75.4.989

Derksen, J., Kramer, I., & Katzko, M. (2002). Does a self-report measure for emotional intelligence assess something different than general intelligence? *Personality and Individual Differences, 32,* 37–48. doi:10.1016/S0191–8869(01)00004–6

Derrick, J. L., Gabriel, S., & Hugenberg, K. (2009). Social surrogacy: How favored television programs provide the experience of belonging. *Journal of Experimental Social Psychology, 45,* 352–362. doi:101016/j.esp.2008.12.003

Dunbar, R. I. M. (1998). The social brain hypothesis. *Evolutionary Anthropology, 6,* 178–190.

Dunbar, R. I. M. (2005). Why are good writers so rare? An evolutionary perspective on literature. *Journal of Cultural and Evolutionary Psychology, 3,* 7–21. doi:10.1556/JCEP.3.2005.1.1

Eaves, L. J., & Eysenck, H. J. (1974). Genetics and the development of social attitudes. *Nature, 249,* 288–289. doi:10.1038/249288a0

Evans, P. D., Gilbert, S. L., Mekel-Bobrov, N., Vallender, E. J., Anderson, J. R., Vaez-Azizi, L. M., . . . Lahn, B. T. (2005, September 9). *Microcephalin,* a gene regulating brain size, continues to evolve adaptively in humans. *Science, 309,* 1717–1720. doi:10.1126/science.1113722

Fehr, E., & Henrich, J. (2003). Is strong reciprocity a maladaptation? On the evolutionary foundations of human altruism. In P. Hammerstein (Ed.), *Genetic and cultural evolution of cooperation* (pp. 55–82). Cambridge, MA: MIT Press.

Folstein, S. E., & Rutter, M. L. (1988). Autism: Familial aggregation and genetic implications. *Journal of Autism and Developmental Disorders, 18,* 3–30. doi:10.1007/BF02211815

Ford, M. E., & Tisak, M. S. (1983). A further search for social intelligence. *Journal of Educational Psychology, 75,* 196–206. doi:10.1037/0022–0663.75.2.196

Fox, S., & Spector, P. E. (2000). Relations of emotional intelligence, practical intelligence, general intelligence, and trait affectivity with interview outcomes: It's not all just 'G.' *Journal of Organizational Behavior, 21,* 203–220. doi:10.1002/(SICI)1099–1379(200003)21:2<203::AID-JOB38>3.0.CO;2-Z

Fryer, R. G., Jr., & Levitt, S. D. (2004). The causes and consequences of distinctly Black names. *Quarterly Journal of Economics, 119,* 767–805.

Gangestad, S. W., & Simpson, J. A. (1990). Toward an evolutionary history of female sociosexual variation. *Journal of Personality, 58,* 69–96. doi:10.1111/j.1467–6494.1990.tb00908

Gangestad, S. W., & Simpson, J. A. (2000). The evolution of human mating: Trade-offs and strategic pluralism. *Behavioral and Brain Sciences, 23,* 573–644. doi:10.1017/S0140525X0000337X

Gardner, H. (1983). *Frames of mind: The theory of multiple intelligences.* New York, NY: Basic Books.

Geary, D. C. (2005). *The origin of mind: Evolution of brain, cognition, and general intelligence.* Washington, DC: American Psychological Association.

Geher, G., & Miller, G. (Eds.). (2007). *Mating intelligence: Sex, relationships, and the mind's reproductive system.* Mahwah, NJ: Erlbaum.

Gilles, G. E., Stough, C., & Loukomitis, S. (2004). Openness, intelligence, and self-report intelligence. *Intelligence, 32,* 133–143.

Goldberg, L. R. (1992). The development of markers for the big-five factor structure. *Psychological Assessment, 4,* 26–42.

Gottfredson, L. S. (1997). Why g matters: The complexity of everyday life. *Intelligence, 24,* 79–132. doi:10.1016/S0160–2896(97)90014–3

Hagen, E. H., & Hammerstein, P. (2006). Game theory and human evolution: A critique of some recent interpretations of experimental games. *Theoretical Population Biology, 69,* 339–348. doi:101016/j.tpb.2005.09.005

Hamilton, W. D. (1964a). The genetical evolution of social behavior. I. *Journal of Theoretical Biology, 7,* 1–16. doi:10.1016/0022–5193(64)90038–4

Hamilton, W. D. (1964b). The genetical evolution of social behavior. II. *Journal of Theoretical Biology, 7,* 17–52. doi:10.1016/0022–5193(64)90039–6

Herrnstein, R. J., & Murray, C. (1994). *The bell curve: Intelligence and class structure in American life.* New York, NY: Free Press.

Hill, K., & Hurtado, A. M. (1996). *Ache life history: The ecology and demography of a foraging people.* New York, NY: Aldine.

Holland, D. C., Dollinger, S. J., Holland, C. J., & MacDonald, D. A. (1995). The relationship between psychometric intelligence and the five-factor model of personality in a rehabilitation sample. *Journal of Clinical Psychology, 51,* 79–88. doi:10.1002/1097–4679(199501)51:1<79::AID-JCLP2270510113>3.0CO;2-P

Humphrey, N. K. (1976). The social function of the intellect. In P. P. G. Bateson & R. A. Hinde (Eds.), *Growing points in ethology* (pp. 303–317). New York, NY: Cambridge University Press.

Jensen, A. R. (1998). *The g factor: The science of mental ability.* Westport, CT: Praeger.

Jerisen, H. (1973). *Evolution of the brain and intelligence.* New York, NY: Academic Press.

Kanazawa, S. (2002). Bowling with our imaginary friends. *Evolution and Human Behavior, 23,* 167–171. doi:10.1016/S1090–5138(01)00098–8

Kanazawa, S. (2004a). The Savanna Principle. *Managerial and Decision Economics, 25,* 41–54. doi:10.1002/mde.1130

Kanazawa, S. (2004b). General intelligence as a domain-specific adaptation. *Psychological Review, 111,* 512–523. doi:10.1037/0033–295X.111.2.512

Kanazawa, S. (2006). Why the less intelligent may enjoy television more than the more intelligent. *Journal of Cultural and Evolutionary Psychology, 4,* 27–36. doi:10.1556/JCEP.4.2006.1.2

Kanazawa, S. (2007). Mating intelligence and general intelligence as independent constructs. In G. Geher & G. Miller (Eds.), *Mating intelligence: Sex, relationships, and the mind's reproductive system* (pp. 283–309). Mahwah, NJ: Erlbaum.

Kanazawa, S. (2008). Temperature and evolutionary novelty as forces behind the evolution of general intelligence. *Intelligence, 36,* 99–108. doi:10.1016/j.intell.2007.04.001

Kanazawa, S. (2010). Why liberals and atheists are more intelligent. *Social Psychology Quarterly, 73,* 33–57. doi:10.1177/0190272510361602

Kanazawa, S., & Perina, K. (2009). Why night owls are more intelligent. *Personality and Individual Differences, 47,* 685–690. doi:10.1016/j.paid.2009.05.021

Kanazawa, S., & Still, M. C. (1999). Why monogamy? *Social Forces, 78,* 25–50.

Kihlstrom, J. F., & Cantor, N. (2000). Social intelligence. In R. J. Sternberg (Ed.), *Handbook of intelligence* (pp. 359–379). Cambridge, England: Cambridge University Press.

King, D. P., & Takahashi, J. S. (2000). Molecular genetics of circadian rhythms in mammals. *Annual Review of Neuroscience, 23,* 713–742. doi:10.1146/annurev.neuro.23.1.713

Klein, D. C., Moore, R. Y., & Reppert, S. M. (1991). *Suprachiasmatic nucleus: The mind's clock.* New York, NY: Oxford University Press.

Kluegel, J. R., & Smith, E. R. (1986). *Beliefs about inequality: Americans' view of what is and what ought to be.* New York, NY: Aldine.

Lake, C. C., & Breglio, V. J. (1992). Different voices, different views: The politics of gender. In P. Ries & A. J. Stone (Eds.), *The American woman, 1992–93: A status report* (pp. 178–201). New York, NY: Norton.

Lee, R. B. (1979). *The !Kung San: Men, women, and work in a foraging society.* Cambridge, England: Cambridge University Press.

Leutenegger, W., & Kelly, J. T. (1977). Relationship of sexual dimorphism in canine size and body size to social, behavioral, and ecological correlates in anthropoid primates. *Primates, 18,* 117–136. doi:10.1007/BF02382954

Levinson, D. (Ed.). (1991–1995). *Encyclopedia of world cultures* (Vols. *1–10*). Boston, MA: G. K. Hall.

Levitt, S. D., & Dubner, S. J. (2005). *Freakonomics: A rogue economist explores the hidden side of everything.* London, England: Penguin.

Lieberson, S., & Bell, E. O. (1992). Children's first names: An empirical study of social taste. *American Journal of Sociology, 98,* 511–554. doi:10.1086/230048

MacDonald, K. (1995). Evolution, the five-factor model, and levels of personality. *Journal of Personality, 63,* 525–567. doi:101111/j.1467–6494.1995.tb00505.x

Marlowe, H. A., Jr. (1986). Social intelligence: Evidence for multidimensionality and construct independence. *Journal of Educational Psychology, 78,* 52–58. doi:10.1037/0022–0663.78.1.52

Marlowe, H. A., & Bedell, J. R. (1982). Social intelligence: Further evidence for the independence of the construct. *Psychological Reports, 51,* 461–462.

Mayer, J. D., Roberts, R. D., & Barsade, S. G. (2009). Human abilities: Emotional intelligence. *Annual Review of Psychology, 59,* 507–536. doi:10.1146/annurev.psych.59.103006.093646

Mayer, J. D., Salovey, P., & Caruso, D. R. (2008). Emotional intelligence: New ability or eclectic traits? *American Psychologist, 63,* 503–517. doi:10.1037/0003–066X.63.6.503

Mayer, J. D., Salovey, P., Caruso, D. R., & Sitarenios, G. (2001). Emotional intelligence as a standard intelligence. *Emotion, 1,* 232–242. doi:10.1037/1528–3542.1.3.232

McRae, R. R. (1994). Openness to experience: Expanding the boundaries of Factor V. *European Journal of Personality, 8,* 251–272. doi:10.1002/per.2410080404

Miller, A. S., & Kanazawa, S. (2007). *Why beautiful people have more daughters.* New York, NY: Penguin.

Miller, G. F. (2000a). How to keep our metatheories adaptive: Beyond Cosmides, Tooby, and Lakatos. *Psychological Inquiry, 11,* 42–46.

Miller, G. F. (2000b). Sexual selection for indicators of intelligence. In G. R. Bock, J. A. Goode, & K. Webb (Eds.), *The nature of intelligence* (pp. 260–275). New York, NY: Wiley.

Neisser, U., Boodoo, G., Bouchard, T. J., Jr., Boykin, A. W., Brody, N., Ceci, S. J., . . . Urbina, S. (1996). Intelligence: Knowns and unknowns. *American Psychologist, 51,* 77–101. doi:10.1037/0003–066X.51.2.77

Nettle, D. (2005). An evolutionary approach to the extraversion continuum. *Evolution and Human Behavior, 26,* 363–373. doi:10.1016/j.evolhumbehav.2004.12.004

Nettle, D. (2006). The evolution of personality variation in humans and other animals. *American Psychologist, 61,* 622–631. doi:10.1037/0003–066X.61.6.622

Ridley, M. (1996). *The origins of virtue: Human instincts and the evolution of cooperation.* New York, NY: Viking Press.

Roberts, R. D., Zeidner, M., & Matthews, G. (2001). Does emotional intelligence meet traditional standards for an intelligence? Some new data and conclusions. *Emotion, 1,* 196–231. doi:10.1037/1528–3542.1.3.196

Sally, D. (1995). Conversation and cooperation in social dilemmas: A meta-analysis of experiments from 1958 to 1992. *Rationality and Society, 7,* 58–92. doi:10.1177/1043463195007001004

Salovey, P., & Mayer, J. D. (1990). Emotional intelligence. *Imagination, Cognition and Personality, 9,* 557–568.

Scarr, S. (1995). Psychology will be truly evolutionary when behavior genetics is included. *Psychological Inquiry, 6,* 68–71. doi:10.1207/s15327965pli0601_13

Shapiro, R. Y., & Mahajan, H. (1986). Gender differences in policy preferences: A summary of trends from the 1960s to the 1980s. *Public Opinion Quarterly, 50,* 42–61. doi:10.1086/268958

Shepard, R. N. (1994). Perceptual-cognitive universals as reflections of the world. *Psychonomic Bulletin & Review, 1,* 2–28.

Spearman, C. (1904). General intelligence, objectively determined and measured. *American Journal of Psychology, 15,* 201–293. doi:10.2307/1412107

Sundquist, J. L. (1983). *Dynamics of the party system* (Rev. ed.). Washington, DC: Brookings Institution.

Symons, D. (1990). Adaptiveness and adaptation. *Ethology and Sociobiology, 11,* 427–444. doi:10.1016/0162–3095(90)90019–3

Tooby, J., & Cosmides, L. (1990a). On the universality of human nature and the uniqueness of the individual: The role of genetics and adaptation. *Journal of Personality, 58,* 17–67.

Tooby, J., & Cosmides, L. (1990b). The past explains the present: Emotional adaptations and the structure of ancestral environments. *Ethology and Sociobiology, 11,* 375–424. doi:10.1016/0162–3095(90)90017-Z

Tooby, J., & Cosmides, L. (1992). The psychological foundations of culture. In J. H. Barkow, L. Cosmides, & J. Tooby (Eds.), *The adapted mind: Evolutionary psychology and the generation of culture* (pp. 19–136). New York, NY: Oxford University Press.

Trivers, R. L. (1971). The evolution of reciprocal altruism. *Quarterly Review of Biology, 46,* 35–57.

Vitaterna, M. H., Takahashi, J. S., & Turek, F. W. (2001). Overview of circadian rhythms. *Alcohol Research and Health, 25,* 85–93.

Whitmeyer, J. M. (1997). Endogamy as a basis for ethnic behavior. *Sociological Theory, 15,* 162–178. doi:10.1111/0735–2751.00030

Whitten, N. E., Jr. (1976). *Sacha Runa: Ethnicity and adaptation of Ecuadorian jungle Quichua.* Urbana: University of Illinois Press.

Wirls, D. (1986). Reinterpreting the gender gap. *Public Opinion Quarterly, 50,* 316–330.

Critical Thinking

1. What is the Savanna Principle?

2. Describe the way in which the Savanna Principle may be used to conduct research on intelligence

3. Describe two different theories about traits such as intelligence.

Create Central

www.mhhe.com/createcentral

Internet References

The hypothesis: Why do people want what they want?
www.psychologytoday.com/blog/the-scientific-fundamentalist/201003/the-hypothesis

Intelligence and liberalism
http://andreaskluth.org/2010/03/31/intelligence-and-liberalism

Article

Prepared by: Eric Landrum, *Boise State University*

Enough about You

When Christopher Lasch's landmark book The Culture of Narcissism: American Life in an Age of Diminishing Expectations *was first published in 1979,* narcissism *was not a term with much popular currency. The book played a large role in changing that, and in the decades since its publication the wide-ranging cultural critique at its core has been embraced by conservatives and liberals alike. While there are sections of* The Culture of Narcissism *that now seem dated—or at least a product of their time—much of the material in the original edition is so spot-on and even prophetic that it could have been written this year. What follows is a general sampling of particularly timely or prescient passages from a book that has become a sort of* Silent Spring *of America's psychological journey inward.* —The Editors

CHRISTOPHER LASCH

Learning Outcomes

After reading this article, you will be able to:

- Describe the characteristics of a narcissist and those conditions by which a narcissist can thrive.

- Define the concept of anxious self-scrutiny and the role it plays to help individuals deal with the demands of daily life.

T his book describes a way of life that is dying—the culture of competitive individualism, which in its decadence has carried the logic of individualism to the extreme of a war of all against all, the pursuit of happiness to the dead end of a narcissistic preoccupation with the self.

Economic man . . . has given way to the psychological man of our times—the final product of bourgeois individualism. The new narcissist is haunted not by guilt but by anxiety. His sexual attitudes are permissive rather than puritanical, even though his emancipation from ancient taboos brings him no sexual peace. He extols cooperation and teamwork while harboring deeply antisocial impulses. He praises respect for rules and regulations in the secret belief that they do not apply to himself. Acquisitive in the sense that his cravings have no limits, he does not accumulate goods and provisions against the future, in the manner of the acquisitive individualist of 19th-century political economy, but demands immediate gratification and lives in a state of restless, perpetually unsatisfied desire.

Storm warnings, portents, hints of catastrophe haunt our times. The Nazi holocaust, the threat of nuclear annihilation, the depletion of natural resources, well-founded predictions of ecological disaster have fulfilled poetic prophecy, giving concrete historical substance to the nightmare, or death wish, that avant-garde artists were the first to express. Impending disaster has become an everyday concern, so commonplace and familiar that nobody any longer gives much thought to how disaster might be averted. People busy themselves instead with survival strategies, measures designed to prolong their own lives, or programs guaranteed to ensure good health and peace of mind.

The contemporary climate is therapeutic, not religious. People today hunger not for personal salvation, let alone for the restoration of an earlier golden age, but for the feeling, the momentary illusion, of personal well-being, health, and psychic security.

Notwithstanding his occasional illusions of omnipotence, the narcissist depends on others to validate his self-esteem. He cannot live without an admiring audience. [His insecurity can be] overcome only by seeing his "grandiose self" reflected in the attentions of others, or by attaching himself to those who radiate celebrity, power, and charisma. For the narcissist, the world is a mirror, whereas the rugged individualist saw it as an empty wilderness to be shaped to his own design.

Today Americans are overcome not by the sense of endless possibility but by the banality of the social order they have erected against it. People nowadays complain of an inability to feel. They cultivate more vivid experiences, seek to beat sluggish flesh to life, attempt to revive jaded appetites. Outwardly bland, submissive, and sociable, they seethe with an inner anger for which a dense, overpopulated bureaucratic society can devise few legitimate outlets.

The popularity of the confessional mode testifies, of course, to the new narcissism that runs all through American culture. Instead of working through their memories, many writers now rely on mere self-disclosure to keep readers interested, appealing not to their understanding but to their salacious curiosity about the private lives of famous people.

The mass media, with their cult of celebrity and their attempt to surround it with glamour and excitement, have made America a nation of fans and moviegoers. The media give substance to and thus intensify narcissistic dreams of fame and glory, encourage common people to identify themselves with the stars and to hate the "herd," and make it more and more difficult for them to accept the banality of everyday existence.

The modern propaganda of commodities and the good life has sanctioned impulse gratification and made it unnecessary for the id to apologize for its wishes or disguise their grandiose proportions. But this same propaganda has made failure and loss unsupportable.

The proliferation of recorded images undermines our sense of reality. We distrust our perceptions until the camera verifies them. Photographic images provide us with the proof of our existence, without which we would find it difficult even to reconstruct a personal history.

Medicine and psychiatry—more generally, the therapeutic outlook and sensibility that pervade modern society—reinforce the pattern created by other cultural influences, in which individuals endlessly examine themselves for signs of aging and ill health, for telltale symptoms of psychic stress, for blemishes and flaws that might diminish their attractiveness. . . . Modern medicine has conquered the plagues and epidemics that once made life so precarious, only to create new forms of insecurity. In the same way, bureaucracy has made life predictable and even boring while reviving, in a new form, the war of all against all. Our over-organized society, in which large-scale organizations predominate but have lost the capacity to command allegiance, in some respects more nearly approximates a condition of universal animosity than did the primitive capitalism on which Hobbes modeled his state of nature.

A society that fears it has no future is not likely to give much attention to the needs of the next generation, and the ever-present sense of historical discontinuity—the blight of our society—falls with particularly devastating effect on the family. The modern parent's attempt to make children feel loved and wanted fails to conceal an underlying coolness—the remoteness of those who have little to pass on to the next generation and who in any case give priority to their own right to self-fulfillment.

The weakening of social ties, which originates in the prevailing state of social warfare, at the same time reflects a narcissistic defense against dependence. A warlike society tends to produce men and women who are at heart antisocial. It should therefore not surprise us to find that although narcissists conform to social norms for fear of external retribution, they often think of themselves as outlaws.

The ethic of self-preservation and psychic survival is rooted, then, not merely in objective conditions of economic warfare, rising rates of crime, and social chaos but in the subjective experience of emptiness and isolation. It reflects the conviction—as much of a projection of inner anxieties as a perception of the way things are—that envy and exploitation dominate even the most intimate relations. The ideology of personal growth, superficially optimistic, radiates a profound despair and resignation. It is the faith of those without faith.

In an age of diminishing expectations, the Protestant virtues no longer incite enthusiasm. Inflation erodes investments and savings. Advertising undermines the horrors of indebtedness, exhorting the consumer to buy now and pay later. Self-preservation has replaced self-improvement as the goal of earthly existence. In earlier times, the self-made man took pride in his judgment of character and probity; today he anxiously scans the faces of his fellows not so as to evaluate their credit but in order to gauge their susceptibility to his own blandishments. He practices the classic arts of seduction with the same indifference to moral niceties, hoping to win your heart while picking your pocket. The happy hooker stands in place of Horatio Alger as the prototype of personal success.

Success in our society has to be ratified by publicity. It is well known that Madison Avenue packages politicians and markets them as if they were cereals or deodorants; but the art of public relations penetrates even more deeply into political life, transforming policy making itself. The modern prince does not much care that "there's a job to be done"—the slogan of American capitalism at an earlier and more enterprising stage of its development; what interests him is that "relevant audiences," in the language of the Pentagon Papers, have to be cajoled, won over, seduced.

The search for competitive advantage through emotional manipulation increasingly shapes not only personal relations but relations at work as well. Personal life, no longer a refuge from deprivations suffered at work, has become as anarchical, as warlike, and as full of stress as the marketplace itself. The cocktail party reduces sociability to social combat.

At the same time that public life and even private life take on the qualities of spectacle, a countermovement seeks to model spectacle, theater, all forms of life, on reality—to obliterate the very distinction between art and life. Both developments popularize a sense of the absurd, that hallmark of the contemporary sensibility. Overexposure to manufactured illusions soon destroys their representational power. The illusion of reality dissolves, not in a heightened sense of reality as we might expect, but in a remarkable indifference to reality.

A number of historical currents have converged in our time to produce not merely in artists but also in ordinary men and women an escalating cycle of self-consciousness—a sense of the self as a performer under the constant scrutiny of friends and strangers. . . . To the performing self, the only reality is the identity he can construct out of materials furnished by advertising and mass culture, themes of popular film and fiction, and fragments torn from a vast range of cultural traditions. In order to polish and perfect the part he has devised for himself, the new Narcissus gazes at his own reflection, not so much in admiration as in unremitting search of flaws, signs of fatigue, decay.

In our society, anxious self-scrutiny (not to be confused with critical self-examination) not only serves to regulate information signaled to others and to interpret signals received; it also establishes an ironic distance from the deadly routine of daily life. On the one hand, the degradation of work makes skill and competence increasingly irrelevant to material success and thus encourages the presentation of the self as a commodity; on the other hand, it discourages commitment to the job and drives people, as the only alternative to boredom and despair, to view work with self-critical detachment. When jobs consist of little more than meaningless motions, and when social routines, formerly dignified as ritual, degenerate into role playing, workers . . . seek to escape from the resulting sense of inauthenticity by creating an ironic distance from their daily routine. They take refuge in jokes, mockery, and cynicism. By demystifying daily life, they convey to themselves and others the impression that they have risen beyond it, even as they go through the motions and do what is expected of them. As more and more people find themselves working at jobs that are in fact beneath their abilities, as leisure and sociability themselves take on the qualities of work, the posture of cynical detachment becomes the dominant style of everyday intercourse.

Critical Thinking

1. What is competitive individualism?

2. What is the relationship between the psychological concepts of narcissism and self-esteem?

3. From a societal perspective, what role does anxious self-scrutiny play?

Create Central

www.mhhe.com/createcentral

Internet References

Emotional competency
 www.emotionalcompetency.com/tyranny.htm

When narcissism meets addiction
 www.theatlantic.com/health/archive/2013/07/where-narcissism
 -meets-addiction/278195/

Political Attitudes Vary with Physiological Traits by Douglas R. Oxley et. al.

179

Prepared by: Eric Landrum, *Boise State University*

Political Attitudes Vary with Physiological Traits

DOUGLAS R. OXLEY ET AL.

Learning Outcomes

After reading this article, you will be able to:

- Understand the possible connection between a person's political views and his or her physiological traits.

- Differentiate between physiological responses that tend to be linked to those with strong liberal or conservative views.

The nature and source of political attitudes have been the subject of much study (*1–3*). Traditionally, such attitudes were believed to be built from sensible, unencumbered reactions to environmental events (*4*), but more recent research emphasizes the built-in, almost "automated" quality of many political responses (*5*), which has been suggested to be based in brain activation variations in limbic regions (*6–8*). The research task is now to determine why some people seem primed to adopt certain political attitudes, whereas others appear primed to adopt quite different attitudes. For example, although images and reminders of the terrorist attacks of 9–11 produce an aggregate shift in political views (*9, 10*), the reasons for individual variability in the degree of attitudinal shifts are unknown.

One possibility is that people vary in general physiology and that certain of these variations encourage the adoption of particular political attitudes. Broad, physiologically relevant traits such as feelings of disgust and fear of disease have been suggested to be related to political attitudes (*11, 12*), and political beliefs can be predicted by observing brain activation patterns in response to unanticipated events, such as one letter of the alphabet appearing on a computer screen when the respondent expected a different letter (*13*). A connection between self-reports of felt threat and political attitudes has also been identified in previous research (*14–19*).

The physiology of response to a perceived threat is an attractive topic of investigation because an appropriate response to environmental threat is necessary for long-term survival and because perceived threat produces a variety of reasonably well-mapped, physically instantiated responses (*20*). If the threat is abrupt, a defensive cascade of linked, rapid extensor-flexor

movement occurs throughout the body within 30 to 50 ms (*21*), presumably to reduce vital-organ vulnerability (e.g., eye blink and retraction of the head). Less immediately, perceived threat causes signals from the sensory cortex to be relayed to the thalamus and ultimately to the brain stem, resulting in heightened noradrenergic activity in the locus ceruleus (*22*). Acetylcholine, acting primarily through the amygdala but also through the hypothalamic-pituitary-adrenal axis (*23*), stimulates release of epinephrine, which in turn leads to activation of the sympathetic division of the autonomic nervous system. Though these basic response patterns apply in all people, individual sensitivity to perceived threat varies widely (*24*).

To test the hypothesis that variations in physical sensitivity to threat are associated with political beliefs, in May 2007, we conducted a random telephone sample of the population of Lincoln, Nebraska. Participants were screened [see supporting online material (SOM)] to identify those with strong political attitudes (regardless of the content of those attitudes), and qualifying individuals were invited to a lab in the city. During the first visit, the 46 participants completed a survey instrument (see SOM) ascertaining their political beliefs, personality traits, and demographic characteristics. During the second session, about 2 months after the first, participants were attached to physiological equipment, making it possible to measure skin conductance and orbicularis oculi startle blink electromyogram (EMG) response (*25*).

Skin conductance "has been closely linked with the psychological concepts of emotion, arousal, and attention" and "provides relatively direct and undiluted representation of sympathetic activity" (*26*). Arousal causes increased moisture in the outer layers of the skin that in turn enhances conductivity, making it possible to assess sympathetic activation by recording changes in the level of skin conductance. Each participant was shown three separate threatening images (a very large spider on the face of a frightened person, a dazed individual with a bloody face, and an open wound with maggots in it) interspersed among a sequence of 33 images. After logging the data to normalize the distribution, we computed the change in the mean level of skin conductance (SCL) from the previous interstimulus interval (10 s) to the stimulus of interest (20 s). This calculation isolates the change in skin conductance induced by the stimulus and reduces the effects of baseline variations across participants (27). We computed the mean change in SCL induced by the three threatening stimuli and determined whether this mean difference was related to variations in preference for socially protective policies (described below). Similar procedures were conducted for three nonthreatening stimuli shown during the series (a bunny, a bowl of fruit, and a happy child).

The other physiological measure was orbicularis oculi startle blink response, an involuntary response to a startling noise. Harder blinks (higher blink amplitudes) are indicative of a heightened "fear state" (28). The threatening stimulus was a loud, standardized level of white noise heard by participants (through headphones) at seven unexpected moments while they were looking at a computer screen containing nothing but a focus point. As is common practice (28), we first took the logarithm of the data and then computed participants' average blink amplitude. Because surprising subjects with a sudden, jarring noise is likely to affect all physiological indicators, we conducted the startle portion of the study after completing separate tests on skin conductance. The order of the images and the timing of the auditory startle were randomized once, and then that program was presented to all participants.

The survey instrument contained a battery of items asking respondents whether they agreed with, disagreed with, or were uncertain toward 28 individual political concepts—the well-known Wilson-Patterson format (29). We identified particular positions on 18 of these policy issues as those most likely to be held by individuals particularly concerned with protecting the interests of the participants' group, defined as the United States in mid-2007, from threats. These positions are support for military spending, warrantless searches, the death penalty, the Patriot Act, obedience, patriotism, the Iraq War, school prayer, and Biblical truth; and opposition to pacifism, immigration, gun control, foreign aid, compromise, premarital sex, gay marriage, abortion rights, and pornography. We do not label these collections of policy positions as either "liberal" or "conservative" because we measure only one aspect of ideologies and exclude other aspects such as positions on economic issues. We take no stance on whether these positions actually promote the stability and cohesion of the social unit; we only assert that, given the common frames of the modern American policy, those most concerned about social protection will tend to be attracted to the particular policy positions listed.

We computed a summary measure of each participant's stances on the 18 political issues such that those positions suggesting a concern for protecting the social unit were given higher scores. To test the skin conductance portion of our analysis, we divided participants into two groups according to their level of concern for protecting the social unit: those above the median and those below. Participants whose policy positions suggest more concern for protecting the social unit were distinguished by an increase in skin conductance when threatening stimuli were presented. Those whose positions suggest less concern for protecting the social unit, by contrast, were mostly

unaffected by those same stimuli and the difference in these two groups was statistically significant ($P = 0.05$). When participants were shown nonthreatening stimuli, there was no statistically significant difference ($P = 0.77$) in skin conductance changes between the two groups.

Uncontrolled, bivariate results have the potential to mislead. We therefore regressed each participant's summary level of support for socially protective political policies on changes in skin conductance as well as on four sociodemographic variables commonly used as predictors of political attitudes: gender, age, income, and education (race and ethnicity were not controlled because all but one participant was self-identified as white and non-Hispanic). With the effects of these sociodemographic variables controlled, the effect of increases in skin conductance when viewing threatening stimuli was positive and significant ($P < 0.01$), with a large standardized regression coefficient (0.377). When nonthreatening images were viewed, however, changes in skin conductance appeared to be unrelated to political attitudes pertaining to protecting the social order. In this multiple regression model, the standardized regression coefficient for skin conductance change was statistically insignificant ($P = 0.96$), small, and slightly negative (-0.007).

A further test of this pattern is possible when, for each participant, mean skin conductance change occasioned by the viewing of the nonthreatening stimuli is subtracted from mean skin conductance change when viewing the threatening stimuli. When this variable was entered into the multiple regression with age, income, education, and gender, it was in the expected direction (greater relative reaction to threatening stimuli correlates with more support for socially protective policies), sizable (standardized regression coefficient = 0.28), and statistically significant ($P = 0.04$). Full results of this analysis are presented in the SOM.

Startle blink EMG responses habituate (28), but the tendency for high blink amplitudes to correlate with respondents supportive of protective policies was consistent across the exercise and was also apparent for the overall means. Although the difference was not significant in the bivariate analysis, when the sociodemographic controls were added to better specify the model, the coefficient for blink amplitude was again in the predicted (positive) direction, sizable (standardized regression coefficient = 0.286), and statistically significant ($P = 0.03$).

Our data reveal a correlation between physiological responses to threat and political attitudes but do not permit firm conclusions concerning the specific causal processes at work. Particular physiological responses to threat could cause the adoption of certain political attitudes, or the holding of particular political attitudes could cause people to respond in a certain physiological way to environmental threats, but neither of these seems probable. More likely is that physiological responses to generic threats and political attitudes on policies related to protecting the social order may both derive from a common source. Parents could both socialize their children to hold certain political attitudes and condition them to respond in a certain way to threatening stimuli, but conditioning involuntary

Political Attitudes Vary with Physiological Traits by Douglas R. Oxley et. al.

181

reflex responses takes immediate and sustained reinforcement and punishment, and it is unlikely that this conditioning varies systematically across political beliefs.

Alternatively, political attitudes and varying physiological responses to threat may both derive from neural activity patterns, perhaps those surrounding the amygdala. There is a connection between localized activation of the amygdala and aversive startle response (*30*). Amygdala activity is also crucial in shaping responses to socially threatening images (*31, 32*) and may be connected to political predispositions. Indeed, given that political and social attitudes are heritable (*33–36*) and that amygdala activity also has been traced to genetics (*37–40*), genetic variation relevant to amygdala activity could affect both physiological responses to threat and political attitudes bearing on threats to the social order.

Our findings suggest that political attitudes vary with physiological traits linked to divergent manners of experiencing and processing environmental threats. Consequently, our research provides one possible explanation for both the lack of malleability in the beliefs of individuals with strong political convictions and for the associated ubiquity of political conflict.

References and Notes

1. A. Campbell, P. E. Converse, W. E. Miller, D. E. Stokes, *The American Voter* (John Wiley, New York, 1960).
2. P. E. Converse, in *Ideology and Discontent,* D.E. Apter, Ed. (Free Press, New York, 1964).
3. J. R. Zaller, *The Nature and Origins of Mass Opinion* (Cambridge Univ. Press, New York, 1992).
4. B. I. Page, R. Y. Shapiro, *The Rational Public* (Univ. of Chicago Press, Chicago, 1992).
5. M. Lodge, C. Taber, *Pol. Psychol.* **26,** 455 (2005).
6. G. E. Marcus, W. R. Neuman, M. Mackuen, *Affective Intelligence and Political Judgment* (Univ. of Chicago Press, Chicago, 2000).
7. R. McDermott, *Perspect. Polit.* **2,** 691 (2004).
8. D. Westen, *The Political Brain* (Public Affairs, New York, 2007).
9. M. J. Landau *et al., Pers. Soc. Psychol. Bull.* **30,** 1136 (2004).
10. S. Fahmy, S. Cho, W. Wanta, Y. Song, *Vis. Commun. Q.* **13,** 3 (2006).
11. J. Faulkner, M. Schaller, J. H. Park, L. A. Duncan, *Group Process. Intergroup Relat.* **7,** 333 (2004).
12. C. D. Navarrete, D. M. T. Fessler, *Evol. Hum. Behav.* **27,** 270 (2006).
13. D. M. Amodio, J. T. Jost, S. L. Master, C. M. Lee, *Nat. Neurosci.* **10,** 1246 (2007).
14. J. T. Jost, J. Glaser, A. W. Kruglanski, F. J. Sulloway, *Psychol. Bull.* **129,** 339 (2003).
15. J. T. Jost, *Am. Psychol.* **61,** 651 (2006).
16. L. Huddy, S. Feldman, C. Taber, G. Lahav, *Am. J. Pol. Sci.* **49,** 593 (2005).
17. S. Feldman, *Pol. Psychol.* **24,** 593 (2003).
18. K. Stenner, *The Authoritarian Dynamic* (Cambridge Univ. Press, New York, 2005).
19. F. Pratto, J. Sidanius, L. M. Stallworth, B. F. Malle, *J. Pers. Soc. Psychol.* **67,** 741 (1994).
20. W. B. Cannon, *Bodily Changes in Pain, Hunger, Fear, and Rage* (Appleton, New York, 1915).
21. M. M. Bradley, P. J. Lang, in *Handbook of Psychophysiology,* J. T. Cacioppo, L. G. Tassinary, G. G. Berntson, Eds. (Cambridge Univ. Press, New York, 2007).
22. M. E. Thase, R. H. Howland, in *Handbook of Depression,* E. E. Beckham and W. R. Leber, Eds. (Guilford, New York, 1995).
23. E. Lemche *et al., Hum. Brain Mapp.* **27,** 623 (2006).
24. G. H. Grosser, H. Wechser, M. Greenblatt, *The Threat of Impending Disaster* (MIT Press, Cambridge, MA, 1971).
25. Materials and methods are described in the SOM.
26. M. E. Dawson, A. M. Shell, D. L. Filion, in *Handbook of Psychophysiology,* J. T. Cacioppo, L. G. Tassinary, G. G. Berntson, Eds. (Cambridge Univ. Press, New York, 2007).
27. A. Miller, J. Long, in *Developmental Psychophysiology,* L. A. Schmidt, S. J. Segalowitz, Eds. (Cambridge Univ. Press, New York, 2007).
28. P. J. Lang, M. M. Bradley, B. N. Cuthbert, *Psychol. Rev.* **97,** 377 (1990).
29. G. D. Wilson, J. R. Patterson, *Br. J. Soc. Clin. Psychol.* **7,** 264 (1968).
30. S. Anders, M. Lotze, M. Erb, W. Grodd, *Hum. Brain Mapp.* **23,** 200 (2004).
31. C. L. Larson *et al., Biol. Psychiatry* **60,** 410 (2006).
32. D. A. Fitzgerald, M. Angstad, L. M. Jelsone, P. J. Nathan, K. L. Phan, *Neuroimage* **30,** 1441 (2006).
33. N. G. Martin *et al., Proc. Natl. Acad. Sci. U.S.A.* **83,** 4364 (1986).
34. L. Eaves *et al., Twin Res.* **2,** 62 (1999).
35. J. R. Alford, C. L. Funk, J. R. Hibbing, *Am. Polit. Sci. Rev.* **99,** 153 (2005).
36. J. H. Fowler, L. A. Baker, C. T. Dawes, *Am. Polit. Sci. Rev.* **102,** 233 (2008).
37. Z. F. Mainen, *Nat. Neurosci.* **10,** 1511 (2007).
38. H. Bracha, D. Yoshioka, N. Masakawa, D. Stockman, *J. Affect. Disord.* **88,** 119 (2005).
39. C. A. Ponder *et al., T. C. Gilliam, A. A. Palmer, Genes Brain Behav.* **6,** 736 (2007).
40. A. R. Hariri *et al., Science* **297,** 400 (2002).
41. We thank E. Whitaker, C. Jacobs, B. Sexton, K. A. Espy, J. Brehm, D. Bulling, and the James Long Company for their invaluable assistance. Financial support was provided by the NSF (SES-0721378 and SES-0721707), the ManTech Corporation, and the University of Nebraska–Lincoln's Strategic Research Cluster Grant program.

Critical Thinking

1. In this study, why do you think it was important that the researchers studied those with strong political beliefs? Might the pattern of results change with those with weaker beliefs or those who held some liberal and some conservative viewpoints? Explain.

2. The height of one's blink (blink amplitude) was measured, and significant differences were found by the authors. What was the interpretation of those results, and do you agree with the interpretation? Why or why not?

Create Central

www.mhhe.com/createcentral

Internet References

Physiological politics

http://languagelog.ldc.upenn.edu/nll/?p=2121

The biology of politics: Is it for real?

http://scienceblogs.com/grrlscientist/2008/09/20/the-physiology-of-politics

Article   Prepared by: Eric Landrum, *Boise State University*

That Elusive Birth Order Effect and What It Means for You

SUSAN KRAUSS WHITBOURNE

Learning Outcomes

After reading this article, you will be able to:

- Understand some of the variables that are influenced by one's birth order.
- Identify some of the research-based differences between first-born, middle-borns, last-borns, and only children.

Only child, first-born, last-born, or somewhere in between. Where do you fit into the birth order of your family? Perhaps you've come to believe the myths both in your family and in psychology as a whole that your character, values, achievement strivings, and life success are determined by the family position that fate, and your parents, awarded to you. Psychology goes through periods of alternatively accepting and rejecting these myths. Although various theories abound, when you come right down to it, the matter is one that requires the right research approach. Methods are everything in studies of birth order and personality.

Of the many factors to control for, there's sex of the children, number of years between them (in multiple-child families), and family history, not to mention the right way to study personality. What about step-siblings, half-siblings, and siblings who don't even know that the other one exists? There are biological and adopted families. Parents vary in their ages and in the ages they were when they had their children. When it comes to psychological variables, the situation becomes even more complex. Do we study actual achievements, and if so, how do we measure them? Income? Education? Occupational prestige or advancement up the career ladder? Should we look at personality, motivation, intelligence, happiness, or mental health?

OK, your methodological head is spinning by now, so we'll try to make some sense of the latest research, much of which does a better job of controlling for all of these factors than was true in years past. We'll look at three recent studies, beginning with a dose of reality from the distinguished University of Georgia psychologist Alan E. Stewart, who wrote what is perhaps the definitive recent work (2012) on the theory and research on birth order. He bases his paper on 529 journal articles published over a 20-year period. The sheer number of studies on birth order is a testimony to the importance of this topic in psychology.

Taking his lead from the original birth order theorist, Alfred Adler (a one-time disciple of Freud), Stewart distinguished between "actual" birth order, or ABO (the numerical rank order into which you are born in your family of origin) and "psychological" birth order, or PBO (self-perceived position in the family). Right away, you've probably learned something useful. Your actual birth order need not have the same impact on you as the birth order you believe you have. Actual and psychological birth order can deviate for a number of reasons, including illness of one child, size of family, and degree of separation between siblings. Your role in the family based on your age may not be same as the role you have come to occupy.

As explained by Stewart, using Adler's framework, the first-born child (or one with the "oldest" role) would be most likely to take on a leadership position, like it when people stick to rules and order, and strive toward achievement goals. The first-born may be sensitive to being "dethroned" by younger sibs who drain away the attention of parents that the first-born enjoyed before they came along.

The youngest child may feel less capable and experienced, and perhaps is a bit pampered by parents and even older sibs. As a result, the youngest may develop social skills that will get other people to do things for them, thus contributing to their image as charming and popular.

Then there's the all-too-easy-to-ignore middle child, who feels robbed of the prized youngest child status, and perhaps feel rejected. On the positive side, the middle child may also develop particularly good social skills in order to keep from being ignored.

For the only child, there's the possible advantage of receiving all the attention from parents, but this is balanced by the feeling of constantly being scrutinized and controlled.

These brief portraits probably sound quite familiar to you, and they should, because they make up much of the stereotyped mythology about birth order. Adler's description of these positions are more nuanced than we typically read about in their pop psych translations, but for now, they'll suffice.

For decades following Adler's writings, researchers working in the tradition of "individual psychology," or the Adlerian school of thought, tried without much success to validate the theory. In part, this was because they lacked statistical methods available now, but also because they focused on ABO (i.e. actual) rather than PBO (i.e. psychological). Much of this changed when the Psychological Birth Order Inventory (PBOI) was developed in 1991 by a research team that included Stewart. The PBOI contains items to assess all birth order positions in the family that individuals rate on an agree-disagree scale.

First-born items on the PBOI tap feelings of being powerful, important, leading, and achieving ("It was important for me to do things right"). The middle-child items focus on competition, having fewer resources, and feeling unimportant ("It seemed like I was less important than other members of my family"). For the youngest child items, individuals rate themselves on being the boss of the family, getting others to do things for them ("I was pampered by my family members"). Finally, the only child scale tapped those feelings of pressure ("I felt like I lived in a fishbowl").

Now we've got the scales sorted out. Let's see whether PBO trumps ABO, as Stewart's model would predict. Taking three examples, rational vs. irrational relationship beliefs, perfectionism, and personality, in each case, the extent of the relationships with PBO were not overwhelmingly large, but they were measurable. Your perceived niche in your family plays a larger role in influencing the adult you've become than the actual timing of your birth.

Stewart's study shows that we're not fated to live out a life dominated by the accident of the timing of our birth. You can't change your actual birth order, but you can change the way you think about your role in the family. Sounds like pretty good news, especially if you felt doomed to a life of middle-child insignificance.

Now we'll take a look at the second contribution, a paper by Daniel Eckstein of Saba University in Netherlands Antilles written with co-author Jason Kaufman (2012). Examining several areas of family life and sibling relationships, Eckstein and Kaufman tested, among other areas, what's known as the "Confluence model" developed by Zajonc (1976). According to this view, first-born are the teachers, and later-borns are the learners. However, as Eckstein and Kaufman point out, first-born aren't necessarily the only ones doing the teaching between sibs. If we use the assumption that perceptions count more than reality, it then becomes clear that second-borns can have much to teach their older sibs. The way they approach the task may be different, but the direction isn't just one-way, as we might otherwise assume.

We'll finish up with the Eckstein and Kaufman paper shortly. The third study bears directly on the point of leadership within the two-child home. Ghent University psychologist Bernd Carette and colleagues (2011) compared the ways that first- and second-borns set goals for themselves. Carette and his fellow researchers limited their study to sibs who were closely spaced in age (averaging 2.5 years). When birth order effects are found, they point out, they tend to be present in this narrow span of time. The theory behind this study was that first-born would set "self-referenced" or mastery goals (ones that they choose for themselves) and second-borns would set "other-referenced" goals or performance goals (wanting to do well on goals set by others). First-born, they argue, would strive for mastery, but second-borns would want to do well to hit the targets that someone else set for them, i.e. the older sib. The measure they used tapped mastery goals by asking participants to indicate, for example, whether in their courses they sought to understand the material as much as possible. Questions about performance goals asked whether they wanted to do well compared to other people.

The findings Carette and team report lend statistically significant, but differences of about 2/10 of a point on a 5-point rating scale. They concluded that the findings "show that birth order lies at the heart of people's goal preferences" (p. 502), Pretty strong stuff. But with the psychological birth order idea in mind, it's hard not to wonder how much perceived family role influenced these motivational ratings. If you're convinced that your birth order leads you to be a leader, you'll behave like a leader.

Let's return, then, to some of the other implications of your self-assigned birth order, but let's flip it and see the role of parental perceptions of their children's birth order. Eckstein and Kaufman point out that perceptions and beliefs about birth order may have their effects, in large part, because parents impose their own stereotypes onto their children. By assigning these stereotyped birth-order roles, which may interact with gender roles, parents create self-fulfilling prophecies among their brood. You come to feel like the leader, if you're a first-born, because you were handed this role early in your life.

Perceptions about birth order can also influence your choice of a future career. Having been given the mantle of the achievement-oriented first-born, you may set your sights higher than do your lowlier, younger, followers. Eckstein and Kaufman cite a study conducted in Poland showing that people believe first-born to be more likely to occupy high prestige occupations to the tune of a correlation of .76 (out of a possible 1.0). That's an almost unheard-of statistic in psychology, where the average reported in a published article is about .3 or .4 at most.

With regard to intelligence, which you have undoubtedly also heard is related to birth order (and fits the Confluence model), the data remain unconvincing. When you add in the stereotype threat effect, which states that people perform on intelligence tests in ways subtly influenced by their self-perceptions, the birth order research becomes even more inherently flawed. If you go around life believing that because you're a first-born you're inevitably smarter, you'll approach any testing situations with the kind of self-confidence boost that can actually boost your score.

This is just one example of the impact that perceptions and stereotypes about birth order can have on apparent birth order effects. The moral of the story for parents is to look for your own biases and stereotypes about birth order as you think about what your children are capable of doing. Encourage them to teach each other, to define their own identities in the family, and to avoid labeling themselves based on their birth order. Don't let the lives of your children be dominated by the random forces that caused them to be born when they were.

Once we define ourselves in terms of who we are, and not when we were born, we'll be able to open up many more opportunities for fulfillment than even our parents might have dreamed for us.

References

Carette, B., Anseel, F., & Van Yperen, N. W. (2011). Born to learn or born to win? Birth order effects on achievement goals. *Journal of Research In Personality, 45*(5), 500–503. doi:10.1016/j .jrp.2011.06.008

Eckstein, D., & Kaufman, J. A. (2012). The role of birth order in personality: An enduring intellectual legacy of Alfred Adler. *The Journal of Individual Psychology, 68*(1), 60–61.

Stewart, Alan E. (2012). Issues in birth order research methodology: Perspectives form individual psychology. *The Journal of Individual Psychology, 68*(1), 75–106.

Zajonc, R. B. (1976). Family configuration and intelligence. *Science, 192,* 227–236.

Critical Thinking

1. Thinking about your own birth order and life outcomes to date, how well does the birth order research desired here accurately describe you? Whatever your conclusion, why do you think this is so?

2. What is the PBOI, and what does it purport to measure?

Create Central

www.mhhe.com/createcentral

Internet References

How birth order affects your personality
www.scientificamerican.com/article.cfm?id=ruled-by-birth-order

College student shakes up birth-order research
http://phys.org/news201004113.html

Article Prepared by: Eric Landrum, *Boise State University*

How Good Are the Asians?

Refuting Four Myths about Asian-American Academic Achievement

Understanding the truth behind the myths is essential for all learners, including Asian Americans.

YONG ZHAO AND WEI QIU

Learning Outcomes

After reading this article, you will be able to:

- Describe the model minor myth and the related evidence.

- Articulate four specific myths about Asian-American academic performance and understand the actual research outcomes rather than the myths.

They have three to five times their proportionate share of college faculty, architects, scientists, teachers, engineers, and physicians. They are overrepresented among winners of National Merit Scholarships, U.S. Presidential Scholarships, Arts Recognition and Talent Search scholars, and Westinghouse Science Talent Search scholars. They are overrepresented at American's most prestigious universities (Flynn 1991), constituting roughly 50% of the freshmen at the University of California at Berkeley and 10% to 30% of students in many other elite universities (Arenson 2007). They score higher on the SAT and ACT, especially in math. In published "school report cards" mandated by the No Child Left Behind Act, they perform much better than other minority groups.

They are called "the model minority." They are Asian Americans.

But, at Cornell University, 13 of the 21 student suicide victims since 1996 have been Asian or Asian American, and a survey at Cornell in 2005 indicated that Asian-American/Asian students seriously considered or attempted suicide at higher-than-average rates (Ramanujan 2006). What is wrong with them? They should be content and happy. After all, they are the model for all other minorities and immigrants.

Much of what has been said about Asian Americans is myth. In recent years, these myths have been strengthened by another set of myths about Asians, especially East Asians, because of their performance in international comparative studies and the economic achievement of these countries.

The myths hurt Asian Americans, a rapidly growing population in American schools. They mask the many problems Asian students encounter in school and society. They justify overlooking the many Asian students who do not fit the stereotype. The myths hurt other minority groups. They are used to deny racism—if the Asians can do it, then race is not a factor in America, so the logic goes. The myths also can hurt education in general as the Asian way of education is imitated—evidenced by the growing popularity of different versions of cram schools in the U.S. and praise for the Asian education system by American education leaders—without consideration of its negative consequences.

Thus, returning some truth to these myths is important.

Myth #1: Asian Americans Have Superior Academic Achievement

Some subgroups of Asian Americans, particularly East Asians, do perform better in a number of areas than other ethnic groups. Chinese Americans are overrepresented in many of the nation's elite universities, receive higher SAT scores in mathematics, are overrepresented among finalists of National Merit Scholars and other recognitions, and are less likely to lag behind their age group.

Other Asian subgroups do not have the same performance. For instance, the 2007 National Center for Educational Statistics (NCES) data show that Cambodian and Hmong students had a higher dropout rate (7%) than did Chinese (2%) and Korean students (2%). Chinese young adults who were foreign born had higher dropout rates than did those of the same subgroups who were U.S. natives (NCES 2007).

Refuting Model Minority Myth

- Not all Asian-American students achieve academic excellence. We must make efforts to treat each student as an independent individual.
- Asian-American students' academic achievement is the result of conscious choice, not genetic determination.
- Asian-American students' academic excellence tends to mask their psychological problems, and thus we must work to acknowledge, identify, and address these problems.
- Asian-American students' academic excellence comes at the cost of other skills and knowledge, thus we must understand the costs and realize Asian-American students are not excellent in all areas.

Moreover, there is an issue of gender equity. According to the 2002 U.S. Census data, about 10% of Asian/Pacific Islander women have less than a 9th-grade education, more than twice the percentage for non-Hispanic whites (4%), while the percentages for Asian/Pacific Islander men are close between those for other Asians (5%) and whites (4%) (Reeves and Bennett 2003).

Even East Asian Americans do not perform equally well in all subjects (Rohrlick et al. 1998). For example, their SAT verbal scores have been consistently lower than their scores in mathematics (Flynn 2007), though these results should be interpreted cautiously due to the confounding factors of language barriers and cultural bias. East Asian Americans earn 45,008 bachelor degrees in the social sciences and humanities, disproportionately fewer than whites (668,782), as well as blacks (84,568) and Hispanics (72,088) (NSF 2007), while they generally excel in quantitative skills and outnumber whites in engineering and computer science disciplines (Hune and Chan 1997). Meanwhile, their academic advantage seems to disappear in college. As indicated by a Cornell study in 2004, Cornell Asian and Asian-American students are more likely to require remedial work in English and reading and they tend to rate themselves lower in public speaking and writing ability (Cornell 2004).

Policy Implications

"Asian American" is a poor label attached to many drastically different subgroups, and not all groups are superior in academic achievement. The people who live in Asia have very different cultures and speak different languages, and their societies have different political systems and economic situations. Thus, Asian Americans differ tremendously in their backgrounds.

They also differ in many other dimensions. For example, some are born in the U.S. as second– or third-generation Americans, while others may have just arrived. Some were refugees; others came initially as students or employees. These differences all can have significant effects on their educational and economic attainment (Ogbu and Simons 1998).

These differences are overlooked in public discourse. Statements made about Asian Americans are usually overgeneralizations from one subgroup, or even a subgroup of the subgroup. As the research indicates, the model minority label is an overgeneralization from the academic and economic achievement of Chinese, Japanese, and Korean Americans. Unfortunately, the U.S. Department of Education, along with other major institutions, usually groups all Asian-American students in their statistics (Magner 1993), even though the U.S. census recognizes over two dozen separate Asian and Pacific Island groups in the U.S. Moreover, these differences are sometimes overlooked even in scholarly writings. Few studies focus on the differences between various Asian-American groups (Lee and Zane 1998).

Meanwhile, attempts in the research to distinguish new immigrants from those of Asian origin who were born in the U.S. are growing but still are rather limited. This can be an especially important distinction for at least two reasons. First, depending on the age when they arrive in the U.S., newly arrived students from Asian countries have received education at various levels in their home country. In addition, their educational experiences and needs would be quite different from those born in the U.S. For example, language and cultural experiences would be essential for new immigrants, while U.S.-born Asian Americans may face challenges learning their heritage language and culture. Second, new immigrants make up a large proportion of the Asian-American population. According to the National Center for Education Statistics, two-thirds of Asian Americans are foreign born, and one-fourth of Asian children were foreign born, a larger percentage than any other race or ethnic group (NCES 2007). New immigrants come to the U.S. at different ages for different reasons with different educational and cultural experiences. Their academic achievement and educational needs naturally vary a great deal.

Thus, education policies should not treat Asian Americans as a homogeneous group. The U.S. Census Bureau's categorization may not be easily changed, but educators can adopt a system of categorization that reflects differences within the Asian-American population.

It is desirable to group Asian Americans based on how long they have lived in the U.S. and the age when they arrived in the U.S. This can be a sensitive indicator of educational needs because the longer a student resides in the U.S. and attends U.S. schools, the more likely that he or she will become "Americanized." Those who are born in the U.S. are certainly different from those who just arrived.

A more appropriate categorization might be the civilization-based framework suggested by Samuel Huntington (1996). Huntington divides the world into nine major civilizations: Western, Latin American, African, Islamic, Sinic, Hindu, Orthodox, Buddhist, and Japanese. Excluding the Russian Federation, which is considered Orthodox, five of these civilizations are present in Asia: Islamic, Sinic, Hindu, Buddhist, and Japanese. Although most of the five civilizations encompass more than one country and education can differ among countries of a particular civilization, the differences within a civilization are likely to be much smaller than differences between civilizations.

A civilization-based framework better captures the educational differences for a number of reasons. First, education is driven by cultural values, and culture is more stable than political systems or political ideology. Culture defines social norms and sets priorities in a society. Although political governments may want to impose certain practices and policies, social norms and rules define people's interactions and behaviors in the long run. Culture thus has a more enduring influence over education than political systems do. For example, despite the different political systems in South Korea and China, the two countries have a lot more in common in their educational practices than do South Korea and India, which are both democracies. Second, though certain geographic regions may share the same civilization, it is not always the case. For example, Singapore, while located in Southeast Asia, has more in common in education with China and Korea than it does with its immediate neighbors, Malaysia and Indonesia. China, Singapore, and South Korea, despite their differences in political systems and geographic locations, are similar educationally because they all belong to the same civilization.

Myth #2: Asian-American Students Are Born Smart, Especially in Mathematics and Science

The truth, of course, is that not all Asian Americans are good at mathematics and science. In a longitudinal comparative study, Stevenson and his colleagues (1993) found no general differences in cognitive functioning in math between Asian students and American students; cognitive capabilities are not the reason behind Asian students' superiority in math. Flynn (1991), through careful analysis of the performance of one subgroup, found that Chinese Americans' high-status positions could be better explained by their group pride, high family incomes, and family influence.

Studies show that Asian-American students benefit from such cultural factors as students' effort in and outside of school, parental expectations and involvement, self-confidence in mathematics and reading, frequency of computer use for activities other than gaming, frequency of book use besides mathematics textbooks, the tendency for hard work and deferred gratification, and the desire for intergenerational social mobility (Coleman 1988; Pearce 2006; Stevenson and Stigler 1992).

Some researchers even propose that the academic excellence of Asian-American students may be a "forced" phenomenon (Du 2008). This echoes Sue and Okazaki's (1990) observation that education is useful for upward mobility when other venues are closed, and Asian-American students choose to make a heavier investment in academic life than in nonacademic activities. "Facing the open or hidden racism and discrimination, there were not many choices left other than the 'hard' way of striving for academic achievements. It was one of the few options that were left open through which they could possibly 'make it'" (Du 2008).

In conclusion, Asian-American emphasis on academic achievement seems to be either the will of individual students and their parents or a choice imposed by their social environments. Either way, the research unanimously suggests that Asian American's academic excellence is really a matter of "choice," not a matter of biological imperative.

Policy Implications

This conclusion should be no surprise to informed educators, but the attribution of academic excellence to biological factors continues to occur in the media and society. An important implication is that educators and policy makers should seriously fight the tendency to attribute academic excellence to racial differences. Effort, not genes, matters in student achievement (Stevenson and Stigler 1992).

This raises the question of whether it is a good idea to categorize academic results by racial background. Although NCLB requires schools to conduct subgroup analysis to identify and bridge achievement gaps, publishing such data can convey the impression that certain ethnic groups always perform better than others. Without further information and deep understanding of the complex web of factors influencing student achievement, it leads to the simplistic interpretation that racial differences account for the academic differences, rather than differences in cultural values, structural conditions, and student and parental efforts.

Unnecessary pressures can fall on Asian-American students and hinder the performance of other ethnic groups if public reports continue to reinforce the stereotypical view that race matters more than effort. Stanford psychologist Carl Steele (1997) discovered that black students and females who are aware of this stereotype perform significantly lower than those who are not aware of it, even though intellectually they are no different. Given this finding, we should keep more students from falling into this stereotype trap.

While many Asian-American families choose to invest in academic performance, others do not. Educators should not be surprised or disappointed when they meet Asian-American students who are not academically excellent or do not excel on all tests. They should also support Asian-American students who make other choices and encourage them to excel in areas outside the core academic subjects.

Myth #3: Asian-American Students Are Trouble-Free Kids

The seemingly superior academic performance of Asian students leads to the belief that they are "super kids," free from psychological and social problems. But Asian students are not trouble free. Despite their superior academic performances, even the successful "model minority" students go through difficult educational and psychological experiences.

Academically, a major stress on Asian-American students is associated with the "model minority" stereotype. For example, Cheryan and Bodenhausen (2000) found that the more conspicuous the stereotype, the lower Asian Americans performed on mathematical problems. In addition, Golden (2006) revealed that colleges held Asian-American students to a higher standard than whites. Golden concluded that some Asian-American students who would have been admitted if they were of any other ethnicity got rejected—often for reasons based on stereotype—to make room for "more desirable" students. Consequently, Asian-American students face by far the lowest admissions rate of any ethnic group (17.6%, compared with 23.8% for whites, 33.7% for blacks, and 26.8% for Hispanics) (Shea 2006), despite the fact that they constitute great numbers of students in some prestigious universities.

Asian-American college students often show increased risk of depression and anxiety, especially among the newly arrived or foreign-born (Chen 1999; Chun et al. 1998). For example, Asian-American students at Cornell are more likely to report significant difficulties with stress (41% vs. 31% overall), sleep difficulties (30% vs. 24% overall), and feeling hopeless (44% vs. 36% overall). They are twice as likely to report being in a sexually or physically abusive relationship, which is a strong predictor of suicidal behavior (Cornell 2004). Even more worrying is that these Asian-American students are least likely to report depression.

The stereotype of "model minority" and cultural reservations about counseling combine to hinder the educational and psychological needs of Asian-American students. A recent analysis of 379 National Institute of Mental Health-funded psychiatric clinical trial studies published between 1995 and 2004 found that Asian Americans made up only 0.6% of the patients studied—the lowest representation of any ethnic group (Morain 2007). In addition, Chinese immigrant students with special needs encounter numerous difficulties, including poor interpretation, lack of professional attention to their needs, culturally insensitive treatment, and a shortage of Asian special educators (Lo 2008).

Policy Implications

Schools, teachers, and the general public need to be aware of the psychological and educational needs of Asian students. Asian children not only face similar psychological and educational needs as their non-Asian peers, they also must deal with their own complicated issues, including the burden of being a model minority.

Raising awareness is a difficult task, but the risks are becoming greater as the Asian population increases rapidly in this country. Educators should work on communicating the urgency and importance of this task through professional magazines, practitioner conferences, and school visits.

Schools also should educate their staff members about how best to meet the needs of Asian students. For example, the nature of a student with high academic achievement is certainly different from those with low academic achievement. Similarly, a student burdened with overly high expectations for academic performance should be treated differently than a student who has too little family support or suffers from low expectations.

Asian students must also deal with the burden of being a model minority.

Finally, a large proportion of Asian students are either new immigrants or born in families of new immigrants, so these students require special attention to issues of adjustment and identity. New telecommunications technologies help new immigrants stay in close contact with their home country and relatives left behind. In addition, there is likely to be travel back and forth between two countries and thus two different cultures—families sending children to be educated in their home country temporarily or families visiting their home countries for extended periods before returning to the U.S. These trends can pose different challenges in cultural adjustment. Thus, schools need new procedures, practices, and policies to help these children and their families.

Myth #4: Asian-American Students Are Good at Everything

Because Asian students and their families invest their efforts and resources in academic achievement, they have fewer resources available for other activities (Cornell 2004; Sue and Okazaki 1990). As Dai argues, "For all the good learning outcomes they have obtained from schooling, there are underdeveloped skills essential for living productively and effectively in the contemporary society" (2008, p. 178).

While their high academic performance may help Asian students get access to higher education, especially prestigious universities, they may lack the creativity and independent thinking skills that make an individual successful in the real world. That also could explain why they begin to lose their competitive edge over other ethnic groups after they enter college (Rohrlick et al. 1998).

Policy Implications

While we admire the academic excellence of Asian-American students, we must recognize the costs associated with it. We should not simply generalize academic performance to other areas and thus believe Asian students are equally strong in all skills and knowledge domains.

More important, the admiration in the U.S. for Asian students' academic excellence mirrors the admiration Americans have for education in Asian countries. The high scores Asians students have obtained in such international tests as TIMSS and PISA have led many Americans to hold up these nations as the model of excellent education (see Stevenson and Stigler 1992, for example). These attitudes ignore the negative aspects of Asian education even as these countries have struggled to abandon those negative aspects (Zhao 2007). We should consider the negative outcomes and costs of these practices and the opportunities lost while chasing academic excellence. And we must consider the harm that stereotypes cause both for Asian students and for others.

References

Arenson, Karen W. "At Princeton, a Parody Raises Questions of Bias." *New York Times,* January 23, 2007. www.nytimes.com/2007/01/23/education/23princeton.html.

Chen, Thomas T. "Asian American Utilization of University Counseling Services: A Review of Current Research." Doctoral Dissertation, Biola University, 1999.

Cheryan, Sapna, and Galen V. Bodenhausen. "When Positive Stereotypes Threaten Intellectual Performance: The Psychological Hazards of Model Minority Status." *Psychological Science* 11 (2000): 399–402.

Chun, Kevin M., Karen L. Eastman, Grace C. S. Wang, and Stanley S. Sue. "Psychopathology." In *Handbook of Asian American Psychology,* ed. Lee C. Lee and Nolan W. S. Zane. Thousand Oaks, Calif.: Sage, 1998.

Coleman, James S. "Social Capital in the Creation of Human Capital." *American Journal of Sociology* 94 (1988): S95–S120.

Cornell University Asian and Asian American Task Force. *Asian and Asian American Campus Climate Task Force Report.* Ithaca, N.Y., 2004.

Dai, David Yun. "Outstanding School Achievement: A Mixed Blessing for the 'Model Minority'?" In *Model Minority Myths Revisited: An Interdisciplinary Approach to Demystifying Asian American Educational Experiences,* ed. Guofang Li and Lihshing Wang. Greenwich, Conn.: Information Age Publishing, 2008.

Du, Liang. "Model Minority as Ethnic Identity and Its Limits: An Ethnographic Study in a Middle-Class Chinese American Community." In *Model Minority Myths Revisited: An Interdisciplinary Approach to Demystifying Asian American Educational Experiences,* ed. Guofang Li and Lihshing Wang. Charlotte, N.C.: Information Age Publishing, 2008.

Flynn, James R. *Asian Americans: Achievement Beyond IQ.* Hillsdale, N.J.: Lawrence Erlbaum Associates, 1991.

Flynn, James R. *What Is Intelligence? Beyond the Flynn Effect.* New York: Cambridge University Press, 2007.

Golden, Daniel. *The Price of Admission: How America's Ruling Class Buys Its Way into Elite Colleges—and Who Gets Left Outside the Gates.* New York: Crown, 2006.

Hune, Shirley, and Kenyon S. Chan. "Special Focus: Asian Pacific American Demographic and Educational Trends." In *Fifteenth Annual Status Report on Minorities in Higher Education, 1996–1997,* ed. Deborah J. Carter and Reginald Wilson. Washington, D.C.: American Council on Education, 1997.

Huntington, Samuel P. *The Clash of Civilizations and the Remaking of World Order.* New York: Simon & Schuster, 1996.

Lee, Lee C., and Nolan W. S. Zane, eds. *Handbook of Asian American Psychology.* Thousand Oaks, Calif.: Sage, 1998.

Lo, Lusa. "Interactions Between Chinese Parents and Special Education Professionals in IEP Meetings: Implications for the Education of Chinese Immigrant Children with Disabilities." In *Model Minority Myth Revisited: An Interdisciplinary Approach to Demystifying Asian American Educational Experiences,* ed. Guofang Li and Lihshing Wang. Greenwich, Conn.: Information Age Publishing, 2008.

Magner, Denise K. "Debate over Woman's Tenure Continues at Berkeley." *Chronicle of Higher Education,* October 20, 1993, p. A16.

Morain, Claudia. "UC Davis to Launch Asian American Center on Disparities Research." University of California News Service, August 14, 2007. www.news.ucdavis.edu/search/news_detail.lasso?id=8285.

National Center for Education Statistics (NCES). *Status and Trends in the Education of Racial and Ethnic Minorities.* Washington, D.C., 2007.

National Science Foundation (NSF). "Table C-6. Bachelor's Degrees, by Field, Citizenship, and Race/Ethnicity: 1995–2004." In *Women, Minorities, and Persons with Disabilities in Science and Engineering.* Washington, D.C., 2007.

Ogbu, John U., and Herbert D. Simons. "Voluntary and Involuntary Minorities: A Cultural/Ecological Theory of School Performance with Some Implications for Education." *Anthropology and Education Quarterly* 29, no. 2 (1998): 155–188.

Pearce, R. R. "Effects of Cultural and Social Structural Factors on the Achievement of White and Chinese American Students at School Transition Points." *American Educational Research Journal* 43 (Spring 2006): 75–101.

Ramanujan, K. "Health Expert Explains Asian and Asian-American Students' Unique Pressures to Succeed." *Chronicle Online,* April 19, 2006. www.news.cornell.edu/stories/April06/Chung.ksr.html.

Reeves, Terrance, and Claudette Bennett. "The Asian and Pacific Islander Population in the United States: March 2002." Washington, D.C.: U.S. Census Bureau, 2003.

Rohrlick, Jeffrey, Diana Alvarado, Karen Zaruba, and Ruth Kallio. "From the Model Minority to the Invisible Minority: Asian & Pacific American Students in Higher Education Research." Paper presented at the 38th Annual Forum of the Association for Institutional Research, Minneapolis, Minn., May 17–20, 1998.

Shea, C. "Victim of Success?" *Boston Globe,* November 26, 2006. www.boston.com/news/education/higher/articles/2006/11/26/victim_of_success.

Steele, Carl M. "A Threat in the Air: How Stereotypes Shape the Intellectual Identities and Performance of Women and African Americans." *American Psychologist* 52 (June 1997): 613–629.

Stevenson, Harold, C. Chen, and S. Lee. "Mathematics Achievement of Chinese, Japanese, and American Children: 10 Years Later." *Science* 259 (January 1993): 53–58.

Stevenson, Harold, and James W. Stigler. *The Learning Gap: Why Our Schools Are Failing and What We Can Learn from Japanese and Chinese Education.* New York: Summit Books, 1992.

Sue, Stanley, and Sumie Okazaki. "Asian-American Educational Achievements: A Phenomenon in Search of an Explanation." *American Psychologist* 45 (August 1990): 913–920.

Zhao, Yong. "China and the Whole Child." *Educational Leadership* 64 (June 2007): 70–73.

Critical Thinking

1. What are some of the measures that are used by researchers to determine academic performance? Do the measures appear to be legitimate? Explain.

2. What are the policy implications for believing in such myths? If a cultural group is believed to possess an overly positive trait, when are the potential harms to that misbelief?

Create Central

www.mhhe.com/createcentral

Internet References

Asian-Americans seek to move beyond the 'model minority' myth
www.ccweek.com/news/templates/template.aspx?articleid=3579&zoneid=7

Moving beyond the model minority myth
www.americanprogress.org/issues/education/news/2011/05/12/9600/moving-education-beyond-the-model-minority-myth

YONG ZHAO is University Distinguished Professor of Education at Michigan State University and director of the U.S.-China Center for Research on Educational Excellence. WEI QIU is a doctoral candidate in the Department of Educational Psychology and Educational Technology at Michigan State University, East Lansing.

Zhao, Yong; Qiu, Wei. From *Phi Delta Kappan*, vol. 90, no. 5, January, 2009, pp. 338–344. Reprinted with permission of Phi Delta Kappa International. All rights reserved. www.pdkintl.org

Unit 9

UNIT

Prepared by: Eric Landrum, *Boise State University*

Social Processes

We humans are particularly social creatures, as are many of the other species with whom we share the planet. We tend to assemble in groups, some large and some small. We form friendships with all sorts of people. Many of these relationships develop naturally from shared interests and common goals. Some of these friendships are long-lasting and endure hardship. Other kinds of friendships are shorter-term that are often soon forgotten. We form highly unique relationships in which we fall in love with another person and decide to commit the rest of our lives, or at least a large chunk of it, to being this person's most intimate companion. And then there are families, perhaps the most interesting social unit full of fascinating dynamics that emerge as children are born, grow up, and form families of their own.

The responsibility for understanding the complicated facets of human social behavior falls to social psychologists. These psychologists, like most research-focused behavioral scientists, are trained to apply rigorous experimental methods to discovering, understanding, and explaining how people interact with one another. During the past century, social psychologists studied some of the most pressing and fascinating social behaviors of the day. For example, social psychologists examined, and continue to study discrimination and prejudice, conformity, and obedience to authority. In addition to these high-profile issues, social psychologists study the more positive side of human social behavior such as liking and loving, attitude formation and change, attributions, and group behavior and decision making. There are fascinating examples available of the impact of positive psychology, such as the effort of an entire country to invest in its own national happiness.

In the past few decades, psychologists have become more aware of the impact of culture on human social relationships and have turned their attention to exploring differences among cultures with respect to social development, social perception, social influence, and social change. As the world seems to become smaller and smaller, the demand for social psychologists to provide explanations for both positive and negative social behaviors that are impacted by cultural influences will only become greater. Interesting challenges and opportunites occur when individuals from different backgrounds have the chance to live and work together, and social psychologists can often offer advice and tips about how to learn and develop in these environments.

Thus, as you study social psychology in your introductory psychology course, apply the principles you are learning not just to better understanding your own social behavior, but also ask yourself how these principles might (or might not) generalize to the social behavior of individuals from different cultures. Doing so might put you in a better position to understand the whys and wherefores of social behavior that would seem (on the surface) to be so radically different from your own. In this unit, we explore the fascinating field of social psychology.

Article   Prepared by: Eric Landrum, *Boise State University*

Replicating Milgram

Last month, we featured IRB best practices ("IRBs: Navigating the Maze" November 2007 Observer), and got the ball rolling with strategies and tips that psychological scientists have found to work. Here, we continue the dissemination effort with the second of three articles by researchers who share their experiences with getting their research through IRB hoops. Jerry Burger from Santa Clara University managed to do the seemingly impossible—he conducted a partial replication of the infamous Milgram experiment. Read on for valuable advice, and look for similar coverage in upcoming Observers.

JERRY BURGER

Learning Outcomes

After reading this article, you will be able to:

- Explain the ethical problems that the original Milgram study posed for psychology and for science.

- Describe the ways in which modern psychologists have tried to reconcile these problems in replicating Milgram's work.

"It can't be done."

These are the first words I said to Muriel Pearson, producer for ABC News' *Primetime,* when she approached me with the idea of replicating Stanley Milgram's famous obedience studies. Milgram's work was conducted in the early 1960s before the current system of professional guidelines and IRBs was in place. It is often held up as the prototypic example of why we need policies to protect the welfare of research participants. Milgram's participants were placed in an emotionally excruciating situation in which an experimenter instructed them to continue administering electric shocks to another individual despite hearing that person's agonizing screams of protest. The studies ignited a debate about the ethical treatment of participants. And the research became, as I often told my students, the study that can never be replicated.

Nonetheless, I was intrigued. Although more than four decades have passed since Milgram conducted his research, his obedience studies continue to occupy an important place in social psychology textbooks and classes. The haunting black-and-white images of ordinary citizens delivering what appear to be dangerous, if not deadly, electric shocks and the implications of the findings for atrocities like the Holocaust and Abu Ghraib are not easily dismissed. Yet because Milgram's procedures are clearly out-of-bounds by today's ethical standards, many questions about the research have gone unanswered. Chief among these is one that inevitably surfaces when I present Milgram's findings to students: Would people still act that way today?

The challenge was to develop a variation of Milgram's procedures that would allow useful comparisons with the original investigations while protecting the well-being of the participants. But meeting this challenge would raise another: I would also need to assuage the apprehension my IRB would naturally experience when presented with a proposal to replicate the study that can never be replicated.

I went to great lengths to recreate Milgram's procedures (Experiment Five), including such details as the words used in the memory test and the experimenter's lab coat. But I also made several substantial changes. First, we stopped the procedures at the 150-volt mark. This is the first time participants heard the learner's protests through the wall and his demands to be released. When we look at Milgram's data, we find that this point in the procedure is something of a "point of no return." Of the participants who continued past 150 volts, 79 percent went all the way to the highest level of the shock generator (450 volts). Knowing how people respond up to this point allowed us to make a reasonable estimate of what they would do if allowed to continue to the end. Stopping the study at this juncture also avoided exposing participants to the intense stress Milgram's participants often experienced in the subsequent parts of the procedure.

Second, we used a two-step screening process for potential participants to exclude any individuals who might have a negative reaction to the experience. Potential participants were asked in an initial phone interview if they had ever been diagnosed with a psychiatric disorder; if they were currently receiving psychotherapy; if they were currently taking any medications for emotional difficulties; if they had any medical conditions that might be affected by stress; if they ever had any problems with alcohol or drug use; and if they had ever experienced serious trauma, such as child abuse, domestic violence, or combat. Individuals who responded "yes" to any of these questions (about 30 percent) were excluded from the study. During the second step in the screening process, participants completed measures of anxiety and depression and were interviewed in person by a licensed clinical psychologist. The clinicians were shown the anxiety and depression data and were allowed to interview participants for as long as needed (about 30 minutes on average). The clinicians were instructed to err on the side of caution and to exclude anyone who they judged might have a negative reaction to the experiment procedures. More than 38 percent of the interviewed participants were excluded at this point.

Third, participants were told at least three times (twice in writing) that they could withdraw from the study at any time and still receive their $50 for participation. Fourth, like Milgram, we administered a sample shock to our participants (with their consent). However, we administered a very mild 15-volt shock rather than the 45-volt shock Milgram gave his participants. Fifth, we allowed virtually no time to elapse between ending the session and informing participants that the learner had received no shocks. Within a few seconds after ending the study, the learner entered the room to reassure the participant he was fine. Sixth, the experimenter who ran the study also was a clinical psychologist who was instructed to end the session immediately if he saw any signs of excessive stress. Although each of these safeguards came with a methodological price (e.g., the potential effect of screening out certain individuals, the effect of emphasizing that participants could leave at any time), I wanted to take every reasonable measure to ensure that our participants were treated in a humane and ethical manner.

Of course, I also needed IRB approval. I knew from my own participation on the IRB that the proposal would be met with concern and perhaps a little fear by the board's members. I work at a relatively small university, and our IRB consists of individuals from a variety of academic backgrounds. I knew that few members would be comfortable or confident when assessing a potentially controversial proposal from another discipline. Given the possibility of a highly visible mistake, the easy response would have been to say "no." To address these concerns, I created a list of individuals who were experts on Milgram's studies and the ethical questions surrounding this research. I offered to make this list available to the IRB. More important, Steven Breckler, a social psychologist who currently serves as the executive director for science at the American Psychological Association, graciously provided an assessment of the proposal's ethical issues that I shared with the IRB.

In the end, all the extra steps and precautions paid off. The IRB carefully reviewed and then approved the procedures. More than a year after collecting the data, I have no indication that any participant was harmed by his or her participation in the study. On the contrary, I was constantly surprised by participants' enthusiasm for the research both during the debriefing and in subsequent communications. We also produced some interesting findings. Among other things, we found that today people obey the experimenter in this situation at about the same rate they did 45 years ago. ABC devoted an entire 60-minute *Primetime* broadcast to the research and its implications. Finally, it is my hope that other investigators will use the 150-volt procedure and thereby jump-start research on some of the important questions that motivated Stanley Milgram nearly half a century ago.

Critical Thinking

1. What ethical problems did the original Milgram study pose for psychology?

2. How have modern psychologists tried to reconcile these ethical problems in replicating Milgram's work?

3. What does it mean to replicate a study, and how did Burger's study differ substantially from the original Milgram study?

Create Central

www.mhhe.com/createcentral

Internet References

Controversy: Ethics in experiments
http://cla.calpoly.edu/~cslem/101/Obey/Ethics.html

Milgram's 1963 obedience experiment is still a disquieting study today
www.twincities.com/life/ci_23674244/disquieting-study-1963-disquieting-study-still-today

JERRY BURGER is a professor of psychology at Santa Clara University. His research interests include social influence, particularly compliance, and the perception of and motivation for personal control.

Burger, Jerry. From *APS Observer*, December 2007, pp. Vol. 64, pp. 1–11. Copyright © 2007 by American Psychological Society. Reprinted by permission via Copyright Clearance Center.

Article   Prepared by: Eric Landrum, *Boise State University*

The Psychology and Power of False Confessions

IAN HERBERT

Learning Outcomes

After reading this article, you will be able to:

- Define false confession and explain the factors that cause it.

- Summarize the ways in which confessions, false or otherwise, corrupt other evidence available in court cases.

On July 8, 1997, Bill Bosko returned to his home in Norfolk, Virginia, after a week at sea to find his wife murdered in their bedroom. A few hours later, Bosko's neighbor, Danial Williams was asked to answer questions at the police station. And after eight hours there, Williams confessed to the rape and murder of Michelle Moore-Bosko.

Five months later, because of inconsistent physical evidence, the Norfolk police became convinced that Williams did not act alone and turned their attention to Joseph Dick, Williams' roommate. Dick confessed as well. He later pled guilty, testified against two other co-defendants, named five more accomplices who were never tried, and publicly apologized to the victim's family. "I know I shouldn't have done it," Dick said just before the judge gave him a double life sentence. "I have got no idea what went through my mind that night—and my soul."

Dick now says that all of that is untrue, and he has a team of lawyers who believe him. In 2005, the Innocence Project filed a petition on behalf of Williams, Dick, and the other two members of the group called the "Norfolk Four." They petitioned Virginia Governor Tim Kaine for clemency on the basis of new physical evidence, and in August 2009, the outgoing governor issued conditional pardons, which set the men free but forced them to be on parole for the next 20 years. It was a decision that Kaine struggled with, and he granted conditional pardons because he said the men failed to fully prove their innocence. "They're asking for a whole series of confessions . . . to all be discarded," Kaine said on a radio show in the fall of 2008. "That is a huge request."

We know that false confessions do happen on a fairly regular basis. Because of advances in DNA evidence, the Innocence Project has been able to exonerate more than 200 people who had been wrongly convicted, 49 of whom had confessed to the crime we now know they didn't commit. In a survey of 1,000 college students, four percent of those who had been interrogated by police said they gave a false confession.

But Why?

False confessions seem so illogical, especially for someone like Joseph Dick of the Norfolk Four, who got a double life sentence after confessing. Why do people confess to crimes they didn't commit? Some do it for the chance at fame (more than 200 people confessed to kidnapping Charles Lindbergh's baby), but many more do it for reasons that are far more puzzling to the average person. In the November 2004 issue of *Psychological Science in the Public Interest,* APS Fellow Saul Kassin looked at the body of research and described how the police are able to interrogate suspects until they confess to a crime they didn't commit.

Generally, it starts because people give up their Miranda rights. In fact, Richard A. Leo found that a majority of people give up the right to remain silent and the right to an attorney. In fact, according to self-report data, innocent suspects gave up their rights more often than guilty suspects (most told Leo either that this was because they felt that they didn't have anything to hide because they were innocent or that they thought it would make them look guilty).

Once a suspect starts talking, the police can use a variety of techniques to make the accused feel as though they are better off confessing than continuing to deny (these include promises of leniency and threats of harsher interrogation or sentences). If a suspect feels like a conviction is inevitable no matter what he or she says, confessing may seem like a good idea.

But, in some cases, the accused comes to believe that he or she actually did commit the crime. It's been shown repeatedly that memory is quite malleable and unreliable. Elizabeth Loftus has repeatedly shown that the human brain can create memories out of thin air with some prompting. In a famous series of experiments, Loftus, APS Past President, was able to help people create memories for events that never happened in their lives simply through prompting. She helped them "remember" being lost in a shopping mall when they were children, and the longer the experiment went on, the more details they "remembered." The longer police interrogate a suspect, emphatic about his guilt and peppering their interrogation with details of the crime, the more likely a suspect is to become convinced himself.

Joseph Dick claims that this is what happened to him. His confession, testimony, and apology to the family were not lies, he maintains, but rather the product of a false memory. "It didn't cross my mind that I was lying," he said. "I believed what I was saying was true."

'Corrupting the Other Evidence'

Despite the evidence that false confessions are a regular occurrence, most jurors struggle with the concept just like Kaine did with the Norfolk Four. Confessions are difficult to discount, even if they appear to be coerced. Years ago, Kassin noticed that cases with confessions have an unusually high conviction rate, and since then he has dedicated his life to studying why that happens and what can be done about it.

In a 1997 study, Kassin and colleague Katherine Neumann gave subjects case files with weak circumstantial evidence plus either a confession, an eyewitness account, a character witness, or no other evidence. Across the board, prospective jurors were more likely to vote guilty if a confession was included in the trial, even when they were told that the defendant was incoherent at the time of the confession and immediately recanted what he said.

Kassin and Neumann also did two simultaneous studies to further explore the power of confessions. In one, they had people watch a trial and turn a dial to rate the extent to which evidence convinced them the defendant was guilty or innocent. The other asked potential jurors after the trial which evidence was most powerful. In both the mid-trial and post-trial ratings, jurors saw the confession as the most incriminating. Other studies have shown that conviction rates rise even when jurors see confessions as coerced and even when they say that the confession played no role in their judgment. "I don't honestly think juries stand a chance in cases involving confessions," Kassin says. "They're bound to convict."

Kassin says he doesn't blame jurors. He travels around the country lecturing on the psychology of false confessions and he says "the most common reaction I get from a lay audience is, 'Well, I would never do that. I would never confess to something I didn't do.' And people apply that logic in the jury room. It's just that basic belief that false confessions don't occur." What's more, the evidence juries are given in conjunction with the false confessions is very damning, Kassin says. False confessions of guilt often include vivid details of how a crime was committed—and why. Confessions sometimes even come with an apology to the family. It's no wonder jurors have trouble discounting them.

What confessions rarely include is an explanation of why the person confessed. In most states, police are not required to videotape the interrogations, just the confessions. So juries don't get to see any potential police coercion and they don't get to see the police planting those vivid details in the minds of the suspects.

And that may be just the tip of the iceberg. Kassin believes that confessions can have a dramatic impact on trials even if they never make it into a courtroom. They can influence potential eyewitnesses, for example, and taint other kinds of evidence.

Kassin recently teamed up with psychologist Lisa Hasel to test the effect of confessions on eyewitnesses. They brought subjects in for what was supposed to be a study about persuasion techniques. The experimenter briefly left the room and, during that time, someone came in and stole a laptop off the desk. The subjects were then shown a lineup of six suspects, none of whom was the actual criminal, and they were asked to pick out which member of the lineup, if any, committed the crime. Two days later, the witnesses were brought back for more questioning. Those who had identified a suspect were told that the person they identified had confessed, another person had confessed, all suspects continued to deny their involvement, or that the identified suspect had continued to deny his involvement. Those who had (correctly) said none of the people in the lineup committed the crime were told either that all suspects denied the crime, that an unspecified suspect had confessed, or that a specific suspect had confessed.

The results show that confessions can have a powerful effect on other evidence. Of the people who had identified a subject from the original lineup, 60 percent changed their identification when told that someone else had confessed. Plus, 44 percent of the people who originally determined that none of the suspects in the lineup committed the crime changed their mind when told that someone had confessed (and 50 percent changed when told that a specific person had confessed). When asked about their decision, "about half of the people seemed to say, 'Well, the investigator told me there was a confession, so that must be true.' So they were just believing the investigator," Hasel said. "But the other half really seemed to be changing their memory. So that memory can never really be regained once it's been tainted." What's more, people who were told that the person they wrongly pinpointed as the culprit had confessed saw their confidence levels soar. After that confirmation, they remembered the crime better and were more sure about details. The implications for inside the courtroom are obvious if eyewitnesses who incorrectly picked someone out of a lineup can become so sure of their choice after learning that the person confessed. "It is noteworthy that whereas physical evidence is immutable (once collected and preserved, it can always be retested), an eyewitness's identification decision cannot later be revisited without contamination," Kassin and Hasel write.

Kassin and Hasel suspect that false confessions may also affect the memories of people who are potential alibis for defendants. Kassin worked on the actual case of John Kogut, who was accused of raping and murdering a 16-year-old girl. Kogut was at a party for his girlfriend at the time the crime was committed, and he had multiple alibi witnesses. But after 18 hours of interrogation, Kogut confessed to the grisly crime. "After he confessed to the crime, [the witnesses] started dropping off one-by-one," Hasel said. "'You know, maybe I saw him earlier in the night but not later; maybe I saw him later in the night but not earlier; it must have been a different night, I must be wrong.'" Kassin and Hasel are currently working on an experiment similar to their eyewitness study to test this theory on a broad basis.

This phenomenon may be explained by the same Loftus research about creating false memories that may have lead to the false confession in the first place. So it is plausible that eyewitnesses or alibi witnesses might begin to remember things differently when told about something as powerful as a confession. But what about scientific evidence? At least confessions can't change something as concrete as DNA evidence or fingerprints, right? Even that belief may be untrue.

In 2006, University College London psychologist Itiel Dror took a group of six fingerprint experts and showed them samples that they themselves had, years before, determined either to be matches or non-matches (though they weren't told they had already seen these fingerprints). The experts were now given some context: either that the fingerprints came from a suspect who confessed or that they came from a suspect who was known to be in police custody at the time the crime was committed. In 17 percent of the non-control tests, experimenters changed assessments that they had previously made correctly. Four of the six experts who participated changed at least one judgment based on the new context. "And that's fingerprint judgments," Kassin said. "That's not considered malleable. And yet there was some degree of malleability and one of the ways to influence it was to provide information about the confession."

The practical importance of this research extends well beyond the laboratory. In a white paper set to be published in *Law and Human Behavior* in 2010, Kassin and four other prominent confession experts make recommendations, including, most notably, mandatory taping of all interrogations in capital cases. Kassin has begun to research this idea. His preliminary data illustrates that, shown two versions of known false confessions (one that just included the confession or another that included the entire interrogation), subjects were significantly less likely to vote guilty when shown the entire interrogation. "The information that the jury doesn't have and needs is how did this guy come to confess and then, when he did confess, how did he know all this information about the crime if he in fact wasn't there," Kassin says. "So yes, I think videotaping is probably the single best protection to be afforded to a defendant."

That would help defendants who were coerced into confessing by police, but would do nothing to help those who lost alibi witnesses or were convicted with the help of eyewitness testimony because of knowledge of a confession. To combat that problem, Hasel and much of the scientific community argues for double-blind testing when handling evidence, meaning that the police officer handling the lineup doesn't know which member of the lineup is the suspect. "So they can't consciously or unconsciously direct [witnesses] to a particular person," she says.

And she wants to investigate whether judges and jurors can understand this topic of evidence dependence—the idea that a confession contaminates other evidence. If jurors are told that a false confession may have tainted other evidence, are they able to look at it objectively and make their own judgment? Can judges grasp its ramifications on appeals? Kassin believes that, because of the persuasive potency of confessions and evidentiary dependence, it's not good enough for judges to look at the other evidence and determine that a jury would have convicted even without the coerced confession.

"If it turns out that the confession corrupted the other evidence, then there is no such thing as harmless error," Kassin said. "I don't think you can look at that other evidence once there is a confession out of the box because once the confession is out there, it corrupts all that other evidence."

Critical Thinking

1. What is a false confession and what causes it?
2. How do confessions, false or otherwise, corrupt other evidence available in court cases?
3. If you were looking to protect a defendant in a criminal case, what would researchers in this area recommend be your first priority?

Create Central

www.mhhe.com/createcentral

Internet References

The false confession
    www.psychologytoday.com/articles/200304/the-false-confession
Can psychology prevent false confessions?
    www.apa.org/monitor/sep06/confessions.aspx
False confessions
    http://forensicpsych.umwblogs.org/issues-and-debates/false-confessions

Herbert, Ian. From APS Observer, December 2009, pp. 10–12. Copyright © 2009 by Association for Psychological Science. Reprinted by permission.

Article   Prepared by: Eric Landrum, *Boise State University*

We're Wired to Connect

Our brains are designed to be social, says bestselling science writer Daniel Goleman—and they catch emotions the same way we catch colds.

Mark Matousek

Learning Outcome

After reading this article, you will be able to:

- Describe the ways in which modern technology is influencing the ways that humans connect to one another and evaluate whether these influences are having positive or negative effects on our ability to relate socially to one another.

Have you ever wondered why a stranger's smile can transform your entire day? Why your eyes mist up when you see someone crying, and the sight of a yawn can leave you exhausted? Daniel Goleman, PhD, has wondered, too, and just as he helped revolutionize our definition of what it means to be smart with his 1995 blockbuster, *Emotional Intelligence,* the two-time Pulitzer nominee and former science reporter for *The New York Times* has dropped a bombshell on our understanding of human connection in his startling new book, *Social Intelligence* (Bantam).

For the first time in history, thanks to recent breakthroughs in neuroscience, experts are able to observe brain activity while we're in the act of feeling—and their findings have been astonishing. Once believed to be lumps of lonely gray matter cogitating between our ears, our brains turn out to be more like interlooped, Wi-Fi octopi with invisible tentacles slithering in all directions, at every moment, constantly picking up messages we're not aware of and prompting reactions—including illnesses—in ways never before understood.

"The brain itself is social—that's the most exciting finding," Goleman explains during lunch at a restaurant near his home in Massachusetts. "One person's inner state affects and drives the other person. We're forming brain-to-brain bridges—a two-way traffic system—all the time. We actually catch each other's emotions like a cold."

The more important the relationship, the more potent such "contagion" will be. A stranger's putdown may roll off your back, while the same zinger from your boss is devastating. "If we're in toxic relationships with people who are constantly putting us down, this has actual physical consequences," Goleman says. Stress produces a harmful chemical called cortisol, which interferes with certain immune cell functions. Positive interactions prompt the body to secrete oxytocin (the same chemical released during lovemaking), boosting the immune system and decreasing stress hormones. As a doting grandparent himself (with author-therapist wife Tara Bennett-Goleman), the author often feels this felicitous rush. "I was just with my two-year-old granddaughter," he says. "This girl is like a vitamin for me. Being with her actually feels like a kind of elixir. The most important people in our lives can be our biological allies."

The notion of relationships as pharmaceutical is a new concept. "My mother is 96," Goleman goes on. "She was a professor of sociology whose husband—my father—died many years ago, leaving her with a big house. After retiring at 65, she decided to let graduate students live there for free. She's since had a long succession of housemates. When she was 90, a couple from Taiwan had a baby while they were living there. The child regarded her as Grandma and lived there till the age of two. During that time, I swore I could see my mother getting younger. It was stunning." But not, he adds, completely surprising. "This was the living arrangement we were designed for, remember? For most of human history there were extended families where the elderly lived in the same household as the babies. Many older people have the time and nurturing energy that kids crave—and vice versa. If I were designing assisted-living facilities, I'd put daycare centers in them and allow residents to volunteer. Institutions are cheating children," he says. "And we older people need it, too."

Positive interactions can boost the immune system: "The most important people in our lives can be our biological allies."

Young or old, people can affect our personalities. Though each of us has a distinctive temperament and a "set point of happiness" modulating our general mood, science has now confirmed that these tendencies are not locked in. Anger-prone people, for example, can "infect" themselves with calmness by spending time with mellower individuals, absorbing less-aggressive behavior and thereby sharpening social intelligence.

A key to understanding this process is something called mirror neurons: "neurons whose only job is to recognize a smile and make you smile in return," says Goleman (the same goes for frowning and other reactions). This is why, when you're smiling, the whole world does indeed seem to smile with you. It also explains the Michelangelo phenomenon, in which long-term partners come to resemble each other through facial-muscle mimicry and "empathic resonance." If you've ever seen a group with a case of the giggles, you've witnessed mirror neurons at play. Such mirroring takes place in the realm of ideas, too, which is why sweeping cultural ideals and prejudices can spread through populations with viral speed.

This phenomenon gets to the heart of why social intelligence matters most: its impact on suffering and creating a less crazy world. It is critical, Goleman believes, that we stop treating people as objects or as functionaries who are there to give us something. This can range from barking at telephone operators to the sort of old-shoe treatment that long-term partners often use in relating to each other (talking at, rather than to, each other). We need, he says, a richer human connection.

Unfortunately, what he calls the "inexorable technocreep" of contemporary culture threatens such meaningful connection. Presciently remarking on the TV set in 1963, poet T.S. Eliot noted that this techno-shredder of the social fabric "permits millions of people to listen to the same joke at the same time, and yet remain lonesome." We can only imagine what the dour writer would have made of Internet dating. And as Goleman points out, this "constant digital connectivity" can deaden us to the people around us. Social intelligence, he says, means putting down your BlackBerry, actually paying full attention—showing people that they're being experienced—which is basically what each of us wants more than anything. Scientists agree that such connection—or lack of it—will determine our survival as a species: "Empathy," writes Goleman, "is the prime inhibitor of human cruelty."

And our social brains are wired for kindness, despite the gore you may see on the nightly news. "It's an aberration to be cruel," says Goleman. Primitive tribes learned that strength lay in numbers, and that their chances of surviving a brutal environment increased exponentially through helping their neighbors (as opposed to, say, chopping their heads off). Even young children are wired for compassion. One study in Goleman's book found that infants cry when they see or hear another baby crying, but rarely when they hear recordings of their own distress. In another study, monkeys starved themselves after realizing that when they took food, a shock was delivered to their cage mate.

Perhaps the most inspiring piece of the social-intelligence puzzle is neuroplasticity: the discovery that our brains never stop evolving. "Stem cells manufacture 10,000 brain cells every day till you die," says Goleman. "Social interaction helps neurogenesis. The brain rises to the occasion the more you challenge it.

Critical Thinking

1. What is the argument that humans are "wired to connect"?

2. How has modern technology influenced the ways that humans connect to one another?

3. Regarding the connection between modern technology and human connections, what is the cumulative impact on social interactions?

Create Central

www.mhhe.com/createcentral

Internet References

Technology, human beings and the fate of the Earth: A social critique of modern life
    www.stateofnature.org/?p=5856

Technology is destroying the quality of human interaction
    http://thebottomline.as.ucsb.edu/2012/01/technology-is
    -destroying-the-quality-of-human-interaction

MARK MATOUSEK is the author of *The Art of Survival* (Bloomsbury).

Matousek, Mark. Reprinted from *AARP The Magazine*, January/February 2007, pp. 32–34. Copyright © 2007 by Matousek, Mark. Reprinted by permission of American Association for Retired Persons (AARP) and Mark Matousek. www.aarpmagazine.org 1-888-687-2227.

Article   Prepared by: Eric Landrum, *Boise State University*

Gross National Happiness in Bhutan: The Big Idea from a Tiny State That Could Change the World

ANNIE KELLY

Learning Outcomes

After reading this article, you will be able to:

- Understand the concept of gross national happiness and understand that it is an alternative to gross national product.

- Articulate the expected outcomes of the GNH project in Bhutan, and know about some of the preliminary outcomes to date.

A series of hand-painted signs dot the side of the winding mountain road that runs between the airport and the Bhutanese capital, Thimphu. Instead of commands to cut speed or check mirrors, they offer the traveller a series of life-affirming mantras. "Life is a journey! Complete it!" says one, while another urges drivers to, "Let nature be your guide." Another, standing on the edge of a perilous curve, simply says: "Inconvenience regretted."

It's a suitably uplifting welcome to visitors to this remote kingdom, a place of ancient monasteries, fluttering prayer flags and staggering natural beauty. Less than 40 years ago, Bhutan opened its borders for the first time. Since then, it has gained an almost mythical status as a real-life Shangri-La, largely for its determined and methodical pursuit of the most elusive of concepts—national happiness.

Since 1971, the country has rejected GDP as the only way to measure progress. In its place, it has championed a new approach to development, which measures prosperity through formal principles of gross national happiness (GNH) and the spiritual, physical, social and environmental health of its citizens and natural environment.

For the past three decades, this belief that wellbeing should take preference over material growth has remained a global oddity. Now, in a world beset by collapsing financial systems, gross inequity and wide-scale environmental destruction, this tiny Buddhist state's approach is attracting a lot of interest.

As world leaders prepare to meet in Doha on Monday for the second week of the UN climate change conference, Bhutan's stark warning that the rest of the world is on an environmental and economical suicide path is starting to gain traction. Last year the UN adopted Bhutan's call for a holistic approach to development, a move endorsed by 68 countries. A UN panel is now considering ways that Bhutan's GNH model can be replicated across the globe.

As representatives in Doha struggle to find ways of reaching a consensus on global emissions, Bhutan is also being held up as an example of a developing country that has put environmental conservation and sustainability at the heart of its political agenda. In the last 20 years Bhutan has doubled life expectancy, enrolled almost 100% of its children in primary school and overhauled its infrastructure.

At the same time, placing the natural world at the heart of public policy has led to environmental protection being enshrined in the constitution. The country has pledged to remain carbon neutral and to ensure that at least 60% of its landmass will remain under forest cover in perpetuity. It has banned export logging and has even instigated a monthly pedestrian day that bans all private vehicles from its roads.

"It's easy to mine the land and fish the seas and get rich," says Thakur Singh Powdyel, Bhutan's minister of education, who has become one of the most eloquent spokespeople for GNH. "Yet we believe you cannot have a prosperous nation in the long run that does not conserve its natural environment or take care of the wellbeing of its people, which is being borne out by what is happening to the outside world."

Powdyel believes the world has misinterpreted Bhutan's quest. "People always ask how can you possibly have a nation of happy people? But this is missing the point," he says. "GNH is an aspiration, a set of guiding principles through which we are navigating our path towards a sustainable and equitable society. We believe the world needs to do the same before it is too late."

Bhutan's principles have been set in policy through the gross national happiness index, based on equitable social development, cultural preservation, conservation of the environment and promotion of good governance.

At a primary school in Thimphu, the headteacher, Choki Dukpa, watches her students make their way to class. She says that she has seen huge changes to the children's emotional wellbeing since GNH principles were integrated into the education system four years ago. She admits that at first she had no idea what the government's policy to change all education facilities into "green schools" meant.

"It sounded good but I wasn't sure how it would work," she says. But after Unicef funded a "green schools" teacher training programme, things improved. "The idea of being green does not just mean the environment, it is a philosophy for life," says Dukpa.

Alongside maths and science, children are taught basic agricultural techniques and environmental protection. A new national waste management programme ensures that every piece of material used at the school is recycled.

The infusion of GNH into education has also meant daily meditation sessions and soothing traditional music replacing the clang of the school bell.

"An education doesn't just mean getting good grades, it means preparing them to be good people," says Dukpa. "This next generation is going to face a very scary world as their environment changes and social pressures increase. We need to prepare them for this."

Despite its focus on national wellbeing, Bhutan faces huge challenges. It remains one of the poorest nations on the planet. A quarter of its 800,000 people survive on less than $1.25 a day, and 70% live without electricity. It is struggling with a rise in violent crime, a growing gang culture and the pressures of rises in both population and global food prices.

It also faces an increasingly uncertain future. Bhutan's representatives at the Doha climate talks are warning that its gross national happiness model could crumble in the face of increasing environmental and social pressures and climatic change.

"The aim of staying below a global two-degree temperature increase being discussed here this week is not sufficient for us. We are a small nation, we have big challenges and we are trying our best, but we can't save our environment on our own," says Thinley Namgyel, who heads Bhutan's climate change division. "Bhutan is a mountainous country, highly vulnerable to extreme weather conditions. We have a population that is highly dependent on the agricultural sector. We are banking on hydropower as the engine that will finance our development."

In Paro, an agricultural region one hour out of the capital, Dawa Tshering explains how the weather is already causing him problems. The 53-year-old farmer grew up in Paro, surrounded by mountains and streams, but has found it increasingly difficult to work his two acres of rice paddy.

"The weather has changed a lot: there is no snow in winter, the rains come at the wrong times and our plants get ruined. There are violent storms," he says. Around 70% of Bhutan's people are smallholder farmers like Tshering.

"The temperature has got hotter so there are more insects in the fruit and grain. I don't understand it, but if it continues we're going to have many problems in growing food and feeding ourselves."

Bhutan is taking action to try to protect itself. Groundbreaking work is being done to try to reduce the flooding potential in its remote glacial lakes. Yet it cannot do it alone. Last week in Doha, campaigners pushed for more support to countries such as Bhutan that are acutely vulnerable to climate change.

"While the world is now starting to look to Bhutan as an alternative model of sustainable economics, all of its efforts could be undone if the world doesn't take action in Doha," says Stephen Pattison from Unicef UK.

"Small and developing countries like Bhutan must get more support, and the UK and other governments must start actually taking action, like pledging their share of money to the green climate fund and get it up and running as soon as possible."

In Paro, teenagers in school uniform heading home from lessons are well aware of the hard times ahead for Bhutan as it tries to navigate a path between preserving its sustainable agenda and the global realities it faces. All say they are proud to be Bhutanese. They want to be forest rangers, environmental scientists and doctors. At the same time they want to travel the world, listen to Korean pop music and watch *Rambo*.

"I want to be able to go out and see the world but then I want to come home to Bhutan and for it to be the same," says Kunzang Jamso, a 15-year-old whose traditional dress is offset with a hint of a boyband haircut. "I think we must keep the outside from coming here too much because we might lose our culture, and if you don't have that then how do you know who you are?"

Critical Thinking

1. How do you think a person can balance the taking from the environment vs. the giving to the environment? Even though countries attempt to do this, individuals are faced with this dilemma daily, even if it isn't thought about daily. How do you resolve this dilemma each day? Are you more of a taker or a giver? Explain.

2. Think about living in a culture where you live on $1.25 a day, and 70% of citizens live without electricity. List at least three ways in which your life would be fundamentally different than it is today.

Create Central

www.mhhe.com/createcentral

Internet References

Gross national happiness
www.grossnationalhappiness.com
Gross national happiness USA
www.gnhusa.org

Article Prepared by: Eric Landrum, *Boise State University*

13 Practical Tips for Training in Other Countries

Growing global opportunities have prompted many workplace learning and development professionals to seek out cross-cultural training opportunities in other countries. While many businesspeople know enough to explore the niceties of business etiquette before entering a new culture, fewer people have developed sufficient cultural intelligence to be sensitive to more profound issues when they embark on efforts to enter, and conduct training in, other countries.

WILLIAM J. ROTHWELL

Learning Outcomes

After reading this article, you will be able to:

- Identify many strategies that are useful for providing education and training services in other countries.

- Understand the importance of doing your homework on the cultural and technological differences between your own country and the educational environment of other countries.

Learning professionals should be cautious when embarking on cross-cultural assignments. Drawing on research and my experiences, here are 13 practical tips for training in cross-cultural settings.

Be Sensitive to Other Cultures

Cultural sensitivity is important, as is realizing that human beings are more alike than they are different. When first working cross-culturally, people are usually tempted to notice cultural differences first. For example, when I visited Saudi Arabia for the first time, I was surprised to learn that men and women are not usually permitted to meet in the same room and that women wearing full-head black coverings cannot travel outside their homes without a male relative or husband as escort.

These rare exceptions aside, the reality is that human beings are pretty much alike everywhere. Most everyone wants a family, a good job, a nice home life, good food, some freedom to speak their minds, and respect and dignity. While modes of dress and beliefs about religion may differ, people are pretty much alike in what they want.

It is wrong to regard people through the narrow lenses of one's own values and cultural views about what is right and wrong. If you question people from other cultures about why they believe or behave as they do, you will find out that their beliefs make perfect sense in the contexts in which they live.

Do Your Homework

Before entering a new country, do some research. Fewer Americans by percentage travel abroad than many other nationalities. Thus, there is a need to teach Americans simple basics about foreign travel. For example, before you embark on a trip, be absolutely sure you know the rules about visas—which countries need them and how to get one. There are easy places to find that information, beginning with a simple web search.

Work your social network to find out if you know anyone who knows people from that country so that you can talk to them before you go. At least find out if there are laws that you may inadvertently break. For instance, be careful about taking prescription medication unless it is in a bottle with your name on the label. Some drugs, such as diet medication or even something as simple as a nicotine lozenge, may be illegal in certain countries.

Also take time to learn about local conditions. When conducting training in South Africa, I was told how much HIV/AIDS affects local business planning on the African continent, a fact that I had known but wish I had researched more fully before my arrival.

Work with Reliable Local Partners and Informants

Spend time to find the right people with whom to work. That can be difficult to do because it is not always easy to check the reputation of others from the United States. But check you must. If you do not, you risk doing the work—and then never getting paid because there are many criminals eager to get you to pony up work first and then give you nothing when it comes time for payment.

When working with a partner for a first time, always ask for money in advance. It is wise to always ask for half the funds due up front to avoid the problem of not being paid anything. Work with people who have a track record of respecting intellectual property, copyrights, and trademarks. Beware of people who wish to partner for the short term and who may be looking for quick and easy ways to steal your products, services, or ideas and use them to their own advantage.

You may have a signed contract, but are you prepared to sue people for nonpayment in foreign courts? Legal recourse may work in America—but not so well elsewhere where networks of informal agreements and personal relationships are far more important than written contracts.

Pay Attention to Marketing

Marketing principles for training and consulting can be different in other countries. In the United States, it is common to send out emails or to offer free webinars as a marketing effort for training. Such relatively impersonal approaches do not work so well with cultures in which who you know is more important than what you can do.

As just one example, I had an experience in which a Chinese partner tried an experiment. On the one hand, the partner invested $30,000 to market seminars in Greater China through classified newspaper advertising, email, and faxes. On the other hand, the same partner marketed directly to key decision makers (vice presidents of HR) by paying them personal visits for seminar sign-ups and by offering free breakfasts with a sample of the training content. The former approach did not work at all; the latter was most effective and resulted in much business.

Consider Language As Well As Cultural Issues

Not everyone speaks English. If you plan to market in other countries, you limit yourself if the market is restricted to English speakers only. But translators are not always equally good. The best translators are not United Nations-trained; rather, they are individuals from the particular country who have some education and experience in the subject matter or industry. They know how to translate for concept as well as for words, and may even be able to cite local examples of how an idea was put into practice.

Be aware that people of other cultures are more comfortable with people like themselves. When in a public seminar, foreign nationals prefer to talk to someone who can speak their language—and is perhaps even the same gender. A particularly powerful solution is to pair up a famous foreign presenter with a local person of a different gender. While that may cost more, it can pay big dividends in the impression it makes.

Recognize Differences in How People Participate

Americans often are quite willing to publicly pose embarrassing business questions directly to senior leaders such as CEOs. But not all cultures are so open. Before arriving to conduct a seminar in a foreign country, ask others who have been to that country what participation style is typical and what strategies might work to get more participation. Do not limit such requests to one person. Ask several because perceptions are sometimes simply erroneous.

The first time I visited China I was told by an experienced Chinese training director that I should use lecture-only methods. After the first hour, my audience had nearly gone to sleep. I started asking participants questions—and giving them small gifts, such as candy bars, when they answered. That worked.

On another occasion I tried to teach public-speaking skills to Chinese graduate students. MBA students, it turned out, were not accustomed to public speaking and were immune to all efforts to use eye contact. So, I told the class that I would wave a 100RMB note (worth about $16) in the back of the room at some point during their individual talks and would give the money to the presenters who saw it. In teaching more than 60 people, I gave away only four bills. I learned that I had to stand right behind aspiring public speakers and direct them to look in specific places to teach eye contact.

Be Prepared to Negotiate

There are two ways to negotiate money in the world. There is the American-style "take-it-or-leave-it" fixed-price approach. And then there is the back-and-forth negotiation style that is used in other countries.

Start higher than you really expect, but allow some room for negotiation. Expect that others will start far lower than you expect; do not be insulted by that. Be prepared to go several rounds before reaching a level of agreement. Before you begin negotiating prices and expenses, determine what your lowest acceptable rate would be.

Would you accept economy travel instead of the much more expensive business or first-class travel? Would you stay in a four-star rather than a five-star hotel? These questions are worth considering. Also be aware that you may have to price your products or services differently if you wish to compete in some foreign markets because they simply cannot afford what they regard as outrageous U.S. or European rates.

Be Sensitive to Different Communication Styles

Realize that people in other cultures don't always communicate as openly as in the United States. In many cultures, there is concern about hurting other people's feelings. It is said in Asia and in the Middle East that there are a thousand ways to say no and a thousand ways to say yes. In fact, if a business problem exists, in some cultures they do not want to share that bad news until the last possible moment for fear of "losing face" or feeling bad about themselves. Sensitivity to communication styles is a key issue when working cross-culturally and occasionally requires exceptional skills to pull out critical information when it is needed.

When training participants who understand English, do not be offended by their slow response times. That's because the people sometimes have to mentally translate what you said to their native language and then translate their answer back into English. People will sometimes apologize to me about their poor English, but I have learned to answer that "your English is much better than my [whatever their language is]."

Recognize the Importance of Personal Relationships

In developed economies, results are important. In developing economies, results also are important—but may be less so or even overshadowed by considerations other than immediate results.

For instance, I was told in South America that "we can predict when a young person joins our company how far he will go—even to the point that we know which 21-year-old will definitely become CEO because he comes from the right family, has the right connections with government officials, attended the right school, and has the right connections in other places."

Be Tenacious in Your Efforts

There is a saying in China that "you can get anything you want in China—if you are prepared to wait long enough." In huge economies, it is possible to make an impact over time. But the buccaneer mentality of "let's go in, make a quick killing, and leave" will usually fail. Local people are waiting to hand you your head if that is your attitude.

Success may depend on being patient and dedicated. That requires long-term investments of time, money, and effort to get results. In India, for example, there are numerous inexpensive training programs offered by well-qualified people who speak very good English. Making an impact takes time, visibility, the right partner, and the most clever marketing approaches possible.

Make Personal Safety the First Priority

Never take safety for granted when you're traveling. Global organizations often have learned to assign a local mentor to someone before he arrives so that foreigners will not end up renting an apartment in an unsafe neighborhood or traveling to unsafe places in a city. Even taking a taxi can turn into a nightmare if not managed properly.

If you are a solitary traveler, make sure that you know how to reach your contacts before you arrive (such as cell phones), who (if anyone) will pick you up at the airport and how you will recognize them, and where you are going. Take nothing for granted.

I once arrived in Pakistan late at night. I was the only Westerner onboard the airplane. Before my arrival I made sure to know who was picking me up—and what to do in case, for any reason, that person was not there. Some countries, such as the Philippines or Indonesia, may have U.S.-style airport screening just to get into a hotel lobby. That speaks volumes about the need to be careful.

On another occasion I traveled to South America to conduct training for a large bank. I told them before I arrived that I was concerned about safety. They did not tell me what they planned to do about it, and I did not ask. Upon my arrival, I was greeted late at night by a large group of burly men with automatic weapons. They asked me who I was. I was a little hesitant to say, but it turned out they were an armed security detachment sent by the bank to ensure my safety.

Be Cautious in What You Take for Granted

In developed economies, HR and training practice may be quite advanced. There may be certifications and even graduate degree programs to ensure professionalism. But in many developing economies, the opportunities to learn about the professions of HR or learning and development may not be so common. Practitioners learn by working in foreign companies and then transferring some of what they have learned into local practice by eventually moving to local companies. Bear that in mind as you consider training in other nations.

Avoid using terms that may seem common—such as training needs assessment, instructional systems design, or even something such as Kirkpatrick's four levels of evaluation. Strive for simple English that is jargon-free and readily transparent in meaning. Always define special terms immediately if you are forced to use them.

Don't Take Training Technology for Granted

Developed economies are in love with technology-assisted training. Everybody wants to try the latest fad or gizmo—whether it is mobile learning, iPad-based instruction, wikis, or even more elaborate approaches such as technology-based simulations or virtual worlds. But the practical reality is that, in many developing economies, either connection speeds are slower than in developed economies or the infrastructure is less reliable. (But it is also true that, in some countries, such as Korea, they make fun of the slow speeds of the Internet in the United States because their infrastructure is newer.) Fewer people have home-based Internet access.

Realize that even something such as offering a virtual meeting may require several rehearsals. I recently offered a virtual training session in Singapore using a popular brand of virtual meeting software. Even though we had two rehearsals, we still had trouble on the day of the training.

The lesson: Never take technology for granted when working abroad. Check and verify what they have, and how well it works, first.

Practical Realities

As globalization continues with the advent of more sophisticated technology and easy travel, more learning and development professionals will work in other countries. As they do, they need to be aware of some practical realities to achieved continued success.

Critical Thinking

1. Do you think you would like to travel abroad someday? Would you rather be a tourist, a worker, or both? Explore and explain your feelings about traveling and working abroad.

2. What are some of the key challenges in providing training abroad? Although your author provided 13 tips, which three do you think are most important, and why?

Create Central

www.mhhe.com/createcentral

Internet References

World business culture

www.worldbusinessculture.com/business-with-other-countries.html

7 tips for foreign business travel

www.inc.com/guides/201103/7-tips-for-foreign-business-travel.html

WILLIAM J. ROTHWELL is a professor of workforce education and development on the University Park campus of The Pennsylvania State University. He also is president of Rothwell & Associates.

Unit 10

UNIT

Prepared by: Eric Landrum, *Boise State University*

Psychological Disorders

Jay and Harry are two brothers who own a service station. Harry and Jay have a good working relationship. Harry is the "up-front" man. Taking customer orders, accepting payments, and working with parts distributors, Harry deals directly with the public, delivery personnel, and other people visiting the station. Jay works behind the scenes. Although Harry makes the mechanical diagnoses, Jay is the mastermind who does the corrective work. Some of his friends think Jay is a veritable mechanical genius; he can fix anything. Preferring to spend time by himself, Jay has always been a little odd and a bit of a loner. Jay's friends think his emotions have always been inappropriate and more intense than other people, but they pass it off as part of his eccentric talent. On the other hand, Harry is the stalwart of the family. He is the acknowledged leader and decision maker when it comes to family finances.

One day, Jay did not show up for work on time. When he finally did appear, he was dressed in the most garish outfit and was laughing hysterically and talking to himself. At first, Harry suspected that his brother was high. However, Jay's condition persisted and, in fact, worsened. Out of concern, his family took him to their physician, who immediately sent Jay and his family to a psychiatrist. After several visits, the doctor informed the family that Jay suffers from schizophrenia. Jay's maternal uncle had also been schizophrenic. The family somberly left the psychiatrist's office and went to the local pharmacy to fill a prescription for anti-psychotic medication.

What caused Jay's drastic change in mental health? Was Jay destined to be schizophrenic because of his family tree? Did competitiveness with his brother and the feeling that he was less revered than Harry cause his descent into mental disorder? How do psychiatrists and clinical psychologists make accurate diagnoses? Once a diagnosis of mental disorder is made (such as schizophrenia), can the individual ever completely recover? Mental disorders affect millions of people throughout the world. Mental disorders impact every aspect of an individual's life, but work, family, and friendships are especially impacted. Because of their detrimental effect on the individual, mental disorders have been a focal point of psychological research for decades. This important work has revealed the likely origins or causes of mental disorders and has led to breakthroughs in the care and treatment of people with mental disorders. This unit emphasis the questions that psychologists have attempted to address in their quest to understand the nature of mental illness.

Article

Prepared by: Eric Landrum, *Boise State University*

The Kids Aren't All Right

New data from APA's Stress in America survey indicate parents don't know what's bothering their children.

CHRISTOPHER MUNSEY

Learning Outcomes

After reading this article, you will be able to:

- Describe the (a) importance of recent research showing that parents do not realize the nature of the stress that their children experience and (b) how men and women tend to differ in experiencing stress.

- Review and explain effective strategies for coping with stress.

There's a disconnect between what children say they're worrying about and what their parents think is stressing them, a gap that could have long-term implications for children's mental and physical health, according to APA's latest Stress in America research.

Children age 8 to 17 say they worry about doing well in school, getting into good colleges and their family's finances. They also report suffering headaches, sleeplessness and upset stomachs.

But these stresses and symptoms are going largely unnoticed by parents, survey findings show.

In fact, more than one in three children report experiencing headaches in the past month, but only 13 percent of parents think their children experience headaches as a result of stress. In addition, while 44 percent of children report sleeping difficulties, only 13 percent of parents think their kids have trouble sleeping.

The survey also found that about one-fifth of children reported they worry a great deal or a lot, but only 3 percent of parents rate their children's stress as extreme (an 8, 9 or 10 on a 10-point scale). In addition, almost 30 percent of children worried about their families' financial difficulties, but just 18 percent of parents thought that was a source of worry for their children.

The findings are troubling because chronic stress left untreated can contribute to psychological problems as well as physical conditions, says Katherine Nordal, PhD, APA's executive director for professional practice. She says parents need to make themselves available and let their children know it's OK to approach them if they're worried about something.

"Parents need to be intentional about setting aside time to be available to their children," she says. "If parents aren't receptive, kids may feel like they're being an additional burden on their parents by talking about their problems."

The online survey, conducted by Harris Interactive for the third consecutive year for the Practice Directorate's ongoing Mind/Body Health public education campaign, polled a nationally representative sample of 1,568 adults in July and August. Results for children age 8 to 17 were drawn from a YouthQuery survey of 1,206 young people conducted online by Harris in August.

Women Still More Stressed

The findings for adults are also troubling:

- Stress levels are high, with 42 percent of adults indicating their stress worsened in the past year. A total of 24 percent said they had an extreme level of stress (8, 9 or 10 on a 10-point scale) over the past month, and 51 percent report moderate stress levels (4 to 7 on a 10-point scale).

- About two-thirds of respondents said they've been diagnosed by a physician with a chronic condition, most commonly high blood pressure or high cholesterol. Seventy percent said a health-care provider recommended lifestyle or behavior changes. That data also show that adults who were advised to make lifestyle changes may not have received enough support from their physicians to do so. In fact, fewer than half were told by their physicians why the changes were important; only 35 percent were given tips or shown techniques for making changes; and only 5 percent to 10 percent were referred to another health-care provider for follow-up.

- Similar to last year's results, women report having experienced more stress symptoms than men, such as irritability or anger, fatigue and depression.

- Among parents of 8- to 17-year-olds, mothers reported higher levels of stress than fathers. On a scale of 1 to 10

Sources of Stress by Age

	Total N=235	Parents 8–12 101	13–17 134	Total 1,206	Youth 8–12 536	13–17 670
Managing school pressures/responsibilities/ homework/grades/Doing well in school	34%	31%	36%	44%	44%	43%
Relationships with siblings/Getting along with my brother(s) or sister(s)	17%	17%	16%	8%	14%	2%
Relationships with peers/Getting along with my friends	20%	20%	20%	16%	22%	11%
Your family's financial difficulties/My family having enough money	18%	20%	17%	30%	28%	31%
His/her physical appearance/weight/The way I look/my weight	17%	17%	17%	22%	17%	26%
Your relationship with your spouse/partner/My parent(s)/ guardian or other family members arguing or fighting more	12%	16%	9%	10%	14%	7%
Pressure managing extracurricular commitments (e.g. sports, hobbies)/Managing activities such as sports, music, clubs, etc.	12%	12%	12%	10%	7%	12%
Peer pressure to engage in risky behaviors (e.g., smoking, drinking, drugs, sex, etc.)/Pressure from friends who want me to try smoking, drinking, drugs, sex, etc.	6%	1%	10%	2%	-	3%
Getting into a good college/determining future/Getting into a good college/Deciding what to do after high school	3%	1%	5%	17%	5%	29%
Non-financial pressures on family members (e.g., health, job frustrations, getting along with extended family, etc.)	3%	3%	4%	N/A	N/A	N/A
Getting along with my boyfriend or girlfriend	N/A	N/A	N/A	3%	1%	4%
My parent(s)/guardian losing their jobs	N/A	N/A	N/A	6%	7%	6%
Other	8%	10%	6%	10%	12%	8%

(with 10 being the highest level), 15 percent of moms rated their stress as a 10, compared with only 3 percent of dads. Mothers were also more likely to report lying awake at night, eating unhealthy foods, overeating or skipping a meal because of stress.

Such findings underscore the need for psychologists to work within the nation's health-care system to help people make needed lifestyle and behavioral changes, Nordal says.

"The key in managing stress effectively for both physical and mental well-being is having effective coping strategies, a combination of relaxation strategies along with exercise, combined with good sleep habits and good eating habits," she says.

This is particularly important for women who often face a "second shift" of caring for children and running a household when they get home from work, says Helen Coons, PhD, a Philadelphia-based clinical health psychologist who works primarily with women. "The reality is, so many women are just too tired. They're running on empty."

That calls for change at several levels to support women, says Coons. Workplaces should offer better access to day care and more flexibility to allow women time for medical checkups and exercise breaks. Spouses or partners need to watch the kids

while mom goes out for a run or a brisk walk, and neighborhood families can rotate babysitting to give parents more flexibility.

"There's that African saying, it takes a village to raise a child. I think it takes a community to support women and families" for healthier lifestyles, she says.

Mile-High Stress

This year's survey also took snapshots of how Americans are faring with stress in eight metropolitan areas—Atlanta, Chicago, Denver, Detroit, Los Angeles, New York, Seattle and Washington, D.C.—comparing results with national findings.

Faring the worst was Denver, where more than 75 percent of residents report that work and money are significant sources of stress, and 35 percent rated their stress as extreme over the prior month.

That distress sounds familiar to Stephanie Smith, PsyD, public education coordinator for the Colorado Psychological Association and a Denver-based practitioner. Although the city's unemployment rate isn't as high as the national average, many of her clients tell her they feel trapped at their jobs. They're working harder for less money because of layoffs and pay cuts,

Getting the Results Out

APA presented the results of the Stress in America survey on Nov. 3 at a New York press conference. Nationally, the research was featured on cable and broadcast news programs, newspapers, radio programs, news and health Websites, and blogs with local psychologists from the Practice Directorate's Public Education Campaign reaching out to local reporters. Coverage of the results reached almost 28 million people.

Outlets that featured articles and discussion of APA's stress survey included:

- NBC, ABC and FOX local affiliates.
- NBC's "Today Show."
- CNN en Espanol.
- "Dr. Nancy" on MSNBC.
- *Wall Street Journal's* The Juggle blog.
- *USA Today.*
- *The New York Times'* Motherlode blog.
- Newsweek.com's "Her Body" column.
- *The Washington Post Express.*

but they're unable to find better jobs and frightened of losing their health insurance.

Smith works with her clients to identify things they can do to relieve stress, such as spending more quality time with family and exercising. "We talk about the things you can control in your life," she says.

In Los Angeles, 71 percent of respondents said they've been told by a health provider they have a chronic condition, compared with 66 percent nationally.

"To me, that's absolutely frightening, because we know the role stress plays in wearing our bodies down," says Michael Ritz, PhD, co-chair of the California Psychological Association's public education steering committee.

Psychologists can help people manage their stress and live healthier lifestyles, Ritz says.

"That underscores so much why psychologists need to be part of our health-care team," he says.

To read more about the 2009 results, go online to www.apa .org/news/press/releases/2009/11/stress.aspx.

Critical Thinking

1. To what extent do parents realize that their children experience stress? Why is this issue important for helping children learn to cope with stress?
2. How do men and women tend to differ in their experiencing of stress?
3. How can a person deal with stress effectively or learn to cope with stress?

Create Central

www.mhhe.com/createcentral

Internet References

Children coping skills

www.stjude.org/stjude/v/index.jsp?vgnextoid=4505b4bc5695a110VgnVC M1000001e0215acRCRD

Signs your child is stressed and 5 ways to help

http://psychcentral.com/blog/archives/2012/06/06/signs-your-child -is-stressed-5-ways-to-help

Article   Prepared by: Eric Landrum, *Boise State University*

The Recession's Toll on Children

Low-income children are more likely to develop cognitive deficits, undermining their chances for successful lives. New psychological interventions could help protect them.

Amy Novotney

Learning Outcomes

After reading this article, you will be able to:

- Explain the relationship between poverty and the development of psychological problems in children.

- Describe the interventions that might help low-income children cope with the stressors they experience.

More than one in five American children now live in poverty, the highest rate in two decades, and one that surpasses that of most other industrialized nations, according to a June report from the nonprofit Foundation for Child Development. Since 1975, the organization has tracked children's overall quality of life with 28 well-being indicators, including infant mortality, preschool enrollment and children's health insurance coverage.

The foundation predicts that the number of children living in poverty will rise to 15.6 million this year, an increase of more than 3 million children in four years. As many as half a million children could become homeless this year, up from 330,000 in 2007.

Perhaps most alarming is that even though the economy is likely to recover in the next few years, a generation of disadvantaged children may not. Today's poorer children could be haunted by the devastating effects of the recession for years to come, as they face an increased risk of engaging in violent crime and illegal drug use, and of experiencing chronic health problems such as obesity.

"Research shows that children who slip into poverty, even for a short time, suffer long-term setbacks even when their families regain their economic footing," says psychologist Ruby Takanishi, PhD, the foundation's president.

These setbacks are especially true for children under 10, she adds. In addition to negative health outcomes—such as a higher susceptibility to asthma, anemia and other health problems—research also shows that children raised in poverty are more likely to experience negative educational and cognitive outcomes, often as a result of less mental stimulation and increased stress in their living situations. Some research even shows that

the brains of poor children may be unable to process information in the same way as the brains of kids in higher-income families.

With the economic downturn forcing more families into poverty, psychologists are using their expertise in child development and cognition to develop evidence-based early-childhood interventions to help improve the prospects for low-income children. They're also advocating for more resources for these children, including better educational and social support, says Martha Farah, PhD, director of Center for Neuroscience and Society at the University of Pennsylvania.

"Our ultimate goal is to understand the complex web of social, psychological and physiological influences that act upon children in low-socioeconomic families and to use that understanding to help them achieve their true potential," Farah says.

> **"Our ultimate goal is to understand the complex web of social, psychological and physiological influences that act upon children in low-socioeconomic families and to use that understanding to help them achieve their true potential."**
>
> —Martha Farah, University of Pennsylvania

Poverty and the Brain

In a classic 1995 study published in the book *Meaningful Differences in the Everyday Experiences of Young American Children* (Brookes Publishing, 1995), University of Kansas psychologists Betty Hart, PhD, and Todd Risley, PhD, found that the average vocabulary of 3-year-old children from "professional" families was more than twice as large as that of 3-year-olds on welfare. Since then, a steady stream of research by psychologists and other scientists has highlighted the gulf between poor and well-off children's performance on almost every measure of cognitive development, including working memory, impulse regulation and language skills. (See "Further Reading, Resources" for more on how poverty affects the brain.)

Last year, researchers at the University of California, Berkeley, presented even more definitive findings on developmental differences between low- and high-income kids: When presented with novel stimuli, EEG readings of 9- and 10-year-olds from poorer homes showed less brain activity in the prefrontal cortex than the brains of children from more well-off families (*Journal of Cognitive Neuroscience,* Vol. 21, No. 6).

"These kids have no neural damage, no prenatal exposure to drugs and alcohol," says cognitive psychologist Mark Kishiyama, PhD, one of the study's authors, who now works at the VA hospital in Martinez, Calif. "Yet the prefrontal cortex is not functioning as efficiently as it should be. This difference may manifest itself in problem-solving and school performance."

Research led by Carleton University psychologist Amadeo D'Angiulli, PhD, provides further evidence of poorer children's deficits in a key ability harbored in the brain's prefrontal cortex—selective attention. In a 2008 study in *Neuropsychology* (Vol. 22, No. 3), D'Angiulli monitored the brain activity of 28 children from grades six to nine while they listened to a random series of four tones. Researchers asked the children to press a button every time they heard two of those tones. The results of the study showed that the brains of the children from lower-socioeconomic backgrounds used more energy when listening to the "other tones" than those from higher-income homes.

A 2009 study in *Developmental Science* (Vol. 12, No. 4), conducted by Helen Neville, PhD, a professor of psychology and neuroscience at the University of Oregon, replicates D'Angiulli's findings. In the study, 32 children listened to two stories simultaneously, one in each ear, and were asked to filter out one. All of the children remembered the story, but the children from disadvantaged homes had more trouble shutting out the distracting stimuli of the other story. Their brains, researchers say, have to work harder to perform the same task, a difficulty that could make it tougher for them to focus on teacher instructions or class assignments.

What's to blame for these disparities? Many researchers suspect it's the stressful home environments and lack of parental education in many low-income homes. "There are, not surprisingly, big differences in the amount of cognitive and linguistic stimulation that children receive in the home," Farah says.

For example, only 36 percent of low-income parents read to their kindergarten-age children every day, compared with 62 percent of upper-income parents, according to a 2002 study by researchers at the nonprofit Educational Testing Service. And in a study co-authored by Farah this year, published in *NeuroImage* (Vol. 49, No. 1), researchers found a direct correlation between hippocampal volume—which is related to memory ability—and the amount of parental nurturance a young child receives; for example, how often a parent holds a child close.

Regardless of the cause, if these cognitive and social performance lags are left unaddressed, they will persist throughout a child's development, says Linda Mayes, MD, a professor of child psychiatry, pediatrics and psychology at the Yale Child Study Center. Her team, which includes Yale child psychologists Michael Crowley, PhD, and James C. McPartland, PhD, is five years into a six-year National Institute of Child Health and Human Development grant to study how economic adversity affects emerging executive control functions in 360 young children in New Haven, Conn.

"It appears that the issue for children from poorer environments is not only a slower start, but rather a slower progression in skill acquisition, so that they stay behind their peers," Mayes says.

Promising Interventions

The good news is that a brain that is vulnerable to the adverse environmental effects of poverty is equally susceptible to the positive effects of rich, balanced learning environments and caring relationships, many psychologists say. While there's clearly no one solution to offset the grave challenges faced by disadvantaged children, evidence-based educational interventions can help poor children achieve cognitive and academic success, research suggests.

One of the most promising programs is the Tools of the Mind curriculum, developed by Metropolitan State College at Denver educational psychologists Deborah Leong, PhD, and Elena Bodrova, PhD. The yearlong program, based on the work of Russian psychologist Lev Vygotsky, helps children build their ability to control their behavior and resist impulses—skills psychologists say are critical for success in school and life. The program's 40 core activities focus on improving executive function through tasks such as "buddy reading," in which students pair up and take turns telling and listening to stories from a picture book. To help the children fight the urge to talk while the other student is telling a story, teachers pass out paper mouths and ears, and remind students that only mouths talk—ears don't.

"With that concrete reminder in front of them, they're able to exercise self-control and listen," says Adele Diamond, PhD, a professor of developmental cognitive neuroscience at the University of British Columbia, who has been testing the program with low-income preschoolers in the Northeastern United States. In her 2007 study published in *Science* (Vol. 318, No. 5,855), Diamond found that Tools students consistently scored higher on tests that require executive function than students enrolled in the school district's long-running curriculum addressing the same academic content. Tools of the Mind is now being used to teach 18,000 prekindergarten and kindergarten students in 12 states around the country.

The Tools program is different from most early education programs, Diamond says, because it encourages children to use executive functioning, while other programs often assume young children can't use those skills. Or, she says, educators in other programs may expect the children to exercise self-control, but don't support them in doing so, leading to failure and criticism. "Instead of getting yelled at for being a poor listener, here the child develops pride in being a good listener," Diamond says.

The Tools program also emphasizes the importance of imaginative, dramatic play, but requires the children to develop a plan for what character they would like to act out—say, an astronaut going to the moon—and holds them to it.

Neville, at the University of Oregon, is also testing an early-child intervention that trains children and their parents about the importance of impulse management and sustained concentration. "If you have control of your selective attention, you can do anything," she says. "You can learn soccer, you can learn to play the cello, you can learn to crochet, you can learn math—it's domain-general."

In the program, Parents and Children Making Connections–Highlighting Attention, parents and their preschoolers attend eight weekly, two-hour evening or weekend attention-training classes. The kids learn to be more aware of their bodies, attention and emotions, as well as how to focus on one thing at a time. In one task, for example, they practice figure-tracing, which requires a moderate amount of concentration, while other students in the room play with balloons, in an effort to challenge the concentration of the figure-tracers. Parents learn to use positive language with their children and remain patient. They also learn strategies to help their children develop their attention control—by pointing out small details on a walk, playing board games and reading books that require them to focus for long periods of time.

In an as-yet-unpublished study, Neville and her team found that children who completed the training improved their IQ, message comprehension and social skills. Parents reported reduced stress and more positive interactions in response to children's crying and temper tantrums.

Overall, Neville says she predicts that programs that include extensive parent training may result in larger gains for children than programs that primarily focus on children. The intervention's initial success also points to the importance of the home environment and the parent-child relationship to children's cognitive development—links that often go unrecognized, she says.

Speaking Out for Kids

But to ensure that low-income children have access to these interventions and others, psychologists must be among those raising awareness of these children's plight, as well as the research that shows there are solutions, Takanishi says.

"Investment during the first decade of life is crucial for the country's well-being, as well as for individual potential," she says. "In the United States, education is the only possibility for escaping from poverty. Thus, the recession's impact on declining availability of prekindergarten programs is very damaging for children in poverty."

Last year, Neville and her team developed a DVD for parents, teachers and policymakers, available at www.changingbrains .org, that explores brain development in children and provides simple techniques caregivers can use to help children reach their full potential.

Takanishi recommends that psychologists contribute newspaper op-eds highlighting research on the effects of poverty. Psychologists might also consider promoting dual-generation programs that focus on increasing literacy among low-income parents—and particularly immigrants—as a way to boost economic status and improve outcomes for children.

"Help other people think more broadly about how to address the issue of children in poverty," Takanishi says. "It's that kind of feeding of ideas and working with other sectors in society that will really help us move toward social change."

Further Reading, Resources

National Center for Children in Poverty: www.nccp.org
Foundation for Child Development: www.fedus.org
Spotlight on Poverty and Opportunity: www.spotlightonpoverty.com
APA Office of Socioeconomic Status. www.apa.org/pi/ses/index.aspx
Hackman, D.A., & Farah, M.J. (2009). Socioeconomic status and the developing brain. *Trends in Cognitive Science, 13,* 65–73.
Jensen, E. (2009). Teaching With Poverty in Mind: What Being Poor Does to Kids' Brains and What Schools Can Do about It. Alexandria, Va.: Association for Supervision & Curriculum Development.
Lipina, S.J., & Colombo, J.A. (2009). Poverty and Brain Development During Childhood: An Approach From Cognitive Psychology and Neuroscience. Washington, DC: APA.
Raizada, R.D., & Kishiyama, M.M. (2010). Effects of socioeconomic status on brain development, and how cognitive neuroscience may contribute to leveling the playing field. *Frontiers in Human Neuroscience, 5,* 1–18.

Critical Thinking

1. How does poverty affect children's intellectual development?

2. Describe the ways that parent training might be used to combat the negative effects of poverty on children's intellectual development.

3. Describe the 'Tools for Life' program and how this intervention is believed to counteract the adverse impacts of poverty on child development.

Create Central

www.mhhe.com/createcentral

Internet References

Recession leads to surge in mental health issues for children
www.thejournal.ie/recession-leads-to-surge-in-mental-health-issues-in -children-573966-Aug2012
Recession causes surge in mental health problems
www.theguardian.com/society/2010/apr/01/recession-surge-mental -health-problems
The long-range impact of the recession on families
www.contemporaryfamilies.org/economic-issues/the-long-range-impact -of-the-recession-on-families.html

Article   Prepared by: Eric Landrum, *Boise State University*

Hypochondria: The Impossible Illness

I am Dying.

Jeff Pearlman

Learning Outcomes

After reading this article, you will be able to:

- Describe some of the typical ideas and beliefs of a hypochondriac.

- Explain some of the challenges in making a diagnostic decision as to whether someone has hypochondriasis.

I know I am dying, because, well, I just know. I'm certain of it. I can feel it.

That pain on the left side of my stomach still hasn't gone away. It's been there for eight or nine months now. The ultrasound came up negative. So did the CT scan, the MRI and the colonoscopy.

"It's probably nothing," said one doctor.

"You likely pulled a muscle," said another.

"I'd ignore it," advised a third.

They are wrong. I know they are wrong. So, with nowhere else to turn, I seek out reassurance. "What do you think my stomach pain is?" I ask. "Do you think I'm OK?"

Eyes roll. "You're fine," my father says. "You're fine," my mother says. "You're fine," my sister-in-law says.

"You're 37 years old. You run marathons. You play basketball every Monday. You've never even broken a bone," my wife says. "You're fine."

I don't believe them. I can't believe them. I refuse to believe them. I wish I could believe them.

This is what it is to be a hypochondriac—what it is to live a life too often based upon the raw, carnal *fear* of inevitable, forthcoming, around-the-bend death. Though I was only recently diagnosed with the disorder, it has plagued me for more than a decade. Over the past 10 years, I have been convinced that I am dying of (in no particular order): *brain* cancer, stomach cancer, pancreatic cancer, testicular cancer, lung cancer, neck cancer, Lyme disease. When one ailment is dismissed by doctors, I inevitably rush to the Internet to learn why they are wrong. What? I don't have colon cancer? Then it must be. . . .

A full-throttle hypochondriac like me convinces himself—beyond reassurance, beyond comfort, beyond anything—that a cut is never merely a cut, that a cough is never merely a cough. He doesn't merely think he feels the pain. He literally feels the pain.

It begins innocently enough. Just recently, for example, I woke up with blurry vision in my left eye. I was OK for a while. I rubbed the eye. Tried lubricating drops. But when the vision remained blurred for several days, my mind began to wander. Is something wrong with that side of my brain? Why is my neck hurting? I mentioned it to my wife, who said, "You're probably fine—don't go to the computer." I went to the computer, where I Googled "blurred vision and tumor." A whopping 199,000 results came up, many of which confirmed my worst *nightmares.*

On cue, I was overcome by dread. Actually, a blackness. I didn't want to talk to anyone. I didn't want to think. Or eat. I was dying. I knew I was dying.

My lowest moment came two summers ago, when—in the midst of an otherwise uneventful trip to Florida to see the in-laws—I was overcome by despair about the Lou Gehrig's disease eating away at my body. What brought it on? I'm not certain. *Stress,* perhaps. Or anxiety. My arms were heavy, my breathing was strained. I locked myself in a bedroom and told my wife to handle our two children without me. Finally, she insisted I get help. "This isn't going well," she said. "You need to talk to someone."

I immediately contacted a therapist, who convinced me of my irrationality. But now there's this pain in my stomach.

This damned pain . . . the Greeks invented the term to describe ailments caused by movement of the upper region of the abdomen—from hypo (below) and chondros (breast bone cartilage). By the late 19th century, however, hypochondriasis had come to mean "illness without a specific cause."

In the year 2010, hypochondriasis is as covert and confounding as ever. Regarded as a mental disorder in the Diagnostic and Statistical Manual (DSM) and categorized as a somatoform disorder, it is defined as "preoccupation with fears of having, or the idea that one has, a serious disease, based on a misinterpretation of bodily symptoms. This preoccupation must have been present for at least six months and persists despite adequate medical reassurance."

It is estimated that one of twenty Americans who visit doctors suffer from the disorder, though all figures are frustratingly inconclusive: One can be a lifelong hypochondriac and never know it, just as one can be convinced one is a hypochondriac and, in fact, be physically ill.

Indeed, hypochondriasis is the Big Foot of disorders—studied, discussed, but persistently elusive. Some people who are hypochondriacs might classify themselves as merely physically sick. "It's very hard to quantify," says Peter T. Swanljung, medical director of the General Adults Unit at Friends Hospital in Philadelphia. Part of the problem is that hypochondriasis exists on a broad spectrum. The worst-case hypochondriacs can delve into the deepest depths of depression—lengthy, unwieldy funks evoked by self-diagnosis and fear of the unknown. Consequently, somewhere in Tulsa, a man is worried that the cut on his foot is a flesh-eating virus. He frets and frets and frets for a week, then gradually forgets about it. A month later, he fears that the spot on his arm is a deadly goose virus. It fades, too.

Despite official recognition in the DSM, those with hypochondriasis are often treated with the respect and seriousness of a Scott Baio film festival. "It's an obsession, and oftentimes people don't want to listen to someone's obsessions," says Gail Martz-Nelson, a Denver psychologist specializing in anxiety disorders. "'I'm terrified I have HIV, I'm terrified I have cancer, I'm terrified I have lymphoma.' People hear that and dismiss it or *laugh* it off. But being a hypochondriac can be crippling. It's not a joke."

Generally speaking, hypochondriacs aren't merely hypochondriacs. Most struggle with anxiety or depression—or both, says Swanljung. "When someone is anxious about having an illness, the anxiety level goes up, the stress level goes up," he says. "That can lead to headaches, to stomach and digestive problems. Anxiety definitely can cause pain, and if you're a hypochondriac you react to that pain in a unique way."

No amount of reassurance helps.

"The brain is so powerful that it really can convince itself of illness," says Caroline Goldmacher-Kern, a New York-based psychotherapist who specializes in anxiety disorders. "You know something is wrong because you believe what you're thinking, and what you're thinking is what you perceive to be feeling. So you can have five people tell you it's all in your mind and that's not good enough."

But in fact, all illnesses are psychosomatic, contends Suzanne Koven, an internist at Massachusetts General Hospital. "All illnesses involve both mind and body," which suggests that one way conditions differ is in the relative contributions of psyche and soma. Koven points out that the simplest sore throat brings a tide of emotion—sometimes fear (What if I miss too much work? Will I lose my job?), sometimes *guilt* (Will anyone catch this from me?), sometimes *anger* (Who did I catch this from?). And conversely, emotions often communicate in the language of the body: a tension headache, for example, or stress-induced upset stomach.

Although hypochondria is formally regarded as a mental disorder, Koven, who sees hypochondriacs every day in her medical practice, has a slightly more expansive view. "We all walk that side of the street a bit. None of us are disembodied; we all have personalities and fears and hopes. It's a matter of degree." One distinguishing factor: Hypochondriacs "get something subconsciously from the illness role," she suggests.

Symptomatology, she adds, may be simply the "flavor" that a person's ruminations take on. "Illness is a very common content of the ruminations in *obsessive-compulsive disorder*, anxiety, and *depression*." For her, an important question is at what point a person's lack of reassurability about health becomes pathological. There's no firm line.

The causes of hypochondriasis seem no more concrete than the symptoms. Some argue that, given the larger axis of anxiety and depression, the condition is largely genetic. Others believe it's learned. "A child is raised by a mother who always fears her kids are sick," says Brian A. Fallon, director of the Center for Neuroinflammatory Disorders and Biobehavioral Medicine at Columbia University. "Then the child becomes an adult and worries irrationally about health issues." Stress is often a catalyst, as is personal tragedy—such as the death of a loved one.

As a boy growing up in Mahopac, New York, I was reared by *parents* who rarely fretted about my health. I've never lost a loved one who was younger than age 80, and my greatest personal injury was a dislocated shoulder 10 years ago (painful, but certainly not tragic). As for stress, well, I cover *sports* for a living. Hardly flying jets into enemy territory.

The one thing I did have, however, was Grandpa Curt, an ornery, brooding man whose night table was topped with a cornucopia of pill bottles and whose hands routinely trembled as if his fingers housed jumping beans. When we visited my grandparents in their Manhattan apartment, I would tiptoe around Grandpa, fearful of brushing against him and drawing his ire.

"He went to the doctor at least once per week," my mother recently recalled. "He'd call the doctors all the time, and after a while they didn't want to take his phone calls. He was never terribly sick, but he always thought he was."

So can I blame this on *genes*? "That'd be hard to say," says Fallon. "There are so many factors."

If the disorder remains mysterious and understudied, treatments do not. As researchers from the University of Groningen reported in late 2008, *cognitive therapy* can be "effective in decreasing hypochondriacal complaints, depressive complaints, and *trait* anxiety." The study cemented the role of what is now the most widely regarded method for tackling the disorder.

"I believe in a cognitive technique called exposure with response prevention," says Martz-Nelson. "You take an obsession and confront it directly. Let's say someone has an irrational fear that he has HIV. That person moves toward the fear, maybe spending time around somebody who has HIV, maybe going to a medical facility. The goal is to do something you've been avoiding."

Initially the process increases anxiety levels. "But over time," she says, "it will settle down and stop meaning so much. You've confronted your fear up close, and you see it for what it truly is: merely a fear, not a reality."

A growing number of doctors are also viewing hypochondriasis as something that can be treated via various *antidepressant drugs*. "In the right cases, medication can certainly help," says Goldmacher-Kern. "Just as anxiety can be treated with medication, hypochondriasis can, too. If it works, fantastic." The trouble is, it doesn't always work.

Eleven years ago, when he was still a medical resident at Columbia University, Fallon was asked to help a man who was convinced, despite medical results to the contrary, that he was saddled with a brain tumor. "He tried Prozac, and it made a dramatic change," Fallon says. "He went from irritable and hostile to *grateful* and happy that something was helping him. I thought, 'Wow, this is fascinating.' Because at that point so little was known."

The use of Prozac and similar medications is now under formal study. Columbia's Fallon and Arthur Barsky, a professor of *psychiatry* at Harvard Medical School, are conducting the largest trial ever undertaken of the disorder. They are enrolling 264 hypochondriacs in a randomized, placebo-controlled clinical trial comparing *cognitive behavioral therapy,* Prozac, and a combination of the two. They suspect that CBT and the drug will be equally effective, but that combination therapy will be even more effective for "this major public health disorder." "I don't know what to expect," says Fallon. "But it will be very interesting."

Two days after speaking with Fallon, I find myself sitting across from a therapist specializing in cognitive therapy. It is our first session, and as I tell him about my health issues, and my troubled mental state, and my grandfather, and my weaknesses, he nods knowingly. I feel naked. Embarrassed. At times, stupid. I am a healthy man with a great family, a great job, a great life.

"What am I doing here?" I ask, dumbly. "What in the world am I doing here?"

"You're getting help," he says, nodding. "And you're trying to end the pain."

Tears stream down my cheeks.

Yes, indeed, I am. —*Jeff Pearlman*

The Struggle to Understand Hypochondria

According to Columbia's Brian Fallon, there are three types of hypochondria. A person with the obsessional-anxious type repeatedly worries, repeatedly asks for assurance, and cannot get out of his mind that something serious may have been missed by the doctor. When we think of a hypochondriac, this is the person we think of, who goes to the doctor over and over again.

The depressive hypochondriac enters the doctor's office with tears in her eyes, insists she's dying and that there's no point even getting tested. Or she might avoid going to the doctor to avoid confirmation of her fears. She might be driven by the guilt of having had an affair and the fear of having contracted HIV. Depressive hypochondria can evolve into a serious delusional type in which the person is convinced of the disorder

and has no insight into the irrationality of her fears. She is at risk for *suicide.*

The somatoform type of hypochondriac has many physical symptoms and assumes there's a serious underlying cause but doesn't necessarily jump to catastrophic conclusions. He just wants the doctor to figure out the cause of the persistent pain and how to get rid of it. Such patients resemble those with somatoform disorder, but worry that there's a significant illness.

Current ways of categorizing somatoform disorders are problematic. They don't capture the large number of primary-care patients—about 25 percent—with unexplained medical symptoms.

People with hypochondria resemble those with OCD: They worry excessively and feel compelled to do something, like visit the doctor over and over. On the other hand, the inability to explain multiple symptoms may be related to medicine's inadequate *understanding* of conditions like *fibromyalgia.* The disorders might be linked by excessive production of pro-inflammatory cytokines.

It may be that the mechanism controlling normal immune response is dysregulated and cytokine production is not turned off, leading to ongoing symptoms of fatigue and malaise. "As we learn more about the relationship between the brain, the immune system, and the *endocrine* system," says Fallon, "a new view will emerge of patients with multiple unexplained symptoms."

Critical Thinking

1. Specifically, what is hypochondriasis?
2. What is the percentage of those in the United States who are believed to suffer from hypochondriasis?
3. What is a "Big Foot" disorder, and why does hypochondriasis fall into this category?

Create Central

www.mhhe.com/createcentral

Internet References

Guide for hypochondria diagnosis, symptoms, and treatment
http://voices.yahoo.com/guide-hypochondria-diagnosis-symptoms-treatment-5820720.html

Confessions of a hypochondriac
www.theguardian.com/lifeandstyle/2010/jan/17/health-and-wellbeing-anxiety

Article   Prepared by: Eric Landrum, *Boise State University*

Bringing Life into Focus

A generation of adults who came of age too early to be diagnosed with childhood ADHD is finding that later-in-life treatment can bring great rewards.

BRENDAN L. SMITH

Learning Outcomes

After reading this article, you will be able to:

- Review some of the effects that ADHD can have on adults.

- Describe some of the treatment options for those adults diagnosed with ADHD.

W hen he was attending law school at Wake Forest University in the 1980s, E. Clarke Dummit couldn't study in the library. It was just too quiet.

"I got in the habit of hanging out at a Krispy Kreme doughnut shop and drinking coffee while I studied my law books," he says. "I needed constant noise around me and a stimulant to focus."

Another decade would pass before Dummit saw a psychologist and was diagnosed with attention-deficit hyperactivity disorder. The diagnosis came as a revelation, and it helped him to fit together some of the jigsaw pieces of his life.

"It was fascinating. I've always had learning disabilities and had to work my way around them," says Dummit, now a 50-year-old criminal defense attorney with his own firm in Winston-Salem, N.C. "I have focus when I really need to for a short period, but then my brain has to relax for a certain amount of time."

Dummit and other adults with ADHD also have to battle a stereotype that ADHD is a childhood mental disorder that doesn't affect adults. Most research on ADHD has focused on children, and the fourth edition of the Diagnostic and Statistical Manual of Mental Disorders (DSM-IV) lists symptoms for ADHD that apply mainly to children, such as losing toys or climbing on things. But a growing body of research is examining the effects of ADHD on adults and documenting that the disorder can have lifelong consequences.

ADHD can cause serious disruptions for adults in their careers, personal relationships and higher education, says J. Russell Ramsay, PhD, an associate professor of psychology and co-director of the Adult ADHD Treatment and Research Program at the University of Pennsylvania School of Medicine. "Society in general values good self-regulation, being able to follow through on things, being reliable, completing tasks on deadline. These skills are important at school and work, and they are equated with good character," Ramsay says. "An individual going through life with ADHD often ends up saying, 'I must not be good enough. I must be lazy. I must be stupid.' These negative beliefs get reactivated and strengthened and may lead people to start giving up or limiting themselves."

Several studies have shown that more than half of children with ADHD will continue to have full symptoms as adults, while some level of impairment may affect up to 80 percent or 90 percent, says Ramsay, who has researched ADHD for more than a decade. "Many adults aren't growing out of ADHD. They're actually just growing out of the childhood definition of ADHD, such as running around and climbing on things," he says. "Adult ADHD research has been hampered because the current symptoms were designed for childhood and adolescence."

Diagnosing Adult ADHD

Many middle-aged and elderly adults grew up at a time when children with ADHD were just considered to be hyperactive or poor learners. ADHD first appeared in DSM-II in 1968, when it was called "hyperkinetic reaction of childhood (or adolescence)." The symptoms included "overactivity, restlessness, distractibility and short attention span, especially in young children."

When Dummit was growing up in the 1960s in Columbia, Tenn., he had trouble focusing in school so his parents took him to Nashville for an evaluation at the Peabody College of Education and Human Development, now part of Vanderbilt University. "No one diagnosed me with ADHD," Dummit says with a laugh. "They said my father was being overbearing and too demanding. My dad said, 'You're damn right,' and we marched out of there."

Today, in contrast, more than 5 million children have been diagnosed with ADHD in the United States, and the percentage of children who are diagnosed has increased each year over the past decade. But for Dummit's generation, who missed the chance to be diagnosed as children, psychologists and psychiatrists must devise a way to identify ADHD in adults.

And even today, some people may not realize the extent of their ADHD symptoms until later in life. ADHD symptoms can sometimes be masked until adulthood because childhood often is structured by parents, school and other activities, says Stephen Faraone, PhD, a clinical psychologist and psychiatry professor at the State University of New York's Upstate Medical University.

"ADHD is a disorder characterized by the inability to regulate one's behavior, emotions and attention. As we get older, we have fewer people telling us what to do," Faraone says. "When we get to college or a job, we're expected to show up without having someone tell us what to do."

Paul Wender, MD, a pioneer in ADHD research, developed one of the first rating scales for measuring ADHD in adults—the Wender Utah Rating Scale—in the 1990s, when he was a psychiatry professor at the University of Utah School of Medicine. The questionnaire, published in the *American Journal of Psychiatry* in 1993, helped retrospectively diagnose adults with ADHD based on their childhood symptoms.

"The diagnosis of ADHD in adults has occurred more and more frequently in recent years, and it has improved dramatically over the past decade," says Wender, now a psychiatrist in private practice in Andover, Mass.

While the DSM-IV lists symptoms for ADHD that are mostly geared toward children, the upcoming fifth edition most likely will contain symptoms that apply more readily to adults, such as having racing thoughts instead of racing around the room. "Adults obviously aren't on top of their desks, but they are restless and unable to sit still," Wender says. Several other scales have been developed to help diagnose ADHD in adults since Wender's work. Faraone helped develop a self-reporting screening scale that was adopted by the World Health Organization. Published in *Psychological Medicine* in 2005, the 18-question survey translates childhood ADHD symptoms from the DSM-IV into adult situations.

In a nationwide telephone survey of 966 adults, published in the *Journal of Attention Disorders* in 2005, almost 3 percent of respondents reported they often had ADHD symptoms, while almost 16 percent reported occasional symptoms. The study by Faraone and Harvard Medical School researcher Joseph Biederman showed that individuals who reported ADHD symptoms were less likely to graduate from high school or college than those who reported no symptoms. Individuals who reported more severe ADHD symptoms were almost three times more likely to be unemployed than adults with no symptoms.

"In the workplace, we know from studies of work productivity and income that adults with ADHD are not likely to achieve as well as their peers," Faraone says. "The estimates range into billions of dollars each year in lost productivity related to adult ADHD."

'Playing Defense Every Day'

Drew Brody, a 39-year-old father with two young children in Santa Monica, Calif., says he used to struggle through his daily routine because of ADHD. As a high-school tutor, he would lose track of time, miss deadlines and feel overwhelmed. "You're walking around with a fog around your brain. Just getting through normal daily behavior is hard, getting up, getting dressed, getting shaved, getting out the door on time," he says. "All of that stuff is 10 times harder than it should be."

Brody was diagnosed with ADHD about seven years ago after his wife, a middle-school vice principal, suggested that he be evaluated. Brody began cognitive-behavioral therapy with a psychologist to identify coping mechanisms, such as time management skills, exercise and a healthy diet. But his persistent symptoms interfered with the therapy. "After a year, I never really got my act together to do any of the improvements on a regular basis," he says.

Brody then was prescribed Concerta, the extended-release version of methylphenidate (Ritalin), and his life changed. He was able to start his own tutoring company, The Scholar Group, which now has 16 tutors who help students in more than 40 academic subjects and on standardized tests such as the SAT.

"It was a revelation," he says. "I don't think I would have created my business if I hadn't started taking Concerta on a daily basis. It's made a substantial change in my life. For bigger life decisions, I am able to think more clearly and work through the steps on how to get there."

His problems from ADHD haven't disappeared, but Brody says his symptoms are more manageable now than they were in the past. "Life with ADHD is like playing defense every day. Things happen to you and you have to address them," he says. "You're not proactively dealing with life. You're waiting to be late or to get in trouble because you can't get ahead."

Brody's experience is common for adults with ADHD who try cognitive-behavioral therapy without medication, says Ramsay, who wrote the 2010 book *"Nonmedication Treatments for Adult ADHD."* Therapy can be very helpful in teaching time management and organization skills, but ADHD symptoms can lead to late or missed appointments, failure to complete homework, and little progress on a treatment plan. Medication in conjunction with therapy can help bring ADHD symptoms under control through life coaching skills and counseling for underlying negative thoughts that can lead to procrastination and frustration, Ramsay says.

The public controversy about overmedication and overdiagnosis of ADHD is really a problem of misdiagnosis, which can result from quick visits to primary-care physicians, Ramsay says. "Some patients may get a diagnosis based on an all-too-brief evaluation and therefore may start treatment with a medication when maybe their symptoms are not a result of ADHD," he says. "Other people with ADHD may be misdiagnosed with some other mental disorder."

Stimulants on Campus

Several studies have shown that stimulants such as Ritalin or amphetamine salts (Adderall) are effective in treating ADHD in adults, but the drugs also can be abused, especially by college students who believe stimulants will boost their academic performance. In a survey of more than 1,800 students at the University of Kentucky, a third of the students reported they had illegally used ADHD stimulants, mainly by obtaining pills from fellow students with prescriptions. Most of the illegal users said the stimulants helped them stay up late and cram for exams, and they believed the drugs increased their reading comprehension, attention and memory. The study was published in 2008 in the Journal of American College Health.

Every college in the United States faces problems with misuse of ADHD stimulants, but most students with ADHD are not faking their symptoms to get medication, says Lorraine Wolf, PhD, a neuropsychologist and director of the Office of Disability Services at Boston University. "Most students with ADHD are serious, hard-working young people who struggle in a college environment, but with accommodations and support they are very successful," says Wolf, an assistant psychiatry professor who researches adult ADHD.

Wolf's office offers time management skills for students with ADHD and provides academic accommodations, including extra time on tests and computer use during exams to help with spelling and grammar. Students must provide extensive documentation of severe ADHD symptoms before accommodations will be granted, Wolf says. "People who come to college with symptoms are pretty much going to have ADHD for the rest of their lives," Wolf says. "People become more refined in how they deal with it. They just get better at handling ADHD."

Almost 5 percent of teenagers in the United States were prescribed stimulants to treat ADHD in 2008, compared with just 2.3 percent in 1996, suggesting that many children aren't outgrowing their symptoms, according to a study by the National Institutes of Health and the Agency for Healthcare Research and Quality. The study was published online in September in the American Journal of Psychiatry.

Some college students who illegally use stimulants may have undiagnosed ADHD, according to a study of 184 college students in northern Virginia, published this year in the Journal of Attention Disorders. The study found that 71 percent of the respondents who misused stimulants also screened positive for ADHD symptoms. Students who illegally used stimulants were seven times more likely to have ADHD symptoms than those who didn't misuse the drugs.

Meanwhile, those symptoms aren't always entirely bad. ADHD can have some beneficial aspects, including the ability to multitask, solve problems quickly and work with people, Wolf says.

Dummit, the criminal defense attorney in North Carolina, says he has embraced his ADHD and believes it helps him hyperfocus on detailed projects for short periods. He only takes a stimulant medication when he needs to concentrate for long stretches, such as during a trial. "I don't accept ADHD as an excuse for bad behavior, but I do try to talk openly about my strengths and weaknesses," he says.

Critical Thinking

1. What are some of the stereotypes that continue to persist concerning attention deficit hyperactivity disorder (ADHD)?

2. What is the linkage between someone having ADHD as a children but then also having ADHD as an adult?

3. What percentages of adults in the general population report that they experience ADHD symptoms?

Create Central

www.mhhe.com/createcentral

Internet References

10 problems that could mean adult ADHD
www.webmd.com/add-adhd/10-symptoms-adult-adhd

Attention Deficit Disorder (ADD/ADHD) test
http://psychcentral.com/addquiz.htm

BRENDAN L. SMITH is a writer in Washington, D.C.

Article　　　　Prepared by: Eric Landrum, *Boise State University*

The Roots of Mental Illness

How much of mental illness can the biology of the brain explain?

Kirsten Weir

Learning Outcomes

After reading this article, you will be able to:

- Understand the ongoing research that is linking the existence of mental illness to the malfunctioning of specific centers of the brain.

- Describe the risk of placing too much emphasis on the hardware (brain) rather than the software (mental processes) in the development of mental illness.

Diagnosing mental illness isn't like diagnosing other chronic diseases. Heart disease is identified with the help of blood tests and electrocardiograms. Diabetes is diagnosed by measuring blood glucose levels. But classifying mental illness is a more subjective endeavor. No blood test exists for depression; no X-ray can identify a child at risk of developing bipolar disorder. At least, not yet.

Thanks to new tools in genetics and neuroimaging, scientists are making progress toward deciphering details of the underlying biology of mental disorders. Yet experts disagree on how far we can push this biological model. Are mental illnesses simply physical diseases that happen to strike the brain? Or do these disorders belong to a class all their own?

Eric Kandel, MD, a Nobel Prize laureate and professor of brain science at Columbia University, believes it's all about biology. "All mental processes are brain processes, and therefore all disorders of mental functioning are biological diseases," he says. "The brain is the organ of the mind. Where else could [mental illness] be if not in the brain?"

That viewpoint is quickly gaining supporters, thanks in part to Thomas R. Insel, MD, director of the National Institute of Mental Health, who has championed a biological perspective during his tenure at the agency.

To Insel, mental illnesses are no different from heart disease, diabetes or any other chronic illness. All chronic diseases have behavioral components as well as biological components, he says. "The only difference here is that the organ of interest is the brain instead of the heart or pancreas. But the same basic principles apply."

A New Toolkit

Take cardiology, Insel says. A century ago, doctors had little knowledge of the biological basis of heart disease. They could merely observe a patient's physical presentation and listen to the patient's subjective complaints. Today they can measure cholesterol levels, examine the heart's electrical impulses with EKG, and take detailed CT images of blood vessels and arteries to deliver a precise diagnosis. As a result, Insel says, mortality from heart attacks has dropped dramatically in recent decades. "In most areas of medicine, we now have a whole toolkit to help us know what's going on, from the behavioral level to the molecular level. That has really led to enormous changes in most areas of medicine," he says.

Insel believes the diagnosis and treatment of mental illness is today where cardiology was 100 years ago. And like cardiology of yesteryear, the field is poised for dramatic transformation, he says. "We are really at the cusp of a revolution in the way we think about the brain and behavior, partly because of technological breakthroughs. We're finally able to answer some of the fundamental questions."

Indeed, in recent years scientists have made many exciting discoveries about the function—and dysfunction—of the human brain. They've identified genes linked to schizophrenia and discovered that certain brain abnormalities increase a person's risk of developing post-traumatic stress disorder after a distressing event. Others have zeroed in on anomalies associated with autism, including abnormal brain growth and underconnectivity among brain regions.

Researchers have also begun to flesh out a physiological explanation for depression. Helen Mayberg, MD, a professor of psychiatry and neurology at Emory University, has been actively involved in research that singled out a region of the brain—Brodmann area 25—that is overactive in people with depression. Mayberg describes area 25 as a "junction box" that interacts with other areas of the brain involved in mood, emotion and thinking. She has demonstrated that deep-brain stimulation of the area can alleviate symptoms in people with treatment-resistant depression (Neuron, 2005).

Maps of depression's neural circuits, Mayberg says, may eventually serve as a tool both for diagnosis and treatment.

Understanding the underlying biology, she adds, could help therapists and psychopharmacologists decide which patients would benefit from more intensive therapy, and which aren't likely to improve without medication. That would be a welcome improvement, she says. "Syndromes are so nonspecific by our current criteria that the best we can do now is flip a coin. We don't do that for any other branch of medicine," she says.

Yet despite the progress and promise of her research, Mayberg isn't ready to concede that all mental illnesses will one day be described in purely biological terms. "I used to think you could localize everything, that you could explain all the variants by the biology," she says. "I think in a perfect world you could, but we don't have the tools to explain all those things because we can't control for all of the variables."

One of the biggest problems, she says, is that mental illness diagnoses are often catchall categories that include many different underlying malfunctions. Mental illnesses have always been described by their outward symptoms, both out of necessity and convenience. But just as cancer patients are a wildly diverse group marked by many different disease pathways, a depression diagnosis is likely to encompass people with many unique underlying problems. That presents challenges for defining the disease in biological terms. "Depression does have patterns," Mayberg says. "The caveat is different cohorts of patients clearly have different patterns—and likely the need for different specific interventions."

Software Malfunction

When it comes to mental illness, a one-size-fits-all approach does not apply. Some diseases may be more purely physiological in nature. "Certain disorders such as schizophrenia, bipolar disorder and autism fit the biological model in a very clear-cut sense," says Richard McNally, PhD, a clinical psychologist at Harvard University and author of the 2011 book *"What is Mental Illness?"* In these diseases, he says, structural and functional abnormalities are evident in imaging scans or during postmortem dissection.

Yet for other conditions, such as depression or anxiety, the biological foundation is more nebulous. Often, McNally notes, mental illnesses are likely to have multiple causes, including genetic, biological and environmental factors. Of course, that's true for many chronic diseases, heart disease and diabetes included. But for mental illnesses, we're a particularly long way from understanding the interplay among those factors.

That complexity is one reason that experts such as Jerome Wakefield, PhD, DSW, a professor of social work and psychiatry at New York University, believe that too much emphasis is being placed on the biology of mental illness at this point in our understanding of the brain. Decades of effort to understand the biology of mental disorders have uncovered clues, but those clues haven't translated to improvements in diagnosis or treatment, he believes. "We've thrown tens of billions of dollars into trying to identify biomarkers and biological substrates for mental disorders," Wakefield says. "The fact is we've gotten very little out of all of that."

To be sure, Wakefield says, some psychological disorders are likely due to brain dysfunction. Others, however, may stem from a chance combination of normal personality traits. "In the unusual case where normal traits come together in a certain configuration, you may be maladapted to society," he says. "Call it a mental disorder if you want, but there's no smoking-gun malfunction in your brain."

You can think of the brain as a computer, he adds. The brain circuitry is equivalent to the hardware. But we also have the human equivalent of software. "Namely, we have mental processing of mental representations, meanings, conditioning, a whole level of processing that has to do with these psychological capacities," he says. Just as software bugs are often the cause of our computer problems, our mental motherboards can be done in by our psychological processing, even when the underlying circuitry is working as designed. "If we focus only at the brain level, we are likely to miss a lot of what's going on in mental disorders," he says.

The danger in placing too much attention on the biological is that important environmental, behavioral and social factors that contribute to mental illness may be overlooked. "By over-focusing on the biological, we are doing patients a disservice," Wakefield says. He sees a red flag in a study by Steven Marcus, PhD, and Mark Olfson, MD, that found the percentage of patients who receive psychotherapy for depression declined from 53.6 percent in 1998 to 43.1 percent in 2007, while rates of antidepressant use stayed roughly the same (*Archives of General Psychiatry*, 2010).

A Nuanced View

The emerging area of epigenetics, meanwhile, could help provide a link between the biological and other causes of mental illness. Epigenetics research examines the ways in which environmental factors change the way genes express themselves. "Certain genes are turned on or turned off, expressed or not expressed, depending on environmental inputs," McNally says.

One of the first classic epigenetics experiments, by researchers at McGill University, found that pups of negligent rat mothers were more sensitive to stress in adulthood than pups that had been raised by doting mothers (*Nature Neuroscience*, 2004). The differences could be traced to epigenetic markers, chemical tags that attach to strands of DNA and, in the process, turn various genes on and off. Those tags don't just affect individuals during their lifetime, however; like DNA, epigenetic markers can be passed from generation to generation. More recently, the McGill team studied the brains of people who committed suicide, and found those who had been abused in childhood had unique patterns of epigenetic tags in their brains (*Nature Neuroscience*, 2009). "Stress gets under the skin, so to speak," McNally says.

In McNally's view, there's little danger that mental health professionals will forget the importance of environmental factors to the development of mental illness. "I think what's happening is not a battle between biological and non-biological approaches, but an increasingly nuanced and sophisticated appreciation for the multiple perspectives that can illuminate the etiology of these conditions," he says.

Still, translating that nuanced view to improvements in diagnosis and treatment will take time. Despite decades of research on the causes and treatments of mental illness, patients are still suffering. "Suicide rates haven't come down. The rate of prevalence for many of these disorders, if anything, has gone up, not down. That tells you that whatever we've been doing is probably not adequate," Insel says.

But, he adds, there's good reason to hold out hope. "I think, increasingly, we'll understand behavior at many levels, and one of those will be physiological," Insel says. "That may take longer to translate into new therapies and new opportunities for patients, but it's coming."

In the meantime, according to Insel and Kandel, patients themselves are clamoring for better biological descriptions of mental disorders. Describing mental illnesses as brain malfunctions helps minimize the shame often associated with them, Kandel says. "Schizophrenia is a disease like pneumonia. Seeing it as a brain disorder destigmatizes it immediately."

Certainly, Kandel adds, social and environmental factors are undeniably important to understanding mental health. "But they do not act in a vacuum," he says. "They act in the brain."

It's too soon to say whether we'll someday have a blood test for schizophrenia or a brain scanning technique that identifies depression without any doubt. But scientists and patients agree: The more we understand about our brain and behavior, the better. "We have a good beginning of understanding of the brain," says Kandel, "but boy, have we got a long way to go."

Critical Thinking

1. If you believe that "all mental disorders are biological diseases," how might that influence your approach to treatment?

2. How does a biological model to mental illness help to describe conditions such as schizophrenia, bipolar disorder, and autism?

3. What is epigenetics, and how does its study contribute to our understanding of mental illness?

Create Central

www.mhhe.com/createcentral

Internet References

Five major mental disorders share genetic roots
www.nimh.nih.gov/news/science-news/2013/five-major-mental-disorders-share-genetic-roots.shtml

Origins of mental illness
www.minddisorders.com/Ob-Ps/Origin-of-mental-illnesses.html

KIRSTEN WEIR is a freelance writer in Minneapolis.

Unit 11

UNIT

Prepared by: Eric Landrum, *Boise State University*

Psychological Treatments

Have you ever had the nightmare of being trapped in a dark, dismal place and no one lets you out? Your pleas for freedom go unanswered and, in fact, are suppressed or ignored by domineering authority figures around you. You keep begging for mercy but to no avail.

You are fortunate to awake to the normal realities of your daily life. Have you ever wondered what would happen if we took perfectly normal individuals and institutionalized them in such a dark, dismal place? In one well-known and remarkable study, that is exactly what happened.

In 1973, eight individuals, including a pediatrician, a psychiatrist, and some psychologists, presented themselves to psychiatric hospitals. Each claimed that he or she was hearing voices. The voices, they reported, seemed unclear but appeared to be saying "empty" or "thud." Each of these individuals was admitted to a mental hospital, and most were diagnosed as being schizophrenic. After admission to the hospital, the "pseudopatients" or fake patients gave truthful information and thereafter acted like their usual, normal selves.

Their hospital stays lasted anywhere from 7 to 52 days. The nurses, doctors, psychologists, and other staff members treated them as if they were schizophrenic and never saw through their trickery. Some of the real patients in the hospital, however, recognized that the pseudopatients were perfectly normal. After their discharge, almost all of the pseudopatients received the diagnosis of "schizophrenic in remission," meaning that they were still diagnosed as schizophrenic, but they weren't exhibiting any of the symptoms at the time of release.

What does this classic study demonstrate about the diagnosis and treatment of mental illness? Is genuine mental illness readily detectable? If we can't always pinpoint mental disorders, how can we treat them appropriately? What treatments are available, and which treatments work better for various diagnoses? Although the diagnosis of schizophrenia is dramatic and often of interest to those studying psychology, what about the diagnosis and treatment of much more common disorders, such as depression or addiction?

The treatment of mental disorders is certainly challenging. As you probably know, not all individuals diagnosed as having a mental disorder are institutionalized. In fact, only a relatively small percentage of people suffering from one or more psychological disorders is confined to a mental institution. The most common treatments for mental disorders involve psychotherapy or counseling, medication, or some combination. Depending on the individual and the severity of his or her symptoms, the course of treatment may be relatively short (less than a year) or quite long (several years or more).

The array of available treatments is ever increasing and can be downright bewildering—and not just to the patient or client! Psychotherapists, clinical psychologists, and psychiatrists must weave their way through complicated sets of symptoms, identify the best diagnosis, and then suggest a course of treatment that seems to best address the client's problems in the context of complex healthcare delivery systems. In order to demystify and simplify your understanding of treatments and interventions for mental disorders, this unit presents some of these concepts.

Article   Prepared by: Eric Landrum, *Boise State University*

PTSD Treatments Grow in Evidence, Effectiveness

Several psychological interventions help to significantly reduce post-traumatic stress disorder symptoms, say new guidelines.

Tori DeAngelis

Learning Outcomes

After reading this article, you will be able to:

- Explain how psychologists approach the treatment of post-traumatic stress disorder.

- Summarize the effectiveness of various methods of treating post-traumatic stress disorder.

It's a bittersweet fact: Traumatic events such as the Sept. 11 attacks, Hurricane Katrina, and the wars in Iraq and Afghanistan have enabled researchers to learn a lot more about how best to treat post-traumatic stress disorder (PTSD).

"The advances made have been nothing short of outstanding," says Boston University psychologist Terence M. Keane, PhD, director of the behavioral science division of the National Center for Post-Traumatic Stress Disorder and a contributor to the original PTSD diagnosis. "These are very important times in the treatment of PTSD."

In perhaps the most important news, in November, the International Society for Traumatic Stress Studies (ISTSS), a professional society that promotes knowledge on severe stress and trauma, issued new PTSD practice guidelines. Using a grading system from "A" to "E," the guidelines label several PTSD treatments as "A" treatments based on their high degree of empirical support, says Keane, one of the volume's editors. The guidelines—the first since 2000—update and generally confirm recommendations of other major practice-related bodies, including the U.S. Department of Veterans Affairs (VA), the Department of Defense, the American Psychiatric Association, and Great Britain's and Australia's national health-care guidelines, he says.

In other PTSD-treatment advances, researchers are adding medications and virtual-reality simulations to proven treatments to beef up their effectiveness. Clinical investigators are also exploring ways to treat PTSD when other psychological and medical conditions are present, and they are studying specific populations such as those affected by the Sept. 11 attacks.

Though exciting, these breakthroughs are somewhat colored by an October Institute of Medicine (IoM) report that concludes there is still not enough evidence to say which PTSD treatments are effective, except for exposure therapies. Many experts, however, disagree with that conclusion, noting that a number of factors specific to the condition, such as high dropout rates, can lead to what may seem like imperfect study designs.

Treatments That Make a Difference

The fact that several treatments made the "A" list is great news for psychologists, says Keane. "Having this many evidence-based treatments allows therapists to use what they're comfortable with from their own background and training, and at the same time to select treatments for use with patients with different characteristics," he says.

Moreover, many of these treatments were developed by psychologists, he notes.

They include:

- **Prolonged-exposure therapy,** developed for use in PTSD by Keane, University of Pennsylvania psychologist Edna Foa, PhD, and Emory University psychologist Barbara O. Rothbaum, PhD. In this type of treatment, a therapist guides the client to recall traumatic memories in a controlled fashion so that clients eventually regain mastery of their thoughts and feelings around the incident. While exposing people to the very events that caused their trauma may seem counterintuitive, Rothbaum emphasizes that it's done in a gradual, controlled and repeated manner, until the person can evaluate their circumstances realistically and understand they can safely return to the activities in their current lives that they had been

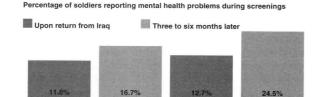

Percentage of soldiers reporting mental health problems during screenings

■ Upon return from Iraq   ■ Three to six months later

11.8%   16.7%   12.7%   24.5%

Active duty   Reserves

Delayed reaction. When troops returning from Iraq are screened a second time, the proportion who report mental health problem rises.

Source: *Journal of the American Medical Association*

avoiding. Drawing from PTSD best practices, the APA-initiated Center for Deployment Psychology includes exposure therapy in the training of psychologists and other health professionals who are or will be treating returning Iraq and Afghanistan service personnel.

- **Cognitive-processing therapy,** a form of cognitive behavioral therapy, or CBT, developed by Boston University psychologist Patricia A. Resick, PhD, director of the women's health sciences division of the National Center for PTSD, to treat rape victims and later applied to PTSD. This treatment includes an exposure component but places greater emphasis on cognitive strategies to help people alter erroneous thinking that has emerged because of the event. Practitioners may work with clients on false beliefs that the world is no longer safe, for example, or that they are incompetent because they have "let" a terrible event happen to them.

- **Stress-inoculation training,** another form of CBT, where practitioners teach clients techniques to manage and reduce anxiety, such as breathing, muscle relaxation and positive self-talk.

- **Other forms of cognitive therapy,** including cognitive restructuring and cognitive therapy.

- **Eye-movement desensitization and reprocessing,** or EMDR, where the therapist guides clients to make eye movements or follow hand taps, for instance, at the same time they are recounting traumatic events. It's not clear how EMDR works, and, for that reason, it's somewhat controversial, though the therapy is supported by research, notes Dartmouth University psychologist Paula P. Schnurr, PhD, deputy executive director of the National Center for PTSD.

- **Medications,** specifically selective serotonin reuptake inhibitors. Two in particular—paroxetine (Paxil) and sertaline (Zoloft)—have been approved by the Food and Drug Administration for use in PTSD. Other medications may be useful in treating PTSD as well, particularly when the person has additional disorders such as depression, anxiety or psychosis, the guidelines note.

Spreading the Word

So promising does the VA consider two of the "A" treatments—prolonged exposure therapy and cognitive-processing therapy—that it is doing national rollouts of them within the VA, notes psychologist Antonette Zeiss, PhD, deputy chief consultant for mental health at the agency.

"Enhancing our ability to provide veterans with the psycho-therapies for PTSD that have the strongest evidence base is one of our highest priorities," Zeiss says. In fact, the VA began training psychologists to provide the two approaches more than a year before the Institute of Medicine released its report of successful treatments, she says. "We're pleased that the report confirms our emphasis on this training."

The VA system's structure and philosophy make it possible to test the results of treatments in large, realistic samples—a clinical researcher's dream, notes Schnurr, who has conducted a number of such studies, most recently in a study of female veterans that led to the rollout out of prolonged exposure therapy. That study was reported in the Feb. 28, 2007, issue of *The Journal of the American Medical Association* (Vol. 297, No. 8, pages 820–830).

"The VA was able to support the science, so the research didn't just sit around in a journal and get discussed," Zeiss says. "They put money toward it, and they asked us to help them do a major rollout of the treatment."

Boosting Effectiveness

Meanwhile, other researchers are experimenting with add-ons to these proven treatments to increase their effectiveness. Some are looking at how virtual reality might enhance the effects of prolonged-exposure therapy. By adding virtual reality, whereby clients experience 3-D imagery, sounds and sometimes smells that correspond with a traumatic event, "we think it might be a good alternative for people who are too avoidant to do standard exposure therapy, because it puts them right there," says Emory University's Rothbaum.

Other researchers are adding a small dose of an old tuberculosis drug, D-cycloserine, or DCS, to treatment to see if it can mitigate people's fear reactions. Rothbaum's team, which includes psychologist Mike Davis, PhD, and psychiatrist Kerry Ressler, MD, PhD, have recently shown that the drug helps to extinguish fear in animals, so they're hoping for a similar effect in people.

In one study with veterans of the current Iraq war, Rothbaum's team is giving all participants a type of virtual reality that simulates combat conditions in Iraq, then randomizing them into a drug condition where they get DCS, a placebo, or the anti-anxiety drug alprazolam (Xanax).

In a similar vein, researchers at the Program for Anxiety and Traumatic Stress Studies at Weill Cornell Medical College are using virtual reality and DCS to treat those directly affected by the 2001 World Trade Center attacks, including civilians who were in the towers or nearby buildings, witnesses, and firefighters and police officers who were first responders.

Participants receive standard cognitive behavioral treatment enhanced with virtual reality, where they see graded versions

PTSD Treatments Demand More Study, Independent Panel Finds

Inserting a cautionary note in the enthusiasm about effective treatments for post-traumatic stress disorders (PTSD), an Institute of Medicine (IoM) panel concluded in October that only exposure therapies such as prolonged exposure and cognitive-processing therapy have enough evidence to recommend them for treatment. The independent review was requested by the Department of Veterans Affairs (VA).

"At this time, we can make no judgment about the effectiveness of most psychotherapies or about any medications in helping patients with PTSD," states Alfred O. Berg, MD, the University of Washington professor of family medicine who chaired the IoM committee. "These therapies may or may not be effective—we just don't know in the absence of good data."

In a review of 53 drug studies and 37 psychotherapy studies, the seven-member panel concluded that many PTSD studies are flawed in terms of design and high dropout rates, which limit their generalizablity. Moreover, most drug studies were funded by pharmaceutical companies, and many psychotherapy studies were conducted by people who developed the techniques or by their close collaborators, the report finds.

Besides listing a number of drugs that need more independent investigation, the panel asserted that the following psychotherapies need better evaluation:

- Eye-movement desensitization and reprocessing.
- Cognitive restructuring.
- Coping-skills training.
- Group psychotherapy.

This said, the findings shouldn't be interpreted to mean that exposure therapies are the only treatments that should be used to treat the condition, the report adds. The reports' authors do suggest, however, that Congress should provide resources to the VA and other federal agencies to fund high-quality PTSD research that includes veterans and other affected groups in research planning.

Psychologists expert in PTSD commended the committee for its critical review and the VA for commissioning the independent study. However, many believe the report is flawed in several ways, including that it fails to address the difficulties in conducting PTSD research and to take into account existing reviews and guidelines conducted by other independent bodies.

"I think [the IoM panel] raised the bar too high and they're not realistic about what PTSD is and how hard it is to study and to keep people in treatment," says PTSD expert Barbara O. Rothbaum, PhD, director of the Trauma and Anxiety Recovery Program at Emory University. "High dropout is endemic in PTSD."

Dartmouth Medical School psychologist Paula P. Schnurr, PhD, well-known for her rigorous, large-scale studies of PTSD populations, says that in her view, the literature "differs from the conclusions of the report, in that there's good evidence that a wider range of cognitive behavioral therapies are effective."

In addition, the panel's findings are at odds with many reviews already done in the field, Rothbaum says. As one example, the committee did not support the evidence base on any drug at all, even though the Food and Drug Administration has approved the selective serotonin reuptake inhibitors paroxetine (Paxil) and sertaline (Zoloft) to treat PTSD. "There have been a number of reviews out there, and none has concluded that only one intervention works," she says.

—T. DeAngelis

---

of a Twin Towers scenario, starting with simple images of the buildings on a sunny day, and progressing gradually to include the horrific sights and sounds of that day. They also randomly receive either a small dose of DCS or a placebo pill before each session.

While neither study is complete, the researchers say the treatments appear to significantly reduce participants' PTSD symptoms. Rothbaum has recently submitted a grant proposal for a study where she plans to compare traditional and virtual-reality exposure therapies—which hasn't yet been done—in combination with DCS or a placebo.

Addressing Comorbidity

Other psychologists are starting to think about ways to treat PTSD when it is accompanied by other psychiatric and health conditions. Psychologist John Otis, PhD, of Boston University and VA Boston, for instance, is testing an integrated treatment that aims to alleviate symptoms of both PTSD and chronic pain in Vietnam veterans and veterans of Operation Iraqi Freedom and Operation Enduring Freedom. The treatment combines aspects of cognitive processing therapy for trauma and cognitive behavioral therapy for chronic pain.

"We think these two conditions may interact in some [psychological] way that makes them more severe and challenging to treat," Otis says. In particular, he and others posit that "anxiety sensitivity"—fear of experiencing one's anxiety-related symptoms—may increase the odds that certain PTSD sufferers have more problems than others.

Again, while the study is not yet finished, results are encouraging, reports Otis. "Many of the veterans who are getting the integrated treatment are experiencing partial or complete remission of both kinds of symptoms," he says.

On a broader scale, the National Center for PTSD's Keane believes that much more research is needed on treating PTSD and psychiatric comorbidities such as depression, anxiety, substance abuse, personality disorders and psychosis—a common situation that escalates the more severe a person's PTSD symptoms are, he says.

He, for one, would like to examine possible applications to PTSD of the concept of a "unified protocol," a theory and methodology being developed by Boston University psychotherapy researcher David Barlow, PhD, to treat concurrent problems such as panic attacks, anxiety and phobias.

That said, the recent advances promise to help many more people suffering from a condition they did not bring on themselves, says Zeiss.

"While there is still more to learn, we have taken significant steps in developing treatments that have been shown to be effective and that will be increasingly provided both in VA and other mental health care settings," says Zeiss. "Those affected by combat stress and other traumas will be able to reach out for care without feeling ashamed or hopeless."

Critical Thinking

1. How do psychologists effectively treat individuals with post-traumatic stress disorder?

2. What is post-traumatic stress disorder, and how is it diagnosed?

3. How does the complication of co-morbidity make the treatment of post-traumatic stress disorder more difficult?

Create Central

www.mhhe.com/createcentral

Internet References

PTSD: Treatment efficacy and future directions
www.psychiatrictimes.com/articles/ptsd-treatment-efficacy-and
-future-directions

Most PTSD treatments not proven effective
www.washingtonpost.com/wp-dyn/content/article/2007/10/18/
AR2007101802186.html

Tori DeAngelis is a writer in Syracuse, N.Y.

Article   Prepared by: Eric Landrum, *Boise State University*

When Do Meds Make the Difference?

For most nonpsychotic conditions, empirically supported therapies and medications yield similarly good results, but therapy is better over the long haul, research finds.

TORI DEANGELIS

Learning Outcomes

After reading this article, you will be able to:

- Discuss the effectiveness of psychotherapy and drug therapy in the treatment of psychological disorders.

- Evaluate the effectiveness of psychotherapy and drug therapy in successfully treating mental disorders.

As new psychotropic drugs enter the marketplace, and more psychologists gain the ability to prescribe, an inevitable question arises: Are drugs, therapy or a combination the best form of treatment?

Research shows fairly consistent results: For most nonpsychotic disorders, behavioral interventions are just as effective as medications, and they hold up better over time.

"When researchers have directly compared empirically supported therapies with drugs in nonpsychotic populations, they hold their own very nicely," says Vanderbilt University depression expert Steven D. Hollon, PhD. Such therapies are also stronger in terms of enduring effects, he says. "People come away from treatment not only having their symptoms relieved, but learning something they can use the next time," he notes.

The British government, for one, is taking strong action with such findings: The United Kingdom's National Health Service is investing millions of dollars over the next few years to train more psychologists in evidence-based practices, making these interventions the treatment of choice over medications.

Meanwhile, research is continuing on combining drugs and therapy in treatment, and there, results are more mixed, says David H. Barlow, PhD, director of Boston University's Center for Anxiety and Related Disorders. In some cases, one treatment may boost the other. In other cases, there is no effect. Other times, combining the two may undermine an effective treatment. In addition, combination studies have been hobbled by theory and design problems, but research is

improving and eventually should lead to clearer outcomes, Barlow says.

As the research continues to unfold, practicing psychologists—whether they prescribe themselves or collaborate with physicians—should educate themselves on psychopharmacological findings, says Jeff Matranga, PhD, one of two psychologists at the group practice Health Psych Maine who has completed postdoctoral psychopharmacology training.

"It is critically important that we gain information about the relative merits of medications, psychotherapy, a combination or a sequence for a given clinical problem," says Matranga, who lectures frequently on the topic. "Thankfully, this type of research has been increasing, and it is quite valuable for the treating clinician to help guide treatment choices."

The Word on Depression

Research on depression shows that medications and empirically supported therapies such as cognitive behavioral therapy (CBT) and interpersonal therapy are equally effective, with each modality helping about 60 percent of clients, notes Hollon. Combined treatments produce even better results: In a literature review in the April 2005 *Journal of Clinical Psychiatry* (Vol. 66, No. 4, pages 455–468), Hollon and colleagues found that, in general, combining medication and therapy raised treatment effectiveness to as much as 75 percent.

"While that's not a huge increment in terms of the likelihood that someone will get better, you get a faster, more complete and more enduring response when you put drugs and therapy together," Hollon says.

One subgroup of depressed clients seems particularly amenable to combined treatment: severely and chronically depressed adults. One large multisite study was reported in the May 2000 *New England Journal of Medicine* (Vol. 342, No. 20, pages 1462–1470), and conducted by Brown University psychiatrist Martin B. Keller, MD, Virginia Commonwealth University psychologist James P. McCullough Jr., PhD, Stony Brook University psychologist Daniel Klein, PhD, and colleagues. In the study, researchers randomized patients with major depression either to a depression-focused CBT developed by McCullough, or to the antidepressant Serzone (nefazodone).

"The combination of the two was whoppingly more effective than either one alone," says Klein. About three-quarters responded to the combination, compared with about 48 percent for each individual condition. "People suffering from chronic depression often have longstanding interpersonal difficulties, and the virtue of combined treatment in this case may be that it simultaneously targets both depressive symptoms and social functioning," he says.

Weighing in on Anxiety Disorders

Likewise, large-scale studies on anxiety disorders find that people do equally well with medication or CBT, but that fewer people relapse with CBT than with medication, says Barlow, a lead researcher in the area. Unlike with depression, however, combined treatments don't seem to confer extra benefits, he notes.

> **"The ultimate positive circumstance is to have as many tools as you can."**
>
> —Richard G. Heimberg, Temple University

The same pattern holds true for social phobia, says Temple University's Richard G. Heimberg, PhD, who has conducted a number of studies in the area. "You might get a bigger short-term burst from medication, but CBT is about as effective, and it's also associated with better protection against relapse," he says.

A long-standing line of research on obsessive-compulsive disorder (OCD) that has tested therapy and medication interventions has yielded what is considered a "best practice" for the disorder: a cognitive behavioral treatment for OCD combining exposure and ritual prevention, known as EX/RP. In this line of research, University of Pennsylvania researcher Edna Foa, PhD, and colleagues have conducted systematic studies to identify the active ingredients of EX/RP. In one set of studies, the team compared separate components of EX/RP and found that exposure only and ritual prevention only were not as effective as the combination of the two. In another line of research, they compared the efficacy of the trycyclic antidepressant clomipramine with EX/RP. They found that EX/RP reduced symptoms more than clomipramine and that EX/RP improved the effects of clomipramine, but the reverse was not the case.

The results of these studies "show that EX/RP is the treatment of choice for OCD, both as a treatment by itself and as an augmentation to medication," says Foa. She has found similar results with children and adolescents, though a related study on young people at Duke University did find an optimal effect by combining the selective serotonin reuptake inhibitor (SSRI) Zoloft (sertraline) and EX/RP, she notes.

Foa and her colleagues are now looking at how to improve OCD treatment further. In a current study, for instance, they're exploring how adding different conditions and more time might

---

Combined-Treatment Research Gains Sophistication

Results of combined-treatment studies can be varied and confusing, as a result of methodology, researcher bias and patient characteristics, experts say. In fact, even the order in which you give treatments may make a difference, as may patients' treatment preference, notes Stony Brook University psychologist and depression researcher Daniel Klein, PhD.

Fortunately, research on combined treatments is becoming more sophisticated in design, theory and potential application, says David H. Barlow, PhD, director of Boston University's Center for Anxiety and Related Disorders. This evolution bodes well both for research and treatment, he believes.

The original studies on combined treatments tested drugs and therapy at the same time. The problem with this approach was a lack of theoretical rationale and hence a conflicting record of results. "No one provided a really good reason as to why these treatments might do better than one treatment alone," Barlow says.

A more sensible strategy that's being increasingly used examines "sequential" treatments, where researchers start with one treatment and either add or substitute a second one if the first isn't producing adequate results. This methodology promises to help tailor treatments and save money, Barlow says.

Now, researchers are launching what Barlow thinks may be the most effective research design yet: combining therapy with drugs developed specifically to work with a given psychological treatment—so-called "synergistic" treatments. For example, scientists are adding D-cycloserine—an old tuberculosis antibiotic recently shown to help extinguish fear in animals—as a complement to psychological treatments for conditions such as obsessive-compulsive disorder and post-traumatic stress disorder (PTSD). (See the January *Monitor* for its application to PTSD.)

Likewise, they're looking into possible applications of the hormone oxytocin to treat people with social anxiety, Barlow says. Traditionally used to stimulate labor and breastfeeding in women, oxytocin also helps to promote trust and bonding, which could help people with social anxiety overcome their fears, he notes.

—T. DeAngelis

---

influence outcome. In the first part of the study, they're examining what happens when they give OCD sufferers not responding well to an SSRI an additional treatment of either EX/RP or the antipsychotic medication risperidone. In the second part, they're extending the length of each additional treatment for those still not experiencing much symptom relief.

Real-World Considerations

Transporting such findings into the real world can, of course, be challenging. Unlike the relative purity of the lab, the treatment world is a teeming bazaar of providers—many of whom do not have the credentials or training of psychologists—turf issues, cost concerns and varying patient inclinations and needs, experts say.

In the provider domain, practitioners both in psychology and medicine often are not as up to date on empirically tested treatments as researchers, Hollon says. "There's a large discussion in the literature about how few people in the real world tend to practice therapies with empirical support, and the same thing is true with pharmacotherapy," he notes.

And, of course, not everyone has access to mental health care. Even if they do, says Foa, "It's not easy for people to find this treatment, because there aren't a lot of experts in the area."

Meanwhile, cost issues can prevent the most effective treatments from being used, those involved say. For instance, therapy may be more expensive up front, though studies show it is often more cost-effective over the long run, Matranga notes.

Insurers are sometimes more willing to pay for medications than for therapy, and some primary-care physicians are more likely to prescribe medications before therapy for a range of psychological conditions, he says, particularly if they don't have easy access to someone trained in these therapies.

Patient variables present a mystery in need of greater understanding as well, says Heimberg: Some people don't believe that "talking" can help, others are too anxious to try medications on one side or therapy on the other, and still others can't tolerate medication side effects, for example.

> **"There's a large discussion in the literature about how few people in the real world tend to practice therapies with empirical support, and the same thing is true with pharmacotherapy."**
>
> —Steven D. Hollon, Vanderbilt University

Likewise, research is beginning to show that clients' preferences make a huge difference in outcome, says Klein. "They're more willing to stick with and invest in something they believe will work," he notes.

Finally, drugs and therapy each carry pros and cons that need to be assessed when finding the right treatment for someone, Hollon says. With therapy, there's a learning curve; with drugs, there are side effects, he says.

Given that we're moving into an era where pharmacological and behavioral strategies will be increasingly used and blended, it's wise to be as informed as possible, Heimberg emphasizes.

"The ultimate positive circumstance," he says, "is to have as many tools as you can."

Critical Thinking

1. Is psychotherapy effective in treating psychological disorders? How does its effectiveness compare to the use of drugs in treating psychological disorders?

2. How does the effectiveness of psychotherapy compared to the use of drugs in treating psychological disorders?

3. Describe the process of a "sequential treatment" and how this methodology is being used to better understand psychotherapy effectiveness treatment.

Create Central

www.mhhe.com/createcentral

Internet References

Mental illness: Treatment and drugs
www.mayoclinic.com/health/mental-illness/DS01104/DSECTION=treatments-and-drugs

Anxiety disorders and effective treatment
www.apa.org/helpcenter/anxiety-treatment.aspx

TORI DEANGELIS is a writer in Syracuse, N.Y.

Article   Prepared by: Eric Landrum, *Boise State University*

More Support Needed for Trauma Intervention

Treatment for child trauma works, but too often, children don't have access to it.

BETH AZAR

Learning Outcomes

After reading this article, you will be able to:

- Describe the consequences and characteristics of children who suffer from abuse.

- Explain the concept of evidence-based treatment and provide some examples of successful evidence-based treatments for those suffering from child abuse.

In the wake of the Penn State sexual abuse scandal, legislators are looking for ways to protect children from abuse. Less than two weeks after Penn State officials were charged with perjury and failing to report suspected child abuse, Sen. Robert Casey Jr. (D-Pa.) introduced legislation that would pressure states to have and enforce laws requiring all adults to report suspected child abuse and neglect.

Decades of research spell out the long-term consequences that abuse can have for children. The ongoing CDC "Study of Adverse Childhood Experiences," for example, shows that children who are abused and neglected have an increased risk of severe mental and physical health problems, including post-traumatic stress disorder (/topics/ptsd/index.aspx), depression (/topics/depress/index.aspx), suicide (/topics/suicide/index.aspx), substance abuse (/topics/addiction/index.aspx), chronic obstructive pulmonary disease, ischemic heart disease and liver disease.

But just as important as identifying cases of abuse is supporting treatments that help victims recover. Psychologists have developed evidence-based interventions that can reduce the harmful effects of child abuse. The key is ensuring that all individuals who experience abuse have access to these evidence-based treatments, so they don't become victims for life, says psychologist Anthony Mannarino, PhD, vice chair of the department of psychiatry, Allegheny General Hospital, Pittsburgh, and professor of psychiatry at Drexel University College of Medicine.

"With treatment, these kids can have the resilience to overcome their experience," says Mannarino, who through APA submitted written testimony to a Dec. 13 hearing on child abuse held by the Senate Health, Education, Labor and Pensions Subcommittee on Children and Families. "Being a victim doesn't have to become who they are or how they define themselves. But if they don't get help and their families don't participate, they can have long-standing difficulties."

Scope of the Problem

The Penn State case serves to remind the public that child abuse is all too common in the United States. Although estimates vary greatly depending on the source, the Fourth National Incidence Study of Child Abuse and Neglect, released in 2010, found that in 2005–06, one child in 25 in the United States, or 2.9 million children, experienced some kind of abuse or neglect. Most of those children—77 percent—were neglected. Of the 29 percent of those children who were abused, 57 percent were physically abused, 36 percent were emotionally abused and 22 percent were sexually abused.

Estimates of the percentage of abused children who will suffer long-term consequences vary widely. One review of research on child maltreatment—including physical and sexual abuse as well as neglect—published in the 2004 "Posttraumatic Stress Disorder In Children and Adolescents: Handbook," found that PTSD rates ranged from 20 percent to 63 percent. In her studies, psychologist Sheree Toth, PhD, director of the Mt. Hope Family Center in Rochester, N.Y., and associate professor at the University of Rochester, finds that as many as 90 percent of maltreated infants have insecure or disorganized attachment. "The bright side is that there are evidence-based treatments that can dramatically improve the prognosis for these kids," says Toth. "We've shown that with intervention we can greatly decrease rates of insecure and disorganized attachment."

Interventions That Work

A study published in 2006 in Development and Psychopathology by Toth and her colleagues showed that before intervention, 90 percent of a group of 137 maltreated infants had disorganized attachment and only one infant had secure attachment. Of the 50 infants who subsequently received one of two evidence-based therapies—infant-parent psychotherapy or a psychoeducational parenting intervention—58 percent had secure attachment a year later. In comparison, only one child among the 54 who received the standard treatment available in the community had secure attachment a year later.

Other researchers have shown positive results using evidence-based treatments to decrease the incidence of PTSD, depression, aggression and other behavioral problems seen in abused children. Mannarino, for example, has spent more than 25 years developing and testing an intervention called Trauma-Focused Cognitive Behavioral Therapy (TFCBT) to treat children age 3 and older who have post-traumatic stress symptoms from abuse. In 12 to 16 sessions, children and their non-offending parents or caregivers learn about the specific effects trauma can have on emotions and behavior, and develop skills to manage their emotional distress, including relaxation techniques and how to use words to express their feelings.

In addition, the therapists help the children construct a narrative about their experience. "We talk about the idea of making the unspeakable speakable," says Mannarino. "By showing them that it's OK to talk about it, it makes the experience less overwhelming."

Many child abuse experts agree that, to date, TF-CBT has a strong base of empirical support as an intervention to treat trauma in children, with 10 randomized controlled trials, all showing its effectiveness. The studies show that as many as 85 percent of children treated with TF-CBT get markedly better on measures of shame, PTSD and depression, says Mannarino. Parents improve as well, showing less depression and emotional distress, better parenting skills and having a better outlook for the future.

Another highly regarded intervention is Alternatives for Families: A Cognitive Behavioral Therapy (AF-CBT), whose senior developer is David Kolko, PhD, professor of psychiatry, psychology and pediatrics at the University of Pittsburgh School of Medicine. AFCBT is designed to address individual and family involvement in conflict, coercion and aggression, including hostility and anger, mild physical force and child physical abuse. Its focus on physical abuse includes joint and individual work involving the alleged perpetrator—in most cases abusing parents or caregivers—and the child at various times throughout treatment. Working with the adult offender makes treatment complicated clinically, says Kolko, and may require additional time, but his team sees good results from this integrated approach.

Kolko also directs a program that provides services to the adolescent sexual offender, called Services for Adolescent and Family Enrichment. His program—which is funded by the local court system—has kept data on more than 250 cases and finds a two-year recidivism rate of only 1.5 percent, he says.

Unfortunately, access to these evidence-based treatments for child abuse is "pitiful," says Toth. Because researchers have developed them in university settings, they're mostly available near big medical centers. In addition, only 45 percent of graduate programs and 51 percent of internships that train psychology students to treat abused or otherwise traumatized children use TFCBT, according to two studies published in December in *Psychological Trauma:* Theory, Research, Practice, and Policy and Training and Education in Professional Psychology.

That's why Mannarino is putting much of his efforts these days into training and dissemination of TF-CBT around the country.

"Despite our ability to treat these kids, the real truth is that most kids who are abused are never properly treated," says Mannarino. "They grow up bearing the scars of unfortunate victimizations and wind up having serious adult problems, including depression, psychiatric hospitalizations and a general overuse of health services because they didn't get the help they needed."

Critical Thinking

1. What are some of the long-term consequences for abused children?

2. Describe the role that resilience can play in providing effective treatment for child abuse victims.

3. When child abuse victims are not treated as children, what are some of the potential long-term problems due to lack of treatment?

Create Central

www.mhhe.com/createcentral

Internet References

Treatment for traumatized children, youth, and families
      www.childwelfare.gov/responding/treatment.cfm
Grief and trauma intervention for children
      www.nrepp.samhsa.gov/ViewIntervention.aspx?id=259

BETH AZAR is a writer in Portland, Ore.

Yes, Recovery Is Possible

APA is participating in a new federally funded initiative designed to spread the word that people can—and do—recover from mental illnesses.

Rebecca A. Clay

Learning Outcomes

After reading this article, you will be able to:

- Differentiate between the typical recovery expectations from individuals who suffer from a heart attack (or other chronic illness) vs. those who suffer from the onset of a mental illness.

- Describe how the focus on a wellness or recovery approach differs from the current traditional treatment approach exhibited by psychologists.

Peter Ashenden was determined not to let his severe depression keep him from finishing his college degree and getting a job. The clinical staff at the day facility where he was receiving treatment in the 1980s had a different idea: a sheltered workshop for people with disabilities. "The workshop was putting caps on lipstick tubes for six hours a day," remembers Ashenden, who now directs consumer and family affairs at the insurance company Optum Health.

To Ashenden, that's a perfect example of what happens when a mental health system hasn't embraced the idea that people can recover from mental illnesses. Now, as part of a team at APA devoted to an initiative called Recovery to Practice, he's working to ensure that psychologists get the training they need to help people with mental health conditions live meaningful lives in the community and achieve their full potential.

Funded by the Substance Abuse and Mental Health Services Administration (SAMHSA), the five-year initiative has a dual mission: to create an online repository of resources on recovery principles and practices and to develop recovery-focused training for mental health professionals.

APA is one of five national mental health organizations to partner with SAMHSA; the other grantees include the American Psychiatric Association, American Psychiatric Nurses Association, Council on Social Work Education and National Association of Peer Specialists. Like the other organizations, APA will share resources and develop a recovery-oriented curriculum that will be used to train its constituency.

"SAMHSA has made Recovery to Practice a priority, and I am pleased that APA is one of the organizations involved in moving this initiative forward," says Gwendolyn P. Keita, PhD, executive director of APA's Public Interest Directorate (/pi/index.aspx). "Recovery is a growing movement, and it is important that psychologists are involved."

Research Changes Minds

"Until fairly recently, it was assumed that people with serious mental illness would never recover," says Mary A. Jansen, PhD, who chairs APA's Task Force on Serious Mental Illness and Severe Emotional Disturbance and is a member of the Recovery Advisory Committee that guides APA's Recovery to Practice initiative. "Individuals were often warehoused in state mental institutions."

When new medications allowed many of those people to return to their communities, most psychologists and other mental health practitioners still believed they would never regain full functioning, says Jansen, director of Bayview Behavioral Consulting in Vancouver. Then research by psychologists and others in the 1970s began to show that people could recover, and individuals with serious mental illnesses began to advocate for services that would help them achieve recovery.

By 2003, mental health recovery had become the overarching goal of President George W. Bush's New Freedom Commission on Mental Health. The commission's 2003 report, *Achieving the Promise: Transforming Mental Health Care in America*, argued that the nation's mental health system was broken and identified the major flaw as the lack of a vision of recovery. The commission also laid out a challenge: "We envision a future when everyone with a mental illness will recover, a future when mental illnesses can be prevented or cured, a future when mental illnesses are detected early and a future when everyone with a mental illness at any stage of life has access to effective treatment and supports—essentials for living, working, learning and participating fully in the community."

Now the Recovery to Practice initiative is working to make that vision a reality.

"It's really no different than if you have a heart attack or another chronic illness," says Jansen. "Once you recover from the acute stage, you generally begin a recovery process, with a team of professionals and interventions all working toward helping you get back to the highest level of functioning you can achieve." Now the push is on to get that same focus on rehabilitation into the mental health field and into the mainstream of psychology, says Jansen.

"In the late 1970s into the 1990s, interventions were specifically designed for people with serious mental illnesses, many of whom had lost considerable functioning in part because they had languished in environments where no one believed they could do anything," she says.

In the same way that cardiologists might encourage heart attack patients to stop smoking, start exercising and work on lowering their cholesterol, she says, psychologists and others committed to a recovery-oriented approach now use psychosocial rehabilitation interventions to assist people with mental health conditions. These services, says Jansen, are designed to involve individuals in a partnership with professionals as they try to gain—or regain—a meaningful life, however they define it.

That recovery-oriented approach shouldn't just be used with people who have severe depression, schizophrenia, bipolar disorder and other serious mental illnesses, adds Jansen. It's also useful for any mental health condition that keeps someone from functioning as well as he or she could.

In 2009, APA's Council of Representatives passed a resolution endorsing the concept of recovery for people with serious mental illness. "This resulted from a commitment by APA's Committee for the Advancement of Professional Practice (CAPP) (/practice/leadership/capp/index.aspx) to place increased emphasis on recovery within psychology practice," says Katherine C. Nordal, PhD, executive director for APA's Practice Directorate.

But the recovery movement hasn't become well integrated into psychology yet, says Andrew T. Austin Daily, the APA staffer who directs the association's Recovery to Practice project.

An analysis by APA staff, the Recovery Advisory Committee and APA's Committee for Assessment and Training in Recovery revealed multiple economic, political, social and technological barriers to integrating recovery into psychology. One obstacle is inadequate reimbursement for providing recovery-related services. Some psychologists are reluctant to change their practice orientation; others may fear people with serious mental illnesses. There's a shortage of affordable housing options, supported employment programs and other services that psychologists can point patients to as they begin re-integrating into their communities. And because few training standards and best practices exist, psychologists simply may not know how to use this orientation to facilitate their clients' recovery.

"The big challenge is addressing psychologists' perceptions of recovery and how it impacts their work," says APA 2011 President Melba J.T. Vasquez, PhD. "But another challenge that APA really cares about is getting recovery into education and training: It's important for both our students in graduate doctoral programs but also for our current providers to learn these recovery concepts and principles and put them into practice."

Working with a recovery mindset is very different from what psychologists traditionally do, adds Vasquez. For example, in therapy sessions with the mother of a son with serious mental illness, Vasquez didn't just focus on helping to ease her distress. She also reached out to a social worker and others in the community to help the woman find housing and a job for her son. "Working collaboratively with others in the community is important," says Vasquez, "and we're not usually trained to work that way."

Training Materials

To help psychologists get that training, APA's Recovery to Practice team is developing a curriculum for doctoral psychology training programs that emphasizes recovery outcomes and explains recovery-related principles and practices.

"This process should be greatly facilitated by the tremendous work of CAPP's Task Force on Serious Mental Illness and Severe Emotional Disturbance, which spent years developing and revising the *Catalog of Clinical Training Opportunities: Best Practices for Recovery and Improved Outcomes for People with Serious Mental Illness,*" says Nordal.

Still in draft form, the curriculum features more than a dozen modules on such topics as the recovery movement's history, the scientific foundations of recovery, health disparities, ethics and how to incorporate recovery principles into such tasks as clinical assessment, treatment planning and interventions.

The APA team will spend the next year developing the curriculum and plans to have it ready for pilot testing by the end of next summer. The hope is to have three or four graduate training directors incorporate the curriculum into their programs and provide feedback. The Recovery to Practice team will then modify the curriculum as needed and either do another round of pilot testing or move ahead with working with the psychology training councils on dissemination and marketing.

APA also plans to go beyond the SAMHSA-funded project in its efforts to spread the word on recovery. In addition to the curriculum for graduate students, APA will develop versions for use in internship programs as well as continuing-education programs for psychologists already in practice.

For Jansen, the focus on recovery is especially timely given the roll-out of health-care reform.

"Health-care reform is all about promoting wellness: getting people to be as healthy and productive members of society as they can be," she says, adding that this will ultimately reduce costs. "If psychology as a profession doesn't embrace the notion of recovery and the need to train psychologists in the rehabilitative interventions needed to assist people to recover, psychology will likely be left behind."

Critical Thinking

1. If you don't believe that individuals can recover from mental illness, what are some of the ramifications of that belief for those with mental illness? What are their life prospects under that scenario?

2. How might the mindset of a psychologist differ when working toward a treatment goal vs. a recovery goal?

3. How might the education and training of current psychology graduate students be modified to encourage more of a recovery/wellness orientation?

Create Central

www.mhhe.com/createcentral

Internet References

Psychology is a behavioral and mental health profession
www.apa.org/about/gr/issues/health-care/profession.aspx

Discover and recover: Resources for mental and overall wellness
http://discoverandrecover.wordpress.com/mental-health-freedom
-and-recovery-act

REBECCA A. CLAY, is a writer in Washington, D.C.

Article   Prepared by: Eric Landrum, *Boise State University*

Addiction Interaction, Relapse and Recovery

CHERYL KNEPPER

Learning Outcomes

After reading this article, you will be able to:

- Articulate the definition of an addiction.

- Identify some of the potential screening tools in identifying addictions.

Substance abuse and dependence rarely occur in a vacuum. Today's addict is faced with a multitude of issues that may co-exist and compromise recovery. Co-existing addictions/compulsive behaviors such as drugs and alcohol, pathological gambling, sex, food, work, internet and gaming can become chronic and progressive if left unidentified and untreated. Many of these addictions don't only coexist, but interact, reinforce and fuse together becoming part of a package known as Addiction Interaction. The term "Addiction Interaction Disorder" was introduced by Patrick Carnes PhD in 2011.

Caron Treatment Centers conducted a research study among adult patients with drug and alcohol addictions to determine what percentage may be at risk for sex and love addiction. The 485 participants were given the SAST-R (Sexual Addiction Screening Tool-Revised a 45 item forced choice (Yes/No) instrument) (Carnes, Green & Carnes, 2010). The findings of this study indicated that 21 percent of individuals being treated for primary substance dependence scored at risk. Another interesting finding from the study showed a higher percentage of cannabis, cocaine and amphetamine abuse or dependence diagnosis in the individuals that scored at-risk for sexual addiction. In addition, at-risk individuals had higher percentages of mood disorder, PTSD and eating disorder diagnoses.

ASAM's definition of addiction is a primary, chronic disease of the brain reward, motivation, memory and related circuitry. Dysfunction in these circuits leads to characteristic biological, psychological, social and spiritual manifestations. This is reflected in an individual pathologically pursuing reward and/or relief by substance use and other behaviors. The neural pathways are altered when drugs or other compulsive addictive behaviors exist. Changes in the neural plasticity occur which alters the brain wiring. Neurons that fuse together wire together which creates an interaction of addictions. When the pleasurable or reward-driven behavior stops, there is a decrease of dopamine (and possibly other neuro-transmitters depending on what the behavioral effect is), therefore causing a sensation of a "crash" or withdrawal, compelling the person to re-engage in the original euphoric behavior (Milkman & Sunderwirth, 1987).

Pleasurable, reward-driven behaviors can serve to self-medicate, fuse, or replace each other just like substances interact. For example, alcoholism is put into remission, and gambling addiction substitutes the absence of alcohol; this is known as "Replacement." This puts the individual at high risk for relapse back to drug of choice. Another process known as "Fusion" occurs when two or more addictive behaviors develop into one episode. For example, when sex and cocaine are combined, the individual cannot engage in either addictive behavior without the other addiction present. This cycle repeats over and over. Addictions can cycle back and forth in a patterned and systematic way, which leaves the co-addicted individual at higher risk for relapse.

The addictive behavior of one addiction can serve as a ritual pattern to engage another. Actions such as buying and preparing drugs can activate the pleasure center of the brain. Alterations in the reward center of the brain could lead to distorted perceptions about people, places, and things, as well as interfere with the brain's ability to process feelings. Furthermore, circuits in the brain found in the reward center have routes to the part of the brain that affect memory, judgment, and our intellect. If all of a patient's addictions are not addressed during treatment, their likelihood of relapsing is much greater. An integrated approach is best. This approach takes a thorough look at what other compulsive behaviors or addictions may be contributing to one's chemical addiction and provides the individual with a broader understanding of potential risk factors.

During a patient's stay at Caron, we use multiple screening tools such as the Minnesota Multiphasic Personality Inventory-2 Restructured Form (MMPI-2-RF), the Sexual Addiction Screening Test—Revised (SAST-R), Sexual Dependency Inventory—R 4 (SDI-R 4.0), South Oaks Gambling Screen-Revised (SOGS-R) and Eating Attitudes Test-26 (EAT-26). Patients are given these screens and assessments if they endorse certain behavioral questions during the psychosocial interview, but can be given a little further into treatment when patients start to be more honest and open about themselves. From these assessments, there is a clearer picture of the addictions and disorders from which the patient suffers.

Because of the interactive nature of multiple addictions, it is necessary to use an integrated multidisciplinary treatment approach. Caron has certified and licensed addictions experts from an array of disciplines: addictions counselors, psychologists, psychiatrists, spiritual counselors, nutritionists, medical team of nurses and physicians. The treatment philosophy at Caron is built on the foundation of the 12 Steps and evidence based practices; for example, CBT (Cognitive Behavioral Therapy), Mindfulness Practice and MI (Motivational Interviewing). In addition, patients are offered specialty groups such as Addiction Interaction groups and tasks, 12 Step lecture series, Family of Origin group, Seeking Safety group, Parenting, Body Image, Grief and Loss. While patient treatment will vary depending on each individual's circumstances, it is important to make them aware if multiple addictions co-exist. Additionally, psycho-education helps patients work through shame and "normalize" behavior based on their history. It is also essential to identify relapse triggers, high-risk situations, relapse signs and symptoms, repetitive patterns and relapse thinking and develop interventions to address these issues along with an integrated continuing care plan.

Patients and their family members are encouraged as part of the treatment process to attend the 5-day Family Education Program which is didactic and experiential in design. The goal is to educate and assist the family in understanding the disease of addiction while providing support and encouragement for their part of the recovery process.

The goal is to give the individual and their family the gift of Recovery for Life!

Critical Thinking

1. There are many different types of addictions beyond those we stereotypically think of, such as drug addiction and alcohol addiction. Can someone be addicted to the Internet? Can someone be addicted to swimming pools? Explain your answer to both of these questions.

2. What are the relationships between drug and alcohol addiction and sex and love addiction? If a person has one addiction, is he or she more likely to have another addiction? Explore this possibility and explain your answer.

Create Central

www.mhhe.com/createcentral

Internet References

A relapse prevention plan: The tools of recovery
    www.addictionsandrecovery.org/relapse-prevention.htm
Is relapse a normal part of recovery?
    www.familyrecoverysolutions.com/articles/relapse

Article   Prepared by: Eric Landrum, *Boise State University*

Post-Prozac Nation: The Science and History of Treating Depression

SIDDHARTHA MUKHERJEE

Learning Outcomes

After reading this article, you will be able to:

- Understand the effects of taking Prozac from the perspective of someone who has taken Prozac.

- Articulate the current status of the serotonin hypothesis of depression.

Few medicines, in the history of pharmaceuticals, have been greeted with as much exultation as a green-and-white pill containing 20 milligrams of fluoxetine hydrochloride—the chemical we know as Prozac. In her 1994 book *Prozac Nation,* Elizabeth Wurtzel wrote of a nearly transcendental experience on the drug. Before she began treatment with antidepressants, she was living in "a computer program of total negativity . . . an absence of affect, absence of feeling, absence of response, absence of interest." She floated from one "suicidal reverie" to the next. Yet, just a few weeks after starting Prozac, her life was transformed. "One morning I woke up and really did want to live. . . . It was as if the miasma of depression had lifted off me, in the same way that the fog in San Francisco rises as the day wears on. Was it the Prozac? No doubt."

Like Wurtzel, millions of Americans embraced antidepressants. In 1988, a year after the Food and Drug Administration approved Prozac, 2,469,000 prescriptions for it were dispensed in America. By 2002, that number had risen to 33,320,000. By 2008, antidepressants were the third-most-common prescription drug taken in America.

Fast forward to 2012 and the same antidepressants that inspired such enthusiasm have become the new villains of modern psychopharmacology—overhyped, overprescribed chemicals, symptomatic of a pill-happy culture searching for quick fixes for complex mental problems. In *The Emperor's New Drugs,* the psychologist Irving Kirsch asserted that antidepressants work no better than sugar pills and that the clinical effectiveness of the drugs is, largely, a myth. If the lodestone book of the 1990s was Peter Kramer's near-ecstatic testimonial, *Listening to Prozac,* then the book of the 2000s is David Healy's

Let Them Eat Prozac: The Unhealthy Relationship Between the Pharmaceutical Industry and Depression.

In fact, the very theory for how these drugs work has been called into question. Nerve cells—neurons—talk to one another through chemical signals called neurotransmitters, which come in a variety of forms, like serotonin, dopamine and norepinephrine. For decades, a central theory in psychiatry has been that antidepressants worked by raising serotonin levels in the brain. In depressed brains, the serotonin signal had somehow been "weakened" because of a chemical imbalance in neurotransmitters. Prozac and Paxil were thought to increase serotonin levels, thereby strengthening the signals between nerve cells—as if a megaphone had been inserted in the middle.

But this theory has been widely criticized. In *The New York Review of Books,* Marcia Angell, a former editor of *The New England Journal of Medicine,* wrote: "After decades of trying to prove [the chemical-imbalance theory], researchers have still come up empty-handed." Jonathan Rottenberg, writing in *Psychology Today,* skewered the idea thus: "As a scientific venture, the theory that low serotonin causes depression appears to be on the verge of collapse. This is as it should be; the nature of science is ultimately to be self-correcting. Ideas must yield before evidence."

Is the "serotonin hypothesis" of depression really dead? Have we spent nearly 40 years heading down one path only to find ourselves no closer to answering the question how and why we become depressed? Must we now start from scratch and find a new theory for depression?

Science may be self-correcting, but occasionally it overcorrects—discarding theories that instead need to be rejuvenated. The latest research suggests that serotonin is, in fact, central to the functioning of mood, although its mechanism of action is vastly more subtle and more magnificent than we ever imagined. Prozac, Paxil and Zoloft may never turn out to be the "wonder drugs" that were once advertised. But they have drastically improved our understanding of what depression is and how to treat it.

Our modern conception of the link between depression and chemicals in the brain was sparked quite by accident in the middle of the last century. In the autumn of 1951, doctors treating tubercular patients at Sea View Hospital on Staten Island with a new drug—iproniazid—observed sudden transformations in their patients' moods and behaviors. The wards—typically glum and silent, with moribund, lethargic patients—were "bright last week with the happy faces of men and women," a journalist wrote. Patients laughed and joked in the dining hall, as if a dark veil of grief had lifted. Energy flooded back and appetites returned. Many, ill for months, demanded five eggs for breakfast and then consumed them with gusto. When Life magazine sent a photographer to the hospital to investigate, the patients could no longer be found lying numbly in their beds: they were playing cards or dancing in the corridors.

If the men and women at Sea View were experiencing an awakening, then a few hundred miles south, others at Duke's hospital encountered its reverse. In 1954, a 28-year-old woman was prescribed Raudixin to control her blood pressure. A few months later, she returned to the hospital, complaining of crying spells, dullness and lethargy. She felt futile, guilty and hopeless, she told her doctors. A few months later, when she returned, the sense of futility had turned into hostility. A 42-year-old woman prescribed Raudixin told her doctor that "God would cause her to become insane" before she could repent. The "feeling blue," as another patient described it, persisted until the drug was discontinued. At another hospital, one patient treated with Raudixin attempted suicide. Several people had to be admitted to psychiatric wards and administered electroconvulsive therapy before the symptoms were alleviated.

Psychiatrists and pharmacologists were quick to note these bizarre case reports. How, they wondered, could simple, seemingly unrelated chemicals like Raudixin or iproniazid produce such profound and opposite effects on mood? It was around this same time that scientists were learning that the brain itself was immersed in a soup of chemicals. In the early part of the century, scientists wondered how nerve cells talked to one another. By the late 1960s, evidence suggested that signals between neurons were carried by several chemicals, including the neurotransmitter serotonin. Might iproniazid and Raudixin have altered the levels of some neurotransmitters in the brain, thereby changing brain signaling and affecting mood? Strikingly so, scientists found. Raudixin—the "feeling blue" drug—drastically lowered the concentration of serotonin and closely related neurotransmitters in the brain. Conversely, drugs known to increase euphoria, like iproniazid, increased those levels.

These early findings led psychiatrists to propose a radical new hypothesis about the cause and treatment of depression. Depression, they argued, was a result of a "chemical imbalance" of neurotransmitters in the brain. In the normal brain, serotonin shuttled between mood-maintaining neurons, signaling their appropriate function. In the depressed brain, this signal had somehow gone wrong. The writer Andrew Solomon once evocatively described depression as a "flaw in love"—and certainly, the doctors using Raudixin at Duke had seen that flaw emerge grimly in real time: flaws in self-love (guilt, shame, suicidal thoughts), love for others (blame, aggression, accusation), even the extinction of a desire for love (lethargy, withdrawal, dullness). But these were merely the outer symptoms of

a deeper failure of neurotransmitters. The "flaw in love" was a flaw in chemicals.

Powerful vindication for this theory came from the discovery of new medicines that specifically elevated serotonin concentrations. The first such drug, Zimelidine, was created by a Swedish researcher, Arvid Carlsson. Following Carlsson's lead, pharmaceutical chemists threw their efforts and finances into finding serotonin-enhancing drugs, and the new giants of the antidepressant world were born in rapid succession. Prozac was created in 1974. Paxil appeared in 1975, Zoloft in 1977 (the trade names were introduced years later).

In 2003, in Boston, I began treating a 53-year-old woman with advanced pancreatic cancer. Dorothy had no medical problems until she developed an ominous sign known to every cancer specialist: painless jaundice, the sudden yellowing of skin without any associated pinch of discomfort. Painless jaundice can have many causes, but the one that oncologists know best, and fear most, is pancreatic cancer.

In Dorothy's case, the mass in the pancreas turned out to be large and fist-shaped, with malignant extensions that reached backward to grip blood vessels, and a solitary metastasis in the liver. Surgical removal was impossible, chemotherapy the only option.

The suddenness of the diagnosis struck her like an intravenous anaesthetic, instantly numbing everything. As we started chemotherapy in the hospital, she spent her mornings in bed sleeping or staring out of the window at the river below. Most disturbing, I watched as she lapsed into self-neglect. Her previously well-kept hair grew into a matted coil. The clothes that she had worn to the hospital remained unchanged. There were even more troubling signs: tiny abrasions in the skin that were continuously picked at, food left untouched by the bedside table and a gradual withdrawal of eye contact. One morning, I walked into what seemed like a daily emotional flare-up: someone had moved a pillow on the bed, Dorothy had been unable to sleep and it was somehow her son's fault.

This grief, of course, was fully provoked by the somberness of her diagnosis—to *not* grieve would have been bizarre in these circumstances—but she recognized something troubling in her own reaction and begged for help. I contacted a psychiatrist. With her consent, we prescribed Prozac.

In the first weeks, we waited watchfully, and nothing happened. But when I saw her again in the clinic after a month and a half, there were noticeable changes. Her hair was clean and styled. Her cuts had disappeared, and her skin looked good. Yet she still felt sad beyond measure, she said. She spent her days mostly in bed. The drug certainly affected many of the symptoms of depression, yet had not altered the subjective "feeling" of it. It healed the flaws in her skin but not all the flaws in love.

Any sane reader of this case would argue that a serotonin imbalance was not the initiating cause of Dorothy's depression; it was, quite evidently, the diagnosis of a fatal disease. Should we be searching for a chemical cause and cure when the provocation of grief is so apparent?

Pause for a moment, though, to consider the physiology of a heart attack. A heart attack can be set off by a variety of causes—chronic high blood pressure or pathologically high levels of "bad" cholesterol or smoking. Yet aspirin is an effective treatment of a heart attack regardless of its antecedent cause. Why? Because a heart attack, however it might have been provoked, progresses through a common, final pathway: there must be a clot in a coronary artery that is blocking the flow of blood to the heart. Aspirin helps to inhibit the formation and growth of the clot in the coronary artery. The medicine is clinically effective regardless of what events led to the clot. "Aspirin," as a professor of mine liked to put it, "does not particularly care about your medical history."

Might major depression be like a heart attack, with a central common pathway and with serotonin as its master regulator? There was certainly precedent in the biology of the nervous system for such unifying pathways—for complex mental states triggered by simple chemicals. Fear, for instance, was found to involve a common hormonal cascade, with adrenaline as the main player, even though its initiators (bears, spiders or in-laws) might have little resemblance to one another.

But such a line of inquiry can't tell us whether the absence of serotonin *causes* depression. For that, we need to know if depressed men and women have measurably lower levels of serotonin or serotonin-metabolites (byproducts of serotonin breakdown), in their brains. In 1975, pathologists performed autopsies on depressed patients to measure serotonin levels. The initial findings were suggestive: depressed patients typically tended to have lower levels of brain serotonin compared with controls. But in 1987, when researchers in Scandinavia performed a similar experiment with newer tools to measure serotonin more accurately, serotonin levels were found to be higher in depressed patients. Further experiments only deepened these contradictions. In some trials, depressed patients were found to have decreased serotonin levels; in others, serotonin was increased; in yet others, there was no difference at all.

What about the converse experiment? In 1994, male subjects at McGill University in Montreal were given a chemical mixture that lowered serotonin. Doctors then measured the fluctuations in the mood of the men as serotonin levels dipped in the blood. Though serotonin was depleted, most of them experienced no significant alterations in their mood.

At first glance, these studies seem to suggest that there is no link between serotonin and depression. But an important fact stands out in the McGill experiment: lowering serotonin does not have any effect on healthy volunteers with no history of depression, but serotonin-lowering has a surprisingly brisk effect on people with a family history of depression. In these subjects, mood dipped sharply when serotonin levels dropped. An earlier version of this experiment, performed at Yale in 1990, generated even more provocative findings. When depressed patients who were already responding to serotonin-enhancing drugs, like Prozac, were fed the serotonin-lowering mixture, they became acutely, often profoundly, depressed. Why would serotonin depletion make such a difference in a patient's mood unless mood in these patients was, indeed, being controlled by serotonin?

Other experiments showed that though depressed patients generally didn't have consistently lower levels of serotonin,

suicidal patients often did. Might contemplating suicide be the most extreme form of depression? Or is it a specific subtype of mood disorder that is distinct from all the other forms? And if so, might depression have multiple subtypes—some inherently responsive to treatment with serotonin-enhancing drugs and some inherently resistant?

We may not understand how serotonin-enhancing antidepressants work, but do we know whether they work at all?

In the late 1980s, studies examined the effect of Prozac on depressed subjects. Several of these trials showed Prozac reduced the symptoms of depression when compared with a placebo. Depression is usually assessed using a standardized rating scale of different symptoms. In general, some patients reported clinically meaningful improvements, although the effects were often small and varied from trial to trial. In real-world terms, such a change could be profound: a transformation in anxiety, the lifting of the ache of guilt, an end to the desire to commit suicide. But for other patients, the changes were marginal. Perhaps the most important number that emerged from these trials was the most subjective: 74 percent of the patients reported feeling "much" or "very much" better on antidepressants.

In 1997, a psychologist, Irving Kirsch, currently at the Harvard Medical School, set out to look at the placebo effect in relation to depression. In part, the placebo effect works because the psyche acutely modifies the perception of illness or wellness. Kirsch wondered how powerful this effect might be for drugs that treat depression—where the medical condition itself happens to involve an alteration of the psyche.

To measure this effect, Kirsch combined 38 trials that included patients who had been given antidepressants, placebos or no treatment and then applied mathematical reasoning to estimate how much the placebos contributed to the improvements in mood. The analysis revealed two surprises. First, when Kirsch computed the strength of the placebo effect by combining the trials, he found that 75 percent of an antidepressant's effect could have been obtained merely by taking the placebo. When Kirsch and his collaborators combined the published and unpublished studies of antidepressants (they obtained the unpublished data from the F.D.A. via the Freedom of Information Act), the effects of the antidepressants were even more diluted—in some cases, vanishingly so. Now, the placebo effect swelled to 82 percent (i.e., four-fifths of the benefit might have been obtained by swallowing an inert pill alone). Kirsch came to believe that pharmaceutical companies were exaggerating the benefits of antidepressants by selectively publishing positive studies while suppressing negative ones.

But there are problems in analyzing published and unpublished trials in a "meta-trial." A trial may have been unpublished not just to hide lesser effects but because its quality was poor—because patients were enrolled incorrectly, groups were assigned improperly or the cohort sizes were too small. Patients who are mildly depressed, for example, might have been lumped in with severely depressed patients or with obsessive-compulsives and schizophrenics.

In 2010, researchers revisited Kirsch's analysis using six of the most rigorously conducted studies on antidepressants.

The study vindicated Kirsch's conclusions but only to a point. In patients with moderate or mild depression, the benefit of an antidepressant was indeed small, even negligible. But for patients with the most severe forms of depression, the benefit of medications over placebo was substantial. Such patients might have found, as Andrew Solomon did, that they no longer felt "the self slipping out" of their hands. The most severe dips in mood were gradually blunted. Like Dorothy, these patients most likely still experienced sorrow, but they experienced it in ways that were less self-destructive or paralyzing. As Solomon wrote: "The opposite of depression is not happiness, but vitality, and my life, as I write this, is vital."

These slippery, seemingly contradictory studies converge on a surprisingly consistent picture. First, patients with severe depression tend to respond most meaningfully to antidepressants, while patients with moderate or mild depression do not. Second, in a majority of those who do respond, serotonin very likely plays an important role, because depleting serotonin in depressed patients often causes relapses. And third, the brain-as-soup theory—with the depressed brain simply lacking serotonin—was far too naïve.

As is often the case in science, a new theory emerged from a radically different line of inquiry. In the late 1980s, a neuroscientist named Fred Gage became interested in a question that seemed, at first, peripheral to depression: does the adult human brain produce new nerve cells?

The dogma in neurobiology at the time was that the adult brain was developmentally frozen—no new nerve cells were born. Once the neural circuits of the brain were formed in childhood, they were fixed and immutable. After all, if new neurons were constantly replacing old ones, wouldn't memories decay in that tide of growth? But Gage and other scientists revisited old findings and discovered that adult mice, rats and humans did, in fact, experience the birth of new neurons—but only in two very specific parts of the brain: in the olfactory bulb, where smells are registered, and in the hippocampus, a curl of tissue that controls memories and is functionally linked to parts of the brain that regulate emotion.

Could there be a connection between emotion and neuronal birth in the hippocampus? To find out, Gage and his collaborators began to study stressed mice. When mice are chronically stressed—by sudden changes in their living environments or by the removal of their bedding—they demonstrate behavioral symptoms like anxiety and lethargy and lose their sense of adventurousness, features that mimic aspects of human depression. Researchers found that in these mice, the burst of nerve cells in the hippocampus also diminished.

The converse turned out to be true as well. When mice are housed in an "enriched" environment—typically containing mazes, nesting materials and toys—they become more active and adventurous. They explore more; they learn faster; they seek pleasure. Enrichment, in short, acts behaviorally like an antidepressant. When Gage examined the brains of these enriched mice, he found that more neurons were being born in the hippocampus.

At Columbia University, another neuroscientist, René Hen, was intrigued by Gage's studies. Hen, working with other researchers, began to investigate the link between Prozac and nerve growth. The birth of neurons in the mice takes about two or three weeks—about the same time it takes for antidepressants to take effect. Might the psychiatric effects of Prozac and Paxil be related to the slow birth of neurons and not serotonin per se?

Hen began to feed his mice Prozac. Over the next few days, their behaviors changed: anxiety they had exhibited decreased, and the mice became more adventurous. They looked for food in novel environments and were quick to adopt newly learned behaviors. And newborn neurons appeared in the hippocampus in precisely the location that Gage found with the environmentally enriched mice. But when Hen selectively blocked the birth of neurons in the hippocampus, the adventurousness and the food-exploration instincts of the Prozac-fed mice vanished. Prozac's positive effects, in other words, depended on the birth of nerve cells in the hippocampi of these mice.

In 2011, Hen and his colleagues repeated these studies with depressed primates. In monkeys, chronic stress produces a syndrome with symptoms remarkably similar to some forms of human depression. Even more strikingly than mice, stressed monkeys lose interest in pleasure and become lethargic. When Hen measured neuron birth in the hippocampi in depressed monkeys, it was low. When he gave the monkeys antidepressants, the depressed symptoms abated and neuron birth resumed. Blocking the growth of nerve cells made Prozac ineffective.

Hen's experiments have profound implications for psychiatry and psychology. Antidepressants like Prozac and Zoloft, Hen suggested, may transiently increase serotonin in the brain, but their effect is seen only when new neurons are born. Might depression be precipitated by the death of neurons in certain parts of the brain? In Alzheimer's disease, areas of the brain involved in cognition degenerate, resulting in the characteristic dementia. In Parkinson's disease, nerve cells involved in coordinating movement degenerate, resulting in the characteristic trembling. Might depression also be a degenerative disease—an Alzheimer's of emotion, a dementia of mood? (Even our language begins to fail in this description. Dementia describes a breakdown of "mentation"—thinking—but we lack a similar word for a degeneration of mood: is it disaffection?)

And how, exactly, might the death of neurons in the tiny caul of the hippocampus (a part of the brain typically associated with the storage of memory) cause this disorder of mood? Traditionally, we think that nerve cells in the brain can form minuscule biological "circuits" that regulate behaviors. One set of nerve cells, for instance, might receive signals to move the hand and then relay these signals to the muscles that cause hand movement. It is easy to imagine that dysfunction of this circuit might result in a disorder of movement. But how does a circuit of nerves regulate mood? Might such a circuit store, for instance, some rules about adapting to stress: what to say or do or think when you are sick and nauseated and facing death and your son has moved a pillow? Did such a degeneration provoke a panic signal in the brain that goaded Wurtzel's deadly reverie: cellular death leading to thoughts of suicide?

And how, then, does the birth of cells heal this feeling? Are new circuits formed that restore vitality, regenerating behaviors that are adaptive and not destructive? Is this why Prozac or Zoloft takes two or three weeks to start working: to become "undepressed," do we have to wait for the slow rebirth of new parts of the brain?

If an answer to these questions exists, it may emerge from the work of Helen Mayberg, a neuroscientist at Emory University. Mayberg has been mapping anatomical areas of the brain that are either hyperactive or inactive in depressed men and women. Tracing such sites led her to the subcallosal cingulate, a minuscule bundle of nerve cells that sit near the hippocampus and function as a conduit between the parts of the brain that control conscious thinking and the parts that control emotion. Think of the subcallosal cingulate as a potential traffic intersection on the road between our cognitive and emotional selves.

When Mayberg stimulated this area of the brain with tiny bursts of electricity using probes in patients resistant to antidepressant therapy, she found remarkable response rates: about 75 percent of them experienced powerful changes in their moods during testing. Seconds after stimulation began, many patients, some of them virtually catatonic with depression, reported a "sudden calmness" or a "disappearance of the void." The stimulator can be implanted in patients and works like a depression pacemaker: it continues to relieve their symptoms for years. When the battery runs low, patients slowly relapse into depression.

At first glance, Mayberg's studies would appear to bypass the serotonin hypothesis. After all, it was electrical, not chemical, stimulation that altered mood. But the response to Mayberg's electrical stimulation also seemed to be linked to serotonin. The subcallosal cingulate is particularly rich in nerve cells that are sensitive to serotonin. Researchers found that if they blocked the serotonin signal in the brains of depressed rats, the pacemaker no longer worked.

A remarkable and novel theory for depression emerges from these studies. Perhaps some forms of depression occur when a stimulus—genetics, environment or stress—causes the death of nerve cells in the hippocampus. In the nondepressed brain, circuits of nerve cells in the hippocampus may send signals to the subcallosal cingulate to regulate mood. The cingulate then integrates these signals and relays them to the more conscious parts of the brain, thereby allowing us to register our own moods or act on them. In the depressed brain, nerve death in the hippocampus disrupts these signals—with some turned off and others turned on—and they are ultimately registered consciously as grief and anxiety. "Depression is emotional pain without context," Mayberg said. In a nondepressed brain, she said, "you need the hippocampus to help put a situation with an emotional component into context"—to tell our conscious brain, for instance, that the loss of love should be experienced as sorrow or the loss of a job as anxiety. But when the hippocampus malfunctions, perhaps emotional pain can be generated and amplified out of context—like Wurtzel's computer program of negativity that keeps running without provocation. The "flaw in love" then becomes autonomous and self-fulfilling.

We "grow sorrowful," but we rarely describe ourselves as "growing joyful." Imprinted in our language is an instinct that suggests that happiness is a state, while grief is a process. In a scientific sense too, the chemical hypothesis of depression has moved from static to dynamic—from "state" to "process." An antidepressant like Paxil or Prozac, these new studies suggest, is most likely not acting as a passive signal-strengthener. It does not, as previously suspected, simply increase serotonin or send more current down a brain's mood-maintaining wire. Rather, it appears to change the wiring itself. Neurochemicals like serotonin still remain central to this new theory of depression, but they function differently: as dynamic factors that make nerves grow, perhaps forming new circuits. The painter Cézanne, confronting one of Monet's landscapes, supposedly exclaimed: "Monet is just an eye, but, God, what an eye." The brain, by the same logic, is still a chemical soup—but, God, what a soup.

There are, undeniably, important gaps in this theory—and by no means can it claim to be universal. Depression is a complex, diverse illness, with different antecedent causes and manifestations. As the clinical trials show unequivocally, only a fraction of the most severely depressed patients respond to serotonin-enhancing antidepressants. Do these patients respond to Prozac because their depression involves cellular death in the hippocampus? And does the drug fail to work in mild to moderate depression because the cause of that illness is different?

The differences in responses to these drugs could also be due to variations in biological pathways. In some people, neurotransmitters other than serotonin may be involved; in yet others, there may be alterations in the brain caused by biological factors that are not neurotransmitters; in yet others, there may be no identifiable chemical or biological factors at all. The depression associated with Parkinson's disease, for instance, seems to have little to do with serotonin. Postpartum depression is such a distinct syndrome that it is hard to imagine that neurotransmitters or hippocampal neurogenesis play a primary role in it.

Nor does the theory explain why "talk therapies" work in some patients and not in others, and why the combination of talk and antidepressants seems to work consistently better than either alone. It is very unlikely that we can "talk" our brains into growing cells. But perhaps talking alters the way that nerve death is registered by the conscious parts of the brain. Or talking could release other chemicals, opening up parallel pathways of nerve-cell growth.

But the most profound implications have to do with how to understand the link between the growth of neurons, the changes in mood and the alteration of behavior. Perhaps antidepressants like Prozac and Paxil primarily alter *behavioral* circuits in the brain—particularly the circuits deep in the hippocampus where memories and learned behaviors are stored and organized—and consequently change mood. If Prozac helped Dorothy sleep better and stopped her from assaulting her own skin, might her mood eventually have healed as a response to her own alterations of behavior? Might Dorothy, in short, have created her own placebo effect? How much of mood is behavior anyway? Maybe your brain makes you "act" depressed, and then you "feel" depressed. Or you feel depressed in part because your brain is making you act depressed. Thoughts like these quickly transcend psychiatry and move into more unexpected and unsettling realms. They might begin with mood disorders, but they quickly turn to questions about the organizational order of the brain.

John Gribbin, a historian of science, once wrote that seminal scientific discoveries are inevitably preceded by technological inventions. The telescope, which situated the earth and the planets firmly in orbit around the sun, instigated a new direction in thinking for astronomy and physics. The microscope, taking optics in a different direction, ultimately resulted in the discovery of the cell.

We possess far fewer devices to look into the unknown cosmos of mood and emotion. We can only mix chemicals and spark electrical circuits and hope, indirectly, to understand the brain's structure and function through their effects. In time, the insights generated by these new theories of depression will most likely lead to new antidepressants: chemicals that directly initiate nerve growth in the hippocampus or stimulate the sub-callosal cingulate. These drugs may make Prozac and Paxil obsolete—but any new treatment will owe a deep intellectual debt to our thinking about serotonin in the brain. Our current antidepressants are thus best conceived not as medical break-throughs but as technological breakthroughs. They are chemical tools that have allowed us early glimpses into our brains and into the biology of one of the most mysterious diseases known to humans.

Critical Thinking

1. How did the early diagnosis of cases of depression influence the testing of new hypotheses? Explain.

2. What is a "meta-trial," and how does it work in advancing our understanding of depression and its treatments?

Create Central

www.mhhe.com/createcentral

Internet References

History of the treatment of depression
 www.macalester.edu/psychology/whathap/UBNRP/depression05/history.html

Research on depression
 http://psychcentral.com/disorders/depressionresearch.htm

SIDDHARTHA MUKHERJEE is an assistant professor of medicine in the division of medical oncology at Columbia University. He is the author of *Emperor of All Maladies: A Biography of Cancer.*